Personality and Social Intelligence

Nancy Cantor
University of Michigan

John F. Kihlstrom
University of Wisconsin

Prentice-Hall, Inc. Englewood Cliffs, New Jersey 07632

Library of Congress Cataloging-in-Publication Data

CANTOR, NANCY.
    Personality and social intelligence.

    (Century psychology series)
    Bibliography: p.
    Includes index.
    1. Personality and social intelligence.
2. Motivation (Psychology)   3. Cognition.
I. Kihlstrom, John F.   II. Title.   III. Series:
Century psychology series (Englewood Cliffs, N.J.)
BF698.9.S64C36 1987   155.2   86-25536
ISBN 0-13-657966-3

Editorial/production supervision and
  interior design: Arthur Maisel
Manufacturing buyer: Barbara Kittle

century psychology series
James J. Jenkins
Walter Mischel
editors

© 1987 by Prentice-Hall, Inc.
A Division of Simon & Schuster
Englewood Cliffs, New Jersey 07632

Printed in the United States of America

10 9 8 7 6 5 4 3 2 1

ISBN 0-13-657966-3   01

Prentice-Hall International (UK) Limited, *London*
Prentice-Hall of Australia Pty. Limited, *Sydney*
Prentice-Hall Canada Inc., *Toronto*
Prentice-Hall Hispanoamericana, S.A., *Mexico*
Prentice-Hall of India Private Limited, *New Delhi*
Prentice-Hall of Japan, Inc., *Tokyo*
Prentice-Hall of Southeast Asia Pte. Ltd., *Singapore*
Editora Prentice-Hall do Brasil, Ltda., *Rio de Janeiro*

for Steve and Maddy and Lucy

Contents

Preface

For quite some time—at least as far back in history as the golden age of Theophrastus and the Greek philosophers, and as recently as the modern era of the Doctrine of Traits—personality has been defined by the individual's set of distinctive, enduring, and consistently exhibited behavioral dispositions, or traits. Scientists involved in the study of personality have expended considerable energy documenting the existence of these traits, and searching for a universally applicable multidimensional scheme for the classification of people. Such schemes comprise, for example, the classic factor-analytic personality theories of J.P. Guilford, Raymond B. Cattell, and Hans Eysenck.

Though few would deny the impressive analytic sophistication achieved in the service of establishing the place of the Doctrine of Traits, even ardent supporters of this tradition are somewhat tired of the search for *the* taxonomy of personality types, or the debate over the *true* state of affairs with regard to behavioral-trait consistency. Recent attempts to broaden the scope of personality research and to resurrect interest in the biological-evolutionary, cognitive-motivational, or social-cultural bases of personality differences have been welcomed in the field.

The present book explores one of these alternative directions for personality theory and research. We place social intelligence at the center of this personality theory and define it as the concepts, memories, and rules—in short, the knowledge—that individuals bring to bear in solving personal life tasks. Of course, by placing intelligence at the center of such an analysis, we too run the risk of narrowing rather than broadening the focus of attention and reducing the cognitive basis of personality to some scheme of "social IQ." Clearly, this is not our intention. In fact, intelligence seems to us to be an appropriate centerpiece of personality precisely because it can be construed as multifaceted in nature, as in the work of Howard Gardner on multiple intelligences. Furthermore, the study of "intelligent" action in motivationally relevant social contexts forces consideration of the *effectiveness* of individuals' coping strategies—joining personality and clinical psychology in a common cause. This approach moves the study of personality back to the questions of adaptation and social adjustment raised by Murray and his contemporaries, and, for the moment, away from psychometric concerns with taxonomies and consistency coefficients.

In such a cognitive-motivational analysis, we hope to illustrate the broadening of the scope of personality research by considering process as well as structure, situations in addition to persons, and the life tasks that provide the motivation for personality change as well as those that promote stability and consistency. With these goals in mind we emphasize the complexity of people's solutions to the tasks of social life and note that often those solutions create new and more frustrating problems that further stretch the limits of individuals' social intelligence.

We present the following analysis of personality and social intelligence in the expansionist spirit of the new directions in personality theory and research. Accordingly, we would very much like to acknowledge the continual influence on our thinking of colleagues who are, themselves, pursuing directions that suggest multiple bases for personality and that integrate the concerns of personality and clinical psychologies. Our collaboration in this effort derives from shared interests in social cognition, social learning, and clinical assessment—interests that have been and continue to be very significantly shaped by inspirations, ideas, and discerning guidance provided by Walter Mischel. His contributions to our work are too numerous to enumerate; we can only hope that this book, written in the spirit of his scholarly tradition, serves as something of a gesture of our enormous appreciation.

We very much want to acknowledge the major contributions to this book of many of our colleagues: Jeanne Sumi Albright, Mark Baldwin, Aaron Brower, David Buss, Beverly Chew, Nancy Denney, Nancy Genero, Pat Gurin, Judy Harackiewicz, Reid Hastie, James Hilton, Irene Hoyt, Stanley Klein, Hal Korn, Chris Langston, Hazel Markus, Paula Niedenthal, Richard Nisbett, Julie Norem, Pat Register, Stephen Ruffins, Carolin Showers, Barbara Smuts, Camille Wortman, Elissa Wurf, and Robert Zajonc lent their intellectual and moral support to this effort. In addition, several of these individuals, James Hilton, Chris Langston, Hazel Markus, Paula Niedenthal, and Julie Norem graciously and repeatedly provided specific comments and additions to drafts of this book; their help was invaluable to us. We acknowledge with thanks the technical assistance of Debbie Francis, Sara Freeland, and Phyllis White, and the innovative artistic contributions of Paula Niedenthal. There are certain individuals without whose support and assistance this book would not have been completed. We extend heartfelt thanks to Nancy G. Exelby, a superb editorial assistant, to Arthur Maisel, a patient and helpful production editor, to Priscilla Battis for her speed and accuracy in compiling the index, to John Isley for his support of our work, and again to Walter Mischel for giving us the opportunity to present our thoughts in this series and for his outstanding editorial efforts. Last, though never least, there is the indispensible and continual support of Steve and Maddy and Lucy, to whom we dedicate this book.

The theoretical and empirical work reported in this book was greatly facilitated by support from Grant #BNS-8411778 from the National Science Foundation; from Grant #MH-35856 from the National Institute of Mental Health; and from an H.I. Romnes Faculty Fellowship from the University of Wisconsin.

NANCY CANTOR
JOHN F. KIHLSTROM

Personality and Social Intelligence

> To use the functionalist's language, perceptual readiness or accessibility
> serves two functions: to minimize the surprise value of the
> environment . . . and to maximize the attainment of sought-after objects and
> events. . . . Readiness in the sense that we are using it is not a luxury,
> but a necessity for smooth adjustment. (Jerome Bruner, 1957, pp. 133, 149)

This is a book about the cognitive expertise—the social intelligence—
that places people in a state of perceptual readiness for the events of
social life, minimizing surprises and maximizing personal gains. It is
about the many creative ways in which individuals may potentially take
control of situations by giving them personal meaning and by finding in
them opportunities to fulfill personal goals. It traces the process by which
customary problems become personalized tasks with idiosyncratic solutions, because individuals bring to bear their own social intelligence to
interpret situations and plan action accordingly. *Social* tasks become the
property of *persons* through the application of their intelligence.

Our objective, following in the tradition of the cognitive style
theorists of the "New Look" period, is to combine motivational and
cognitive perspectives on personality in an analysis of social intelligence.
Since the time of the "New Look" movement, many personality theorists
have spoken of the need for more integrated approaches to questions of

individual adaptation in the social world. While different theorists find their sources of integration in different domains of psychological inquiry (Pervin, 1985), we look to the study of *human intelligence* as a source of inspiration in the present integrative endeavor (Baron, 1982).

THE INTELLIGENCE MODEL

Recent approaches to intelligence focus on three aspects of problem solving that provide a useful organizing framework for a cognitive-motivational analysis of personality. First, of course, there is the content and structure of the *expertise* necessary for solving problems (e.g., Sternberg, 1980). Here, theorists focus on *declarative knowledge*—concepts and memories of events, and *procedural knowledge*—rules that operate on those concepts and memories; as well as *metacognitive skills* of planning, monitoring, and evaluation of alternative solutions. This is the expertise that allows individuals to answer analogy questions on intelligence tests and, also, to try a new strategy when the first response seems a bit off the mark. As might be expected, this part of the intelligence literature builds nicely on earlier psychometric work, extending that work on the basis of theories and findings in cognitive psychology (Anderson, 1981).

The next trend in the study of intelligence takes it a bit further from the psychometric routes and considerably closer to questions that intrigue social and personality psychologists—that is, to questions of *context:* What are the contexts that constitute important and demanding tasks for individuals and their cultures? Here the aim of intelligence theorists is to discover the critical contexts in which intelligence is learned, used, and refined over the life-span. Analyzing the contexts in which people really use their intelligence frequently provides insight into the very nature of expertise (Scribner & Cole, 1978). What expertise, for example, does a baseball manager draw upon in framing a strategy for beating an opposing team? Can he adapt his expertise to the tasks of a parent attempting to outsmart a rebellious adolescent? Once meaningful task contexts are found, it is possible not only to test the limits of individuals' performance on ecologically valid tasks, but also to identify novel tasks that may challenge that expertise in new ways.

Closely related to the contextualist approach is a concern with the effectiveness of individuals' solutions to life problems in these familiar contexts. This interest, which we will label as a concern with the *pragmatics* of intelligence (Baltes, 1986), is at the heart of an analysis of *social* intelligence. When close attention is accorded to the contexts in which people use their intelligence everyday, it becomes clear that these contexts present ill-defined problems with multiple avenues for satisfactory solutions. Even within a relatively mundane problem of daily living, such as stretching one's budget to meet the month's bills, there are several plausible angles to embrace, each directed at a slightly different goal (Denney, 1984). Therefore, characterizing a "good" or a "poor" solution to challenging, everyday problems (with their alternative plausible constructions) is a difficult enterprise, indeed. Yet the concern with pragmatics is precisely what makes the intelligence model a viable one for the study of personality and adjustment.

INTELLIGENCE AND PERSONALITY

The questions about expertise, context, and pragmatics raised by an analysis of intelligence fit well within the concerns of personality psychology. Phrased in another way, these are questions about personality structure, person-by-situation interaction, and adaptive/maladaptive personalities (Pervin, 1985). These are the questions around which the present book is organized and on which we hope that the intelligence model will shed some light.

Social Intelligence Expertise

From this view, the cognitive basis of personality can be conceptualized as the declarative and procedural knowledge that individuals bring to bear in interpreting events and making plans in everyday life situations. These *concepts, personal memories,* and *interpretive rules* are the cognitive structures of personality; together they constitute the expertise that guides an individual's approach to the problems of social life. We refer to this knowledge repertoire as *social intelligence.*

These, for example, are the concepts of "self-as-parent" and "self-as-ideal-parent," and the interpretive rules of attribution and social comparison, upon which individuals draw when they strive to be patient and loving parents at even the most exasperating of moments. These are the scripts and episodes about parenting, learned through vicarious experience with siblings and friends, that "prepare" individuals for the trials of parenting, while reminding them of the long-term "benefits." This is the expertise that may encourage the setting of realistic goals in this taxing domain and force attention to strategies of emotion-management and conflict resolution well before the children can even communicate a discrepant opinion. It is this social intelligence—these structures of personality—upon which individuals rely in trying to cope with the present, and to come to some understanding of the past that will motivate continued effort at the task.

Life-Task Contexts

In order to realize the full potential of a social intelligence analysis, this expertise must be considered within the light of an appropriate set of social life contexts. Social contexts, whether defined in terms of interpersonal relationships, cultural institutions, or organizations, afford opportunities for and encourage certain expertise by placing normative demands on individuals in those contexts (Veroff, 1983). Erikson (1950) made this point when he described the cultural rituals in families, schools, social and religious groups, and the like, with which each individual has to coordinate the ego tasks of development. As Joan Miller (1984) recently demonstrated in an elegant cross-cultural study of attribution rules among Americans and Hindus, cultures communicate a world view, part of which limits the kinds of interpretations of social events and situations that individual members will be likely to make. Those interpretations, in turn, specify the sorts of goals and strategies that individuals will be able comfortably to embrace in commonplace social contexts—consensual interpretations that lead to widely-accepted goals and strategies will be favored and reinforced accordingly.

Hence, it is critical to settle on a sample of relevant social life contexts that appropriately engage the energy of individuals in a specified culture and age-group. For that purpose, we frequently consider the social intelligence of individuals as they encounter a new set of normative demands in a life transition period—e.g., the harried new parent, the newly independent first-year college student, or the upwardly mobile young professional.

Though quite normative, these life transition tasks still constitute *ill-defined* problems which are given specific form by each individual. In fact, a central thesis of this approach is that individuals turn these customary life situations into unique problems when they apply their social intelligence (Kelly, 1955; Bowers, 1973). The social tasks of parenting or of striving for a career promotion are given personal meaning in the context of each individual's history of experiences. For one person the task of parenting suddenly provides a much-needed ego boost from the inevitable disappointments of work, while another new parent suffers from role overload and feels exhausted by the burden.

In our view, individuals see different tasks in similar situations as a function of the content of their expertise—their social intelligence—at that point in time. We refer to these self-defined problems as individuals' current *life tasks*. These are the problems which a person sees himself or herself as working on and devoting energy to solving during a specified life period. These are the struggles over career and family and identity which all individuals face in one form or another, but which surface in different ways and at different times for each person. Life tasks constitute a set of personal incentives that motivate and give *unique* meaning to current *social* activity (Klinger, 1977).

The analysis of social intelligence must be embedded within a broader understanding of both the normative demands in a life period and the idiographic life tasks of individual members of that subculture. It is the normative demands that engage the intellectual resources of individuals. Yet, it is an understanding of the personal meaning given to normative demands that will permit us to make more accurate predictions about individuals' responses in social situations. For one person a dinner party clearly taps into current life-task goals of affiliation or even intimacy, while for another person (of the same age and subculture) it will be meaningful in an entirely different way as a self-presentational test of achievement, not intimacy (Jones & Pittman, 1982). The ways in which these individuals act will be most predictable from our knowledge of the "tasks" which they desire to accomplish in each situation. In other words, we must pursue a nomothetic and an idiographic approach to the study of social intelligence in life-task contexts.

Pragmatics and Personality

Adopting an intelligence perspective on social interaction brings to light pragmatic concerns about the adaptiveness of personality—or all too often the *maladaptive* nature of social intelligence in a particular task context. As individuals apply their social intelligence in the form of strategies for handling life tasks, some strategies (and, hence, some aspects of their social intelligence) are likely to be more effective in social interactions than are others. Parents who were "naturals" at coping with the "terrible twos" may be devastated by the rebellion of an adolescent. While it is often easy to see good and poor solutions as they unfold in such social interactions, it is far more difficult to pinpoint the features of individuals' strategies that result in effective problem solving.

Taking a bold position on personality adjustment, we argue that the adaptiveness of goals and strategies largely is determined by the extent and nature of people's knowledge in task-relevant domains, i.e., their social intelligence expertise. Individuals differ in the elaborateness and accessibility of their knowledge in task-relevant domains and in the social consensuality (with relevant others) of their world view in those particular domains (Markus & Smith, 1981; Kihlstrom & Cantor, 1984). One person is a virtual "expert" in "achievement-at-work," seeing easily and quickly several different strategies for impressing the boss in subtle ways. This "achievement expert" has extensive knowledge of the ins and outs of achievement situations, most of which is fairly well-appreciated by co-workers and clients. By contrast, that same person is a clear and rather clumsy "novice" in family dynamics, especially by comparison with peers who, despite similar backgrounds, have taken a more detailed interest in developing that domain of expertise.

The content of a person's expertise in a particular domain can be more or less adaptive, in that the outcomes it suggests may motivate activity in task-relevant situations, debilitate the person with hopelessness, or immobilize with anxiety (Carver & Scheier, 1985). For example, as Bandura (1986) recently argued, the self-serving attributions that non-depressed individuals frequently endorse in difficult achievement contexts may be objectively inaccurate, but still serve an adaptive purpose by motivating continued task effort. Often, the utility of expertise is evaluated more in terms of its motivating value for the individual than in the light of normative standards for prescriptive accuracy (Miller & Cantor, 1982).

We believe that these characteristic patterns of domain-specific expertise, much of which is typically evoked without conscious awareness (Bargh, 1982), still can be unearthed (with some effort) through extensions into the clinical assessment arena of many techniques from laboratory studies of social cognition (Kendall & Hollon, 1981; Ingram, 1985). Moreover, an analysis of the characteristic ways in which individuals confront their life tasks can be of substantial clinical interest (Nasby & Kihlstrom, 1985). Of course, attaining some modicum of self-insight is a necessary, but not sufficient step towards effecting clinical change in this model and in most other approaches. The obstacles to change, as construed here, come from both personal and social sources.

On the personal side, there is a clear "double-edge" to social intelligence expertise. While it is generally adaptive to know a great deal about a task domain, to have considered alternative goals and strategies, and to have arrived at a favorite course of action, it can also be especially hard to effect change in (dysfunctional) expertise. Almost by definition, expertise is hard to change because the person has so many relevant concepts and memories in that domain and such well-practiced rules of interpretation in those situations. In other words, expertise *usually* helps a person arrive at a pragmatic solution to a pressing life task. However, if that expertise leads to a less than satisfactory solution to a life-task problem then difficulties may arise when the person tries to change those habitual ways.

On the social side, the obstacles to change in one person's habitual routines and ways of working on life tasks usually stem from partners' reluctance to give up on well-worn expectancies for social interaction, i.e., to change their expertise. While the spouse of a stereotypically "self-centered achiever" may despair in private about his absent-minded interactions with the children, she has developed an expertise in child-rearing that functions (perhaps too well) to compensate for his "ignorance." Any real change in their parenting roles will have to be accomplished with great effort and flexibility on *both sides*. Individuals have to provide socially-acceptable and negotiable "accounts" of their intentions to effect self-change (Tetlock, 1986)—for what appears to one person to be solely a personal matter, often turns out to involve the cooperation of others as well.

GOALS AND ORGANIZATION

It should be clear, even with this preliminary examination of social intelligence, that we see little point in making global comparisons of individuals on any single dimension of social intelligence or adaptiveness of personality. Social intelligence expertise is multidimensional in form, domain- or task-specific in content, and potentially quite dynamic as it is negotiated anew in each significant life context. This is not a scheme to help people "know their *social I.Q.*"

A second point is related to the first one: We are not committed to developing a taxonomy of people. Such classificatory schemes, often formulated at a highly abstract level, may miss the flexibility and discrimination of experience, thought, and action that is central to human life. We assume, by direct analogy to language, that an infinite variety of individual differences can be produced by the interactions among a finite set of general principles of social learning, social cognition, and social interaction. Therefore, the primary task of a cognitive personology, from our point of view, is to describe the general processes out of which individual differences are constructed.

Nevertheless, this is a model about intelligence and personality, and in that respect we do not intend to shun individual difference comparisons, however multidimensional and domain-specific the assessments must be. The complexity of personality certainly should not lead to the conclusion that social interactions are random and haphazard, and that persons are unpredictable. To the contrary, individuals often are able to make very subtle discriminations among their life situations, to give meaning to these situations through the operation of their cognitive processes, and on some occasions even to respond flexibly to the shifting, evolving patterns of possibilities and constraints that they encounter. In fact, this patterned variability in individuals' construals of situations is precisely the reason to believe that people use *intelligent* action in some life contexts. Intelligent action, as contrasted with the instinctual or the reflexive, is flexible rather than rigidly stereotyped, discriminative rather than indiscriminant, and optional rather than obligatory. As such, it stands as a marker of human potential.

Accordingly, one goal of a social intelligence analysis is to highlight, for each individual, ways in which his or her expertise is functional ("intelligent") in some domains and dysfunctional in others; well-suited for some life tasks and unsatisfactory for others. These assessments, we feel, are most profitably applied to (clinical) issues of adjustment, and therefore, we present a schematic outline of social intelligence assessment procedures in the context of a discussion of personality change.

It seems that there have always been two sides to the study of both personality and intelligence: Theorists have aligned themselves with either an interest in psychometrics and prediction or in remediation and change. In the end it probably does not matter from which direction the interest stems; the data on human behavior force consideration of all angles (cf. Cronbach, 1957). Meanwhile, however, we have chosen to pursue personality and intelligence with goals more in line with understanding the processes of personality change than with improving predictions about cross-situational consistency in social behavior.

With this goal in mind, the organization of the present book follows fairly closely the schema of an intelligence model outlined above. We begin by placing this approach in its most natural historical context, with a brief look at several prior *cognitive* treatments of personality (Chapter 2). Comparisons between work in the cognitive style tradition and that of the "social-cognitivists" (Kelly, Mischel, Rotter, and Bandura) raise issues of stylistic consistency and discriminative flexibility that lead to a discussion of intelligence from a psychometric and an expertise perspective (Chapter 3).

Having, then, announced our intention to pursue the expertise model in the social life domain, we begin the analysis of social intelligence with two chapters on people's knowledge of themselves and others, and their characteristic ways of interpreting social experience (Chapters 4 and 5). Of course, social intelligence expertise cannot be understood *out of context;* therefore, in Chapter 6, we consider individuals' application of their expertise in strategies for working on current life tasks.

In considering the complexity and utility of people's social expertise it is also apparent that the process of translation of intentions into action requires special attention as well (Kuhl & Beckman, 1985). Accordingly, we turn next to questions of development and dynamics, focusing in particular on the contexts of social negotiation out of which social intelligence develops and within which it must work (Chapter 7).

Finally, we (re)turn to questions of pragmatics and social intelligence, asking again about the cognitive expertise that underlies functional and dysfunctional patterns of social interaction (Chapter 8). In this context, we look at techniques for explicating the life-task intentions that motivate an individual's current behavior and the favorite ways in which he or she chooses to work on those pressing problems. We argue that the first step towards corrective change is to understand something about the concepts of self and other and the interpretive rules that shape those problematic interaction strategies; even though change only gets enacted within social contexts. Further, we acknowledge the disappointing fact that the expertise most in need of change will, unfortunately, be the least amenable to a speedy revision.

This "double-edge" to personal expertise should, of course, come as no surprise to personality theorists. Traditionally, it is often assumed that processes of normal personality functioning are not qualitatively distinct from mechanisms that produce maladaptive behavior. Consequently, theoretical frameworks as diverse as psychoanalysis and social learning theory describe the central processes of normal personality—be they drives and defenses or expectancies and values—as potential impediments to effective coping, rather than simply as facilitators of constructive behavior. The present framework is consistent with this tradition in highlighting both the adaptive and the maladaptive potential of individuals' social intelligence.

The impediments to effective coping within the social intelligence framework take somewhat different form than do the id drives and oedipal schemata of psychoanalysis or the classically conditioned phobias analyzed by early learning theorists; yet their effects may be similarly disturbing. The attribution literature, as one example, demonstrates people's tendencies to preserve sometimes inaccurate perceptions of self and others by discounting information and ignoring social feedback (Harvey & Weary, 1984). These "biased" perceptions and beliefs can cause considerable interpersonal difficulties when individuals then draw automatically on scripts for social interaction that necessarily "misjudge" a partner's intentions (Kelley, 1979). Within the social intelligence framework, declarative and procedural expertise, often accessed without conscious control, can serve to "blind" individuals to their mistakes as frequently as it provides the basis for new self-understandings and personality change (Kihlstrom & Nasby, 1985).

In the light of these and other impediments to effective coping that are documented in the pages of this book, it is quite possible that increased understanding of the cognitive processes that typically underlie social behavior eventually will support a somewhat pessimistic outlook on the *realistic* potential for intelligent action. Clearly it is not easy for individuals to effect substantial changes in their characteristic modes of living, even though small steps towards change are noticeable in family, peer group, and organizational settings.

Satisfactory answers to such questions about the force behind the "light" and the "dark" sides of human nature will come only after a more comprehensive understanding of people exists; one that can provide an integrative view of the cognitive, biological, and social bases of human personality. However, the intentions of this book are far more modest in scope. We hope to provide a beginning roadmap of the social intelligence brought to bear in life-task problem solving, as well as some insights about the variations from person to person in the content and form of that map. For the time being, resolution of debates about the extent to which individuals reach the potential of their intelligence in solving social life tasks remains itself a task for the future.

2

Personality and Cognition:

Earlier Treatments

One way to approach the study of individual differences is to argue that personality provides the mechanisms for an individual's adaptation to the demands of social life and personal growth (Murray, 1938). Since the process of adaptation is not the same for all people—individuals confront these intrapsychic and interpersonal demands in very personal ways—personologists work to find the mediating mechanisms that give shape to the person-by-situation interaction. One approach to specifying the person-by-situation interaction is to place cognition at the center of the adaptation process. In its boldest form, this position states that individuals confront these normative tasks of social life differently because they *see* them differently: having construed the situation in a personally meaningful way, the individual *works* to be consistent with that construal. As Allport (1937) put it, individuals are not all consistent in the same way; rather, individuals are consistent with themselves. People's actions are predictable from our knowledge of the meaning they ascribe to the situations in which they are located and the solutions they have favored in the past. Individuals bring to bear different personal constructs (Kelly, 1955), expectancies (Bandura, 1986; Rotter, 1954), and competencies (Mischel, 1973) in making sense of their life environments. Therefore, the study of personality can be viewed as a study of the ways in which people *interpret situations* (and set goals) and *plan and execute behavior* to be consistent with their interpretations (Cantor & Kihlstrom, 1982, 1985). In this chapter we will review some ways in which cognition has been related to personality by other theorists, as a prelude to a detailed consideration of social intelligence and personality.

COGNITIVE STYLES AS PERSONALITY

One of the most long-standing cognitive-personality traditions goes under the broad rubric of *cognitive styles* or cognitive controls (Kagan & Kogan, 1970). According to the cognitive style tradition, individuals develop characteristic styles of perceiving and thinking: one person may be a "leveler" for whom different perceptual objects merge together (level out differences), while another is a "sharpener" who tends to be very sensitive to differences between objects (Holzman, 1954). In a related vein, one person may sort objects using very broad categories, while another makes very fine distinctions between groups of common objects (Pettigrew, 1958). While these cognitive styles are measured on perceptual or conceptual tasks of visual acuity, size and shape discrimination, object matching and sorting, and so on, the assumption is that cognitive style mediates social behavior as well. For example, the style of using broad categories in which to sort objects was believed to be reflective of a risk-taking personality (Kogan & Wallach, 1964), while the leveling extreme, on the style dimension of leveling-sharpening, was seen as associated with a repressive personality type (Holzman & Gardner, 1959; see Byrne, 1964, for a more recent treatment of the style dimension of repression-sensitization). In other words, the cognitive style proponents suggested that performance on standard perceptual and conceptual laboratory tasks was indicative of broader personality characteristics; cognitive style was assumed to mediate the ways in which a person would interpret and respond to information and events in his or her social world. Thus began a very important tradition of personality research in which perceptual and conceptual styles were given center stage in the individual's adaptation in the social world (see Kagan & Kogan, 1970).

The early cognitive style theorists were very much influenced by the ego psychology tradition in psychoanalytic thinking (Gardner et al., 1959). Therefore, styles of perceiving and thinking were associated in their work with the regulating functions of the ego—hence the term *cognitive controls*. Cognitive styles like leveling-sharpening or impulsive-reflective thinking were assumed to serve critical functions in modulating the expression of motivational drives (defensive functions) and in providing for comfortable ways in which to find personal gratification (adaptive functions). On the one hand, characteristic styles of perceiving and thinking reflected characteristic ways of defending against overwhelming intrapsychic drives, as, for example, when the "leveler" engaged in repression. On the other hand, cognitive styles also demonstrated the more adaptive functions of the ego, as the individual worked (unconsciously) to adapt to "reality demands" from the social world (e.g., repression can also be a functional way of handling personal loss or injury). Cognitive styles reflected the ego's activity as the regulator of motives and the mediator between the person and his or her environment. Therefore, this tradition of research not only placed cognition at the center of the person-by-situation interaction but also emphasized the notion of *motivated cognition* (see, also, Bruner & Goodman, 1947)—cognitive styles reflected the person's attempts to regulate and fulfill intrapsychic drives and interpersonal demands.

Exemplar Cognitive Styles

Recent work in the cognitive style tradition has tended to emphasize the mediating role of styles in social behavior rather than pursue the earlier focus on styles of defending against intrapsychic drives (see Shapiro, 1965, for an exception to this trend). In this vein, effort has been directed towards demonstrating that cognitive styles—characteristic ways of perceiving situations and reasoning about solutions to problems—are associated with distinctive patterns of social behavior. The importance of this work in the present context lies not so much in the claims made about the existence of such broadly-defined cognitive styles, or in the data supposedly suggestive of the utility of these style constructs in the prediction of a diverse set of social behaviors, but rather in the precedent set by this tradition for placing interpretive and reasoning processes at the center of a theory of personality. The cognitive style tradition has been justifiably criticized on both conceptual and empirical grounds (see discussion below); however, there is no lessening of interest in the centrality of cognitive processes to the study of personality (Cantor & Kihlstrom, 1981, 1982, 1985). In the following discussion we will briefly summarize two lines of work on cognitive styles—one that emphasizes a *perceptual style* and the other that focuses on a *style of reasoning*—and then turn to a critique of the style approach that hopefully points the way towards another fruitful direction in the study of personality and cognition.

1. Field-embeddedness. One of the most vigorously researched cognitive styles is that of field-embeddedness, also often referred to as field-dependence, or as an analytic-global style, and more recently as psychological differentiation (Witkin et al., 1962). This is a perceptual style that describes the tendency for the individual's perception of a stimulus object to be overcome by the context in which it is embedded (field-dependent, global, undifferentiated) or to be independent of that context or field (field-independent, analytic, differentiated). The style is assessed by performance on three perceptual tasks: the Body Adjustment Test (BAT), the

Rod-and-Frame Test (RFT), and the Embedded Figures Test (EFT). These
tests have been described by Kagan & Kogan (1970) as follows:

> In the case of the BAT, the subject is seated in a tilted chair within
> a tilted room, and his task is to adjust his chair to the true vertical while
> the room is tilted. . . . In the RFT, the subject is seated in a completely
> darkened room facing a luminous rod suspended within a luminous frame.
> The subject is required to adjust the rod to the true vertical, when
> his body is tilted or upright, and when the rod and frame are tilted in the
> same or opposite directions . . . . Finally, the EFT consists of a series
> of complex geometric figures in which a series of simple figures is
> embedded . . . . The subject's score on the EFT represents the mean amount
> of time required to locate each of the simple figures. (P. 1323)

Each of these tasks is supposed to tap the common stylistic tendency to
separate (or merge) the stimulus (i.e., body, rod, or geometric designs) from
the field in which it is embedded. A composite perceptual style index is
derived based upon an individual's performance across the three types of
tasks. The perceptual style index—degree of field-independence/dependence
or global/analytic style—is then assumed to be correlated with patterns of
social behavior which are conceptually related to the style (Witkin &
Goodenough, 1977).

The links between the field-embeddedness style and the criterion
behaviors are typically derived conceptually from the construct of
"psychological differentiation"—the separation of self from environment
(Witkin et al., 1962). Field independent individuals—who tend to separate
the perceptual figure from its embedding field—should perceive themselves
as quite independent from their social context and take their cues for
behavior from internal, not external, referents. The opposite pattern of
behavior would be expected for individuals with a diffuse or global
perceptual style that tends to merge the stimulus (self) with its field
(environment). For example, Witkin & Goodenough (1977) argued that
"the main perceptual tests used to assess extent of field dependence reflect
degree of reliance on internal or external referents" (p. 661). They noted
that in the RFT "some people tend to use the external field as the main
referent for judging rod position, aligning the rod with the tilted frame
in order to perceive the rod as straight; others, using the felt position of
the upright body as a referent, bring the rod close to the vertical. . . . These
contrasting ways of perceiving the upright are expressions of a broad
difference among people in focus on self or field" (p. 662). This "broad"
stylistic difference should, in turn, be reflected in a variety of interpersonal
behaviors which tap extent of focus on self or others as the standard for
behavior.

Witkin & Goodenough (1977) review a large assortment of studies
suggestive of a relationship, albeit a complex one, between field-depen-
dence/independence (measured as a perceptual style) and an interper-

sonal–other-directed/intrapersonal–inner-directed style of social interaction. In general, while the evidence is suggestive of such a cognitive-behavioral style link, there are many qualifiers in this relationship. For example, field-dependent individuals do seek information from others in the process of making decisions, but only when there is ambiguity about the best decision. Field-dependent people attend more to the faces of those with whom they are interacting than do field-independent people; they also do better at picking up nonverbal social cues. However, they are *not* globally more likely to seek social approval or to be emotionally dependent or to desire attention from others. They will conform more to the socially normative opinion in a group interaction context (when the "correct" decision is ambiguous), but will not be especially susceptible to persuasive communications from experts (see Witkin & Goodenough, 1977, p. 663).

Research on this style construct has been quite prolific and important in setting a precedent for fruitful analyses of the links between perception-cognition and social behavior. For example, it makes good sense to see if an individual's proclivity for attending to contextual cues in the RFT generalizes to his or her attentiveness to social cues from facial expressions in the course of a social interaction (Witkin & Goodenough, 1977). If the person makes use of visual-field stimulation as a frame of reference in the RFT, then he or she might well draw similar information from the nonverbal reactions of people in the social "field." However, the argument for the generality and utility of a perceptual *style* of field dependence/independence, with wide-ranging implications for all sorts of (sometimes vaguely) related social behaviors, has gone considerably beyond analyses of perceptual-behavioral links based directly on common task elements. For example, the person who is labeled as "field-dependent" on the standard perceptual tasks (RFT, EFT, BAT) is then expected to demonstrate all kinds of personal traits characteristic of an *interpersonal orientation* (conformity, dependence, other-directedness), traits that go well beyond the simple attentiveness to social-field information implied in the field-dependence perceptual measure. And it is precisely these *broad style* assertions that have led people to question the utility of the field-dependence construct.

Most critiques have been focused around questions of *generality*: Is there really a *style* of perceiving at issue here? If so, what general *process* variable is at the heart of all of these disparate behaviors? (Baron, 1982; LCHC, 1982). The answer to the style question depends on the consistency of performance on tasks in which the common element is presumed to involve the tendency to separate a stimulus (including the self) from an embedding field. In order to convincingly argue for a perceptual style which generalizes to cognitive and social-behavioral tasks, proponents of the field-dependence construct need to show that people are relatively consistent in their preferred "styles" both within task domains and across related domains (i. e., within and across perceptual, cognitive, and social tasks). This pattern of generality has not always been demonstrated. While it has been especially difficult to show consistency in performance within the domain of social behavior (Jahoda, 1980; Werner, 1979), there have even been problems in attempts to find consistency across the three standard perceptual tasks in cross-cultural contexts (Dasen, Berry, & Witkin, 1979). For example, Wober (1966) found no relation between performance on the EFT and the RFT in certain West African countries. While these inconsistencies have typically been explained away by reference to certain mediating socialization factors (which presumably make these tasks *different* for the participant cultures), the defense of the style construct is on shaky grounds as it becomes clear that such socialization factors can not easily be isolated. Researchers from the Laboratory of Comparative Human Cognition (see Sternberg, 1982, Ch. 11) report many cross-cultural failures to find consistency across the EFT and RFT. Moreover, performance on these tasks rarely seems to be related as expected to the conceptually relevant socialization factors. For example, Witkin and his colleagues have pointed to mother's traditionalism as an antecedent to field-dependent behavior, but studies of child-rearing patterns rarely reveal the expected relationship (LCHC, 1982). Such questions about the consistency of performance even within the perceptual domain and about the empirical support for the logically-relevant socialization antecedents have led some researchers to doubt the utility of using the *style* construct to describe performance on these tasks. Serpell (1976) even went so far as to suggest that these tasks simply measured skill at dealing with pictorial stimuli, while Irwin et al. (1976) suggest that availability of intellectual stimulation is the key antecedent determining performance on the EFT (see also Streibel & Ebenholtz, 1982).

Doubts about the generality of an underlying perceptual style in the case of field-dependence research have been bolstered by failures to find expected consistencies across conceptually-related tasks in different domains. Kagan & Kogan (1970), for example, report that performance on *visual* field-embeddedness tasks does not generalize to performance on tasks involving disembedding *verbal* material (p. 1327). Such failures of generality suggest that the so-called global/analytic style revealed in the visual-spatial tasks may be restricted to select perceptual tasks. If these restrictions are prevalent, and even sympathetic reviews of this work suggest that they are, then it becomes especially difficult to find a parsimonious description of the *style-variable* that supposedly underlies such performance differences as are found on the embeddedness perceptual tasks.

The picture becomes even more complex when one considers the web of confirming and nonconfirming findings about the performance of field-dependent and field-independent individuals on *social tasks*. In their review of this literature, Witkin & Goodenough (1977) argue on the basis of Lewin's early work on psychological differentiation that the critical factor underlying the field-dependent *style* is a merging of self with environment, a global or nondifferentiated perceptual attitude towards the world. However, if the field-dependent style is a nondifferentiated one, then why are field-dependent individuals not more emotionally dependent or more likely to seek social approval than are field-independent people? It is the case, as Witkin & Goodenough are quick to point out, that in some contexts field-dependent people conform more to group norms than do field-independent people. But why, if psychological differentiation is the critical variable here, are they only more conforming in group inter-actions with *ambiguous* task demands/solutions? Similar problems occur in translating from the conceptual framework of psychological differentia-tion theory to the empirical evidence gathered in other social tasks in which the dependent measure ostensibly taps a reliance on or attentiveness to external social (as opposed to internal) cues as a frame of reference (e.g., memory for faces, see Witkin & Goodenough, 1977, p. 670). In fact, the pattern of data generalizing from the perceptual to the social domain is so complex that it is hard to feel sanguine in calling field-dependence a "style" with all of the implications of breadth and consistency denoted by that construct (see Zigler, 1963; Sternberg & Salter, 1982; LCHC, 1982).

Attempts to add a cross-cultural dimension to the work on field-dependence/independence have also raised the concerns that there is a value-bias in this style construct (i.e., field-*dependence* is often equated with a less-developed or sophisticated mode of perceiving [see Scribner & Cole, 1973, for a review]). Of course, Witkin and his colleagues have claimed that the construct is value-free, since field-dependence is well-suited for environments that value an interpersonal orientation and field-independence works well when cognitive analysis is prized. However, this claim is difficult to defend in practice. The value-free argument seems to boil down to demonstrating that different cultures socialize different styles which, in turn, become more adaptive in those environments. But, can we really show that cultures present individuals with such clear-cut messages as to make one or another style more valued (adaptive) and, thus, more likely to be exhibited across a variety of situations? Would the Eskimos, who as a group tend to score as field-independents on the perceptual tasks, really preserve an "object-oriented" analytic style when dealing with inter-personal, "people-oriented" problems? Would they be less interested in people than would be a "field-dependent culture"? (LCHC, 1982). And, as noted above, it is very difficult to isolate the socializing agents/factors that result in these stylistic differences in perception, let alone find the environments in which it is *generally* "better" to be field-dependent or independent as a rule. Once again, even arguments about the value-laden versus value-free nature of the field-embeddedness construct return in the end to questions about generality, again leading one to be cautious about suggesting that people really preserve a consistent *style* of perceiving across their everyday interactions.

2. *Impulsivity-reflectivity.* Another popular approach focuses on styles of problem solving as manifest in reasoning tasks. This approach is perhaps best exemplified in the work of Kagan and his colleagues (see Messer, 1976) on the dimension of impulsivity-reflectivity. In this case, instead of focusing on styles of perception and interpretation as in the field-embeddedness work, the concern is with information processing occurring further along in the problem-solving process. As Messer (1976) notes: "Reflection-impulsivity describes the tendency to *reflect* on the validity of problem solving . . . when several possible alternatives are available and there is some uncertainty over which one is the most appropriate" (p. 1026, our italics). In other words, this style is intended to capture the process of *evaluation* in problem solving, the extent to which individuals think about alternative solutions to problems and weigh the pros and cons of different approaches to an uncertain situation. Accordingly, the measures of this style, which are intended to get at this "conceptual tempo" in problem solving, always involve the evaluation of multiple alternative answers with the "correct" one left unspecified. The measure of reflectivity is then taken to be a joint function of response time and errors on the task. For example, the most popular measure of reflectivity, developed initially for use with children, is the Matching Familiar Figures Test (MFFT; Kagan et al., 1964). In this task, the individual is presented with a drawing of a familiar object (e.g., a chicken) and with a number of facsimiles that differ in subtle details from the standard; the task is to select the alternative that exactly matches the standard, and the measure of reflectivity is the time to the first response and number of errors overall—the "reflective" individual scores above the median for the group on response time and below the group median on errors. As in the case of field-embeddedness, there are other related tasks used to provide convergent evidence of reflectivity-impulsivity; for example, in the Design Recall Task (DRT) the figures are pictures of geometric forms (instead of familiar objects), and the testee has to choose the correct alternative from memory to match the standard. According to Messer (1976), there is fairly good convergence in individuals' performance across these different versions of the matching task.

Once again, in order to demonstrate that this is a *style* of being *impulsive or reflective* in evaluating plausible alternative problem solutions, proponents of this construct have worked to show generality in performance across different tasks and domains. The tendency to be reflective or impulsive seems to generalize from the standard-matching task to some other reasoning tasks (e.g., solving analogies) and to tasks involving motor inhibition and self-regulation using self-speech to guide behavior (see Messer, 1976, for a review). Ironically, the wider the net of generalization from the MFFT to other conceptual and perceptual tasks (e.g., MFFT performance correlates with performance on the RFT and EFT), the less clear it is that *conceptual tempo* is actually the underlying style factor controlling performance. This is especially worrisome because standard IQ measures also often correlate with both performance on the MFFT and with performance on the other generalization tasks (Messer, 1976, p. 1036).

As always, the picture becomes even more complicated when tests of generalization of the conceptual tempo style are performed in the social domain. For example, while reflectiveness/impulsiveness is related to attentiveness and aggressiveness in play for children, there is no relation observed with measures of risk-taking and very mixed results with measures of delay of gratification—again, it is not entirely clear why some of these tasks *do* seem to be influenced by the conceptual tempo "style" and other, ostensibly similar tasks *do not* show the generalization pattern. Moreover, there are the usual problems of interpretation and cause and effect assignment. Reflectivity is related to anxiety about intellectual performance and self-competence image; but these "emotional dispositions" may actually be the critical determinants of response time and errors on the conceptual tasks (Messer, 1976, p. 1039). It is very difficult indeed to support a style argument (with generalization data) when the style is as globally-defined as conceptual tempo (or perceptual field-dependence). Inevitably, the pattern of generalization will be mixed and it will be difficult to specify the real style factors determining performance.

Critiques of this conceptual style dimension have raised issues very similar to those discussed in the case of the field-dependence perceptual style: Is there really a single style dimension of tempo underlying performance on the MFFT and other generalization tasks? Why does one get a mixed pattern of generalization if there is a global style variable at issue here? Shouldn't the style characterization be less value-laden (i.e., equating reflectiveness with correctness) since individuals will also differ in the importance they place on accuracy versus speed in particular task contexts? These qualms about the global style approach have prompted proponents to work on developing a "style-like" analysis of individual differences in problem-solving strategies, but one that allows for more concrete specification of the perceptual and cognitive components of the style and more latitude for domain-specificity of performance and variability in the value placed on the alternative modes of problem solving (see Sternberg & Salter, 1982).

The recent work of Baron (1979, 1982) on the cognitive style of reflectivity/impulsiveness exemplifies this trend towards a *more concrete, less general,* and *less value-laden* description of modes of problem solving.

Following the scheme set forth by John Dewey (1933), Baron suggests that we analyze problem solving in terms of phases of thinking which involve problem recognition, enumeration of possible solutions, evaluating these plausible alternative paths towards a desired outcome, and revising the list of solutions on the basis of evidence gathered in the course of thinking about the problem. In the context of these phases, individuals may be more or less *reflective* or *impulsive* in particular phases of problem solving, across all phases for particular types of problems, or generally so on certain phases across many types of problems—there is much room in the phase analysis for defining consistency in reflectivity in different ways for different people and problems.

The phase analysis also allows for a more concrete and varied definition of reflectivity in different phases of problem solving. For example, reflectiveness in the enumeration phase involves the amount of search engaged in for plausible alternative solutions; an impulsive response in the evaluation phase would involve jumping to an action plan without a protracted consideration of the evidence for and against each alternative plan. Furthermore, the analysis of reflectivity proposed by Baron is considerably less value-laden than is the case in most style approaches. It is quite clear that reflectiveness in problem solving is highly dependent on the level of involvement and motivation to succeed at the task in question (Messer, 1976, p. 1032). Baron (1982) suggests that in most problem-solving contexts a moderate level of reflectiveness is actually optimal, balancing the desire for accuracy with the need for action. Beyond this normative criterion, individuals set their own optimum parameter for reflectiveness as a function of personal values in specific problem contexts. *Impulsiveness* becomes problematic when it hinders a person from reaching his or her *own goals* in a particular problem context; similarly, *reflectiveness* can also interfere with adaptive problem solving if one becomes immobilized in a context that demands quick action. The analysis of the cognitive style of conceptual tempo needs, therefore, to be much more concrete, more value-open or relativistic, and more open to variations in preferred style across different task domains or times in a person's life.

New Directions: Learning from the Cognitive Styles Approach

The cognitive style tradition has made a considerable contribution to the study of personality in that a precedent has been set for the analysis of individual differences in modes of problem solving. This tradition has made it respectable to look for consistencies in the ways in which people perceive situations and reason about problems; in so doing, it has paved the way for the pursuit of a cognitive approach to personality—an approach that places central emphasis on the processes of interpretation and reasoning at the basis of individuals' adaptations to life. Although the cognitive style theorists never fully equated those styles with the *primary* structures of personality, and always looked for relationships between a person's characteristic cognitive style and his or her personality (traits), it seems plausible to pursue that equation. Why must *"personality"* be limited to social and emotional traits when cognitive processes of interpretation and reasoning are critical in shaping a person's unique approach to the problems of social life?

In their review of the literature on cognitive styles, Kagan and Kogan (1970) make a claim for the field-embeddedness style dimension that seems equally relevant to the general pursuit of a cognitive personology. They say: "Its importance derives in large part from its fertility: the dimension is not confined to perception but impinges upon cognition, intelligence, personality, and social behavior. The boundaries between these various domains—so often treated in isolation from one another in psychology—are shown to be permeable . . ." (p. 1340). The cognitive style tradition has been instrumental in convincing personality psychologists to widen their purview and make those boundaries truly permeable. No longer must we think of the study of personality and of cognition as separate pursuits.

Work in the cognitive styles tradition has also provided some important lessons about possible pitfalls in the study of cognition and personality. There seem to be three things to watch for in particular in developing a systematic approach to individual differences in modes of interpretation and reasoning about the problems of social life. First, it is critical that the characterization of a "cognitive style" (broadly defined to include perceptual-interpretive processes) be as concrete as possible with a detailed account of the multiple cognitive components involved in the problem-solving effort. Rather than attempting to uncover a small set of basic cognitive styles derived from very abstract individual difference constructs like psychological differentiation or reflectivity, it may be more fruitful to consider in more detail a larger variety of problem-solving strategies that different people may use in arriving at solutions to common problems.

Second, in a related vein, there should not be the expectation in such an analysis that "styles" of problem solving will in fact be highly generalizable and, therefore, consistent across very different problem contexts. Individuals confront different problems with different histories of experiences and with different values and goals in each context; these variations in experience and motivations produce variability in styles of approaching problems in different domains of a person's life, at different times in life, or involving different task requirements. The complexity of these intra-individual differences in modes of problem solving across domain, time, and task seems particularly evident when the problems at issue involve central aspects of people's lives. Hence, it would probably be unwise to expect broad patterns of stylistic regularity in the domains of problem solving most relevant to the study of personality.

Finally, if we are to take seriously the proposition that modes of thinking may be influential in shaping an individual's adaptation in important arenas of social life (Baron, 1982), then we must also loosen the criteria for *effectiveness* in problem solving. Although cultures and social groups certainly impose normative standards for problem solving and normative values with regard to optimal solutions, individuals ultimately set their own goals and standards, especially in important domains of life. In order to characterize the adaptiveness of a person's interpretation of a problem or plan for a solution, we need to be very sensitive to that person's history and goals in the particular context in question. After all, the thesis of a cognitive approach to the study of personality is that individuals impose their own meaning (and motives) on situations, just as they attempt to adapt to the normative demands of those situations.

THE SOCIAL COGNITIVISTS: KELLY, MISCHEL, ROTTER, AND BANDURA

There are several other major traditions in personality research for which interpretive and reasoning processes play a central role in individual differences. In the next section we will concentrate on four theorists—George Kelly, Walter Mischel, Julian Rotter, and Albert Bandura—whose work complements that of the cognitive style tradition in the emphasis on construal and reasoning processes as central in social adaptation. Here, however, the attempt is to link the interpretive and problem-solving processes to quite idiographic sources—to personal constructs and expectancies and plans and competencies acquired through observation of, and contact with, specific socio-cultural environments. Their social cognitive orientation seems to suggest a more contextualized, less global treatment of the cognitive basis of personality. Hence this work provides a natural transition from the cognitive style tradition to more recent cognitive approaches.

George Kelly: Idiographic Declarative Knowledge

George Kelly (1955; Mair, 1977) was the first major theorist to provide a thoroughly cognitive and fully idiographic treatment of personality. He characterized people as *naive scientists* constantly engaged in *anticipating events* on the basis of hypotheses derived from *personal constructs* about the self and the world. In so doing he placed the interpretive process at the very center of individual differences: *Fundamental Postulate.* "A person's processes are psychologically channelized by the ways in which he anticipates events" (Kelly, 1955, p. 46). Moreover, since he posited a full repertoire of personal constructs particular to each individual, Kelly emphasized the potential for considerable intra-individual and interindividual variability or flexibility in the construals of social situations and events. He spoke of the potential for "constructive alternativism"; people differ in terms of how many alternative constructs they have available, and which they choose to apply at any given time. There are many possible ways of viewing an event since there are many different constructs seen as applicable in any situation.

According to Kelly, at the heart of anticipations or predictions of events are *constructs*—abstract cognitive frameworks, composed of similarities and contrasts, used for perceiving objects and interpreting events. The process of interpretation consists of finding the similarities (and differences) between current and past events via application of some construct(s) that captures a recurrent theme. For one person, being sent to jail as an adult is like being sent to detention as a schoolchild; for another, jail is seen as similar to a period of solitary meditation, more a matter of spiritual testing than of enforced punishment. These two people, construing jail in such different ways, are likely to react quite differently when threatened with imprisonment. For the latter individual one might assume that conscientious passive resistance might be an acceptable form of adult activity; for the former person such activity would be likely to raise too many threatening constructs to be easily accommodated. Their reactions are determined by the application of highly personal and subjective constructs, only remotely tied to objective common features of the event in question. For Kelly, then, what is importantly different about these two people is that they anticipate this event (and, presumably, most other events as well) in quite different ways. As he stated in the *Individuality Corollary:* "Persons differ from each other in their constructions of events" (p.55). Those cognitive constructions derive, in turn, from each person's quite unique repertoire of personal constructs.

In keeping with his emphasis on construals and constructs, Kelly considered in some detail the particulars of a construct repertoire from which such individual differences in social perception and behavior might follow. In so doing he anticipated many features of the *content, organization,* and *structure* of social knowledge also emphasized in recent cognitive approaches to personality. The following discussion reviews some of the features that give Kelly's idiographic-cognitive theory such a "modern" flavor.

1. Idiographic content.   The most basic assumption in Kelly's system is that individuals develop highly personalized, unique content associated with core constructs in their repertoires. He was committed to the idiographic-content perspective in several respects. First, any two individuals are quite likely to apply different constructs to construe the same objective event (as in the jail example given above). Each individual has *core* constructs, basic components in his/her construct system, and other more *peripheral* constructs, less essential in day-day existence. The likelihood that two people would draw on exactly the same core constructs in interpreting a single event is rather slim. Further, even when a common verbal label is applied by two people in describing a single event, the name may refer to a different underlying meaning for each. In the jail example, both individuals might well draw on the construct of "intimidation" (vs. facilitation") in characterizing the anticipated jail experience. For one person, however, intimidation refers to physical and verbal abuse from authority, while for the other person the construct of intimidation taps feelings of awe at the prospect of testing the limits of one's spiritual-personal reserves. Again, the differences in underlying meaning, like the differences in preferences for core constructs, will surely lead to differences in subsequent behavior.

In order to understand an individual's reaction to an event it is critical at least to attempt to gain insight into the often idiosyncratic content of those central personal constructs, i.e., to uncover the underlying meaning. While Kelly acknowledged that all constructs are not easily verbalizable by the construer—he called these implicit constructs *preverbal constructs*—he also considered it critical to uncover those underlying constructs in order to accurately characterize personality. [The notion of preverbal constructs is about as close as Kelly ever came to acknowledging the existence of unconscious mental contents and processes. His position on this matter resembles many recent treatments of highly overlearned declarative knowledge and automatized procedural processes (Smith, 1984).] Like Freud before him, Kelly essentially believed that what appear to be surface inconsistencies (or, to use his word, fragmentations of constructs) in a person's construct system, typically make sense in terms of some overarching construct in the system—the outside observer simply has to adopt the construal system of the person in question in order to see the underlying consistency or coherence in the individual's system.

In the light of the importance he accorded to unveiling both verbal and preverbal personal constructs and to revealing the core consistency in a construct system, it is not entirely surprising that Kelly turned away from traditional inventory self-reports and developed the *role construct repertory test* as an assessment tool for mapping a person's core constructs and their idiographic content (Bannister & Mair, 1968). In the REP test, individuals provide attributes (and the opposing contrast) that distinguish two important people in their lives from a third significant person, repeating this process for a sample of about fifteen such triads. From such a collection of descriptions one can easily get a sense of how the person classifies important people in his or her life. The individual's core constructs, defined by highly personal attributes and contrasts, are assumed to emerge as he or she delineates the important figures in the social world. Then, in a subsequent part of the REP test administration, the participant rates the relevance of every construct generated in the session to every person in the list, thus mapping out the "range of convenience" or applicability of each core personal construct with regard to his or her important social world.

The matrix of person-by-construct applicability ratings from the REP test can also serve as input to a factor analysis or multidimensional scaling analysis in order to derive sets of persons-constructs with similar underlying meaning for the participant. Hence, the idiosyncratic content and organization of personal constructs can emerge, allowing for comparisons between individuals who, for example, inhabit similar environments which they construe and structure in fundamentally different ways (Kihlstrom & Nasby, 1981). The REP test has considerable flexibility as an assessment tool; constructs can be elicited to describe important people, situations, or even self-in-situations. While the procedure was quite labor-intensive in Kelly's time, the advent of high-speed computers makes the process far less cumbersome today. As we will describe in later chapters, the REP test is a precursor to several techniques popular today in the assessment of personal schemas and social prototypes (e.g., Rosenberg & Gara, 1985).

2. Idiographic organization.   Kelly also suggested that individuals' repertoires of personal constructs constitute well-organized systems. Constructs don't exist in isolation from each other: they are organized in some way, and this organization is also an important feature of personality. Kelly assumes that this organization is *hierarchical* in nature, such that some constructs *imply* other, more specific ones in the system. And, of course, the exact nature of the implication structure is highly idiosyncratic from person to person: for one person, "good" may imply positively valued intellectual traits, such as intelligent, creative, cultured, and artistically sensitive; for another person, the same label may subsume attributes such as friendly, agreeable, responsible, and nurturant. Accordingly, these organizational differences would lead to differences in behavior displayed toward a person labeled as "good."

Constructs are arranged in contrasts as well as in hierarchies in Kelly's system. Just as a construct at a particular level in the hierarchy carries positive implications for certain constructs that are subordinate to it (e.g., good people are also friendly), so each construct carries negative implications for some construct that is opposite to it (e.g., good people are not bad). Thus, constructs are more correctly expressed in terms of opposing pairs, with one *emergent* construct and its *contrast*. And, as with hierarchical organization, even when two people give their constructs the same names, the exact nature of the contrast will likely differ from one to the other. For one person, the opposite of "friendly" may be "hostile"; for another, the opposite is closer to "disagreeable" in intended meaning.

Again, the default assumption in Kelly's view is always in favor of idiographic meaning underlying common language. Nor is there any expectation that a person's chosen contrast match the antonym in the dictionary. Constructs are personal, and their meanings are not the same for everyone.

3. Idiographic structure.   Kelly also assumed that individuals differed in the *complexity* of their construct systems. Some individuals have highly differentiated systems, involving many different constructs—and thus many different ways of construing events. Others have very simple systems consisting of only a few constructs, and thus have little opportunity for constructive alternativism. In some individuals the system may be so simple that it is monolithic—the same construct is applied to everything. Taken to an extreme, simple construct systems may spell trouble for the individual. Monolithic construct systems are characteristic of paranoid psychiatric patients, who tend to filter experience through rigid delusional systems. Recent cognitive theories of depression have made a similar argument with respect to the negative depressive schema (Beck, 1976) or the overapplication of an evaluative, good-bad construct by depressive patients (Pietromanoco, 1983). While Kelly assumed a wide range of construct complexity in the systems of well-functioning adults, he did suggest that too simple a system inhibits flexibility in the construal of like events. Individuals differ not only in the sheer number of core constructs but also in the range of application ("range of convenience") of any given construct in everyday life. This additional aspect of structural complexity adds quite a bit of potential for construct system variability—a person may have many very specific constructs in a certain domain of life, while applying only a few constructs quite broadly in other domains. Hence, the assessment of complexity is itself very complex in Kelly's highly idiographic system.

The degree of complexity of structure of a personal construct system has direct implications for personality change in Kelly's theory. Constructs change over time through a process of progressive refinement: *Experience Corollary.* "A person's construction system varies as he successively construes the replications of events" (p. 72). No event is totally novel, in that it can always be construed as similar to something that happened before. However, some events are quite surprising, and don't fit comfortably within an existing personal construct system. When this happens, the person either forces the event into the system, or changes the system in some respect. While the push will always be towards preservation of the system, some events do encourage the addition of new constructs to a system, the refinement of definitions of old constructs, and the widening or narrowing of the range of application of core constructs.

The links between system complexity and personality change arise in this refinement process: *Modulation Corollary*. "The variation in a person's construction system is limited by the permeability of the constructs within whose range of convenience the variants lie" (p. 72). In other words, some constructs are less amenable to this refining process than others—in Kelly's terms, are less *permeable*. For example, core constructs will be harder to alter than peripheral ones, because relatively fewer events will have to be *re*construed in the latter case. Similarly, subordinate constructs will be easier to modify than superordinate ones, because the former carry fewer implications that will also have to be changed. Consequently, personality change—in the form of construct-system change—will be hard to achieve for individuals with relatively simple construct systems, that is, when the system is organized around a few very central core constructs with many interwoven implications.

Regardless of complexity, personality change is at least theoretically possible through the revision of the content and organization of core personal constructs; though for some persons the refinement process will be arduous because of the special significance of a few constructs. Even so, the potential for construct system refinement—*permeability* of the system as a whole—is a key facet of the Kelly system; one that allows for interindividual comparisons along a dimension of "social adaptiveness." And, once again, this is a feature of Kelly's theory that makes it quite "modern" in tone and thrust.

In summary, Kelly demonstrated that it is possible to give central weight to the interpretations that people make of their social world without necessarily assuming that individuals are to be characterized by cognitive dispositions or styles of perception and reasoning that generalize across all life domains. Kelly drew a highly differentiated and idiographic picture of social cognition in his theory of personal constructs. His description of personal construct systems predated, in its details of content, organization, and structure, many recent treatments of declarative social knowledge (e.g., Kihlstrom & Cantor, 1984; Markus, 1983; Rosenberg & Gara, 1985). Individual differences in the *content* of core or central personal constructs, in the *organization* of networks of those constructs, and in the *structure* or elaboration of those constructs in particular content areas, are still viewed as promising sources of variation in defining the cognitive basis of personality.

In subsequent chapters we will incorporate all three of those sources of variation in outlining ways in which people bring to bear different repertoires of declarative social knowledge as they work on personal life tasks. And we will point to ways in which the REP test, or variations on its basic form, is being used to assess the core constructs, domains of applicability, and organization of constructs of individuals with regard to central life-task domains. Kelly's notions of personality change via construct refinement will also be reconsidered as part of comprehensive programs of cognitive-behavior modification. Particularly relevant to those efforts are Kelly's warnings that core constructs with many implications within the construct system—domains of personal expertise and heightened self-relevance—remain especially intractable or impermeable to pressure for change, even when reliance on those constructs in the interpretive process seems to cause personal discomfort. As Kelly noted, individuals work very hard to force the social world to fit within the interpretive framework of core personal constructs.

Walter Mischel: Procedural Knowledge and Competencies

While George Kelly emphasized the themes and constructs underlying social perception and behavior, his student, Walter Mischel, has further explicated the construal process with studies of *procedural* social knowledge (Mischel, 1973; 1977; 1984). Working from a theoretical position similar to Kelly's, in which the task of the personologist is to discover the unique meaning that an individual gives to an event or situation, Mischel has pursued his idiographic-cognitive personology within the framework of the social learning tradition, all the while moving that perspective in more and more "cognitive" directions.

He argued early on, in his now classic critique of the Doctrine of Traits, that the pattern of discriminativeness apparent in diverse domains of social behavior is a natural extension of the idiographic construal process. As Mischel stated then: "[O]ne must know the properties or meaning that the stimulus has acquired for the subject. Assessing the acquired meaning of stimuli is the core of social behavior assessment" (1968, p. 190). Social behavior is not variable because it is *indiscriminate;* it varies across stimulus situations because people are accutely responsive in their readings of those situations to small variations in events. Moreover, behavior varies across persons in a predictable fashion, reflecting the uniqueness of their histories of social learning: "Idiosyncratic histories produce idiosyncratic stimulus meanings"(Mischel, 1973, p. 259).

Mischel chose to study those idiosyncratic acquired stimulus meanings and the construal process itself within the context of a social learning framework of social behavior analysis—analyzing the process by which objective stimulus attributes or reinforcement contingencies impact differently on persons with varying values, expectancies, and personal constructs, derived from particular learning histories. Like his social learning colleagues—principally, Rotter and Bandura—Mischel de-emphasized the direct impact of objective contingencies on behavior and noted, again, that: "The meaning and impact of a stimulus can be modified dramatically by *cognitive transformations*" (1973, p. 260, emphasis in the original). Hence, the critical task is to study the cognitive operations or processes that produce mental representations of stimulus situations, serving, in turn, as the source of individual differences in behavior.

These *cognitive transformations* may be illustrated in an experiment on delay of gratification in children. Children were promised a reward of a highly preferred snack food for performing a task. After completing the activity, they were asked to wait for the reward, though if they preferred not to wait they could immediately receive a less-preferred snack as a reward instead. Those children who were seated in front of the promised reward delayed gratification only a relatively short time—especially if they were instructed to focus on such consummatory qualities as its taste. In contrast, children who were instructed to mentally transform the food into something without consummatory qualities were able to delay considerably longer. Those children who imagined the desired marshmallows as white clouds floating in the sky gained sufficient cognitive control over their behavior to achieve their most preferred outcome. Thus, at least in this instance, behavior is brought under the control of mental representations of the reward, rather than following the pull of the objective stimulus input. Accordingly, the child who can perform the proper cognitive transformation will be able to delay longer than the child who does not have that transformation rule and self-control strategy in his or her repertoire.

In order to understand individual differences in self-control it is critical to assess the person's repertoire of procedural knowledge, both at the level of specific rules (for example, the ones that produce a mental image) and more molar or strategic routines (for example, the goal-setting, planning, and monitoring underlying the successful effort at self-control in the delay paradigm). It is through the operation of these procedures, both the specific rules and the more molar plans and strategies, that individuals achieve volitional control over their own behavior—in Mischel's words: "persons can overcome stimulus control . . . what a situation does to people depends on just how they think about it, on their ideation more than on what they are actually facing" (Mischel, 1984, p. 353).

1. Charting the transformation process.   Using the delay of gratification paradigm as an exemplar instance of individuals exerting *cognitive control* over situations, Mischel has worked to chart the procedural knowledge at the core of successful self-control (Mischel, 1985). At the level of specific ideation rules, he has shown that cognitive distraction (e.g., "think fun") works quite well for preschoolers as a means of overcoming the debilitating effects of having the reward object present in the room. An even better self-control procedure is to think about the nonconsummatory aspects of the reward object (e.g., thinking of pretzels as sticks); a far worse strategy is to focus directly upon the consummatory aspects of the desired reward (e.g., thinking how crunchy and salty the pretzels are). As he suggests, "A child's momentary mental representation of the outcomes in the delay paradigm influences his or her waiting time" (1984, p. 354).

Procedural knowledge of a more molar or strategic sort is also at the base of successful self-control—children do not delay effectively until they develop some self-reflective or metacognitive expertise (Mischel, 1981). For example, most preschoolers are unaware that cognitive (or even physical) distraction is a viable strategy for self-control; by third grade, however, they spontaneously describe elaborate distraction techniques and even occasionally hit on the value of "negative ideation" about the reward object ("think about gum stuck all over them"). Self-instructions and self-monitoring in line with these preferred techniques increases the children's ability to delay gratification and reach their stated goals. As Mischel notes, "They systematically come to prefer, instead of hot ideation, distraction from temptation, self-instructions about the task contingency, and cool ideation about the rewards themselves" (Mischel, 1979, p. 751). In other words, they develop self-reflective insight into actions that help and actions that hinder self-control.

In addition to demonstrating considerable metaknowledge about self-control strategies in the delay paradigm itself, Mischel and his colleagues have shown that children, even as early as age ten in some cases, have quite a bit of sophistication about the nature of *plans* and *planning* in general. Some very young children distinguish between

> the intentional aspect of a plan ("I'm planning to clean up my room tomorrow because I'm planning to have a friend over"), its informative function ("a plan tells you what to do and when and where and how to do it"), and its execution ("you have to make yourself do it when the time comes: planning is the part you do beforehand, but then doing it is the actual right there part"). At older ages, children seem aware of many strategies for forming and implementing effective plans (e.g., elaborate mental rehearsal, public commitment . . .). With greater age, there also may be increasing reliance on a kind of cognitive shorthand . . . without requiring extensive or explicit self-instruction . . . . (Mischel, 1979, p. 749)

This developmental progression, in turn, helps to clarify the role of metacognition in self-control and to underscore the multiplicity of procedures whereby adults gain cognitive control over their behavior.

2. Competencies and consistencies. Consistencies in individuals' behavior, within Mischel's cognitive-social learning perspective, derive from the consistent application of particular personal constructs and cognitive procedures in the construal of different situations. A central concept in this analysis is that of *cognitive and behavioral competencies—* procedural knowledge and action strategies that permit effective handling of particular situations. For example, in isolating the procedural and strategic knowledge associated with effective delay behavior, Mischel posits a set of competencies having to do with the control and diversion of attention, the proclivity to plan and self-monitor in a waiting situation, the characteristic use of ideation strategies to focus on the "cool" aspects of rewards, and so forth. These competencies, once acquired and demonstrated in delay-type situations, will presumably stay in the person's repertoire, such that when a situation with similar meaning and possibilities for action for the individual arises, similar behavior will be evoked.

Mischel and his colleagues have traced the temporal stability in self-control behavior from preschool to adolescent testing. They find that "the correlations give a general picture of the child who delayed in preschool developing into an adolescent who is seen as attentive and able to concentrate, able to express ideas well, responsive to reason, competent, skillful, able to plan and think ahead . . ." (Mischel, 1984, p. 355). While the objective delay situations have presumably changed from preschool to adolescence, the acquired meaning of delay settings remained relatively consistent across time for the individuals.

Behavioral coherence or stability follows from the elicitation of common meaning across time and contexts and the desire on the part of the individual to use his or her acquired competencies to guide behavior. Acting on these competencies may be under the control of incentives—though the incentives themselves are subjectively interpreted by the individual—but the competencies themselves are not acquired anew every time they are used, and they remain available even in the face of considerable periods of disuse. In fact, for Mischel, the stability of these competencies constitutes a central part of the stability of personality as a whole.

In contrast to the presumption of stability of cognitive competencies, Mischel, like Kelly before him, has emphasized the adaptive side of behavioral variability across contexts—individuals demonstrate the intelligent application of their competencies by making fine-tuned discriminations in their interpretations and actions in different situations. For Kelly, rigid consistencies in behavior across situations derived from excessively simple, even monolithic, construct systems and their application indiscriminately across a wide range of ostensibly different situations. In his current work, Mischel adds to this picture of the maladaptive side of nondiscriminating behavior with an analysis of the overuse of too few cognitive and behavioral strategies across too many situations by individuals with problems in adjustment.

For example, when Wright and Mischel (1985) intensively followed the behavior of children with emotional adjustment problems across numerous situations over a two-summer period at a sleep-away camp setting, they found considerable cross-situational consistency (one is tempted to say rigidity) in the children's behavior, but only when measured in situations that placed considerable strain on them and surpassed their competencies in particular "problem domains" of aggression or social withdrawal. It is as if these children consistently fell back on inappropriate or ineffective cognitive-behavioral strategies when pushed to their competence limits by highly demanding situations. In less demanding contexts or in behavioral domains for which they had more sophisticated competencies (e.g., prosocial behavior), they demonstrated a more "typical" level of behavioral variability/consistency (with cross-situation correlation coefficients hovering around .30 instead of sky-rocketing to .73, as in the case of behavior measured in taxing situations in problematic domains).

As Mischel argued some time ago, behavioral flexibility across situations is the norm—and an intelligent one at that—not the exception. People typically have quite intricate and finely-tuned constructs, values, and procedural strategies that enable them to cope with the shifting requirements of different life situations. As both Kelly and Mischel have stressed, the intelligence of human beings is demonstrated by the diversity of interpretations they give to ostensibly similar events and situations; from those diverse interpretations follow highly specialized behavioral responses characteristic of a particular person in a particular context. In subsequent chapters we will try to remain faithful to this conception of individuals' social intelligence, incorporating Mischel's account of procedural social knowledge so as to underscore the creativity in people's strategies for negotiating the tasks of social life.

Julian Rotter: Motivation and Choice Behavior

Working at the same time and place as George Kelly, Julian Rotter presented in his book *Social Learning and Clinical Psychology* (see 1954; also Rotter, 1966, 1971; Rotter, Chance, & Phares, 1972), the first major treatise on *cognitive social learning* in which individuals' behavioral *choices* followed from their interpretations of the stimulus situation and the contingencies for reinforcement. Rotter's is a theory of choice behavior in which the individual responds to the subjective meaning of events and to his or her expectations for reinforcement.

In presenting this theory, Rotter broke with the behaviorist view of social learning in a number of critical respects. Although the behaviorists defined reinforcements objectively in terms of their effects on behavior (Thorndike's empirical law of effect), he defined them subjectively: the value attached to any potentially reinforcing event is subjective, and one person's meat can be another person's poison. Moreover, whereas behaviorists defined reinforcement contingencies objectively in terms of the contingent probability of the event given a particular response, Rotter defined them subjectively, in terms of the individual's cognitive expectations. Finally, Rotter defined the situation in psychological terms, as it is experienced by the individual, and as the individual ascribes meaning to it. As with Kelly and Mischel, objective reality is not as important to Rotter as is subjective reality.

Rotter's expectancy-by-value theory of choice behavior does much to bridge the competence/performance gap apparent in social behavior. People do not always *apply* their cognitive competencies effectively and forcefully to work towards a desired outcome. Therefore, what is needed is an analysis of people's expectancies for reinforcement, along with a view of the meaning and value they associate with the available "reinforcement" in a situation. A central part of the process of interpretation and planning in situations is the evaluation of the likelihood of achieving different potential outcomes and an assessment, however rapid and unarticulated, of the personal value placed on reaching those ends.

While Rotter principally uses "motivational" constructs, his theory is not incompatible with the "cognitive" process of situation construal and strategic self-regulation emphasized by Kelly and Mischel. In fact, it is probably best to consider the full *interpretive process* as one in which events are construed (via the application of constructs and procedures) and, simultaneously, assessed for personal meaning in the light of salient task values/goals. Plans and strategies of action are always formed in the light of expectancies about possible reinforcements in a given context (see Bandura, 1985; Carver & Scheier, 1981; Norem & Cantor, 1986b). To get a handle, then, on this interpretive-planning-action cycle—that culminates in the *choices* of central concern to Rotter—it is important to characterize not only the *constructs* and *competencies* of the individual but the *values* and *expectancies* that guide the choices made in particular contexts.

1. Goals and psychological needs.   Rotter was quite clear in placing goals, and the basic *psychological needs* from which they derived, at the heart of the interpretive and choice process. He argued: *Postulate 6.* "Behavior as described by personality constructs has a directional aspect. It may be said to be goal-directed . . ." (1954, p. 97). Individuals make the choices they do because certain end-states are expected to bring them closer to fulfilling the particular psychological needs that press most upon them at the time. For Rotter, underlying the particular set of goals and values of a person in a particular context is a set of more abstract psychological needs derived at some early age through learning from physiological drives such as hunger, thirst, and warmth. He defined (1954, p. 132) six broad categories of needs, which may be compared to the more extensive list offered by Murray (1938):

> *Recognition-Status* The need to be considered competent or good in a professional, social, occupational, or play activity. Need to gain social or vocational position—that is, to be more skilled or better than others.

Protection-Dependency The need to have another person or group of people prevent frustration or punishment and to provide for the satisfaction of other needs.

Dominance The need to direct or control the actions of other people, including members of family and friends. To have any action taken be that which he or she suggests.

Independence The need to make own decisions, to rely on oneself, together with the need to develop skills for obtaining satisfactions directly without the mediation of other people.

Love and Affection The need for acceptance and indication of liking by other individuals. In contrast to recognition-status, not concerned with social or professional position of friends, but seeks their warm regard.

Physical Comfort The learned need for physical satisfaction that has become associated with the gaining of security.

These abstract needs serve as a basis for interpreting the more specific goals that individuals develop in particular life contexts. A basic need will be played out in very particular ways, and even defined in very circumscribed ways, for any given individual. For example, a person could have a high need for recognition of her achievements in school, but not for her achievements in sports; or a person could seek protection from his friends but not from his family. The important thing, for Rotter, is that people differ in terms of the extent to which they possess each of these needs—their levels of *need value*. Differences in need value, in turn, determine differences in the value of different potential reinforcers.

Hence, Rotter presented a position that combines a set of basic need categories with rather idiographic instantiations of need-goals as played out in the lives of individual persons. Rotter's theory emphasizes the goal-directed nature of social behavior: people engage in activities in order to satisfy their particular set of pressing psychological needs in the contexts in which they have learned to expect to be able to gain some reinforcement—basic psychological needs will never, of course, be fully satisfied, and they may emerge in different specific forms for an individual in different life contexts.

2. Expectancies and cognitive dispositions. For Rotter, there is another very critical component in the cognitive repertoire that shapes choices: *Postulate 7.* "The occurrence of a behavior of a person is determined not only by the nature or importance of goals or reinforcements but also by the person's anticipation or expectancy that these goals will occur" (1954, pp. 102-103). In fact, following Tolman and Postman, Rotter defined learning as the building up of expectancies or hypotheses concerning behavior-reinforcement relationships. The individual's behavior is goal-directed precisely because he or she acts with the expectancy of future reinforcements— environmental events that will lead to the satisfaction of certain psychological needs—consequent upon certain actions in his or her repertoire. Those expectancies (about the consequences of certain actions) are, however, quite subjective and may be at variance with objective probabilities—and with the subjective expectancies of other people. In many cases, the expectancies are rather general hypotheses about the typical outcomes expected in general classes of situations (*generalized expectancies*); with more and more actual experience in particular situations the generalized expectancies are refined and become *specific expectancies* tailored to the particulars of the situation. Of course, the process of repeated refinement of expectancies does not ensure increased "objectivity" or "accuracy"—at least in terms of coordination with the views of other participants/observers.

Rotter placed a fair measure of emphasis on those *generalized expectancy orientations* that individuals bring to situations in the absence of specific experience with the operative contingencies. One of the most important expectations that a person develops concerns the sources of reinforcement: whether they are a function of his or her own actions, or rather dependent on the acts of other people. *Locus of control* amounts to the person's generalized expectancy about the causal relation between behavior and reinforcement (Rotter, 1966; Phares, 1976, 1978). Interestingly, he posited consistent individual differences in *internal* versus *external* locus of control, with locus of control serving as a cognitive rather than a behavioral disposition. However, while locus of control is highly generalized by definition, and thus displays consistency over different situations, the individual's orientation towards causation can change from internal to external or the reverse in accordance with his or her life experiences. Rotter suggested a similar pattern of generalized expectancy (with the potential for dramatic change) about interpersonal trust—with this cognitive disposition defined as one's expectation that he or she can rely on another's promises (Rotter, 1966). Again, the belief (about trust) need not be stable, and can change depending on the individual's specific life experiences.

While Rotter outlined a set of generalized cognitive dispositions on which individuals are assumed to differ consistently, he also clearly viewed these as *learned* beliefs and accorded considerable emphasis in his work to promoting personality *change* in a therapeutic context (Rotter, Chance, & Phares, 1972). Just as personality emerges as individuals interact with their environments, personality changes through a process of interaction, as people have the opportunity to practice certain behaviors and experience reinforcement. Therapy is itself a problem-solving process similar to other social interactions: discussions in therapy allow the client to examine his or her values and expectancies about the consequences of action, and to consider alternate interpretations of situations and different ways of achieving personal goals.

For Rotter, problems of adjustment occur under a number of different conditions. First, the person may place very high value on the satisfaction of some particular need, but have a very low expectation that need-relevant goals will be achieved. In this case, treatment would be directed toward revising either the values or the expectations. Alternatively, a person may value two needs that are incompatible, resulting in conflict; or the person may lack the skills needed to obtain satisfaction in some area. In each instance, the therapeutic dialogue is geared toward a refinement of the person's cognitive orientation to allow for a smoother coordination between the individual's goals in a particular setting and expectations about the action that will bring him or her closest to achieving those needs. For Rotter, as for Kelly and Mischel, personality change derives ultimately from a refinement or redirection of one's interpretations of situations and one's plans for reaching goals in settings that tax the person's competencies and force some accommodation or fine-tuning of standard responses. Rotter firmly believes in the potential for real changes to occur as people confront new life experiences or familiar ones in new settings.

Rotter's theory of choice behavior predates recent efforts to consider the motivational foundation of cognitive strategies (see Showers & Cantor, 1985). As we will detail later, a central task for any cognitive personality theory is to articulate connections between "motivational" elements (like needs, goals, and values) and "cognitive" elements (like expectancy orientations) in social problem solving. Rotter's theory provides a particularly cogent account of these connections, one that avoids labeling the processes of interpretation and choice as the purview of either motivational or cognitive theorists (Nuttin, 1984). In so doing, Rotter sets a precedent by paying attention to the personal goals, tasks, and values which create the "hot" atmosphere for making choices given "cold" appraisal of the expectancy of reinforcement. This is a precedent which we too will follow in the present account of social intelligence.

Albert Bandura: Self-Efficacy and Social Learning

Kelly, Mischel, and Rotter all stress the active role of the self as construer, hypothesis-tester, and planner of behavior. Albert Bandura has added to this picture an explicit emphasis on the *self as interpreter of the self,* that is, on the central role played by self-expectancies and self-reflection in self-regulation and social behavior. For Bandura, "the human capacity for reflective self-consciousness provides a prominent mechanism of human agency. By reflecting on their experiences and on what they know, people can derive knowledge about themselves and the world around them. They also evaluate and alter their own thinking by reflective thought. In verifying thought by this means people generate ideas, act on them or predict from them what should happen, judge from the evident results the adequacy of their thoughts, and change them accordingly" (1986, p. 1).

While Kelly portrayed the construal process as one primarily focused from person to world, Bandura reminds us that people spend much time interpreting themselves as well. Whereas Rotter focused upon the critical role of outcome expectancies—anticipations of particular action-outcome-reinforcement relationships—and Mischel characterized the planning involved in guiding action accordingly ("if I do this, then . . ."), Bandura's recent work has centered on the predominance of *self-efficacy expectations* and *self-reflection* in self-regulation and learning and change. The emphasis on self-knowledge and self-reflective thought has always been implicit in these social-cognitive models, but Bandura has brought the "cognitive self" more explicitly to center stage and in so doing has added another key element in a characterization of the cognitive basis of personality.

1. Self-efficacy and action.   In considering the expectancies that guide behavior in particular settings, Bandura has distinguished between *outcome expectancies* (of the sort traditionally studied by social learning theorists) and *efficacy expectancies*. It is self-efficacy expectancies—judgments about one's ability to carry out the actions required to achieve control over events in a situation—that serve as the primary force or mechanism guiding social behavior. As Bandura says: "Among the types of thoughts that affect human motivation and action, none is more central or pervasive than those concerning personal efficacy" (1986, p. 2). While it is obviously important that the individual expects that a particular behavior will lead to a certain outcome (outcome expectancy), it is equally important that the person has the expectancy that he or she can reliably produce the behavior in question (efficacy expectancy). Note that it is not the actual state of affairs that is relevant here. It does not matter whether the person can, in fact, perform some particular action. What matters is whether the person *thinks* he or she can.

Individuals' expectancies about personal efficacy influence performance, persistence at tasks, experiences of stress, and the success of efforts at learning and behavior change. The efficacy-action relationship has been demonstrated in numerous diverse circumstances: phobics gain greater performance attainments as self-efficacy with regard to the feared task increases (Bandura, Reese, & Adams, 1982); children's level of perceived self-efficacy at mathematics influences their speed of learning, persistence at difficult problems, and overall performance level independent of actual level of mathematics ability (Collins, 1982); and, physical stamina in competitive situations is closely coordinated with perceived self-efficacy at the task (Weinberg, Gould, and Jackson, 1979).

Interestingly, the efficacy-action link is strong even in cases where the judgment of self-efficacy is actually out of line (either under- or overestimation) with some "objective" assessment of past performance or ability. For example, subjects who have been exposed to unsolvable anagram problems are slowed in completing subsequent problems that are solvable. Although this learned helplessness effect is quite complex, it appears to involve the subject's belief that he or she cannot master the situation. In fact, that is not objectively the case: the second set of puzzles is soluble and the students have the competence to solve them. Yet, experience has taught the subject to believe otherwise, and this belief controls behavior. The subjective expectancy is the powerful self-regulator of motivation and performance, not the objective skill or performance base rates (Norem & Cantor, 1986a).

Bandura is quite clear about the centrality of efficacy expectancies in performance: an individual is only as skilled as he or she thinks is the case; without the requisite sense of mastery at the task, the person will not do an optimum job of orchestrating the necessary subskills, nor will he or she work particularly hard at the task. Fortunately, self-efficacy expectancies are not necessarily generalized across different task contexts—repeated failure may lower the person's expectancy that he or she can effectively control outcomes in *those* task settings, but may not necessarily foster a "helpless" attitude generally. Bandura is far more context-specific in his treatment of self-efficacy expectancies than was Rotter in his discussion of generalized expectancies about outcomes (see, also, Metalsky & Abramson, 1981, on attributional style and depression).

Perceived self-efficacy can also change on a moment-to-moment basis, depending upon the person's immediately prior experiences and emotional state. Feelings of elation may increase feelings of mastery (sometimes beyond all reason, as in the megalomania of a manic patient), while anxiety or depression may reduce them. In fact, the "typical" state of nondepressed individuals seems to be conducive to self-appraisals that err in the direction of an overestimation of capabilities (Lewinsohn et al., 1980). Bandura considers this to be a cognitive benefit rather than a failing: "If efficacy beliefs always reflected only what people can do routinely, they would rarely fail but they would not mount the effort needed to surpass their ordinary performances" (1986, p. 14). Once again, it is wise to recall that it is the *perceived* state of mastery, not necessarily one derived directly from past performance, that mediates future behavior and motivates (or debilitates) persistence at specific tasks.

One of the most intriguing influences of self-efficacy expectations comes in the domain of stress and coping. Bandura and his associates have suggested that self-efficacy serves as the cognitive mechanism through which individuals gain feelings of controllability that reduce stress reactions in risky situations. Or, to state it differently, "It is mainly perceived inefficacy to cope with potentially aversive events that makes them anxiety provoking" (Bandura, 1986, p. 6). For example, Bandura, Taylor, Williams, Mefford, and Barchas (1985) demonstrated that people's beliefs about their coping efficacy in phobic domains affect the release of catecholamines, which, in turn, signal autonomic stress reactions. When phobic subjects confronted tasks in their "strong efficacy range" their epinephrine and norepinephrine levels were relatively low; levels of these stress indicators soared when the tasks exceeded their self-perceived levels of coping efficacy. Most importantly, after treatment in which perceived levels of coping efficacy are raised via guided mastery experiences, these same individuals experience and demonstrate no particular stress reactions (measured subjectively or physiologically) when they confront those same previously taxing task situations. As Bandura notes: "perceived coping efficacy rather than tasks, per se, is the source of variance in affective reactivity" (1986, p. 8).

2. Self-efficacy and cognitive motivation.   For Kelly, Mischel, Rotter, and Bandura, the motivation to perform is at least as much cognitively based as derived from primary biological drives/needs. As Rotter suggested, the anticipatory motivation associated with playing through in one's mind the likely outcome of a behavior and considering the likely reinforcement in the light of personal values (also cognitively represented) is considerable. It is this process of *forethought,* often quite automatic and sometimes "preconscious," that turns objective reinforcements into subjective incentives, enabling the individual to take control over outcomes (Kelly, 1955; Bandura, 1986) and to potentiate effective strategies of self-control (Mischel, 1984).

While the anticipation of response outcomes is a central form of cognitive motivation and self-control, Bandura, in keeping with his emphasis on self-efficacy expectancies, has also considered in detail the role of internal standards and self-evaluation processes in motivating performance. As individuals work towards a goal, they engage in a cognitive comparison process, matching their progress with a standard of performance and evaluating it in the light of their perceived sense of efficacy at the task. They may value an outcome very highly and be quite sure of its occurrence given the successful performance of a particular action, but without a belief in their personal efficacy at the task even a small discrepancy-from-standard will be discouraging. On the other hand, when a person evaluates his or her progress at a task and feels quite discontented over a substandard performance, he or she will be even more motivated than ever to work for the desired outcome *when* a sense of high personal efficacy for the task exists.

The self-regulation cycle is a very dynamic, ever-shifting one: As standards are set and revised and performance monitored and evaluated, the individual's motivation to persist rises and falls in accordance with his or her assessments of self-efficacy and task progress. Feelings of self-esteem derived from the self-evaluation of progress, and of self-efficacy, derived from evaluation of prior experience and from tutelage and observation of similar others in similar contexts, conspire to set the affective-motivational context for further performance. Self-reinforcement, in the form of self-praise (or self-reproach or denial of rewards in the face of substandard performance) can be a highly effective means of motivating (or discouraging) optimal orchestration of one's skills and effort.

3. Self-efficacy, learning, and change.
In the writings of all four of these theorists, expectancies about the future—be they outcome expectancies, self-efficacy expectancies, personal constructs, self-plans—help to determine the preferred course of action in a particular context. Hence it is particularly critical to consider the social learning roots of such cognitive expectancies, and Bandura has spent considerable time at that project (1977; 1985). In general, he has distinguished between two forms of learning. *Learning by response consequences* is the kind of trial-and-error acquisition of knowledge familiar from the operant behaviorism of Skinner. However, this learning is given a cognitive emphasis. Direct experience provides information concerning environmental outcomes and what must be done to gain or avoid them. As a result, the person forms mental representations of experience that permit anticipatory motivation in the form of outcome expectancies.

Modeling involves learning through vicarious experience—by observing the effects of others' actions. While a term such as "modeling" encompasses learning through *example,* Bandura also uses it to cover learning through *precept*—deliberate teaching and learning, often mediated by linguistic communication. In other words, reinforcement is merely one way for the person to gain information about the outcomes of action—the other ways being example and precept. In either case, the learner is an active participant in the process, interpreting this "information" in the light of current goals, skills, and opinions about the "teacher." The learning process, and the expectancies derived from it, will be quite specific to the history and current state of the individuals involved, forming an idiographic record of direct and vicarious experience.

Self-efficacy can serve as an example of how anticipatory expectations develop through social learning. Obviously, one source of self-efficacy is *performance accomplishments:* the personal experience of success and failure. Repeated success experiences will raise the person's expectancy that he or she can effectively control outcomes in similar task contexts. But the same sorts of expectancies can be generated through *vicarious experience.* Observing other people's success or failure will lead to appropriate expectations about oneself—at least to the degree that one perceives oneself to be similar to those other people and to possess the requisite subskills that they modeled. (In fact, observations of others' performances can be diagnostic both for assessments of efficacy and outcome expectancies and for teaching skill procedures painlessly.)

Perceived self-efficacy can also be shaped in the absence of any experiential basis whatsoever, merely through *verbal persuasion*. A person who is repeatedly told that he or she is incapable of accomplishing some goal, especially if that information comes from an authoritative source, may actually come to believe it about him- or herself. That person, in turn, may come to struggle with an entirely novel problem in the future, precisely because it closely resembles the sorts of problems diagnosed as beyond his or her competence limits by others in the past. While perceptions of personal efficacy can and do vary across time and task, certain formative past experiences with self-evaluation or tutelage and persuasion may indeed be very hard to ignore.

Accordingly, this brings us to the question of "personality change" in the form of modifications in expectancies and values and skills. Bandura, like the other theorists described here, ascribes to a dynamic, modifiable conception of human personality: one in which action (in the form of mastery experiences), cognition (most particularly with regard to perceived self-efficacy), and environmental forces (of social support and social models) interact to produce personality change. Consistent with his interactive model of cognitive motivation, Bandura eschews efforts to pit cognitively-based treatments versus behavioral treatments: *mastery experiences* are critical both for teaching skills and for developing efficacy at a task; *efficacy*, in turn, is critical in ensuring behavioral change that persists beyond the initial guided demonstrations with a model. As Bandura notes: "Changes result from cognitive processing of performance information rather than from the performances per se" (1986, p. 26). He cites as one example driving phobics who have been successfully guided to master one route but remain incapable of going beyond that terrain. These individuals, by comparison to more successful treatment cases, remain immobilized by their perceived inefficacy, even in the face of performance successes.

The process of change with regard to perceived self-efficacy, as with the (re)mastery of skills and the modification of incentives for performance, is slow—slower, perhaps, than the original acquisition process—and not likely to result in highly generalized transformations. Yet, the recalcitrance of self-debilitating thought in the face of mastery experiences should not be taken as support for more "purely" behavioral-oriented efforts at change—for, as Bandura argues, "it is by analyzing thinking patterns that one can best discern the type and amount of mastery experiences needed to alter self-debilitating thought . . . . By ignoring cognitive interactants, one sacrifices understanding of the mechanisms mediating change, retards the rate of progress which depends upon optimally persuasive behavioral tests, and jeopardizes generalization of change" (1986, p. 27). As a diehard "social cognitivist," Bandura places cognition at center stage in the behavioral process; as a strong proponent of the "active cognitive self" he attributes primary agency for change to the ameliorative powers of self-reflection in a supportive social and behavioral environment.

New Directions: Learning from the Social Cognitivists

There is much that is common across the cognitive style and social cognitivist treatments of personality: most particularly, personality adaptation is presented as a process of cognitive problem solving with interpretive and reasoning expertise at the center of the process. The core structures of personality are, to borrow from Mischel's terminology, mental representations; the core dynamics are procedures for interpreting, goal setting, planning, and self-monitoring of performance, and evaluating feedback. These cognitive structures and procedures, in turn, serve motivational functions, enabling the individual to fulfill some basic needs (as in Rotter's expectancy-by-value theory), to regulate the expression of those needs (as in Mischel's work on self-control processes), to gain some degree of control over events (as in Kelly's theory of anticipations), and to assert personal agency through self-regulation and reinforcement (as in Bandura's depiction of cognitively-based motivation).

In other words, these cognitive problem-solving processes serve the self-regulatory functions of concern to cognitive style theorists from the psychodynamic tradition (i.e., serve as *cognitive controls*). Moreover, the analyses of the cognition-action links, as presented, for example, by Mischel or Bandura, fit well with the concerns of the style theorists more interested in demonstrating that cognitive styles are associated with distinctive patterns of *social behavior*. Finally, at the most general level, there is continuity between the cognitive styles theories and those of the social cognitivists, because in both traditions cognition and personality are inextricably intertwined.

While these traditions are similar in the basic framework for studying personality adaptation as social problem solving, there are many differences in the specifics of the approaches. One way to see these differences is to consider how the social cognitivists fare with respect to the critiques frequently leveled at cognitive style approaches. For example, as noted earlier, many have argued that the central problem with traditional cognitive styles is that they are described in very general, abstract terms (e.g., field-embeddedness as a global versus analytic perceptual style) and yet assessed with very specific (nonsocial) laboratory tasks (e.g., EFT or RFT). There is a need, therefore, for more molecular analyses of the components of a "cognitive style" and for assessments taken directly in socially mean-ingful task contexts.

The social cognitivists do seem to provide fairly concrete, molecular specifications of the cognitive structures and procedures underlying social behavior in different life domains. For example, Kelly's REP test provides a very detailed account of the content, organization, and areas of com-plexity/simplicity of an individual's personal construct system. Those constructs, in turn, are generated with reference to significant people and situations in the person's current (or past) life environment. Similarly, Mischel traces the effectiveness of different procedures for self-control—distraction, "hot" and "cold" ideation—and assesses children's competence at self-control with regard to their (meta)knowledge of, and intention to use, effective plans and strategies in demanding delay situa-tions.

Rotter, perhaps the most prone to describing the cognitive basis of personality in general terms, still emphasizes the formation of spe-cific outcome expectancies as the individual gains experience in a situ-ation and posits abstract needs (like those for recognition and status) only as a guide to understanding individuals' more specific values (and associated goals). Bandura fills in more details about individuals' an-ticipatory cognitions with his characterization of self-efficacy expectations as finely-tuned, changeable, and highly potent estimates of one's ability to master the right action in a particular task setting. He charts the ups and downs of individuals' efficacy expectancies directly in the midst of very self-relevant social tasks, e.g., following individuals with driving phobias as they navigate new roads.

For the social cognitivists, then, cognitive expertise of the sort that enables effective social problem solving—the regulation of needs and the control over outcomes—comes in fairly specific forms. Components of social problem solving, such as constructs and plans and efficacy and outcome expectancies, are directly assessed within tasks that at least simu-late the operative demands and incentives of naturally occurring social situations.

Another way in which the social cognitivists are quite specific and concrete in approach is in the emphasis on highly personalized social learning as the basis for the acquisition of constructs, expectancies, and rules for social problem solving. The stress on individualized learning histories translates into idiographic cognitive expertise with regard to the content and organization of those constructs and expectancies and procedures. As Kelly noted, the potential for complexity in individuals' construct systems is increased substantially by the personalized meaning that common constructs acquire and the different patterns of associations across constructs for different individuals. Similarly, for Mischel, there is no single effective/ineffective style of delay of gratification; individuals acquire procedures for distraction, ideation, and planning and then create personally effective strategies by combining those procedures in novel ways to fit their particular state and the particulars of the current context. (Hence, the "delayer" may be quite discriminative in the use of various different strategies to meet his or her goals and the demands of each delay task—much like Baron's reworking of the "reflective style.") For Rotter, each person acquires a very individualized set of need values and outcome expectancies, which function in consort to produce highly specialized patterns of choice behavior. Similarly, Bandura frequently notes that the social learner makes *creative* use of multiple sources of information (from direct experience and precept and example) in *constructing* expectancies and goals and plans in each different context.

For each of these theorists the emphasis is more on the complexity and diversity of constructs and expectancies and procedures in an individual's repertoire than it is on delineating basic cognitive styles necessarily defined at a highly abstract level of discourse. Their systems all allow for cross-situational generalization—Kelly's suggests a comparison between monolithic and complex construct systems, Mischel's suggests an analysis of a "planfulness" dimension, Rotter's explicitly develops the locus of control distinction, and Bandura's suggests that self-efficacy expectancies may well generalize across contexts and tasks. However, in each case the thrust of the analysis is to demonstrate that social behavior is highly discriminative across context and task precisely because individuals respond to the *personal meaning* that each situation holds for them; and those meanings are derived from personalized construct and rule systems. Those construct and rule systems, of course, are reflections in part of ritualized social-cultural themes acquired over a lifetime via observation and tutelage. But each person's reading of those themes has a personal mark, as reflected in a particular way of construing situations and discriminating between situations. That thrust leads these social cognitivists to place more weight on idiosyncratic ways of interpreting and reasoning about social life, rather than emphasizing generalized cognitive styles.

The cognitive style tradition has also been taken to task for being too value-judgmental, such that certain styles are generally assumed to be more functional for certain types of tasks than are others (e.g., reflective style over impulsive style for reasoning tasks; field-dependent style over field-independent style for social perception tasks). As noted earlier, this critique is based on the notion that individuals will bring to bear different goals in a task context and, hence, it will be quite difficult to judge a priori which style best fits a given task. This critique is a particularly interesting one to consider in the light of social cognitivist theories. While the social cognitivists strongly argue for the idiographic nature of people's specific task goals, it is also the case that certain characteristic patterns of task-construals are seen as more/less adaptive than others in these theories, too. For example, there is little doubt that Kelly views monolithic or simplistic construct systems as a hindrance in social adaptation, that Mischel views effective self-control as an important outcome of adaptive cognitive strategies, that Rotter values generalized *internal* expectancy orientations over *external* ones, while Bandura emphasizes the adaptive side of the nondepressed person's "illusory" glow of confidence and task mastery. The cognitive components at issue here are different from the traditional style dimensions—more multifaceted, concretely specified and assessed, and idiographic in content and form—but not altogether value-free, either.

Of course, there is good reason for some value-judgments to surface in any cognitive theory of personality. After all, a central function of individuals' constructs and rules for self-regulation is to allow for effective social adaptation, as well as to promote personal satisfaction. Hence, it would be shortsighted to avoid value distinctions altogether by taking a thoroughly relativistic stand. The social cognitivists do take value stands; however, they typically adopt a value position that differs somewhat from the cognitive style position.

Consider, for example, the value-judgments made by Witkin et al. about the field-embeddedness style: field-independent individuals do well at analytic thinking, while field-dependence is a style optimally geared to performing well at social life tasks. While such a position does allow for variety in the optimal style-task match, preventing some styles from being consistently identified as optimal (i.e., both field-independence and dependence have their place), it also ignores the possibility that different styles may be optimal in a single task when they are used in the service of different goals. In other words, the style-value position assumes that a task goal can be identified a priori (on the basis of some external, accuracy criterion) and that the "best" style for the task will then follow clearly because the task goal remains constant.

Suppose, however, that the task goal varies across people and for a given person over time. In that case, standard style-task optimal matches would not generalize over time and persons, and the "best" cognitive style would be one that enabled a flexible approach to be taken in response to the particulars of the moment. That is, the individual might need to call on both field-independent and dependent orientations to reach his or her goal; and, it would not always be the case that a dependence-social task and independence-analytic task equation could be assumed a priori just from knowledge of the ostensible task purpose. Moreover, in any given task context, two individuals might well pursue the same goal with contrary styles, each style being best-suited to the individual's skills. For example, one person might maximize accuracy on a reasoning task with a slow reflective analysis, while another person does best with top-of-head responding so as to control performance anxiety. The characteristically best-suited styles for those two persons in that task setting might even change dramatically as they get experience with the task—the valued orientation is not set in stone either for the individual, the task, or even the individual-task pair.

Accordingly, at an abstract level, the value that pervades the social cognitivists' writings is one of *cognitive flexibility* and *malleability* enabling behavioral adaptiveness. In this vein, Kelly wrote about constructive alternativism, Mischel emphasized individuals' discriminative facility, Rotter posited a learning process from generalized expectancy orientations to specialized, context-sensitive ones, and Bandura placed considerable store in the potential for self-reflection to facilitate behavior change (and vice versa). In all four cases, the value is on flexibility and malleability of thought—and, consequently, on cognitive "styles" conducive to change—because the assumption is that when the cognitive structures of personality are fluid and dynamic then individuals will be in the best position to fulfill their own particular goals in a variety of social life contexts. For example, while Bandura sees much that is positive in an "optimistic glow" that encourages risk-taking in problem solving, he would most certainly not place positive value on a rigidly optimistic orientation that prevents a realistic self-appraisal of efficacy and performance in the course of a problem-solving effort. It is the rigidity of styles and the assumption that a given style is to be valued a priori for a given kind of task without regard to the specifics of the person-in-context—the person's history, goals, current state—that would bother a social cognitivist.

Hence, by implication if not explicitly, the social cognitivists argue for a premium on "intelligent" thought—in the sense of unprogrammed, nonrigid, creative thinking (Gould, 1981). Moreover, they evaluate intelligent responses with reference to maximizing personal goals not necessarily of the sort typically viewed as prescriptively optimal (Miller & Cantor, 1982) or generally assumed to be stable and applicable across all persons in a given task context (Baron, 1982). While it is certainly difficult to avoid value judgments in discussions of personality adaptation, it is possible to place the value on flexible thinking—both in the goals associated with tasks and in the cognitive styles applied in the solutions to those tasks. The cognitive style theorists began that process by considering the optimality of particular style-task matches; the social cognitivists have gone a step further by stressing multiple task goals and the need for flexible "styles" to fit those ever-changing task demands and goals.

In turn, these accounts of the cognitive bases of personality suggest that the next appropriate step in this tradition is a thorough analysis of what *intelligent* social problem solving would look like. What are the criteria of flexible thinking when applied in the context of pressing life tasks of individuals? How are we to analyze *social intelligence* and judge its value? In the service of making some progress on these issues we turn now to a consideration of recent developments in the study of intelligence.

chapter
3
Personality and Intelligence

In keeping with the traditions of Kelly, Rotter, Mischel and Bandura, and the cognitive style theorists, our intention in the chapters to come is to outline a cognitive personology based upon the unique meaning that individuals ascribe to the situations of their lives and the solutions that they prefer in attempting to adapt to the demands of social life. With this purpose in mind, it seems appropriate to permeate the boundaries between the study of personality and of cognition and to place *intelligence* at the center of such a theory. We focus on intelligence because people use their intellectual resources to frame problems and search out solutions in their life contexts; in so doing they give meaning to their life situations and adapt to the demands of those settings. Intelligent action seems to have all the features which characterize adaptive behavior—it is purposive, flexibly attuned to the goals most salient in each problem context, not rigidly stereotyped or indiscriminate in nature—and adaptive behavior is the natural domain for a study of personality.

More specifically, as cognitive personologists, we want to think about the intelligence that individuals bring to bear in solving their personal life tasks—*social intelligence*. We want to focus on the characteristic ways in which individuals interpret their currently pressing life tasks and evaluate options and plan action in important arenas of their ongoing social lives. Individuals use their social intelligence to work explicitly and implicitly on a wide range of problems, from decisions about career and marriage to the everyday tasks of which those more monumental ones are made, i.e., tasks like learning to relax before job interviews or finding a suitable date for Saturday night. It is that repertoire of social intelligence, and the dynamics of its use and the processes by which it is learned and changed, that contribute to individuals' attempts to adapt to their life environments.

There is some fair measure of irony in the fact that we propose to place intelligence, albeit social intelligence, at the center of a cognitive theory of personality. The analysis of social traits has proceeded in the past by analogy to the analysis of intellectual traits; in fact, in many ways intelligence is often viewed as the super-trait (factor) of them all. Accordingly, placing so much emphasis on social intelligence could doom this approach to the same critique advanced against the cognitive styles and social traits traditions. Although this is a point about which we must remain cognizant, new directions in the study of intelligence suggest that it may well be both appropriate and fruitful to pursue social intelligence as a centerpiece of personality. Therefore, before describing our approach further, we will first consider some of the different ways in which *intelligence* can be conceptualized; which, we hope, will pave the way for an analysis of personality based upon the social intelligence that people bring to bear in the service of their personal life tasks.

CONCEPTUALIZATIONS OF INTELLIGENCE

The Psychometric Approach

When we think about the meaning of intelligence, or the features of intelligent action, two somewhat different conceptions come to mind. On one hand, intelligence is measured by intelligence tests. Intelligence is constituted of a set of basic mental abilities (Thurstone, 1938) concerned with the capacity to perceive relationships, organize and remember information efficiently, draw logical inferences, and reason through problems (Horn, 1980, on fluid intelligence). Individuals differ in these capacities, and performance on intelligence tests should provide a clue to the rank-order of a set of people with regard to intelligence. In fact, according to some psychometricians, the basic abilities that comprise an intelligence test cohere in a meaningful way into a single unitary entity of general intelligence or "g" (see Gould, 1981, p. 24). Therefore, test performance should provide a window on an individual's standing with respect to intelligence. As Gould (1981, pp. 24–25) suggests, for some theorists the psychometric approach to intelligence is about "the abstraction of intelligence as a single entity, its location within the brain, its quantification as one number for each individual, and the use of these numbers to rank people in a single series of worthiness. . . ." If the tests are good tests, producing reliable assessments that validly tap the basic abilities independent of education, experience and cultural values, then performance on the tests should provide an indication of the "upper limit" of problem-solving ability of the individual (relative to others in the population). The emphasis is on stable capacities, not on proclivities or skills that can be trained to improve with experience and motivation (Baron, 1981). In fact, patterns of decline with age would be more reasonably expected than would evidence of improvement with tutelage (Horn, 1980). In its prototypic form, then, intelligence is the ability to see and think; different people have different amounts of this ability (or collection of abilities), and tests should provide a relatively "pure" look at a person's level of ability untarnished by training or momentary fluctuations in involvement or effort.

A hallmark of this psychometric approach to intelligence testing is the characterization of the basic architecture of an individual's intelligence, independent of the amount and content of specific knowledge about different domains in the real world. The desire is to capture those primary mental abilities, the "essence" of intelligence (Baltes, 1986). For example, Cattell and Horn, two central theorists of intelligence, measure *fluid intelligence* with tests of perception and reasoning using materials that are either familiar to all participants or novel for everyone (Cattell & Horn, 1978; Horn, 1980). Hence, spatial abilities may be tested with a novel paper-folding task or a hidden figures test with relatively commonplace figures. Tests of abstract reasoning ability will include analogies with nonsense materials, word association tasks with totally commonplace words, and so forth. The expectation is that these tests will reveal the "true" rank order of individuals on a cluster of primary abilities without consideration of advantages accrued by certain individuals who may have had special *exposure or practice or tutelage* during the course of everyday social life. Ideally, the tests should measure fluid intelligence *outside of the life context* of the individual, tapping those abilities that do not depend on experience with the particular norms of a specific culture or the language and facts accepted by that culture. Moreover, since the items on the test do not relate to the everyday tasks and life goals of the participants, people should be equally motivated to work on these items—in theory, the tests should not be more or less meaningful to different individuals.

Cattell and Horn (1978) compare fluid intelligence to a form of intellectual performance, which they call *crystalized intelligence*, that is heavily influenced by social experience and cultural norms. Tests of crystalized intelligence tap the individual's knowledge of the language and norms and beliefs accepted as "facts" in his or her particular culture—the amount and content of a person's real-world knowledge. Such tests stress vocabulary, general information, and reading comprehension and there-fore are heavily influenced by the extent of social learning, tutelage, and experience in the culture. Moreover, since the items measuring crystalized intelligence do relate directly to a person's everyday life experiences, some people will be more motivated by and involved in these tasks than will others for whom the material fits less well with their life goals and activities. For example, Horn (1980) describes two tests of crystalized intelligence that are likely to be of more interest to some people than to others: the common uses task requires that people think of new ways to use commonplace objects, and one test of verbal comprehension utilizes newspaper articles as stimulus material to be understood and paraphrased. In other words, while tests of fluid intelligence purposely avoid reference to commonplace events and objects, tests of crystalized intelligence draw directly from the individual's repertoire of real-world knowledge. In some respects, crystalized intelligence fills in the specific *content* and *form* within the fluid *structure* for each individual.

The Lay Approach

The other approach to the description of intelligence, *the lay conception*, is based on a characterization of individuals in their everyday life contexts without reference to performance on standardized tests intended to measure intelligence. For example, Sternberg et al. (1981) make reference to "people's conceptions of intelligence" which they study by asking people in supermarkets and railroad stations and college libraries simply to describe the characteristics of a prototypically intelligent person. According to these descriptions, the lay conception includes a large number of characteristics of intelligence which seem to break down into three categories: practical problem-solving ability, verbal ability, and social competence. Table 3-1 summarizes the attributes frequently mentioned in these descriptions. Interestingly, while the lay conception is similar to the psychometric one in its emphasis on problem-solving skills (fluid intelligence) and verbal ability (crystalized intelligence), these skills are described with reference to social tasks (e.g., "deals effectively with people") and practical life problems (e.g., "listens to all sides of an argument"). Moreover, the interpersonal features of intelligence—the characteristics that allow a person to comfortably interact in his or her social context—are given particular weight in the lay conception, especially in the set of features labeled here as "social competence" (e.g., "is sensitive to other people's needs and desires").

The lay conception includes a rather large number of characteristics of intelligent people, many more features than any one intelligent person would be expected to possess. In this sense, the concept of intelligence is a "fuzzy" one (Neisser, 1979) based on a set of typical features of intelligent people rather than a set of defining features possessed by all such individuals. Intelligent people, whom we would consider to be equally adept in their handling of their life tasks, may differ considerably in their

TABLE 3-1   Factors Underlying People's Conceptions of Intelligence

FACTOR	EXAMPLES
I. Practical problem-solving ability	Reasons logically and well.
	Identifies connections among ideas.
	Sees all aspects of a problem.
	Keeps an open mind.
	Responds thoughtfully to others' ideas.
	Sizes up situations well.
	Gets to the heart of problems.
	Interprets information accurately.
	Makes good decisions.
	Goes to original sources for basic information.
	Poses problems in an optimal way.
	Is a good source of ideas.
	Perceives implied assumptions and conclusions.
	Listens to all sides of an argument.
	Deals with problem resourcefully.
II. Verbal ability	Speaks clearly and articulately.
	Is verbally fluent.
	Converses well.
	Is knowledgeable about a particular field of knowledge.
	Studies hard.
	Reads with high comprehension.
	Reads widely.
	Deals effectively with people.
	Writes without difficulty.
	Sets aside time for reading.
	Displays a good vocabulary.
	Accepts social norms.
	Tries new things.
III. Social competence	Accepts others for what they are.
	Admits mistakes.
	Displays interest in the world at large.
	Is on time for appointments.
	Has social conscience.
	Thinks before speaking and doing.
	Displays curiosity.
	Does not make snap judgments.
	Makes fair judgments.
	Assesses well the relevance of information to a problem at hand.
	Is sensitive to other people's needs and desires.
	Is frank and honest with self and others.
	Displays interest in the immediate environment.

Source: From *People's conception of intelligence,* by R.J. Sternberg, B. Conway, J. Keton, & M. Bernstein (Table 4). Copyright 1981 by the American Psychological Association. Adapted by permission of the publisher and the author.

specific intelligent characteristics. There is no one *right* way (or even two or three right ways) to be intelligent (Cantor, 1978; Cantor & Mischel, 1979). For example, Sternberg et al. (1981) found that the features of an intelligent person differed when people described "academic intelligence" versus "everyday intelligence." Similarly, different subject populations (for example, college students versus people questioned at a railroad station) placed different emphasis on academic and practical skills in their descriptions of a generally intelligent person. As might be expected, students placed considerably more weight on academic intelligence and less emphasis on practical intelligence than did people questioned about their conceptions of intelligence at a railroad station. When laypeople consider the attributes of an intelligent person, those attributes vary according to the life contexts in which the individual operates. There are many ways to be intelligent and part of being intelligent is being able to adapt one's behavior smoothly and easily to the varying demands of different social situations. Intelligence is a truly fuzzy concept.

The lay conception of intelligence places considerable emphasis on the content and amount of knowledge that a person possesses in different life domains; intelligence is *expertise* at particular tasks (Baltes, Dittman-Kohli, & Dixon, 1984; Siegler & Richards, 1982). For example, researchers have looked at chess masters and exceptionally creative scientists as case studies of intelligence and expertise (Chi, 1978; Larkin et al., 1980). In these cases, the intelligent person is not simply the older one, for ten-year-old chess "experts" can outperform adult novices without much trouble (Chi, 1978). Moreover, intelligence defined as expertise in a specific domain of knowledge is not restricted to skill in domains that involve direct tutelage like chess or physics. Sternberg (1984), for example, talks about "tacit knowledge" such as knowing what it takes to succeed at a particular job, while Baltes et al., 1984, speak of "expertise in the pragmatics of life" (p. 66). Moreover, we all know people with exceptional skills at very complex social tasks such as listening to another person and quickly seeing their problem so as to empathize fully with their situation. In fact, we tend to label such persons with descriptions that resemble those applied to experts at nonsocial tasks; we say "he's good with people" as readily as we remark on his expertise in chess or mechanics or cooking (Schneider et al., 1979).

Although such displays of "social intelligence" are not as easily associated with years of tutelage and experience as are performances in chess or physics, still it is assumed that social experience in a particular culture is critical to building social expertise as well (Scribner & Cole, 1978). In fact, intelligence in the lay sense of the word is so linked to performance within a specific social-cultural environment that one definition of an intelligent person might well be a person who really knows and understands his or her culture. For example, the subjects in the Sternberg et al., 1981, study stressed that intelligent people are good at sizing up a situation and figuring out what action is called for in a particular context (see Table 3-1). Intelligent people with expertise at social tasks seem almost instinctively to do the right thing at the right moment in their particular arena of expertise. Some people seem to know exactly when to get angry openly and when to stifle discontent for the sake of smoothing an interaction; others are "experts" at leadership or at competition, and so forth. This aspect of social intelligence requires an exquisitely developed appreciation of the nuances of situations and the cultural norms and demands associated with the types of situations common to one's area of social expertise. Just as masters of crystalized intelligence know their vocabulary and masters of chess know their moves, these social experts know the rules of the game in particular contexts (Argyle, 1981).

The lay conception of intelligence also includes a characterization of the proficiency of the individual's basic reasoning processes and problem-solving capacities—the realm of fluid intelligence (see Table 3-1). Intelligent people are thoughtful rather than hasty, sizing up a situation rather than reacting instinctively solely on the basis of past experience. They see the nuances to every problem and develop new solutions instead of reacting in a stereotyped fashion. Yet, intelligence is also linked to action; intelligence allows one to get things done (Sternberg & Salter, 1982). Intelligent people can also see the "big picture" and act pragmatically to achieve their goals instead of remaining "lost in thought." Hence, even the characterization of "basic intelligence" from the lay perspective is embedded within the pragmatics of everyday life; therefore, Sternberg et al. (1981) labeled the cluster of features generated to describe an intelligent person's problem-solving skills as "practical problem-solving ability" (see Table 3-1).

The lay conception of intelligence seems, then, to stress expertise in a knowledge domain, particularly in an area of social competence, and practical problem-solving ability. The inference that someone is intelligent derives from the ways in which he or she handles the mundane as well as the monumental tasks of social life. Accordingly, Baltes (1986), for example, conceptualizes *wisdom* as "expertise in the domain of life planning, life management, and life review" (p. 20); the wise person has "good judgment about important matters of life" (p. 20). A person who is "socially wise" seems to have a sixth sense about other people; he or she knows, for example, exactly when to offer help and when to wait to be approached in a tense interpersonal situation. He or she uses social wisdom to solve important life problems, although those problems may be confronted in the very mundane circumstances of everyday life.

One of the most interesting features of the lay conception of intelligence is that it is difficult to devise a test that adequately captures an individual's intelligence or wisdom at social life tasks (Denney, 1984). While we all feel capable of recognizing and characterizing intelligence (Siegler &

Richards, 1980), translating from the context of naturalistic social problem solving to a testing context is not a simple matter. As Sternberg et al. (1981) note: "Most assessment and training of intelligence that transpire in the real world are based on implicit rather than explicit theories of intelligence. For example, many more assessments of other people's intellectual abilities are made in the course of interviews and even everyday social interactions (such as cocktail parties, conversations at coffee breaks, and the like) than are made in the evaluation of scores from intelligence tests" (p. 38).

First of all, the problems in social life that best tap an individual's practical intelligence are not obvious. For example, it is difficult to come up with paper and pencil intelligence tests that capture vividly the questions involved in practical problem solving in domains of social life. In one recent study of social intelligence, the questions involved reasoning about abstract moral dilemmas and about the appropriate responses to interpersonal social dilemmas (Keating, 1978). Although these questions certainly tap some aspects of social problem solving, the author concluded that "accurate assessment of social competence may require a different approach to measurement, presumably one that capitalizes on systematic in situ observation" (p. 222). While it may not be necessary actually to observe an individual in the process of a social interaction to assess social intelligence, it is likely that measurements of intelligence should be based not on abstract questions about social dilemmas but, rather, on questions about the real-life tasks confronted by the individual. For example, in order to assess business people's "tacit knowledge" about their profession, Wagner & Sternberg (1985) recently asked a group of executives to answer questions about realistic occurrences in their work world—questions about the priorities for different job-related tasks for an inexperienced person, the criteria for judging success in their field, and so forth. They found that knowledge and understanding of the "hidden agenda of their field of endeavor" was a good predictor of objective success in the field—a good measure of social intelligence in that life domain. However, devising such questionnaires in order to reveal expertise about the "ins and outs" of problem solving in a social setting is by no means a straightforward task. While psychometricians may agree that a vocabulary test gets to the heart of crystalized intelligence (Horn, 1980), there is likely to be less consensus among people as to the critical problems in everyday life that tap intelligence (Neisser, 1979).

Also, it is rarely clear what problem-solving skill or cluster of skills is most critical to arriving at an intelligent solution to a pressing personal or social problem. For instance, even when there is agreement that a particular situation constitutes a "test" of social intelligence—such as the negotiation of an interpersonal conflict among a married couple—there is no guarantee that everyone will define the problem the same way and even less likelihood that people will agree on the optimal solution. When asked to discuss the antecedents of a particularly intense argument, spouses will frequently "see" the problem in very different ways, pointing to different critical events and attributing blame for the negative outcome to different key behaviors emitted by their partners (Kelley, 1979). As Baltes (1986) suggests, judgments about intelligent solutions to complex real-life problems are relativistic—there are multiple ways to "do it right" and different perspectives on the desired outcome.

It is also the case that slight changes in the context in which a problem arises can result in substantial variation in the preferred mode of intelligent problem solving. In fact, the lay definition of intelligence seems to imply responsiveness to the subtleties of social contexts, such that a solution that is intelligent for one person or in one situation may be absolutely stupid in another instance. Marital therapists are often confronted with the necessity of explaining that it takes a special intelligence to see that what one partner wants in a particular context will hurt or even anger the other partner. The problems of social life that are most taxing and important are ill-defined, with multiple construals and alternative solutions depending on the particular experiences and goals of the individuals involved.

Stability and Consistency of Intelligence

As Sternberg et al. noted in their study of lay and expert conceptions of intelligence, the two perspectives do not differ that much in the content of the features attributed to intelligent people—intelligence is manifest in verbal ability, problem-solving skills and some form of social competence or practical, real-world sensitivity (see Tables 4, 5 in Sternberg et al., 1981, pp. 45, 46). In fact, the lay conception's dual emphasis on knowledge-expertise and problem-solving skill is mirrored in the psychometrician's common distinction between crystalized and fluid intelligence (Horn, 1980). However, there are clear differences as well between these two perspectives on intelligence. Clearly the lay conception emphasizes the *pragmatic goals* to which intelligence is applied in the context of everyday life tasks and problems; the psychometric approach aims at shedding the intricacies and ambiguities of ill-defined social problems and achieving an elegant characterization of "pure" intelligence. The psychometric approach wants to characterize intelligence with a few basic tasks and optimal solutions accessible to individuals in a variety of social and cultural contexts. The lay conception preserves the nuances of intelligent behavior because it characterizes problem solving *in vivo*, allowing for a diversity of goals and optimal solutions for different people in different contexts.

Since the psychometrician aims to characterize an individual's basic intellectual resourses (e.g., fluid intelligence) abstracted from social-cultural learning and experience, the expectation is that intelligence will remain relatively stable over most of the life span and then decline in old age (Baltes, 1986). By contrast, the lay conception of intelligence, which does not distinguish clearly between a basic intellectual reserve and skills and knowledge learned through social experience, allows for considerable growth in intelligence over the whole life course (e.g., Baltes, 1986; Sternberg, 1984). As a function of social tutelage, exposure to the culture, and trial and error practice, individuals get wiser and smarter about the pragmatics of social life. Problems that were hard to face and solve at one time in life often do become more tractable later in life. It is difficult to point to a stable core of intelligence that has remained unchanged in the face of this growth in the capacity to confront the problems of life in a specific domain.

Of course, the psychometricians argue that the wisdom of age is simply an accumulation of more skills of crystalized intelligence and that the elderly may appear particularly "wise" precisely because many of the problems of social life are best handled by an application of crystalized intelligence (see Horn, 1980, p. 313). However, the changes in problem solving are not really confined to problems tapping crystalized intelligence alone. For example, Baltes (1986) describes data from his laboratory suggesting substantial improvement in the performance of older persons on traditional tests of fluid intelligence. This improvement comes in the face of training programs designed to make these types of tests as familiar and commonplace in the experience of the elderly as in the lives of young adults. As Baltes et al. (1984) note: "Performance enhancement in elderly subjects based on five one-hour training sessions, then, is roughly equivalent to twenty-year longitudinal age decline observed in the same age range for subjects not participating in any known training activities. Such evidence shows further how relatively minor the naturally observed aging decline in intellectual functioning appears to be when compared with information based on plasticity research" (p. 43). (Ironically, as Gould [1981] points out, Alfred Binet himself believed strongly in the plasticity and propensity for growth in basic intelligence.) Similarly, Baron (1982), extending the teachings of John Dewey, suggests that adults can be trained to think more reflectively and less impulsively across a variety of content domains. In addition, some evidence has begun to accumulate suggesting that the standard decline in fluid intelligence with age abates when tests of reasoning and memory rely on materials that are familiar in the everyday experience of the elderly (Denney, 1984; Hultsch & Dixon, 1984). In other words, performance on a wide variety of basic reasoning tasks may be subject to effects of familiarity and may change and improve with tutelage, exposure, and practice. Hence, more recent conclusions about the stability of intelligence seem to be moving towards the lay conception of a fairly fluid system, one that benefits from social learning.

Another difference between these two conceptions of intelligence concerns the amount of cross-domain or cross-task consistency in intellectual performance assumed by the two positions. While the psychometrician would be discouraged if an individual performed very differently on two tasks tapping an aspect of practical intelligence, for example, the lay person expects individuals to be "smart" in some domains of life and rather "dull" or "dense" in others. This is true even in the case of problem solving in two domains that seem to involve common reasoning skills. How many parents do we all know well, for example, who are masters at role-playing and empathizing with a distraught child but claim to be at a total loss when a subordinate at the office acts out of sorts. Rather than assume, as a psychometrician might, that the individual is not as socially perceptive and competent as we thought from his or her parenting performance, most of us simply acknowledge that the person's role-playing and empathy skills themselves will vary considerably as a function of prior experiences in different life domains. It isn't just that the person is having a bad day at the office; instead, we suspect that he or she never cultivated that aspect of social intelligence in the work domain of life, never worked to shape those particular social skills at work.

Intellectual performance and intelligence itself, from a lay perspective, rest on experience that is very specific to a particular domain of social life. Hence it is not surprising, from this viewpoint, to find considerable intraindividual variability or domain specificity (Baltes, 1986, p. 14). The recognition of domain specificity in intelligence is less characteristic of current psychometric conceptualizations of intelligence (see Baron, 1982, for a review). The recent treatments of cognitive styles, like reflectivity, cognitive complexity, or repression-sensitization, allow for improvement via practice in a person's performance on problem-solving tests, but still do not emphasize variation in performance across such tests (see Sternberg & Salter, 1982, for a discussion of this point). In fact, as we noted earlier, the very notion of a cognitive style seems to imply consistency in performance for one person across different problem-solving domains that all tap the style in question. By contrast, the lay conceptualization is somewhat more flexible in that the expectation is that people will vary in intelligence in different life domains, even when the requisite skills are similar, simply because their social experience (that shapes the intelligence) has been different in those areas of life. For example, the parent mentioned above who freezes in the face of discontent among his or her co-workers but is masterful in handling a distressed child, may have had very different social-learning experiences in the two domains. He or she may have watched closely and learned well the specifics of interpersonal communication between parents and children on the home-front, while fine-tuning a different set of problem-solving skills for the office. The message in his or her childhood may well have been that problem solving in families is qualitatively different than problem solving in the work-world; empathy is appropriate in one case and wouldn't even occur to the individual in the other context, even though the problem to be solved requires empathetic role-playing in both cases. Differential social experience shapes not just transitory performance, leaving basic intelligence untouched, but, rather, leaves a fundamental imprint on the content and structure of the problem-solving skills brought to bear in different life domains.

The lay viewpoint also leads one to expect considerable variability between groups of people on standardized intelligence tests (Baltes, 1986). From this perspective, we should expect to find differences between groups of people of different ages, social-cultural background, social roles, and so forth—cohort effects—that are of comparable magnitude to individual differences in intelligence. These differences would be expected because the norms and goals of the particular social-historical-cultural context in which an individual gathers problem-solving experiences shape his or her intellectual skills and proclivities, and these norms and goals will change with major variations in roles or life contexts (Veroff, 1983). For example, consider again the individual described earlier who demonstrates considerable perceptiveness as a parent and is rather "socially dense" at work. According to Veroff's (1983) report from a national survey, Americans in 1956 construed their work tasks in very different terms than did Americans questioned in 1976: the earlier sample was quite task- and product-oriented, while the latter group emphasized personal actualization more than organizational productivity. Suppose the socially sensitive parent in this example learned his or her world view about work in the 1950s. He or she may find the implicit norms of the work world today, stressing interpersonal sensitivity and group process, to be quite foreign and uncomfortable. Moreover, the problem-solving strategies that his or her cohort practiced for the work world are entirely different and ill-suited to the present-day scene—the skills once valued by that cohort are less functional today. Consequently, it is not particularly surprising to see the 1950s individual at a loss for "intelligent" solutions to the 1970s problems in the work arena.

As Baltes (1986) suggests, the social ecology in which an individual conducts his or her life will impact enormously on intelligence by setting up certain tasks or problems as worthy of attention and certain solutions as worth striving to reach. "The social environment sets the problems that intelligence is used to solve" (Sternberg & Salter, 1982, p. 16). Those problems may be quite different—in terms of the task demands and optimal solutions valued in that environment—than the ones valued by and practiced in earlier times. The same argument, of course, holds true for variations not in historical norms and context, but in the composition of one's social group or organizational context or family group and so on

(Veroff, 1983; Baltes, 1986). The strategies valued in one group and worked on by one individual may leave a person ill-suited to handle ostensibly similar problems that crop up in a new life context in which different implicit norms are operating. Those new social demands and optimal solutions then, in turn, constitute the context in which an individual's intelligence is tested anew. Some of these new "intelligence tasks" will map directly onto familiar problems and the person will still do well on them; other tasks will not tap as clearly the socially-valued and well-practiced skills of that person's familiar social group. When a poor match between the currently valued strategies and solutions and the person's well-practiced skills occurs, then a seemingly intelligent person may seem less than masterful at some life tasks.

In sum, then, the lay perspective allows for much more variability in intellectual performance on reasoning tasks—variability within individuals over the life course, variability for a given person across domains of problem solving that ostensibly tap common skills but map onto different life problems and experiences, variability between groups of people on tasks that engage highly valued and well-practiced skills for some and not for other social groups—than does the psychometric conception of (fluid) intelligence. The basic features of the lay concept of intelligence seem to demand a more "fluid" (or, perhaps, fuzzy) definition of intelligent behavior in a problem-solving context. Intelligent solutions are defined *relativistically* with personal and social-cultural goals in mind—a smart solution for one person or culture may be rather stupid in another case. The problems that tap intelligence are, themselves, *ill-defined*, representing different "problems" for different people and in different cultures. And the problems that elicit intelligent behavior change dramatically in content and difficulty level when they occur in different *social contexts*—the "same" task takes on different meaning for a person or culture when it is embedded in a different social setting. All of these features conspire to demand a rather complex and malleable approach to the meaning and the measurement of intelligence (Baltes, 1986; Sternberg, 1984).

INTELLIGENCE: EXPERTISE, CONTEXT, AND PRAGMATICS

Recent approaches to the study of intelligence (see Sternberg, 1982, for a review), upon which we will model our treatment of social intelligence, borrow eclectically from the psychometric and the lay conceptions of intelligence. The objective is to study intelligence as problem-solving-in-context, even though it is clear that capturing the essence of an intelligent performance in vivo is much more difficult than is providing a characterization based on a score on a standardized IQ test. However, difficult or not, the goal is to avoid the error of reification (Gould, 1981) in which "the intelligence tests come to be viewed as better indicators of intelligence than the criterial, real-world intelligent behaviors they are supposed to predict" (Sternberg, 1984, p. 270). As Sternberg (1984) reminds us: "there seems to be a need to study intelligence in relation to real-world behavior..." (p. 270), and, we would add, in relation to the goals encouraged by an individual's social life context. We need to adequately characterize the *expertise* that people bring to bear in solving their life tasks, the *context* in which they operate such that certain problems become important, and the *pragmatics* of those life contexts that define the goals to be achieved in an intelligent solution. For the ultimate meaning of intelligence is not to be captured in a single number representing "g" (or even in a set of numbers depicting the person's standing on a collection of primary mental abilities), but rather in the ease with which a person can develop and utilize an expertise in a life domain that is adequate to face changes in the intra- and interpersonal demands of that environment.

1. Expertise.   At the core of any characterization of intelligence, be it the psychometrician's fluid and crystalized intelligence or the lay conception of a smart person, is a repertoire of knowledge used in solutions to problems. Recent treatments of the intelligence repertoire by cognitive psychologists draw a distinction between declarative knowledge and procedural knowledge (Anderson, 1981; Hastie & Carlston, 1980). Declarative knowledge is comprised of the set of *concepts* (facts, beliefs, attitudes) about real and imagined objects and events in the world. It includes knowledge about different kinds of animals, trees, cars, people, social situations, and so forth (Rosch & Lloyd, 1978); knowledge of historical happenings and of events from one's personal autobiographical history (Neisser, 1979); knowledge of how mechanical objects work and of the typical sequence of events in restaurants, birthday parties, and the like (Abelson, 1981). Clearly, an individual's store of declarative knowledge will be highly elaborate in some content domains and rather sparse in other areas—each person has a very personal profile of declarative knowledge which varies across domains as a function of his or her particular learning history. Accordingly, any characterization of intelligence as expertise must be quite fine-tuned (domain specific), capturing the variability in a person's declarative knowledge across domains. Experts in an area not only have a great deal of knowledge and experience in that area upon which to draw, but the knowledge is also well-organized with many interconnections between facts such that it is easy to use in appropriate contexts (Sternberg & Salter, 1982).

Procedural knowledge, the other part of the core intelligence repertoire, includes the rules (procedures) for acquiring, manipulating, and retrieving information in order to solve problems and plan behavior (Anderson, 1981). These rules specify the basic cognitive operations that people perform in order to learn and remember information and make inferences about real and hypothetical events. In addition to the tradition-ally studied rules of "formal" inductive and deductive reasoning—e.g., the component processes used in solving analogies on intelligence tests (see Sternberg, 1984)—the procedural repertoire includes a number of more "informal" cognitive heuristics for making judgments and attributions and inferences about people and events (Tversky & Kahneman, 1974; Nisbett & Ross, 1980). For example, we often predict the behavior of an individual on the basis of stereotypes about that kind of a person, rather than by relying on base rates for the behavior in question. Additionally, the repertoire includes a set of higher-order or meta-rules for planning and monitoring and making decisions about what needs to be worked on and how to go about solving the problem now and in the future (Sternberg, 1984). For example, Baron's (1981, 1982) arguments about reflectivity suggest that some people engage in more "meta-thinking"; they consider multiple angles on a single problem and play through alternative strategies for working on the problem and critically evaluate the outcome in order to improve on future solutions. In some senses, the reflective problem-solving "style," utilizing meta-rules of problem definition, solu-tion, and evaluation, can be considered analogous, in the procedural domain, to expertise in terms of amount and organization of knowledge in the declarative domain (Sternberg, 1984, p. 283). However, as Baron (1982) points out, in this case "more is better" may not be true—the "intelligent" problem-solver knows when to be reflective and when to stop thinking and take action; he or she has a good sense of what problems require considerable thought and at what stages of problem solving that reflection is best aimed.

The expert in some procedural domain can execute the appropriate mental operations automatically without conscious effort in the context of a familiar problem and yet can take the time to be reflective and ensure accuracy in the face of novel or more difficult problems (Smith, 1984; Sternberg, 1984). Expertise or intelligence in the procedural domain in-volves balancing the trade-off between speed or effort and accuracy or completeness: the intelligent person knows when to keep plugging and when to be satisfied with a current solution (Simon, 1954). For example, Larkin et al. (1980) found that experts at physics problems actually spend more time than do novices at "encoding" the problem and planning a general approach to it, although they are also likely to be quicker than novices at carrying out a solution once that plan of attack has been settled upon (Sternberg, 1984, p. 283). Of course, individuals are not likely to be uniformly reflective or impulsive across all domains of problem solving; in some contexts a person will consider all angles on a particular problem, while the same person might impulsively jump to a conclusion in another problem-solving context. Individuals are not likely to be uniformly intel-ligent or stupid in the procedural domain—in some contexts they will show enormous (metacognitive) wisdom in exerting just the necessary amount of problem-solving effort at the right stage in a problem, while at other times in other places they will clearly overdo attention to a particular aspect of a particular problem (Siegler & Richards, 1982). As in the case of declarative knowledge expertise, metacognitive or procedural expertise is likely to be a function of explicit and implicit training and experience in specific problem-solving domains; hence, such expertise or intelligence may well vary considerably across domains and over the life course for any given individual.

   2. Context.   Recently, theorists have demonstrated a special concern that intelligence be measured on tasks that are *relevant* to the life contexts of the individual (Neisser, 1976; Sternberg, 1984; Baltes, 1986). The "contextualist" concern stems in part from the suggestion that optimal performance on tests of intelligence depends upon the enlistment of well-practiced cognitive skills (see Baltes et al., 1984, on strategies for testing-the-limits; Denney, 1984, on optimally exercised potential) and that the life contexts of a person establish the tasks on which those skills get practiced (Baltes, 1986). In other words, it is terribly important that theorists of intelligence study the life contexts of an individual both because those contexts tend to selectively foster the growth of declarative and procedural expertise in certain culturally-valued domains and because an individual may only perform up to optimal potential if and when those expert skills are tested in "appropriate" or well-exercised tasks. As Sternberg (1984) comments: "I define intelligence in terms of behavior in environments relevant to one's life. The intelligence of an African pygmy could not legitimately be assessed by placing the pygmy in a North American culture and using North American tests, unless it were relevant to test the pygmy for survival in a North American culture" (p. 271).

   The contextualist position requires a careful analysis of the life contexts that have special status in setting the tasks on which individuals typically bring to bear their intelligence. Veroff (1983), in an analysis of the contextual determinants of personality, suggests five contexts that may well hold that special status: historical, cultural, developmental, organizational, and interpersonal (see Baltes et al., 1984, for a similar discussion of age-graded, history-graded, and nonnormative life events). For example, life-span theorists have argued that different life tasks become normatively appropriate and self-relevant for an individual at different stages across the life course (Erikson, 1950; Ryff, 1982). While an adolescent may develop considerable declarative and procedural expertise in working on problems of interpersonal intimacy, the young adult may be an expert at career work. These normatively age-graded tasks will then constitute the life contexts in which the individual is most frequently exercising his or her problem-solving intelligence. Similarly, particular cultures (or subcultures) will place special emphasis on certain problem-solving tasks regardless of an individual's age, e.g., Americans stress self-reliance and productivity for little children almost as much as for adults (Erikson, 1950). The culture defines in some sense the contexts in which intelligence is exhibited.

These life contexts shape not only the general problem domains given special emphasis but also the specific tasks on which an individual will be well-practiced (Sternberg & Salter, 1982). In order to obtain optimal task performance it is helpful to frame a problem in such a way that it taps naturally into the person's life experience, i.e., into domains of optimal exercise (Denney, 1984). For example, in a developmental study of problem solving with young adults and middle-aged and elderly adults, Denney, Pearce, & Palmer (1982) used three sets of problems: the "young adult" problems were designed to tap directly into the problem-solving experience of young adults (e.g., how to get home at Christmas with no money and no car); the "middle-aged adult" problems tapped similar skills of logical reasoning but the content of the problems were likely to be most familiar to middle-aged adults, and similarly for the "elderly adult" problems. The expectation was that each age-cohort would perform best on the problems that most directly tapped dilemmas that were realistic possibilities of concern in its life context. This expectation was confirmed, at least for the young and middle-aged adult cohorts: middle-aged adults had just as fine-tuned skills of problem solving as the young adults who consistently out-performed them on "traditional problem-solving tests," but those skills were best exhibited on well-practiced problems within their realm of life experience. (The elderly adults, whom Denney et al., 1982, expected to have some loss of potential for problem solving, in general did not outperform the other two cohorts even on the "elderly adult" problems.) In order to "test the limits" of intelligence it is extremely important that relevant problems be used, problems which fit nicely into the general life domains of special interest to the individual and whose content makes sense to the person so as to maximally elicit his or her problem-solving expertise.

Another striking example of the influence of life contexts on problem-solving performance is provided by the study of different subcultures and the intellectual experiences of their members. For example, Turkle (1984) suggests that for a segment of college students—the "hackers"—computer programming has become a metaphor for problem solving across their life domains. These young adults work on problems of intimacy as if they were solving a tricky computer puzzle; "debugging a relationship" is a commonplace occurrence, a well-exercised skill in their intelligence repertoire. Hence, in order to truly test their intelligence in social life dilemmas, it would be helpful to tap into their special form of problem-solving expertise by phrasing the problems so as to elicit declarative and procedural knowledge about programming. The hackers know how to deal with problems of intimacy—they simply frame the problems and the solutions in terms familiar to their own most well-exercised life experience. Problems that tap both "formal" and practical reasoning capacity can be framed in multiple ways; often, a frame that violates the life experience of the individual will also fail to elicit the full intelligence of that person.

3. Pragmatics.   Individuals respond to the pressures of their various important life contexts by setting goals, whether explicitly or implicitly. Those goals, in turn, help to guide problem-solving behavior, delineating the important from the trivial problems on which to work, and constraining the nature of the preferred solutions. An analysis of the pragmatics of intelligence recognizes the central role that motivation and choice (in the form of values and goals) play in intellectual performance (Baron, 1982). As Sternberg (1984) says: "Intelligence is purposive. It is directed toward goals, however vague or subconscious those goals may be" (p. 272). In order to fully understand why an individual works with particular intensity on a problem, or how that person goes about trying to solve the problem, it is critical to appreciate the objectives that he or she has in mind. Appreciation of the pragmatics of intelligence in a particular life context can dramatically alter the criteria for a "wise" or "intelligent" solution to a particular problem (Baltes, 1986). Baron (1982), for example, argues that while in most instances a reflective attitude results in better problem solving, there are some contexts in which impulsive solutions are actually more intelligent (e.g., in emergency settings; in the throes of an intimate moment). Similarly, Simon (1955) argued that it was not always intelligent for a person (company) to work to maximize the expected value of a decision, when a somewhat less spectacular outcome achieved with less effort would suffice. And the same could be said for many of the solutions to thought problems that are generated via quick and dirty cognitive heuristics in the place of more tedious, but technically more accurate rules of formal logic and inference (Miller & Cantor, 1982). Analyses of intelligence must be relativistic, recognizing that solutions which are intelligent for one person in one context may well be unwise for another person facing an ostensibly similar problem with a different set of goals in mind. To be intelligent is to be pragmatic, and pragmatics change with variations in life contexts (Baltes et al., 1984). Sternberg & Salter (1982) describe the newer approach to intelligence as follows: ". . . this conception has a fundamentally pragmatic character to it: Solving the problems of life is placed at the center of the conception of intelligence" (p. 17).

Measuring Intelligence: Novelty Versus Familiarity

We have suggested that the study of intelligence focuses on the *expertise* that individuals develop in their *life contexts* in the service of *personal goals.* The intelligence repertoire is comprised of declarative and procedural knowledge (expertise) that enables a person to comprehend a problem in a life context—to "see" a problem in context—and to carve out a solution that makes sense in light of his or her particular life goals, i.e., to find a pragmatic solution. Accordingly, the measurement of intelligence centers in large part on the expertise required by the tasks confronted in relevant life contexts. What is it that people know about a particular life domain that allows them to identify problems in that context and plan appropriate (pragmatic) solutions? How do they use that knowledge in the service of goals that are salient at that time in their lives? An intelligent person in a particular life domain knows a great deal about that domain (declarative expertise) and has at his or her fingertips well-developed procedures for handling situations in that domain (procedural expertise). Moreover, the intelligent person uses that expertise wisely, devoting the most attention to important problems which are relevant to pressing goals (metacognitive expertise) in that domain. Consequently, intelligence should be measured in domains that tap relevant tasks and goals for the individual in question. In other words, individuals develop expertise for particular purposes in specific life domains; familiar tasks in familiar domains will tap that expertise.

However, as both psychometricians and lay persons have pointed out, intelligence also involves the ability to handle novel task demands or familiar tasks in novel circumstances (Sternberg, 1984). The intelligent person can use his or her expertise in a particular domain in such a way as to be sensitive to variations in task demands and in optimal solutions. Intelligent people are flexible; they see alternative ways to define a problem and alternative solutions to pursue (Spivak, Platt, & Shure, 1976), rather than being locked mindlessly into familiar routines (Langer, 1978). Moreover, intelligent people are sensitive to feedback that suggests the necessity for revisions in their approach to a situation or problem (Piaget, 1972; Haan, 1982). These aspects of intelligence support the importance of measuring intelligence with tasks that are not so much a part of a person's everyday routines that he or she will fall back automatically on familiar solutions—tasks labeled by Sternberg (1984) as "nonentrenched" tasks which make demands outside of the person's ordinary experience.

The measurement of intelligence as construed here is particularly tricky, then, because of the need to balance familiarity and novelty in the selection of tasks and task contexts. On one hand, the tasks and contexts have to be familiar enough so as to tap into relevant issues and the expertise of the individual. On the other hand, in order to see how the person accommodates to variations in task demands and social feedback, it is important to present the person with some novelty either in the actual task or the circumstances in which it occurs. The psychometric approach achieved this balance in task selection by measuring fluid intelligence with novel tasks and crystalized intelligence with more familiar, commonplace materials. But how can one achieve a balance without resorting to a position which suggests two separate kinds of intelligence? One solution preferred recently by several theorists is to mix task novelty with practice at the task, allowing the person to confront novel demands slowly over the course of many practice trials (Smith, 1984; Sternberg, 1984). Another solution that we favor is to follow a person as he or she works on a familiar and important task in a new life context. The novelty of the context changes the specific demands of the task and the concrete goals to be worked towards without presenting a totally unfamiliar problem to be solved. For example, a high school student who is a virtual expert at the tasks of social intimacy may well find it necessary to accommodate that expertise to the slightly different pressures of social life at college (Cantor, Brower, & Korn, 1984). In a sense, the new life context defines a new task for the individual, but one that is familiar enough to tap the relevant expertise and yet novel enough to assess the person's capacity for accommodation. This is a tricky but not impossible balance to achieve in task selection.

Social Intelligence: A Separate Entity?

The emphasis recently on measuring intelligence (problem-solving expertise) in relevant life contexts that tap relevant pragmatic goals has brought with it a reconsideration of the importance of "social intelligence" as contrasted with "academic intelligence" (Neisser, 1976). Quite some time ago, Thorndike (1920) argued that we should be concerned with social intelligence, which he dubbed "the ability . . . to act wisely in human relations" (p. 228). Contemporary theorists have picked up this interest in the intelligence directed at the tasks of social life, rephrasing the earlier definitions in order to build on present evidence about intelligence. For example, Baltes et al. (1984) refer to wisdom as "an expertise in the pragmatics of life" (p. 66); and Weinstein (1969) speaks of the "ability to accomplish interpersonal tasks" (p. 755). Moreover, there is on the part of lay people a strong belief in social intelligence as a component of general intelligence. An intelligent person "accepts others for what they are; admits mistakes; displays interest in the world at large; thinks before speaking; makes fair judgments . . ." (Sternberg et al., 1981, p. 45). There is clearly a renaissance now in the study of social intelligence (Ford & Tisak, 1983).

For the most part, psychometricians and lay people alike conceptualize *social intelligence* as a separate set of primary mental abilities to be contrasted with the abilities of academic or formal intelligence (e.g., Keating, 1978). Guilford (1967), for example, built on Thorndike's suggestion "that there is a social intelligence apart from ordinary intelligence" (p. 77); the province of social intelligence (or behavioral cognition as Guilford labeled it) is the "awareness of attention, perceptions, thoughts, desires, feelings, moods . . . of other persons and of ourselves" (p. 77). This special sensitivity to intra- and interpersonal information is assumed to constitute a distinct form of intelligence which, in turn, facilitates mature social functioning (Gough, 1968) and behavioral effectiveness (Ford & Tisak, 1983). The socially intelligent person, for example, would be able easily to use nonverbal cues, as presented in photographs, to judge the seriousness of a relationship between a mixed-sex couple (Sternberg & Smith, 1985). He or she would be described by peers as reliable, tactful, capable, and foresighted (Keating, 1978), and he or she would be judged as very "competent, smooth, poised" in an interview situation (Ford & Tisak, 1983, p. 200). In a wide variety of social settings, the socially intelligent person exhibits sensitivity, competence, and maturity about the problems of social life.

Since social intelligence is concerned with cognition about other people and social events, psychometricians have measured this aspect of intelligence with tests that are intended to tap social perceptiveness. For example, Guilford (1967) reviews a series of such tests in which the main task is to identify the feelings, traits, actions of another person on the basis of a photograph. The test, called Faces, was designed by analogy to a vocabulary test; the subject views four faces and has to pick the one that depicts a certain mental state. Similarly, Expressions is a test in which the subject has to match descriptions of figural gestures to line-drawn pictures of the gestures of a person (see Figure 3-1). In Questions, the subject

FIGURE 3-1   Guilford's Expressions Test. An item from the Expressions test. Which of the four alternative expressions conveys the same information about the state of mind of the person as in the lone figure above? Answer 4 is keyed, because it also gives the impression of emphasizing a point. From *The nature of human intelligence*, by J. Guilford (Figure 4.3). Copyright 1967 by McGraw-Hill. Adapted by permission.

 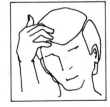  

decides which of four alternative questions might have been asked of an individual shown in a picture with a particular facial expression (e.g., a leering expression goes with a question about a sex scandal). As is clear from these examples, the typical test of social intelligence is based on some aspect of (nonverbal) person perception in which a social stimulus, like a person's face or a picture of a social scene, is abstracted from the social context or behavioral scenario in which it is normally embedded, and the testee must fill in that context and guess what is going on in the picture.

Another form of social intelligence test is designed by analogy to abstract reasoning problems used to tap "academic" intelligence. For example, Keating (1978), in his "search for social intelligence," looked for measures that would tap "formal reasoning about the relationship of the individual to society . . . (i.e., moral or ethical reasoning), and interpersonal reasoning or insight (i.e., appropriate choices in a situation involving interpersonal conflict) . . ." (p. 219). For this purpose, he used the Defining Issues Test, in which the person's level of moral reasoning is assessed on the basis of responses to stories depicting moral dilemmas, and the Social Insight Test in which social judgment is assessed on the basis of the person's decisions about the appropriate action to take in different social dilemma situations. The key, then, to these reasoning tasks is that the content depicts a social or ethical dilemma involving interpersonal actions as compared to the typical test of abstract reasoning in which the problems are "nonsocial" in nature. However, it is important to note that social intelligence is still being measured by tests that present a generic set of social dilemmas to the testee, independent of that person's relevant social life contexts and experiences.

More recently, however, there has been an attempt to measure social competence or intelligence with problems that are familiar in the lives of the testees and that tap goals that are relevant to their effective social functioning. Ford & Tisak (1983), for example, asked ninth and twelfth graders to nominate peers who would be particularly effective in handling social dilemmas that occur in their school life, such as "persuading a group of teachers not to give homework over Christmas vacation, being fun and easy to be with on a date as well as sensitive to the signals of a double-dating companion, sincerely expressing condolences to the family of a favorite teacher who had recently died . . ." (p. 199). The problem situations each depicted "performance in challenging, developmentally salient social contexts involving peers, parents, or teachers" (p. 199). As another measure of social intelligence, Ford & Tisak asked the same adolescents to rate their effectiveness in attaining a set of relevant goals: "getting along with my parents, having a lot of close friends, being romantically involved with someone, helping other people with their problems, and getting involved with other people in activities outside of school" (p. 200). These self-ratings constituted another measure of social intelligence in the context of pressing life tasks for these students.

The objective behind all of these measures of social intelligence has been to demonstrate that social intelligence represents a distinct and coherent set of mental abilities concerned with the processing of "social" information; a set of abilities that differ fundamentally from those underlying the more "formal" reasoning tapped by tests of "academic" intelligence (Keating, 1978). If social intelligence is a separate form of intellectual capacity—a separate entity—then individuals should perform relatively similarly across a set of measures of social perception and reasoning (coherence), and performance on the social intelligence tests should provide a better prediction of social functioning and maturity than would performance on more traditional nonsocial intelligence measures (distinctiveness). Unfortunately, in most recent studies, neither of these conditions for the conceptual integrity of social intelligence has been met (Keating, 1978; Sternberg & Smith, 1985). Keating (1978), for example, who used the measures of moral and social reasoning described above and related them to a measure of social maturity (Gough, 1966), concluded that the "putative domain of social intelligence lacks empirical coherence, at least as it is represented by the measures used here" (p. 222). When relatively abstract (and, thus, formal) social and moral dilemmas constitute the problems in the measurement of social intelligence, there is little evidence that a special, coherent set of mental abilities underlie performance on these tests. Moreover, traditional measures of academic intelligence, such as a concept mastery test of word association and the Standard Progressive Matrices Test of nonverbal reasoning ability, seem to do just as well (or poorly, depending on one's perspective) in predicting scores on a trait measure of social maturity, as do the measures of social intelligence. Hence, are we to conclude that there is no such thing as "social intelligence"?

In one respect the answer to this question is obvious: individuals draw on their intelligence to work on the mundane and monumental tasks of social life—there is certainly expertise involved in forming an impression of the character of another person based on minimal nonverbal cues or in reasoning through a moral dilemma. However, it is by no means clear that social intelligence is best tapped by tasks of person perception or social reasoning that are abstracted from the full social context in which they typically are confronted; nor is it clear that global measures of traits of social maturity provide the best criterion measures of the predictive utility of social intelligence. For example, Ford & Tisak (1983), who measured social intelligence with tasks of reasoning about "real world" social problems confronting their subjects and tested the predictive utility of those measures with an actual criterion behavior—social functioning in an interview situation—came to a more optimistic conclusion about the viability of the social intelligence construct. They concluded that "at least within the adolescent age range, one can identify an empirically coherent domain of social intelligence if a behavioral effectiveness criterion is used . . ." (p. 203).

Interestingly, while Ford & Tisak (1983) provide evidence that seems to support the conceptual and empirical viability of the social intelligence domain, they also point to the need for a fundamental shift in the standard approach to the meaning and measurement of social intelligence. First, they suggest that social intelligence may involve component cognitive processes and skills that are not fundamentally different than those implicated in measures of nonsocial intelligence. As they note, "there is little reason to believe that the cognitive processes underlying effective performance in social tasks are necessarily unique or limited to those tasks" (p. 202). Rather, what gives the social intelligence measures their empirical unity and efficacy—when such unity is observed—may well be that they tap more directly into reasoning about "real world" behavioral problems and, therefore, do better in predicting behavioral effectiveness and social functioning. Hence, the "search for social intelligence" (Keating, 1978) should not center on identifying distinct cognitive components different from those representing academic intelligence; instead, the focus should be on uncovering ecologically valid interpersonal problems that tax the intellective powers of the individual and guide his or her social functioning.

Ford and Tisak (1983) also caution against reifying social intelligence in the form of a general "social IQ" quotient:

> In simple terms, there are many different ways of being socially intelligent. One might be intelligent in one social setting but not another (e.g., a professor might shine at a faculty meeting but be an embarrassment at a dinner party). Or, within a given setting, one might be effective at accomplishing certain kinds of social objectives but not others (e.g., a "teacher's pet" may be successful at winning the approval of teachers but fail miserably in terms of being liked by classmates) (p. 204).

Social intelligence is just as multifaceted, domain-specific, and subject to the effects of experience and tutelage as is nonsocial intelligence. Individuals develop particular expertise in specific *social* tasks and domains; it is in those special contexts that they are especially effective at accomplishing their goals.

The move away from characterizing social intelligence as a fundamentally unique kind of intelligence is also necessitated by changes in the conceptualization and measurement of nonsocial intelligence (Baltes et al., 1984; Sternberg, 1984). As we reviewed earlier, recent approaches to intelligence emphasize the need to make the measures less abstract by using more realistic material. For example, Denney et al. (1982) assessed formal reasoning with problems that depicted hypothetical social dilemmas similar to those problems confronted by individuals in their daily lives. The problems are often presented in a rich social context, one that is appropriate to the age and culture of the individual. Moreover, successful problem solving is assessed by more than accuracy and efficiency of cognitive processing alone; an intelligent display is sensitive to the pragmatic goals implicit in the problem even when these goals lead to violations of some axioms of formal logic (Baltes, 1986; Ford & Tisak, 1983). There is also a move toward a more domain-specific, content-specific view of intelligence (Baltes, 1986): Intelligence as declarative and procedural knowledge expertise is conceptualized and measured within a delimited content domain (for example, a person may be expert at chess or intelligent at anagrams or wise about personal relationships). By taking account of the role of context and pragmatics in intelligence, "nonsocial" intelligence moves closer to the province of "social" intelligence. By conceptualizing the intelligence repertoire as content-specific expertise, "social" intelligence can be more easily defined with regard to the social content of the relevant expertise. In other words, the distinction between academic and social intelligence is getting fuzzier by the moment; even as we acknowledge the importance of "social" knowledge expertise in solving the problems of life.

SOCIAL INTELLIGENCE: EXPERTISE, CONTEXT, AND PRAGMATICS

It seems that the trend in the conceptualization of both "social" and "nonsocial" intelligence is towards the study of intelligence as expertise developed in particular life contexts in the service of pragmatic goals. Social intelligence, in particular, can be construed as declarative and procedural expertise for working on the tasks of social life in which social goals are especially salient. While such a conceptualization is faithful to the intuitions of early researchers like Thorndike and Guilford, who believed that social intelligence was intelligence that permitted one to "act wisely in human relations," it also does not necessitate a search for *unique* cognitive processes underlying "social" tasks of person perception, moral reasoning, and the like. Instead, the emphasis shifts towards achieving a better understanding of the content and form of social knowledge, of the social life tasks, and of the goals that drive problem solving. In a sense, "social intelligence" becomes a convenient organizing principle for the study of individuals at work on social life tasks. By placing this study within an *intelligence* framework, individual differences in social problem solving and the determinants of solutions which are relatively more or less adaptive receive proper attention. Wisdom, then, entails a tortuous process of finding and shaping a social environment that fits comfortably with one's current expertise and, simultaneously, developing new expertise to fit the demands of an everchanging social life (Piaget, 1972). With this perspective in mind, the mandate of theorists of intelligence (Sternberg, 1984; Baltes, 1986) and of personologists (Pervin, 1985), seem quite compatible (Cantor & Kihlstrom, 1985).

1. Social expertise. The social intelligence repertoire contains declarative and procedural knowledge directed at the tasks of social life.

Individuals have well-developed concepts about people, social situations, and themselves (declarative knowledge expertise), concepts which help them make sense of social events. People also have a great deal of such expertise about specific events in their own lives (autobiographical knowledge). This declarative expertise is complemented by much procedural knowledge about how to form impressions of people, make attributions about the causes of events, predict the likely events in a social situation, remember critical features of past events so as to plan future action, and so on. Moreover, there is much metaknowledge underlying individuals' strategies for working on social tasks—procedures for setting goals, planning, monitoring, and evaluating action in the context of unfolding social events. When people face personal crises in their lives or attempt to delay gratification or fulfill a dream of career achievement—when they confront the pressing tasks of social life—their declarative and procedural expertise is brought to bear in the hopes of making progress towards implicit or explicit personal goals.

While it is convenient to think of this intelligence repertoire as somehow distinctively "social" in content, there is really no reason to believe that social concepts, rules for making inferences or retrieving information about people or planning and monitoring one's behavior are fundamentally different in structure and function from the knowledge applied to nonsocial objects and events. Instead, we suggest that there is an intensity and immediacy or salience to this knowledge that makes it seem special and unique, because it concerns tasks and goals that are closest to questions of personal survival and growth and comfort—it is those tasks and goals that make social intelligence so important. When we think about the personality of a person whom we are about to meet we draw on concepts about types of people that are probably structured in ways similar to our concepts about such nonsocial objects as chairs and tables (see Chapters 4, 5), but those person concepts contain thoughts that are more intense and perhaps affectively charged because they have implications for the self that are unavoidable (Niedenthal, 1985). When we form an impression of that person in the first few moments of the interaction, the cognitive processes of categorization and inference are not likely to be unique to interactions with people as opposed to nonsocial objects or events (Smith, 1984). However, such processes may evoke intense feelings (Fiske, 1985) and necessitate the use of cognitive shortcuts or heuristics (Nisbett & Ross, 1980) precisely because the pressure of a personal response is great in the context of a *social* interaction. And, as one plans and monitors and evaluates that response, the metaknowledge that one draws upon is not unique to social problem solving; though again the process involved may feel more tortuous since the goals are somehow "closer to home" and the "right" solution somehow less clearly defined than in the case of most "nonsocial" problems (Baltes et al., 1984, on the uncertainty characteristic of the problems of social life). While it has become unpopular recently to argue that *social* knowledge can be studied by analogy to *nonsocial* knowledge (e.g., Lingle et al., 1983), perhaps the analogy can be made more palatable if we conceive of "nonsocial" knowledge as a special case of "social" knowledge (Zajonc, 1982a), a case in which the *content of the expertise*, the *contexts of the relevant tasks*, and the *pragmatics of usage* are less directly and obviously linked to our ever-present needs of personal and social survival (Plutchik, 1979; Niedenthal, 1985; Norem & Cantor, 1986c). The former is, then, a more "watered-down" version of the latter, just as "academic intelligence" may turn out to be a stripped-down version of "social intelligence" when it is studied in richer contexts with more of the pragmatics of social life in mind (Sternberg, 1984).

   2. Social context and life tasks.   The contextualist position on intelligence stresses the importance of measuring intelligence as expertise developed for tasks that are prevalent in the life contexts of the individual (see Sternberg, 1984, for a review). This point seems especially critical to a conceptualization of *social* intelligence, since there are frequently quite intense pressures exerted by the social environment in the setting of priorities for social problem solving (Higgins & Parsons, 1983). A historical example of this point resides in Freud's (1925) discussions of the antagonistic relationship between the individual, beset with primitive needs for sexual and aggressive gratification, and society with its requirements for individual sublimation towards group ideals. By virtue of participation in social-group contexts, the individual becomes an "expert" at defensive gratifications. (As others have noted, much of Freud's thinking on ego defense mechanisms is quite consistent with contemporary cognitive psychologists' accounts of automatic procedural knowledge—see Erdelyi, 1985; Smith, 1984). More recently, others have stressed the centrality in American culture of skills for delaying gratification; tasks of self-regulation are some of the earliest "social problems" on which children are urged to work by family and school cultures (Erikson, 1950). Accordingly, in light of those cultural-social pressures, children develop quite complex rules (procedural expertise) for planning, monitoring, and evaluating behavior on "delay tasks" (Mischel, 1983).

   The contextualist position applied in the domain of social intelligence suggests the importance of isolating some critical life contexts and charting the social tasks that are especially highly valued in those contexts (e.g., Veroff, 1983; Baltes, 1986). To state the point a different way, it is useful to know what expertise—declarative and procedural knowledge—is particularly well-suited to enabling a person to be a competent member of a particular social-age-cultural group. For example, it would not be surprising to find that traditionally socialized males have finely-tuned expertise in "emotion management" (Hochschild, 1979), since there often is an emphasis in this culture on the regulated expression of emotion in "appropriate" contexts. Rather abstract cultural and social values are played out in the specific tasks and solutions most prized in a particular life context.

3. Pragmatics and social goals.   Perhaps the most salient and universally agreed upon feature of intelligent behavior is that it is *purposive,* directed towards an explicit or implicit goal (Sternberg, 1982). We would argue further that social intelligence is special precisely because it is expertise for life tasks which are relevant to some very basic social goals with special evolutionary significance, perhaps even to goals of territoriality, dominance, safety, and identity (Plutchik, 1979, 1980). Of course, these are goals defined at a very abstract level, but it is not hard to translate the commonplace concrete tasks of social life into problems of self-esteem management and social identity (Little, 1983). What is difficult is to pinpoint the *individual's* special construction of a normative social task and goal— pragmatics is a very personal feature of intelligent social behavior. One person, for example, may "see" parenthood as a problem about achievement and hierarchy and may develop expertise in the service of those goals, while the other person is "working on" affiliation and safety and fine-tuning his or her social intelligence repertoire accordingly. The study of social intelligence is challenging precisely because those basic goals are implicated and yet there is substantial individual variation to be accounted for in the framing of concrete tasks and the specification of those goals. It makes it all the harder to define a normatively "intelligent" solution to an ostensibly common life task (Baron, 1982).

4. Intelligence in social environments.   One way or another the study of intelligence always raises questions of "good" and "poor" solutions, adaptive and maladaptive behavior. This is even more true of the pursuit of social intelligence, probably because some basic social goals are often at least implicitly implicated in the problems of social life. In this regard the "intelligent" solutions to social life tasks seem, as noted earlier, to involve a balance between the individual's accommodation to environmental demands and the shaping of those demands in line with personal goals (Piaget, 1972). The "intelligent" person in a particular context seems to know when to bend his or her expertise to fit the requirements of the situation: he or she sees when it is desirable to cultivate new knowledge in the service of new goals (Cantor & Kihlstrom, 1985). Yet it is also intelligent to "know one's limits"—to know one's expertise—and to be able to shape and select environments which foster the expertise with which one is most comfortable (Snyder, 1981a). Consider, as one example of the delicate balance in social problem solving between accommodation and assimilation, the predicament of many American men as the social value on emotional expression and interpersonal sensitivity in the workplace has become more prevalent. An "intelligent" solution to this predicament is difficult to achieve: the person has to "see" the lack of match between his expertise—his concepts and rules for handling human relations in the workplace—and the normative goals currently being promoted. Having identified the problem, he has to find somehow those contexts in which he feels comfortable learning to be more expressive and, simultaneously, learn to express his reservations about such behavior in other less "suitable" contexts, i.e., accommodate his expertise to some demands and shape the norms towards a more personally comfortable solution in other contexts. Wisdom about social life is based on achieving this often awkward balance between personal proclivities—the state of one's expertise at this time—and prevalent or emerging social norms.

4

Social Concepts and Interpretive Rules

In the present account the study of personality begins with the *social intelligence* that individuals have and use in order to solve the problems of social life: How will I find a date for Saturday night? How will I find a spouse? How will I find intimacy in my life? The problems of social life vary from mundane and perhaps inconsequential ones to quite monumental, sometimes frustrating or even highly painful tasks; however "easy" or "difficult" the problem is to solve, the individual is likely to draw on a rich and complex repertoire of social intelligence in order to tackle it. In this model that repertoire constitutes the structures of personality. The intelligence repertoire is stored in memory as knowledge which the individual uses in the service of setting goals, construing situations, accomplishing life tasks. The intelligence repertoire serves the dynamics of life-task problem solving. In the next two chapters we consider the structures of personality—concepts about the world and the self and rules for interpreting events and planning action. Subsequent chapters concern the more dynamic aspects of personality, as individuals frame their current life tasks and embrace strategies of action in relevant life-task settings.

SOCIAL INTELLIGENCE AS PERSONALITY STRUCTURE

When the structures of personality are equated with the knowledge about people and events and oneself that individuals gather across the lifespan, there is necessarily an assumption of complexity and fluidity about personality. This is not the kind of framework likely to produce an elegant distillation of personality down to a few basic dimensions that provide for a parsimonious taxonomy of personality types. In keeping with Kelly, the cognitive framework assumes that the generative power of language is reflected in idiographic variety in content and organization of social concepts. In line with Mischel, the emphasis is on the diversity of construals and plans that serve common ends for different people. As Gould (1981) noted, intelligence is about creativity and evolution; a social intelligence framework must try to preserve those degrees of freedom for personality structure. At the same time it would be a mistake to imply so little structure that the resultant behavior is viewed as generated by a random access machine. Some assumptions and distinctions about structure are clearly in order here.

In considering the content and organization of social knowledge we look for assumptions and distinctions that allow for idiographic variety and creative evolution while still providing some structural guidelines. Our primary assumption is one of *continuity* across social and nonsocial domains in the structure of knowledge. In keeping with this assumption we draw on the models of cognitive psychology and nonsocial intelligence in elaborating the models of concept and rule knowledge provided by Kelly, Mischel, and the social cognitivists. While there are no doubt substantive differences across these domains of intelligence (Pervin, 1985), these differences do not seem to us major enough to warrant positing fundamentally different knowledge systems. For example, concern has recently been voiced about the appropriateness of studying social concepts—their structure, content, and function—with models primarily developed to describe nonsocial concepts (see Lingle et al., 1983; Ostrom, 1984). These warnings seem well taken; there are certainly features of social concepts unlikely to be matched in nonsocial concepts—e.g., the importance of affective content, the fluidity of membership in social categories, and the fuzziness of taxonomies of social concepts in the face of multiple category membership. However, we will argue below that these features of social knowledge can be faithfully represented in models of social concepts that are not fundamentally discontinuous with those applicable to the presumably more cleanly structured world of objects. Operating with a continuity assumption does not imply, however, blind equation of social and nonsocial knowledge as it is structured and used to navigate in the social and object world.

A similar cautionary note may be in order in the study of procedural social knowledge. Is it useful and/or appropriate, for example, to study rules for drawing inferences about the social world by analogy to statistical decision theory and the cognitive heuristics relevant in the nonsocial problem-solving world (e.g., Nisbett & Ross, 1980)? There are clearly features of the social decision context that make some prescriptively optimal rules of inference nonfunctional (see Miller & Cantor, 1982, on social goals and cognitive heuristics; see Borgida & Brekke, 1981, on task motivation and social inference). Hence, it is reasonable to wonder if we are misguided in characterizing social inference rules as some looser cousin of nonsocial procedural knowledge (Smith, 1984). Again, we believe that this is true only insofar as an attempt is made to rigidly equate the rules of thought used to solve social and nonsocial problems and to evaluate them without sensitivity to the contextual and pragmatic constraints that shape problem-solving behavior.

Our continuity assumption implies, of course, the need to work in both directions in developing this analogy across the nonsocial and social intelligence domains (see also, Zajonc, 1980a). As we learn about the centrality of affective features in the definition of social concepts it may well seem reasonable to consider such content in the representation of nonsocial concepts (after all, apples may not be inherently "hot" objects, but we either like them or not, and to different degrees). Similarly, as the structure and function of informal pragmatic inference rules are better understood, some features of that social intelligence may well serve as appropriate standards by which to judge more formal rules. As long as there is room for seeing distinctive features of these domains of knowledge, it seems reasonable purely in terms of cognitive economy to assume a fair measure of continuity in the structure and even function of social and nonsocial intelligence.

DECLARATIVE AND PROCEDURAL SOCIAL KNOWLEDGE

In keeping with the "continuity assumption," we borrow here from the language of cognitive psychology, in distinguishing between declarative and procedural social knowledge (Smith, 1984). The social intelligence repertoire contains both *concepts* about the social world, people and places, the self and autobiographical events (declarative social knowledge) and *rules* for manipulating and transforming that information and for putting it to work in the construal of events and the planning of action (procedural social knowledge).

While it is convenient to consider declarative and procedural knowledge as separable, rules do operate on concepts and, therefore, models of concepts should allow for easy coordination with rules and vice versa. For example, the fuzzy structure of person concepts, as illustrated in the different degrees of prototypicality of category exemplars, suggests that rules for forming impressions of others be sensitive to differences in goodness-of-fit between the target person and the category ideal (Cantor & Mischel, 1979). Conversely, since rules of impression formation seem to compute cross-temporal stability of behavior more thoroughly than cross-situational consistency of behavior (Mischel & Peake, 1982), one might reasonably expect to see more information about stability than generalizability either in concepts about types of people or in memories about particular category exemplars. While it is difficult continually to coordinate the study of declarative and procedural knowledge, it is essential to do so, for the distinction may be more one of convenience than substance in actuality.

Another distinction made for convenience of exposition is that between knowledge about the *social world* (people and situations and events) and knowledge about the *personal world* (the self and one's autobiographical experiences). While some have argued that the structure and function of concepts about the self and rules of self-inference are fundamentally different from those applicable to the social world in general (e.g. Rogers, 1981), we suspect that here again the differences are more quantitative than qualitative in nature. For example, self-concepts may be *more* resistant to revision, but causal social theories are fairly recalcitrant as well (Anderson, 1982; Swann, 1984). Similarly, though individuals have especially *strong* affective reactions associated with aspects of their self and experience (Markus, 1983), social stereotypes also evoke affective reactions toward strangers (Fiske, 1982).

In the following discussion we will preserve some separation between the discussion of social and personal knowledge by considering them in sequential chapters. However, we also believe that many of the same issues apply in each case, and most of the time social knowledge is indistinguishable from personal knowledge in the way it is used in the construal of social life events. In the present chapter we will consider concepts and rules evoked in the interpretation of information about other people and situations; in the next chapter we will move to a consideration of the repertoire of self-knowledge. Ultimately, we will attempt to consider the coordination of self- and social knowledge as individuals work on their current life tasks (Chapter 6).

PEOPLE AND SITUATIONS AND EPISODES

To begin our consideration of social intelligence, we build on the insights of George Kelly and strive to integrate his model of personal constructs with recent structural models of natural category knowledge. In this account, *social concepts* are accorded central status as structures of personality. These social concepts are organized bundles of knowledge about "kinds of people," "kinds of situations," and "kinds of social episodes," which facilitate the interpretation of social events. Some common social concepts include: social stereotypes of men and women, Jews and WASPs (e.g., Deaux & Lewis, 1984; Hamilton, 1979, 1981); personality types such as achievers and altruists (e.g., Cantor & Mischel, 1979; Hampson, 1982; Buss & Craik, 1983); and situations such as *blind dates*, *bar mitzvahs*, and *job interviews* where we typically encounter such individuals (e.g., Cantor, Mischel, & Schwartz, 1982a; Pervin, 1976). Examples of social episodes or scripts include: the "dating script," the "failing a test" episode, or the "getting married" ritual (e.g., Abelson, 1981; Forgas, 1982).

In keeping with the continuity assumption noted above, we assume that social concepts, like nonsocial concepts, are "fuzzy" representations of the characteristic features of category members (Cantor & Mischel, 1979; Smith & Medin, 1981). This model of fuzzy concepts recognizes the natural variability in the features of actual category members ("all women are not meek"), as well as the social consensus about the prototypical attributes that define the concept ("the prototypical female is meek, nurturing, and not especially analytic in style of thought"—Deaux, 1985). In fact, the mental representation of the concept may be organized around multiple typical exemplars (Ebbesen & Allen, 1979) or abstract prototypes consisting of sets of features more or less correlated with category membership (Cantor & Genero, 1986). For example, the concept of "achiever" may be represented by a relatively full list of characteristic features of achiever-types (such as workaholic, dreams of power, values competition, very verbal) or by a set of descriptions of typical "achievers I have known."

These concepts, whether structured around exemplar instances or abstracted feature lists, include much affect-laden ("hot") social information. The features can represent the goals, emotional reactions, and behavioral plans typically associated with that "kind of person" or elicited in that "kind of situation." Moreover, person and situation concepts are found at multiple levels of abstraction (Kelly, 1955; Cantor, Mischel, & Schwartz, 1982b); the prototypic features of subordinate concepts are more concretely specified than those of more superordinate concepts. Person and situation concepts also contain much information in common, as they concern the dynamics of social interaction—people playing out different roles and creating a socio-emotional atmosphere in a familiar social setting.

Individuals also have well-structured beliefs about the prototypical form of different types of interpersonal interaction rituals, most commonly referred to as "social episodes" (Forgas, 1982) or "social scripts" (Abelson, 1981). These episode concepts are the most "procedural" form of declarative social knowledge because they sometimes serve directly as guides to action (Smith, 1984; Langer, 1978). Concepts of episodes, like those representing persons or situations, are structured around prototypic features or exemplars, yet allow for considerable variation in the actual form that the real episodes take. The features of episode concepts describe the typical roles of participants, the normative sequence of actions, the goals, intentions, and feelings associated with the episode, and, sometimes, the underlying strategies that seem to be guiding the interaction (Trzebinski et al., 1985). Again, episodes may be represented at multiple levels of abstraction (e.g., from the "intimacy episode" to "the date" to "the *first* date") with more detailed elaborations of prototypical interaction scripts associated with more subordinate concepts.

Episodes and scripts are especially interesting knowledge structures because the information in them is organized both conceptually and sequentially, in terms of a canonical order in which the various exchanges occur. As declarative knowledge structures, they are used to help characterize the social rituals or interaction sequences in which people find themselves, and to facilitate inferences about what has happened in the past and what will happen in the future; as procedural knowledge structures, they help to guide behavior in the episode from start to finish. Episode concepts also have special status in the social concept repertoire because they serve as a bridge uniting knowledge about persons and situations. By focusing attention on stereotypical action sequences and interaction exchanges, episodes capture the dynamics of persons-in-contexts and permit "interactionism" to be represented in the social concept repertoire (Zuroff, 1982).

Clearly the repertoire of social declarative knowledge—concepts about persons, situations, and episodes—is rich with content unique to the domain of social life (Lingle et al., 1983). The knowledge represented in these social concepts is used in coordination with procedures for forming impressions, making attributions, predicting future events, and the like: i.e., in the context of social perception and social problem solving. Therefore, it seems wise at this point to examine the *content* of these concepts more closely in order to be sure that any further structural assumptions are consistent with the uniquely social content and functions of this declarative knowledge.

THE CONTENT OF SOCIAL CONCEPTS

What does one need to know about people, situations, and episodes, in order to interpret social events and plan behavior? Or, to take a more empirically-guided approach, given what we know about how people categorize and make inferences and remember other people and events, what features of the social world emerge as important in the construal process? In taking a brief look at the content of social concepts we will consider knowledge about people, situations, and episodes separately, despite their obvious interrelationships in the concept repertoire. After consideration of content, we will return to a discussion of the structure and organization of social concepts within the full repertoire.

Knowledge of Persons

One rather obvious complicating feature of persons is that they are categorized and remembered according to *multiple schemes:* social group and role membership are important (Brewer & Kramer, 1985); biological and constitutional features like gender and height or body type are noted quite readily (Deaux, 1985); and dispositional-trait categories pervade our language and our characterizations of persons (Hampson, 1983). As Kelly (1955) reminded us, constructive alternativism is the rule in people's construals of others.

More interesting in some ways than the complexity of schemes for classifying persons, is the considerable detail of attributes associated with each category type. Concepts about person types are defined in part by informal *population norms* for characteristic attributes (e.g., Sternberg et al., 1981, on intelligent persons; Deaux & Lewis, 1984, on women and men; Cohen, 1981, on librarians and waitresses). Literature on implicit personality theory (Bruner & Tagiuri, 1954; Schneider, 1973) documents the intricacy of these beliefs about the co-occurrence likelihoods of different attributes in different types of persons (see also Shweder, 1982, on the systematic distortion hypothesis). For example, within American culture at least, it is widely believed that talkative people also tend to be adventuresome, that dominant people tend to be cold, that smart people tend to be friendly, and that when we feel pleasure we also tend to feel contentment (Norman, 1963; Rosenberg & Sedlak, 1972; Russell, 1980; Wiggins, 1979). Those co-occurrence relationships are even more strongly and clearly articulated when central traits (Asch, 1946; Hamilton & Zanna, 1974) are implicated or when a particular organizing scheme (like the concept of an "extrovert" or an "old person") is made salient in a specific impression formation context (Schneider & Blankmeyer, 1983). Beliefs about the implications of possessing central dispositions allow people to make sense rather easily of apparent contradictions in personality (Asch & Zukier, 1984). Multidimensional scaling analyses of personality descriptions (e.g., Rosenberg & Sedlak, 1972; Wishner, 1960), along with factor analytic studies in the personality assessment tradition (e.g., Norman, 1963; Goldberg, 1978), suggest certain candidates for central dimensions/domains of denotative meaning in the description of persons (see, for example, Norman's "big five" factors of personality).

Similarly, studies of impression formation suggest that *general evaluations* (on a global good/bad dimension) and more *specific dimensions of connotation* underlie categorizations of persons (Rosenberg & Sedlak, 1972; Osgood et al., 1957; Fiske, 1981; Anderson, 1968). Rosenberg and his colleagues (Rosenberg & Gara, 1985) observe dimensions of evaluative meaning, such as activity, potency, and positiveness, in most of their MDS analyses of implicit personality theory. Norman Anderson's 1974 work on information integration in impression formation supports the role of evaluative meaning associated piecemeal with specific attributes of personality (see also Fiske, 1980 on piecemeal processing of affective information). In addition, recent work by Susan Fiske and her colleagues (Fiske & Pavelchak, 1986) suggests a role for "summary" evaluative impressions associated with person concepts and applied to particular targets as a consequence of categorization (e.g., a new acquaintance who fits the "old flame" stereotype quickly acquires a full-blown evaluative reputation). This "schema-triggered affect" may be more or less diagnostic of particular target persons' evaluative attributes, just as the summary evaluative tag on the concept may be more or less close to an average of the evaluative information associated with familiar category exemplars.

People also associate particular *goals* or *intentions* with concepts of different types of persons: the achiever competes with the intention of outstripping the competition; the shy person creates a private world in order to protect him- or herself from social embarrassment; the fat person diets so as to lose weight, and the short person speaks loudly so as to compensate for his or her insignificant physical presence. Trzebinski et al. (1985) provide convincing evidence, from studies of social inference, that knowledge about particular persons is frequently organized in an "action-oriented" fashion, that is, structured in the light of the basic *goals* and *action strategies* associated with the person's current social role.

Trzebinski et al. note, for example, that "in an individual's schema of career life, *boss* is an important actor category and *carrying out supervisory activities* is an important category of goals associated with that actor. Moreover, the trait *good leadership ability* might be an important condition for realizing the goal of supervision" (1985, p. 1387). Hoffman, Mischel, & Mazze (1981) found that organizing information about a person's actions in terms of relevant goal categories facilitated recall for the behavioral information ("Jane is refusing a chocolate sundae offered at a dinner party because she is trying to lose weight"). In other words, there is increasing support for the centrality of goal and action-strategy information in the structuring of person concepts. People with particular trait dispositions and those who fill particular social roles are perceived to have specific underlying goals that organize their behavior in relevant social interaction contexts. When we see those people in those contexts, basic goals and the strategies of action most associated with them become readily accessible as schemes for organizing information about social actors.

In sum, studies of impression formation, attribution, and person memory suggest that person concepts incorporate multiple categorization schemes; intuitive norms for person attributes and their co-occurrence relationships; affective information associated with attributes and with person types; and considerable expertise concerning underlying intentions, causes of behavior, and goals that motivate behavioral episodes (see Fiske

& Taylor, 1984, for a review). Moreover, knowledge about types of persons is complemented by consideration of the social situations in which they are typically observed. While the intuitive scientist does not always sufficiently recognize the constraining power of situations over people (Nisbett & Ross, 1980), there is no paucity of information about situations (and the persons and episodes that define them) in the lay repertoire (Magnusson, 1981).

Knowledge of Situations

The traditional focus in the study of personality and of social knowledge has been on categorization schemes centered around concepts of people. This has occurred, in part, because the lexicon is so rich in terms descriptive of persons (Allport & Odbert, 1937; Goldberg, 1978). However, despite the 18,000 trait terms descriptive of persons, there is still a rich lexicon to describe social situations shared within common subcultures. In fact, early in the 1950s, Brunswik (1956) was already urging personologists to take seriously the classification of life situations, in order to achieve a "representative" design in the study of individuals and their lives [as, of course, did Lewin (1935) and Murray (1938), even earlier]. Currently, there is somewhat of a revival in interest among personologists in the analysis of persons-in-situations (Magnusson, 1981). Similarly, despite a longstanding tradition of focus on the *person* in person perception (see Schneider et al., 1979), social cognition research has recently turned more concertedly to a study of knowledge of social life situations and social episodes (Forgas, 1982). The study of *situations* is back in fashion and for good reasons; individuals have well-articulated and well-structured concepts about the situations in their lives (Cantor, Mischel, & Schwartz, 1982a). Knowledge of situations forms a substantial part of the social intelligence repertoire (Cantor & Kihlstrom, 1985).

As with persons, there are multiple schemes for the classification of social life situations. People know about the *physical settings* in which episodes take place (Barker, 1968; Frederiksen, 1972; Moos, 1973). Barker (1968), for example, characterized the life of a small town in Kansas with a taxonomy of all the important physical settings in the town and the behavioral episodes associated with them. In addition to being conceived of as *behavioral* settings, situations are often defined by the types of *persons* (and their characteristic *goals*) who typically inhabit the physical setting or make the social episode happen (Cantor, Mischel, & Schwartz, 1982a; Forgas, 1976; Zuroff, 1982). A dinner party is a recreational situation for most guests, an achievement exercise for the nervous host, and a forum for self-promotion for the ingratiating local politician. As with person concepts, some of the richest categorization schemes for situations are those organized around the goals, intentions, and action strategies that characterize the prototypical participant(s) (Abelson, 1981).

As Barker (1968) observed in his study of the Kansas town, one of the things that people know about situations in their own social world is the set of *behavioral norms* associated with different settings or interactions. People know the typical behavioral scripts for situations (Abelson, 1981); the range of behavior "appropriate" for commonplace situations in their lives (Price & Bouffard, 1974); the types of people who will most successfully master a situation (Bem & Funder, 1978); and the "rules of the game" for each situation-ritual (Argyle, 1981). Children's birthday parties involve gift giving, cake eating, and group play; singing "happy birthday" is quite appropriate, though cake throwing might not be much appreciated; cooperative children will be rewarded and hyperactive children restrained in this setting, and the ritual exchange of birthday gifts and party favors signals a successful negotiation of the birthday party "game." Within particular subcultures there is often substantial consensus about these behavioral norms; in some sense, they serve as a signal of appropriate socialization (Goffman, 1974).

While most commonplace social situations have behavioral norms, scripts, and rules associated with them, situations are perceived to differ in the degree of *behavioral constraint* implied by those norms. Constraint is a very important dimension of meaning associated with situations; the exact meaning of constraint varies from the range of permissible behavior (Price & Bouffard, 1974) or the number of different types of persons comfortable in the situation (Cantor, Mischel, & Schwartz, 1982a), to the formality of the situation with respect to the strictness of the rules, the intensity of expression encouraged, or the degree of intimacy displayed by participants (Harré & Secord, 1973; Forgas, 1982). Forgas (1982), for example, found that perceptions of commonplace social episodes varied along three dimensions of connotative and denotative meaning: an *involvement or intimacy* dimension (defined by episodes such as having an intimate conversation with a significant other versus chatting with an acquaintance); a *"know how to behave or not"* dimension (defined by episodes such as watching TV with friends versus meeting new people at a sherry party in college); and an evaluative dimension of *pleasantness* (defined by episodes such as going out for a walk with a friend versus visiting a doctor).

Interestingly, the dimensions of meaning typically associated with social life situations are quite similar to those derived from studies of person perception. Some situations, like some interaction partners, are easier to read ("to know how to behave"), allow for more freedom of expression and individuality ("less constrained or formal"), and encourage closer interpersonal contact between participants ("allow for intimacy"). Perhaps most importantly, situations are perceived to vary considerably in their typical affective atmosphere from pleasant to unpleasant, tense to relaxed, or risky to safe (Price, 1981).

The perceived *affective-evaluative atmosphere* of a situation is a key ingredient in individuals' definitions of situation concepts. When people—be they housewives in Oxford, England (Forgas, 1982), Swedish students (Magnusson & Ekehammar, 1973), or psychiatric in-patients (Moos, 1968)—provide clusters of types of situations in their lives, they quite often focus on commonalities in affective atmosphere associated with exemplar situations. While some common dimensions of affective meaning emerge in all of these studies (e.g., warm-cold, pleasant-unpleasant, anxious-calm, involved-dull, and so forth), individuals often have very personal readings of the feelings elicited by particular situations. Pervin (1976) elegantly demonstrated, using an adaptation of Kelly's REP test, that individuals have clearly demarcated, often idiosyncratic, affective reactions characteristically associated with commonplace situations (e.g., family dinners are occasions of pleasantness for some and grief for others). These affective impressions of situations are often intensely felt, remembered for long periods of time, and reflected upon repeatedly in the course of everyday life. The meaning of situations is quite "hot."

Without question, there is increasing attention being accorded in both the personality and social cognition literatures to people's conceptions of everyday life situations (Pervin, 1985; Hamilton, 1981). Personologists have returned to the Kellyian position that individuals behave differently, one from another, in common life contexts, at least in part because they construe those situations in different ways. For social cognition theorists it is becoming clear that part of the richness of the social knowledge repertoire derives from intuitive concepts of situations and the typical persons, behavioral episodes and affective impressions associated with them (Forgas, 1982). Moreover, perceptions of persons are not devoid of information about context; impressions of familiar persons—their dispositions and central attributes—are constructed in the light of the social contexts in which they are observed (Cantor, 1978; Zuroff, 1982). In other words, research in these two traditions reminds us of the importance of the "social side of situations" (persons, episodes, affects) and of the "contextual side of persons" (habitual contexts, consistency of behavior, context-dependent goals and episodes).

Knowledge of Episodes and Tasks

Intuitive knowledge of persons and situations is united and given common purpose by a concern with the *behavioral episodes* and *social tasks* that typify individuals and their life contexts. This common ground is organized around the dynamics (motivational content) of social life. As Trzebinski et al. (1985), Hoffman et al. (1981), and others (e.g., Abelson, 1981) have suggested, it is time to consider an "action-oriented" representation of social knowledge, one that emphasizes the intentions and motives that underlie social behavior. In so doing, one would focus upon the primary or recurring social episodes that occupy individuals' energies—episodes of affiliation and competition, rituals of communication and self-presentation, tasks of establishing intimacy and managing impressions.

There are, of course, *multiple schemes* that people use in order to organize the social episodes or rituals or tasks that consume their energies. As Barker (1968) did, one can catalogue the episodes and rituals that consume daily social life activities; these *"mundane" events* typically have well-defined behavioral social scripts commonly associated with them (Abelson, 1981). On the other hand, one can consider, as Plutchik (1980) did, the set of *basic evolutionary tasks* for human adaptation—tasks like establishing a dominance hierarchy, exploring one's territory, maintaining control, finding out "who we are" and "with whom we belong," coping with loss and separation. Working from this more "lofty" set of basic life tasks, it is still possible to see associations between basic tasks and the constituent episodes that define them. For example, Plutchik (1980) traces associations between life tasks and the problem-solving episodes that characterize these tasks in specific human contexts, replete with motives and feelings that give form to such striving.

Episode schemes can also be organized around *basic motives* (like power, affiliation, achievement) or *needs* (like self-esteem maintenance, personal control, safety) and the constituent episodes, rituals, and tasks that map onto fulfilling these goals (power tactics; self-control procedures; coping strategies). Additionally, individuals often identify different *domains of social life*—domains like work and play, or love and family—that also implicate certain scripted social relations and interactions. These multiple schemes for chunking social life episodes each serve to highlight different spheres of intentionality and action in our everyday lives (such as domains of achievement striving or intimacy or stress and coping); thus constituting the basis for an action-oriented social knowledge repertoire.

The content associated with these "spheres of intentionality" includes *scripts* for social interaction (e.g., Abelson, 1981), *roles* for different players in the episode (e.g., Higgins, 1981; Argyle, 1981), *plans* for reaching desired goal-states (e.g., Mischel, 1983), and *norms* regulating social exchange (Kelley & Thibaut, 1978). These scripts, roles, plans, and norms tell one how, when, where and in what sequence to make a move in the game of social interaction; they also allow even the casual observer to infer the next move and take notice when a rule violation occurs (Bower, Black, & Turner, 1981). Consider, for example, how disconcerting it is when a person violates the "rules of polite conversation" by launching into a devastating tale of woe in response to a passing remark ("How are you?"). Or, how comforting it is when someone whom one has labeled as ingratiating turns out to have "a small favor to ask of you" (Jones & Pittman, 1982). Shared knowledge of the rules and norms of a culture give considerable cognitive order and a sense of personal control in the face of complex events and interactions (Athay & Darley, 1981).

Studies of attribution and person memory suggest that inferences about *intentions* and *goals,* as well as feelings and thoughts, follow rather automatically from observation of behavior in these kinds of (ritualistic) social interaction episodes (Kelley & Michela, 1980). When a target person seems willingly to take part in a "classic power struggle," inferences about competitive strivings follow naturally (Passer, Kelley, & Michela, 1978); engaging in an ingratiation script (Jones & Wortman, 1973) in the context of a mixed-sex dyadic interaction is more likely to instantiate an intimacy motive than a Machiavellian power play. Inferences about the underlying goals and intentions of actors in commonplace interaction episodes, in turn, serve to organize memories of the participants' behaviors and to generate plausible candidates for future actions (Hoffman et al., 1981; Trzebinski et al., 1985).

Additionally, observers associate distinct *emotional reaction patterns* to target individuals who take particular roles and play out particular scripts in familiar social interaction episodes (e.g., Schwartz & O'Connor, 1984, on interpersonal intimacy scripts and inferences about emotions). Weiner (1985), for example, suggests that attributions about performance in highly familiar achievement episodes extend beyond descriptions of underlying causes to inferences about accompanying affective and motivational states. For example, consider Weiner's example of a Little Leaguer who fails miserably at a game in such a way as to evoke a stable, internal, uncontrollable attribution of poor ability. The stereotypical episode (including past behavior, present context, social reactions) that consistently elicits that attributional inference will also evoke the inference that the child will "feel ashamed and hopeless" and "withdraw effort and give up." Behavioral episodes that follow certain highly stylized forms (such as failing at an important task in public when one has practiced hard for it and when there is a record of similar failures in the past) are taken as quite diagnostic of emotional and motivational states by actors (Schachter & Singer, 1962) and by observers (Weiner, 1985).

Plutchik (1980) even goes so far as to define eight *basic emotions* on the basis of highly structured episodes involving thoughts, feeling states, and action in the service of a fundamental adaptive task (for example, *sadness* maps on to a problem-solving episode derived from a basic task like *coping with loss or separation*). Similarly, Shaver et al. (1985) find that basic "emotion episodes" (such as experiencing fear or sadness) have a characteristic structure, beginning with an interpretation of a situation that evokes a basic personal motive or project and leading automatically to sequences of stereotyped response tendencies, including physiological, behavioral, and expressive reactions; as in Plutchik's model, this entire cycle constitutes the experience (or perception) of a basic emotion. For example, in the Shaver et al. work, the "sadness prototype" contains the following stereotypical emotion episode: "loss of a valued relationship; separation followed by 'tired, rundown, low in energy,' 'withdrawing from social contact,' 'crying, tears, whimpering,'" as well as "blaming, criticizing oneself." People agree on the prototypical components of such basic emotion episodes; they are more confident that a target person has actually experienced a basic emotion if those prototypical components of the episode are observed, and they will fill in the gaps with regard to likely reaction patterns on the basis of even partial evidence that points to the unfolding of an emotion episode (Shaver et al., 1985). There is powerful consensus in intuitions about emotions and the social episodes that define them (Fehr & Russell, 1984).

In sum, stereotypical social episodes are frequently believed to provide invaluable insights into the underlying dynamics—goals, emotions, motivational state—shaping the behavior of actor-participants. Many have argued that concepts about social episodes (the rituals of which they are comprised and the life tasks which they serve) have special status in everyday social cognition (Trzebinski et al., 1985) precisely because of the insight into the dynamics of behavior which is gained. When we observe actors taking part in scripted episodes that evoke "classic" motives in our culture—e.g., an adolescent fighting an authority figure—it certainly feels as if we have learned a great deal about the person and the situation from that episode.

Concepts of social episodes have heuristic value in the present account because they seem to forge a natural structural bridge between concepts of persons and concepts of situations. In revealing the personal dynamics of behavior, an episode leads one to think about the type of person involved (i.e., to access a person concept) and about the type of situation in which such a person typically operates (i.e., to access a situation concept). When you see a young adult engaged in a ritualistic battle of wits with an authority figure, the episode evokes images of adolescents and parents and family scenes at dinner (Baldwin & Holmes, 1985). The episode serves a networking function, bringing to mind a collection of person and situation concepts relevant to the construal of that particular social event. In the construal of social events, diverse sets of person and situation concepts might conceivably be used to give meaning to the events; concepts about episodes may well serve as a guide, channeling the thoughts of the construer in particular directions (Hoffman et al., 1981). As Kelly (1955) postulated in his notion of "constructive alternativism," individuals construct different interpretations of an event because they bring to bear different collections of constructs (concepts) in the construal process. Perhaps concepts about episodes play a central role in initiating the process of accessing particular sets of social concepts in particular instances.

Such consideration of the complexity of the construal process—with multiple plausible readings of the same event—brings us back to questions of structure and organization in the social concept repertoire. The repertoire must be organized in such a fashion as to permit constructive alternativism, encouraging flexibility in the (person, situation, episode) concepts brought to mind in the interpretation of any given event. At the same time, once a given interpretive path is followed, people seem quite adept at accessing a coherent prototype for the kind of person/situation/ actions that typically characterize such an event. In other words, the social concept repertoire must be structured, both at the level of inter-concept connections and intraconcept organization, so as to provide the observer with a diverse collection of potential interpretations, each rich and well formed in its own right, for any given social event.

STRUCTURE AND ORGANIZATION IN THE SOCIAL CONCEPT REPERTOIRE

We began this discussion of the repertoire of social concepts with an analogy between the structure of nonsocial and social concepts. In order adequately to test that analogy it seemed wise to consider first the content of social concepts, and then to see if available models of structure and function adopted from the literature on nonsocial cognition could reasonably be expected to incorporate the special features of social concepts (cf. Lingle et al., 1983; Holyoak & Gordon, 1984). In particular it seems that consideration of content raises questions about both the *internal structure* of social (vs. nonsocial) concepts and the *organization* of concepts within a repertoire of social (vs. nonsocial) concepts. We will now consider those two kinds of structural issues in turn.

Internal Concept Structure

The notion that social concepts about persons, situations, and episodes are structured as *fuzzy sets* around central prototypic exemplars seems to be the least problematic aspect of the cross-domain analogy (Holyoak & Gordon, 1984). Concepts about persons, for example, may be organized around a collection of *representative exemplars* (with attribute descriptions of each) who epitomize the category (such as Teddy Kennedy, Mario Cuomo, Geraldine Ferraro, Strom Thurmond for "national politi-cal figures"). Comparison across the exemplar descriptions reveals both the coherent gist (special-interest constituency; some personal scandal to worry over; well-oiled machine; power tactics) and the variability in the actual instantiations of the concept (for example, Ferraro and Thurmond epitomize the politician in strikingly different ways). Similarly, the gist-coherence and variability of membership in fuzzy person categories can also be represented via more abstract *summary prototypes* organized around the relatively large set of characteristic features of the category. As an example, Miller, Wattenberg, & Malanchuk (1982) analyzed data from a national election study and found that "political candidate" prototypes commonly contained attributes concerned with five features of personal character: integrity, competence, reliability, charisma, and demographic background and appearance. These classes of features are differentially descriptive of current aspiring candidates ("What ever happened to the honest politician?") and voters place different weight on their importance in defining a "good candidate" prototype (e.g., "Charisma without competence doesn't go far, or does it?"). The abstract representation might well contain information about the perceived centrality of each characteristic feature to the concept definition.

As many have noted (Smith & Medin, 1981; Cantor & Genero, 1986) both exemplar and summary prototype models have advantages and disadvantages as representations of fuzzy social concepts. Exemplar models are attractive in that they directly represent the variability in characteristics among category members (Walker, 1975; Lingle et al., 1983; Genero & Cantor, 1986). When one considers a set of prototypical politicians, it is striking exactly how different they can be and still typify the category. The exemplar model also emphasizes the pattern of correlation *between* characteristic features in the set of category members (Lingle et al., 1983), that is, the repeated co-occurrence of certain sets of features across different exemplars conveys such information rather clearly (Genero & Cantor, 1986). Moreover, as Lingle et al. (1983) also point out, thinking about the features of typical category exemplars allows one to easily update a summary impression of characteristic category features; if no exemplar readily comes to mind with a given feature then it can probably be discarded from the summary representation.

While the exemplar model clearly has many attractive features, it is also the case that people frequently have quite elaborate concepts about categories of persons, situations, and social episodes without really having had much experience with a variety of exemplars (Lingle et al., 1983). Novice psychology students begin clinical training with quite elaborate (though frequently misguided) conceptions of the typical features of schizophrenics, paranoids, depressives, and so forth (Cantor & Genero, 1986). And it is frequently easier for novices to learn the gist or central tendency of a social category (e.g., manic-depressives) by abstracting a summary representation rather than attempting to keep in mind the variety of specific exemplars in the category (Genero & Cantor, 1986). This may be particularly true in the case of social categories (vs. nonsocial object categories) for which there may be a wider range of exemplars to learn and more restricted opportunities to directly observe category instances (Lingle et al., 1983).

The above line of reasoning suggests that individuals may well represent some concepts with exemplar prototypes—for example, concepts in domains of personal expertise and familiarity—and think in more abstract terms for other concepts such as those about which they have indirect, vicariously learned knowledge (e.g., American vs. Soviet politicians). In fact, Lingle et al. (1983) propose a *mixed exemplar-sum-mary representation* to provide flexibility in capturing both the gist and variability of natural categories.

The representation of concepts may also change from exemplar to abstract prototypes (and perhaps, then, back to exemplar) as a person acquires experience in a domain (e.g., Homa, Sterling, & Trepel, 1981). The schoolchild learns in history class about one or two Soviet politicians (e.g., Lenin and Stalin) and then gradually abstracts a person prototype for the Soviet politician from years of exposure to the evening news; later, as the face of Soviet politics changes (from Brezhnev to Gorbachev) the global prototype gets fine-tuned or even replaced with specific figures (perhaps of a more representative sort than those that sparked the initial discovery of the concept). Moreover, one can imagine a person stopping at different points in this acquisition process for different concepts (such as cocktail party concept vs. spacewalk concept) and in different domains of social experience (such as concepts about interpersonal experience vs. concepts about athletic experience). In the domain of social knowledge it seems especially critical to consider models of structure and process that permit maximum variation from individual to individual (Kelly, 1955).

Regardless of the exact form of category representation, social concepts, probably even more than their nonsocial counterparts, must be represented in such a way as to highlight both the central tendency and the extreme variability in exemplars that characterizes the real-world instantiations of these concepts (Buss & Craik, 1983; Pervin, 1976; Abelson, 1981). People know that there is a prototypic dominant person, a typical family dinner, and a classic birthday party script; but they also expect to see much variability from person to person, situation to situation, and episode to episode.

The internal structure of social concepts also must highlight varia-tion in "goodness of fit" of exemplars in the category (Cantor & Mischel, 1979; Cantor et al., 1980). Not only do people take note of the variability among exemplars, but there is also substantial agreement among lay observers about the *degree of prototypicality* of these different category members (e.g., Cohen, 1981; Cantor, 1978; Sternberg et al., 1981). Social categories, like their nonsocial counterparts, can be organized in terms of a continuum of category membership, from the clearest to the fuzziest of exemplars. Just as "tomatoes" are problematic exemplars of the "vegetable" category (overlapping as they do with people's conceptions of "fruits"); so, too, are "cruise ship hostesses" borderline exemplars of the "hostess" category (sharing as many characteristic attributes with "salespeople" and "waitresses" as with "hostesses").

In fact, this *continuum of prototypicality* may be an essential struc-tural feature of social categories if there really is more variation in exemplars and more overlap in membership across categories in the social than nonsocial domain (Holyoak & Gordon, 1984). "Tomatoes" may be atypical cases as unprototypical representatives of object categories; for social categories, instances like "cruise ship hostess" may be more the rule than the exception. Once again, the structure of social concepts must serve to represent the complexity of instances apparent in the social world.

The fuzzy sets model does a nice job of characterizing *coherence* and *variability* in social concepts (see Wittgenstein, 1953, on the concept of a "game" as similar to a family with overlapping networks of family resemblances). As such it can be used to represent intuitive knowledge about the *network of co-occurrence of acts* (and other attributes) that define types of persons, situations, or episodes in the social world (e.g., Buss & Craik, 1983; Barker, 1968; Forgas, 1982). However, what about the *dynamic content* of social concepts—the evaluative side of person perception; the behavioral constraint or informality associated with situations; the material about goals and intentions that unfolds in an episode—can this be represented in social (exemplar or summary) prototypes?

At the present time, models of social prototypes (schemas or scripts) represent the dynamic content of social cognition as meaning attributes. The evaluative content of person concepts is represented both by the set of features characteristic of that type of person and by summary evaluative "tags" that mark the perceiver's overall impression of the "goodness" of that type of person in general (Fiske, 1981; Kinder et al., 1980). Similarly, classes of situations have specific features that convey information about atmosphere (opera houses are stuffy and ornate) and people often express summary evaluative judgments of situations (Pervin, 1976). And, as noted earlier, interpersonal episodes are defined in part by the intentions and goals of the participants, as well as representing emotion cycles identified with the whole unfolding set of events (Plutchik, 1980).

These descriptive features of concepts represent the dynamics of social cognition in relatively static and "cold" form. Recently, several theorists have suggested that the dynamic, motoric, and arousal features of individuals' experience with these social "objects" are represented directly in the concept structure (e.g., Gilligan & Bower, 1984; Leventhal, 1984). Lang (1979) talks about the motor-arousal images associated with hot social concepts and Zajonc & Markus (1985) discuss the "hard interface" of motor-affective memory. For example, the "old flame" prototype could be represented by something as close to the actual feeling state of a "pit in one's stomach," as by a global negative evaluative tag and specific prototypical affective features of "uncaring," "detached," "out-of-love." Or, alternatively, the affective memory could be represented as nodes in a procedure for actually generating these feelings. In other words, social concepts frequently seem to evoke patterns of arousal and motor schemes rather directly and immediately. Why not represent that hot content directly in the concept structure? Such models of "hot concepts" remain to be fully developed;

however, they do present a potentially radical departure from the propositional form typically assumed in models of nonsocial concept representations (Holyoak & Gordon, 1984).

Interconcept Organization

One of the ways in which the construal of persons or situations or episodes becomes complex quite quickly is that people bring to bear *many* concepts in trying to make sense of any given stimulus (Srull & Wyer, 1980; Higgins & King, 1981). For example, when we observe another person, it is common to think about his personality in a variety of interpersonal trait domains, his role in several social groups, his age and gender and the characteristics associated with those categories, and the kinds of other persons with whom he typically associates (Schneider, 1973; Schneider et al., 1979). In so doing, we are likely to bring to mind a variety of person categories of different content (e.g., trait categories, social group categories, social caricatures or personas) and different levels of conceptual abstraction (e.g., he is an extrovert, a comic, an inveterate practical joker).

Therefore, when we portray the structure and organization of concepts in the social concept repertoire, it is critical to consider the relations between concepts that facilitate *collections* of related concepts becoming accessible together. These interconcept associations occur not only between different related concepts *within* a conceptual domain (e.g., person or situation or episode domain) but also *across* concept domains (e.g., connecting particular person-situation-episode concepts). When we think about a person, episodes and situations are just as likely to come to mind as are different relevant categories of persons (Trzebinski et al., 1985; Hoffman et al., 1981). The organizational principles that connect concepts in different domains may not differ markedly from those underlying the interconcept associations within the person, situation, or episode domains (Andersen & Klatsky, 1986). However, for the sake of simplicity of presentation, we will consider the organization of concepts within a domain first and then move to the ways in which person, situation, and episode concepts are interrelated within the repertoire.

One of the obvious but important ways in which social concepts are organized to provide ample room for collections of related concepts is in terms of links between concepts at different levels of *abstraction*. As Kelly (1955) pointed out in his personal construct theory, people bring to bear concepts at different levels of abstraction in construing events—a person is described in fairly general terms as *expressive* and also in more specific terms as *witty* (Hampson, John, & Goldberg, 1986). Kelly also noted that the relations between these multiple constructs are fairly well-specified; that is, there are asymmetries in implications such that the more abstract construct is implied by the more specific construct (e.g., "to be witty is a way of being expressive") while the broader construct does not as clearly imply the more specific construct (e.g., "to be expressive is a way of being witty"). Hampson et al. (1986), in a series of elegant studies, have verified the Kelly propositions in the domain of interpersonal trait concepts. For a wide variety of trait categories they are able to specify three levels of category abstractness or "breadth" (operationalized as the diversity of behavioral manifestations of the trait concept) and then construct three-tier hierarchies based upon class-inclusion principles assessed with the asymmetry of implication measure (e.g., extroverted, sociable, talkative).

Hierarchies of social concepts appear to be "fuzzy," however, in a number of respects. Most important, as Hampson et al. (1986) point out, these hierarchies typically include some "good" examples of class-inclusion relations (e.g., punctual–conscientious) and some "poor" examples (e.g., neat–conscientious) in which the feature-nesting property of a well-defined hierarchy is violated. For example, in the domain of situation concepts, Cantor et al. (1982a) found many examples of specific situation categories (e.g., fraternity party) whose characteristic features did not always include those typical of a relevant superordinate category (e.g., party). However, just as these hierarchies are not perfect, they are also far from randomly structured: categories closer together in the hierarchies (e.g., frat party and party) share more characteristic features in common than do categories farther apart in the same hierarchy (e.g., frat party and date).

Hampson et al. (1986) suggest a model of *"fuzzy hierarchies"* with *degrees* of class-inclusion relations between superordinate and subordinate categories, a model very much in line with the fuzzy internal structure of social (and nonsocial) concepts. These fuzzy hierarchies are well structured in that predictable relations between categories at different levels of breadth are observed; but they are imperfectly structured in that some specific categories are poorly nested within the appropriate superordinate category (e.g., office party–party) and admit multiple potential inclusion relations (e.g., office party–interview) (Cantor & Mischel, 1979; Holyoak & Gordon, 1984). Interestingly, as Hampson et al. (1986) note, Hampton (1982) has suggested that similar violations of strict hierarchical structure are also true of taxonomies of natural object categories (e.g., wheelchair as a chair; wheelchair as a vehicle). The fuzzy internal structure of natural language concepts would seem to dictate some fuzziness in the structure of concept hierarchies as well. However, as we have noted elsewhere (Cantor & Mischel, 1979; Cantor, Smith, Mezzich, & French, 1980), fuzzy structure does not imply chaotic structure or no structure at all—people operate quite well with these fuzzy hierarchies.

There are several other principles of *interconcept connections,* in addition to fuzzy class-inclusion, which facilitate the construal of social stimuli by enabling *collections* of related concepts to be easily brought to mind. Imagine, for the moment, a network of interconnected concepts about types of people, including concepts at different levels of abstraction (e.g., extroverts and practical jokers) portraying a *fuzzy hierarchy* with different degrees of *class-inclusion relations* (e.g., extroverts and comic-jokers versus extroverts and bullies). Figure 4-1 presents a hypothetical hierarchy used in prior work on personality prototypes (Cantor & Mischel, 1979). It should be noted that this hierarchy also includes a variety of types of person concepts, some organized around trait constructs and some organized around social group constructs or caricatures (Andersen & Klatsky, 1986). This mixture of person concepts is intentional and seems wise in order to capture the range of construals observed in person perception studies (cf. Hampson et al., 1986). We will discuss this point in detail below.

The first panel of Figure 4-1 portrays a fuzzy hierarchy with inter-concept connections based on class-inclusion relations. It is clear from studies of implicit personality theory (Rosenberg & Sedlak, 1972) that this network must also be enriched by interconcept connections based on *perceived similarity* in *denotative* and *connotative* meaning. For example,

FIGURE 4-1 Fuzzy and Idiosyncratic Person Hierarchies.

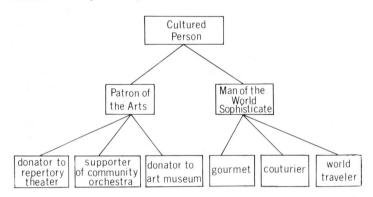

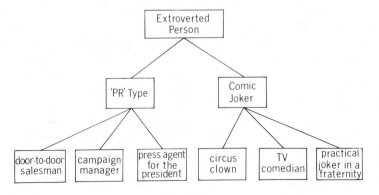

Panel One

as illustrated in the panel of Figure 4-1, many of these person concepts are strongly associated in people's minds on the basis of intuitive beliefs about similarity in descriptive features and/or evaluative connotations (e.g., extroverts and cultured persons) regardless of class-inclusion relations. Moreover, these interconcept connections have a substantial component of *idiosyncratic relations* in them. As Kelly (1955) pointed out some time ago, the meaning connections between constructs will vary enormously based on individual experience. This idiosyncratic component is true not only for evaluative associations (e.g., one person sees both extroverts and cultured persons as positive in nature, while another person construes cultured persons in a highly negative light) but also for semantic meaning connections (e.g., the former person thinks of cultured persons as knowledgeable, creative, intellectually curious, while the latter person views them as snobbish, elitist, superficially well-versed in coffee-table reading).

These idiosyncratic meaning associations derive, of course, from variations in people's direct and vicarious experience with exemplars of the concepts in question (Bandura, 1986). They are reflections of the diversity of exemplars that comprise social categories and the substantial overlap in membership across different categories (Holyoak & Gordon, 1984). As the third panel of Figure 4-1 suggests, one person (Jack) may see very little similarity between extroverts (construed in highly positive terms) and cultured persons (construed as weak, passive snobs), while for another person (Jill) the meanings are quite close (and positive in both cases). These meanings derive presumably from differences in their social learning histories. Jack, for example, might well have met a number of "weak snobs" as a child and modeled the negative reaction of his father towards these individuals. From his experience with cultured persons who seemed passive-withdrawn-quiet (i.e., more introverts than extroverts) the inter-category overlap in membership suggested a very different set of concept connections than it did for Jill, who interacted, perhaps, with a

FIGURE 4-1 *(continued)*

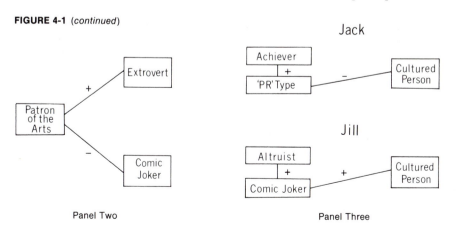

Panel Two   Panel Three

number of warm-talkative-extroverts who also loved drama and opera and the glitter of performances. Again, the variety of exemplars and the number of different multiple memberships in person categories allows for idiosyncratic experiences to shape different concept networks.

Descriptive and evaluative associations (both consensually-validated and idiosyncratic in form) are assumed in most models to constitute the primary interconcept connections in the networks of social concepts (e.g., Fiske & Pavelchak, 1986). However, research on construct accessibility (see Higgins & King, 1981; Bargh & Thein, 1985) suggests other principles that appear to connect concepts typically accessed in tandem in the course of social construal. For example, individuals seem to have their own set of *highly familiar*, frequently brought to mind constructs used to describe other persons (Higgins et al., 1985); those personally-accessible constructs often are *self-descriptive* as well (Lewicki, 1985). Hence, we might imagine that social concepts are linked according to frequency of use, self-relevance, familiarity in everyday life, or *importance* to personal goals (Kunda & Cantor, 1986; Wyer & Srull, 1981). Similarly, social concepts, particularly those organized around prototypical social episodes, might be linked by associations marking *contiguity* in time/space of occurrence in social life events (e.g., ingratiation episodes typically precede—not follow—favor-asking episodes). Just as one can imagine networks of nonsocial concepts with links based on a variety of connections (e.g., part-whole; word associates; see also Andersen & Klatsky, 1986), so, too, is it likely that descriptive and evaluative associations do not exhaust the set of structural links between concepts in the social domain.

One illustrative model might work as follows: concepts in the social concept network would each be tagged for frequency of use, self-relevance, and the like; but accessibility would operate through links from other domains of concept knowledge (e.g., self-knowledge). This kind of an associative marking model would serve to create high probability collections of accessible concepts (based on principles other than descriptive or evaluative similarity) but only under conditions when another, in a sense more primary, form of conceptual knowledge guided the construal process (see, for example, Lewicki, 1985; Holyoak & Gordon, 1983; on self-referent processing of social information). While the exact form of the network links remain at issue, there is little doubt that Kelly was right in suggesting multiple dimensions underlying connections between accessible constructs about the social world.

Basic Levels and Basic Units

Consideration of these fuzzy hierarchies, with concepts at different levels of abstraction or category breadth, leads us to ask, as Eleanor Rosch and her colleagues did in the nonsocial domain (Rosch et al., 1976), whether a preferred or *"basic" level* of categorization exists in social construal

(Cantor & Mischel, 1979). Of course, in shaping this question for the social domain, certain criteria of basic level categories applied in the nonsocial domain become more or less relevant—e.g., basic level person categories might not be identified by simple linguistic labels or common motor movements or precedence in the language acquisition process. However, the thrust of the basic level category notion can be preserved: Is there a level of category breadth in social *perception* represented by concepts that typically (though not always) convey particularly rich, distinctive, vivid, and easily accessible prototypes for persons, situations, or social episodes (e.g., Cantor et al., 1982b)?

The answer to this question, stated in its boldest form as above, is clearly negative. In the midst of social construal, different processing goals emerge, such as communicating a quick comparative portrait of two types of persons or providing a detailed prediction about forthcoming behavior-in-context, to make one or another level of categorization most preferred, easily accessible, and useful (Higgins, 1981). Similarly, individuals have their own particular content domains of expertise and ignorance and the level of category breadth that maximizes cue validity of prototypic features will vary across these domains (Higgins & King, 1981; Cantor & Mischel, 1979). In order to be faithful to the flexibility of social construal it is essential that we assume a great deal of movement up, down, and across these fuzzy concept hierarchies in the course of construal.

Yet, as much as it now seems wrongheaded to expect to isolate *a* basic level of social concepts (preserved across content domains and construal contexts and individuals), there is something naggingly right about the notion that a middle-level of abstraction has special utility (Cantor & Mischel, 1979). When we consider the *content* of social construals it is not the highly abstract trait factors or task-episodes or situations that convey the richness and vividness of intuitive social knowledge—it isn't extroversion or social belongingness episodes or affiliation settings that organize our day to day thoughts and plans and behaviors (Little, 1983; Cantor & Kihlstrom, 1985). Moreover, somehow we typically know not to expect day to day life events to fit neatly into highly specific subordinate categories— the fast-food waitress never quite fits the Burger King script from T.V. Instead, it may well be that, typically, our level of social expertise, our processing goals of anticipatory self-regulation and social prediction, and the fairly high degree of variability in the stimulus itself from context to context, are indeed well matched by some more middle-level of conceptual breadth. While the exact identity of the middle-level will surely shift from one person to another and one content domain to another, it may still make sense to speak of a "default" preference that moves to the middle (cf. Hampson et al., 1986).

The same question also arises with respect to the existence of "basic" units of social perception, because of people's ability to organize social experience with a *diversity of conceptual units* (e.g., personality vs. action-oriented representations). For example, in the domain of person categories, some researchers have argued for the dominance of "social caricatures" as units of organization rich in behavioral attributes and easily brought to mind in the construal process (Andersen & Klatsky, 1986); while others build a case for the utility of personality trait categories as representations of patterns of behavior co-occurrence organized in fuzzy hierarchies at different levels of abstraction (Hampson et al., 1986; Buss & Craik, 1983).

In fact, the argument for preferred units of person construal is quite parallel to that considered in the literature on basic levels of social construal. As argued above, it is clear that people make use of multiple organizational principles in structuring and unitizing social experience. Much as we would all like to identify *the* units of social construal the true state of affairs may be more messy than pristine. Each person undoubtedly has a set of well-structured, highly accessible person concepts that constitute a mixed bag of dispositional categories (e.g., dominant persons) and caricatures (e.g., the class bully) and biologically-based classifications (e.g., adolescent boy). As units of person construal, "social caricatures" (like class bully or macho male) are particularly compelling because of their natural connections to social episodes and typical social situations (e.g., it is easy to *see* the macho male coming to the rescue of the helpless female whose car is stalled on the highway) (Andersen & Klatsky, 1986). Yet, as Buss & Craik (1983) have clearly demonstrated, in some domains of social experience, personality disposition categories are especially rich in behavioral features and also provide nice links to contexts of occurrence in daily life (e.g., the shy person at a party is a quite vivid, accessible concept).

Interdomain Organization

This analysis of constructive alternativism in social construal underlines one form of flexibility: people have access to well-structured concepts organized in different forms for the same stimuli. Another impressive feature of social construal is that while a person may organize information about an event in terms of one kind of conceptual unit (e.g., an intimacy episode), other relevant units come quickly to mind as well (e.g., a candlelight dinner and an adoring lover). Since these collections of person and episode and situation concepts appear to function together in the construal process, it seems reasonable to assume another level of structure in the social concept repertoire—*interdomain associations*.

As we noted earlier, analysis of the content of person, situation, and episode concepts suggests natural dimensions of overlap on which to base connections across conceptual domains in the concept repertoire. Situations are frequently defined by the persons and episodes commonly found in them (e.g., Cantor, Mischel, & Schwartz, 1982a; Barker, 1968); person categories, be they based on personality dispositions, social roles, or caricatures, typically evoke contextualized images (e.g., "the frat type at a frat party"; Niedenthal et al., 1985; Zuroff, 1982) with powerful action scripts (e.g., "the animal house" episode). Episodes, as we argued earlier, provide a quite natural bridge between person and situation concepts, as they tend to evoke images of the typical persons filling the action roles and the typical settings in which such scripts can unfold (Trzebinski et al., 1985). One need only imagine thinking of episodes without filling in the relevant person and situation category information to see how closely these units are linked (e.g., what is a "test of wits" episode without a "brain" and her "audience"?). Moreover, to the extent that episode concepts carry special implications for the dynamics of social life—goals, strategies, intentions, and emotions—they must serve as conduits linking the actors and settings of social interaction.

In considering the content of social episodes we noted that they may be especially powerful units of organization in the construal process because of their association with basic life tasks (e.g., intimacy; identity; territoriality; dominance; loss/separation; see Plutchik, 1980). At an abstract level, hierarchies of episode concepts may well be organized around different content domains of *social life tasks* (Cantor & Kihlstrom, 1985). Such an organization would provide the basis for quite natural links at an abstract level across concept domains of persons, episodes, and situations; for person and situation hierarchies can also be arrayed in terms of a taxonomy of adaptive tasks fairly easily (e.g., dominance tasks that map onto power-hungry people and settings of interpersonal conflict). Of course, person, situation, and episode concepts also have ready connections at more concrete levels of construal (e.g., the "schoolchildren scapegoating" episode brings readily to mind the "class bully" and the "playground at recess").

In reality, the interconnections across concept domains probably constitute quite a *tangled web*, with interconcept connections across levels of abstraction and domains going in all directions and substantial idiosyncratic organization in these interlocking networks. Figure 4-2 presents a schematic version of a chunk of one hypothetical tangled web in the intimacy domain. This tangled web of concepts includes interconnections between person, situation, and episode concepts that vary in strength, that jump across hierarchical levels, and that allow for asymmetries in the direction of association. While this may appear to be a rather messy network, the key to organization in the social concept repertoire is to preserve room for idiographic elaboration—each person's web has its unique stamp—and to allow easy access to *different* bundles of concepts at once (i.e., to permit constructive alternativism). We suspect that to meet such objectives a rather tangled conceptual web must be assumed to exist in the social concept repertoire.

Person Concepts   Situation Concepts

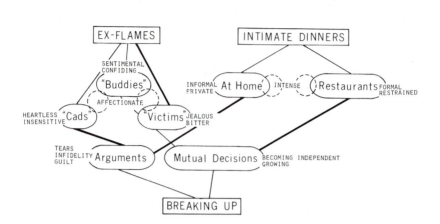

Episode Concepts

FIGURE 4-2 Tangled Intimacy Web.

Fuzzy Concepts in Fuzzy Hierarchies
in Tangled Webs: Useful?

We have seen that it is quite possible to accommodate models of concept representation of nonsocial objects in order to handle the complexity of social concepts. At the level of internal concept structure, "mixed models" comprised, to varying degrees for different concepts, of both summary abstract feature lists and descriptions of category exemplars have been proposed (Lingle et al., 1983). With regard to interconcept associations, "fuzzy hierarchies" with class-inclusion relations that vary in degree of relatedness and links between concepts based upon other similarity principles have emerged as viable candidates to capture the implication relations between concepts (Hampson et al., 1986; Andersen & Klatsky, 1986). At the level of interdomain (person, situation, episode) connections, a tangled web, with many crossover links that define different construal paths from the same entry concept, seems necessary, even though some "cleaner" links exist at the more abstract level of basic adaptive tasks that structure each concept domain into semi-independent parts. These accommodations seem reasonable (in the light of the complexity of social concepts) and, with the exception of dimming the prospects for a "basic level" or "basic unit" of social construal to emerge, do not appear to challenge the analogy between social and nonsocial concepts severely. In fact, along the way in this analysis, we have noted that in many instances these accommodations to the "pure" fuzzy sets model (Rosch et al., 1976) seem appropriate in the nonsocial concept domain as well as in the case of social concepts (e.g., Hampton, 1982; Lingle et al., 1983; Labov, 1973; Andersen & Klatsky, 1986).

While these accommodations do not seem severe to us, they still raise several important questions about the utility of this approach to social concept structure: Do the special features of this model capture important aspects of the social construal process? Is this model faithful to constructive alternativism in social construal? We will now consider these critical questions in turn.

1. Gist and variability. In our view the primary contribution of the fuzzy sets model of concept structure is in highlighting the coexistence of *gist* and *variability* in the attributes of category members. Such a model captures the common intuition about social concepts—implicit in the phrase that there is a kernel of truth to stereotypes—that it is possible to know the central tendency of a category and yet confront in actuality exemplars that only partially fit that idealized model. This seems especially critical in the case of social concepts because these concepts often represent categories comprised of a very wide range of exemplars, with a variety of different patterns of feature co-occurrence and many cases of "unclear" exemplars in which the instance partially fits a number of alternative categories at once (Holyoak & Gordon, 1984; Cantor & Genero, 1986). Yet, with all this internal variability, social concepts do have a coherent gist as represented in people's summary prototypes (e.g., Cantor et al., 1980; Cantor et al., 1982a).

A summary prototype provides for an accessible set of "default knowledge" about the category when specific exemplars are not easily brought to mind, when it comes time to update the concept in the face of new data, and when predictions of a general sort are required and no one exemplar can serve as a clear model (Ashmore & DelBoca, 1980; Deaux & Lewis, 1984). Knowledge of a range of actual exemplars keeps one's inferences in check, serving to remind us that most people or episodes or situations do not in fact fit the stereotypic expectations (Locksley et al., 1980). In other words, the fuzzy sets model, instantiated in the mixed prototype representation, seems ideal as a model of social concepts—a model that can tolerate variety, poor category fits, and dynamic shifts in concept meaning, and still communicate a coherent message about the central tendency of the category.

2. Multiple construal paths. In essence, the fuzzy hierarchy and tangled web models of interconcept structure arise because there do not exist clean one-one mappings between social stimulus objects (persons, episodes, or situations) and the concepts developed to summarize them.

One has the impression (perhaps mistaken) that there is a basic category to which each nonsocial stimulus object belongs (e.g., the fundamental *chair* concept; Rosch et al., 1976) and that shifts in context of usage or observation only slightly obscure the real one-one mapping for a moment without fundamentally changing the object's rightful place. This impression of clarity of belongingness and stability of meaning does not as easily extend to the world of social objects (Cantor & Mischel, 1979; Holyoak & Gordon, 1984). The meaning (and rightful conceptual place) of social objects really does change with corresponding shifts in context of observation and in the perceiver's processing goals (Hampson et al., 1986). There clearly are multiple paths through the social concept repertoire traversed by a perceiver as he or she thinks about a single object or event but in a different light (Kelly, 1955). Fuzzy hierarchies and tangled conceptual webs seem well-suited to represent a shifting set of associations between concepts with multiple paths going in all directions and varying in strength of connection (see Figure 4-2 above). Most important, this model, as in the case of the mixed prototype model of internal structure, incorporates some of the apparently highly stable connections between social concepts (e.g., sociable people and dominant people) and frequently traversed paths (e.g., the birthday girl, gift-giving episode, surprise party) and clear cases of class-inclusion implications (e.g., bossy type and dominant person) without ignoring the potentially more variable and idiosyncratic interconcept associations (e.g., the silent moral-leader type and dominant persons, the "manager behind the man," and the "political campaign speech"). In a tangled web of fuzzy hierarchies entirely different conceptual paths can be traversed with apparent ease, as when a particular social interaction (e.g., an apparently genuine personal appeal) takes on an unusual meaning (e.g., a slippery salesman approach) given the context of observation (e.g., a campaign press conference). Moreover, characteristics of the perceiver, such as mood state, familiarity with the event in question, intentions in the situation, can guide the construal process in strikingly different conceptual directions (e.g., Isen & Clark, 1982; Markus, Smith, & Moreland, 1985; Showers & Cantor, 1985; Higgins & King, 1981). This model allows for constructive alternativism and richness of interpretation—breadth and depth in social construal.

INDIVIDUAL DIFFERENCES IN SOCIAL CONCEPTS

One of the main advantages of this approach is that the same assumptions that are compatible with constructive alternativism also serve to highlight dimensions of individual difference in the content and organization of a social concept repertoire. As Kelly (1955) pointed out some time ago, individuals differ in their construals of events because they differ in the form and content of their construct systems. In the same vein, more recently, theorists have argued that people have their own favorite content areas of social experience (Markus, 1977, 1979, 1983), favorite concepts that evoke those experiences (Higgins & King, 1981), and personal meanings for those concepts (Rosenberg & Gara, 1985; Gara, 1986). One way to characterize these individual differences in the social concept repertoire is as differences in the areas of *social expertise* (Showers & Cantor, 1985). Accordingly, everyone has areas of expertise and of ignorance about social life experience (i.e., about persons, situations, episodes) and their profile of expertise is reflected in the content and organization of the social concept repertoire. In fact, social expertise may well be reflected in the content and structure of knowledge at three levels in the repertoire: at the concept level; at the fuzzy hierarchy level; at the tangled web level. We will consider these kinds of individual differences, and their relation to the structural assumptions presented earlier, in turn.

1. Concepts.   Perhaps the easiest way to see expertise reflected in the social concept repertoire is in the degree of elaboration and the content of features of particular concepts. A person who is an "expert" about "joggers" has a rich and distinctive jogger prototype, many exemplars to concretize the meaning of the concept, and, probably, clearly delineated evaluative-affective associations to the concept (Markus, 1979). This expertise most likely derives from personal experiences (directly confronted or vicariously modeled) and indicates some form of self-relevance of the concept in question (Markus, 1979; Lewicki, 1985). Familiarity with exemplars of the concept may translate also into elaborations of the concept at quite specific levels of abstraction (with multiple related concepts to capture fine distinctions in meaning) and, perhaps, may be reflected in the choice of especially vivid conceptual units that go beyond common language terms (e.g., social caricatures vs. dispositional categories; see Andersen & Klatsky, 1986). The jogger expert may make distinctions that most novices would not consider important, between "faddish joggers," "marathoners," "fitness joggers," and more (Rosch et al., 1976; Fiske & Kinder, 1981; Higgins & King, 1981).

2. Fuzzy hierarchies.   Expertise at the concept level may also "spread" to the broader content area reflected in a fuzzy hierarchy (e.g., the jogger expert may actually be quite knowledgeable about a broad array of "achievers" with a four-tier hierarchy including "achievers"/"athletes"/"joggers"/"marathoners"). Here, the expertise is reflected in the number and diversity of concepts within the hierarchy, the number of levels of abstraction covered by such concepts, and the number, strength, and multi-directionality of the interconcept connections in the hierarchy. These structural features enable the expert to "see" relevant social events from many angles (Sternberg, 1984) with multiple construal paths and concepts at different levels of abstraction (Hampson et al., 1986). The fuzzy structure of the hierarchy (with degrees of class-inclusion represented) also enables the expert to know when a related concept in the hierarchy is truly relevant in a particular context and when not to fill in the gaps too broadly (e.g., the "achiever" concept, and all that it implies, is not particularly relevant to understanding the behavior of a "faddish jogger"). Moreover, the associative network connecting concepts within the hierarchy probably reflects the idiosyncratic meaning that this life arena has come to have in the mind of the expert; novices may stay closer to the culturally-defined, consensual meanings and associations (Rosenberg, 1977).

3. Tangled webs. Individual differences in social concept expertise are also likely to be reflected in the density of cross-domain connections linking different types of concepts across different hierarchies in the web. For example, social expertise may translate into very strong and elaborate connecting paths between person and episode and situation concepts in related conceptual hierarchies (e.g., the "marathoner" takes us to a "competition" episode and a "marathon race" setting). In particular, these links establish the "action-oriented" and "interactionist" content of social expertise (Trzebinski et al., 1985; Zuroff, 1982). And, to the extent that these paths extend throughout the different hierarchies (implicating rather abstract person, situation, and episode concepts along the way), then experts may be expected to see the implications for basic adaptive life tasks rather quickly in the course of common social experience. Perhaps this is what is meant when we say that an "intelligent person goes right to the heart of the matter" (Sternberg et al., 1981).

These individual differences in social expertise (as reflected in the content and organization of the social concept repertoire) are important because they are likely to influence the nature and outcome of the social construal process. The impact of such repertoire differences on the interpretive process can be imagined simply by considering the set of concepts that two people—a "school brain" and a relative novice in this arena of social experience—would be likely to bring to mind when confronting a "test-taking" competition at school. Figure 4-3 presents a comparison between these two individuals, illustrating the various ways in which their different social learning histories and personal involvement in the "academic achievement" domain might be reflected in differences in the meaning and structure of some of their social concept hierarchies.

Of course, in order to see the full import of these structural differences in individuals' concept repertoires, it is necessary to consider the coordination of conceptual and rule knowledge in the construal process. We need to look closely at the reflection of these conceptual differences in the *rules* of interpretation used by individuals in the course of social experience.

Expert Representation:
Scholarship Competition

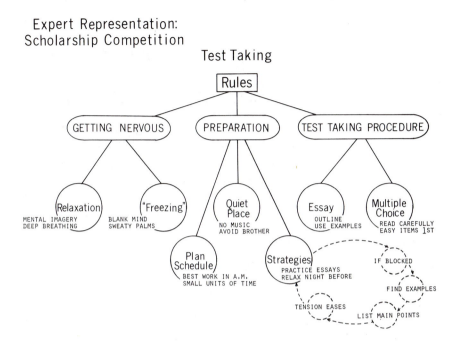

Novice Representation:
Scholarship Competition

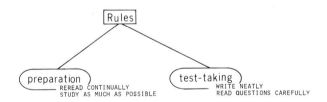

FIGURE 4-3 Expert and Novice Representations.

INTERPRETIVE RULES IN SOCIAL CONSTRUAL

A substantial portion of the social intelligence repertoire consists of *interpretive rules* for making sense of social experience. These rules are properly considered as procedural knowledge for encoding, manipulating, retrieving, and utilizing declarative concepts in the service of interpreting events in the social world. These are the rules involved in perception, categorization, memory, causal attribution, judgment, and inference in both social and nonsocial domains. The individual uses these rules in coordination with the concept repertoire; for, as Nasby & Kihlstrom (1985) note: "while declarative knowledge refers to *knowing that*, procedural knowledge represents *knowing how*" (p. 6). However, while people frequently can articulate the "facts" that they know to be "true" of different types of people, episodes, and situations (i.e., declarative concepts are available to conscious introspection, at least in principle), interpretive rules are typically *implicit* such that a person isn't aware of having this "knowledge." Or, if the person does infer its existence, there is no direct awareness of when it is applied, and no control over its application (Kihlstrom, 1984; Nasby & Kihlstrom, 1985). Procedural rules for social construal can be inferred through laboratory analysis, and, through interpersonal exchanges or in therapy, some of our most habitual interpretive rules (and "hidden" concepts) may surface and receive explicit attention.

The set of interpretive rules, inferred from observation of lawful patterns of performance in various social construal tasks, is sizable (see Fiske & Taylor, 1984, for a thorough review). Indeed, in the social domain, interpretive rules allow us to categorize people, situations and events (e.g., Cantor & Mischel, 1979); infer others' emotional states from interaction episodes (Weiner, 1985; Shaver et al., 1985); evaluate the likability of other people (Anderson, 1974; Fiske, 1980, 1982); infer dispositions underlying people's behaviors (Jones & Davis, 1965) and evaluate the causes of events (Kelley, 1967, 1972; Weiner et al., 1972); encode and retrieve information about people, events, and situations (Hastie, 1980, 1981); make predictions about the future (Nisbett & Ross, 1980); and test those hypotheses (Snyder, 1981b). The set of interpretive rules is rich, diverse, and easily adapted to meet the needs of social life construal. This knowledge is also so routinely relied upon in the course of an interaction or reflective moment, that it is easy to ignore it in considering the cognitive structures in personality.

In fact, a very large portion of research in social cognition is devoted to explicating these interpretive rules, more than exists for the self-regulatory rules that personality psychologists with a cognitive bent have typically emphasized (Bandura, 1986; Mischel, 1981). This research suggests quite clearly that individuals have an enormous repertoire of interpretive rules and that this is an arena of knowledge ripe for an individual difference analysis (e.g., Peterson & Seligman, 1984; see Nasby & Kihlstrom, 1985).

Many of these rules suggest that fairly extensive "calculations" are run off quite automatically in the course of construal. People seem willing and able to perform these calculations when provided with a "cognitive set" to be thorough and accurate, to make sense of all of the available data, or to remember each piece of social datum. For example, we know that there is a calculus for making causal attributions, such that information about behavioral consistency, distinctiveness of behavior, and social consensus around the observation figure heavily in judgments of causal responsibility (Kelley, 1967). We also know that to judge the likability of people, individuals act as if they "compute" the average of the likability ratings associated with the target's various attributes, considering as well initial biases toward that person (Anderson, 1974). Similarly, when people are confronted with incongruent information about another person, they seem to have a variety of procedures for making sense of the incongruities (Devine & Ostrom, 1985; Hastie, 1984). Asch & Zukier (1984) describe several such "reconciliation" procedures. People can "segregate" the information, assigning incompatible attributes to different spheres of a person's life; infer a "cause-effect" relation between incompatible attributes (e.g., "he is hostile because he is dependent"); find a "common source" for the incompatible attributes; suppose a "means-end" relation between the attributes ("he is strict in order to be kind"); or "interpolate" some mediating attribute ("he is intelligent but has become discouraged and so is unambitious"). All three of these instances of construal—in causal attribution, likability evaluation, impression formation—invoke interpretive procedures that involve calculation and information integration.

However, in the course of this research investigators have also uncovered systematic departures from or shortcuts around these interpretive rules. So, for example, the "fundamental attribution error" leads us to attribute a person's behavior to internal dispositions, even in the face of clear situational constraints or without evidence of cross-situational consistency in the target behaviors (e.g., Ross, 1977; Mischel & Peake, 1982). Similarly, the arduous procedure of information integration in evaluating the likability of another person is often bypassed, replaced by a simple summary evaluation garnered from readily accessible knowledge of the pleasantness of "people like that type" (Fiske, 1982). There is also a tendency for people to preserve a coherent personality impression by ignoring incongruent behavioral evidence, especially when a readily believable situational attribution is brought directly to their attention (e.g., Crocker, Hannah, & Weber, 1983; but see also Hastie, 1981; White & Carlston, 1983). Procedural shortcuts have been identified in practically every domain of social perception, memory, and judgment (Nisbett & Ross, 1980).

In these examples, the loss in accuracy of judgment seems hardly to impact at all on the efficiency and/or utility of such procedures for social construal—one rarely, if ever, sees a lay person (or even an expert) complain about the margin of error in judgments based upon these cognitive shortcuts (Miller & Cantor, 1982). In some respects this is rather surprising since one assumes that the underlying motives for social construal are prediction and control—the cognitive work here is presumably in the service of accurately anticipating social events (Kelly, 1955; Pittman & Pittman, 1979). Yet people function quite well relying almost exclusively, and typically without much conscious thought, on these shortcut interpretive procedures that are often obviously off the mark in predictive precision (Swann, 1984).

This paradox raises a number of intriguing questions about in-dividuals' tolerance for error and the salutory effect of "illusory cognitive control" that are beyond the scope of the present discussion. However, for our purposes, the paradox is of interest because it leads us to consider possible reasons for engaging in shortcut processing that derive from the structure of the concept repertoire and processing goals beyond those of achieving control through accurate prediction. Moreover, the analysis of shortcut procedures naturally suggests an analysis of individual differences in interpretive expertise; i.e., do some people rely on shortcuts less than others in some construal contexts? We will consider these issues in turn.

Fuzzy Concepts and Shortcut Rules

Interpretive rules operate with the social concepts in the declarative knowledge store in order to make sense of stimuli. To the extent that individuals automatically retrieve person, episode, and situation concepts in the course of processing social stimuli—i.e., bring their personal con-structs to bear as Kelly suggested—then the reliance on "shortcut" rules may derive from the "fuzzy" nature of those concepts. In other words, given that there is a coordination between rules and concepts, it may be that shortcut rules match fuzzy concepts particularly well.

First, there is little doubt that people have quite rich (if tangled) associative networks in the social concept repertoire, such that col-lections of concepts are brought to bear easily in the course of construal. In fact, Winter et al. (1985) report that people tend to infer personality dispositions automatically, without awareness or drain on processing capacity. They asked subjects to perform a digit-memory task and then, during a retention interval, to read sentences about actors' behaviors. On a surprise cued-recall test, personality disposition cues led to the best recall for the sentences, and memory was unaffected by the difficulty of the digit-memory task. These results suggest that subjects automatically en-coded the sentences in terms of relevant personality dispositional concepts without any interference from the digit task, without awareness of the inference process, and without instructions from the experimenter to do so. These "unintentional" personality inferences are apt to be comple-mented by inferences that implicate episode and situation concepts as well (Trzebinski et al., 1985). The associative links across concept domains are quite strong and plentiful, and we know that people find it very easy and useful to organize information about social behavior in terms of the information about goals and context highlighted in episode and situation concepts.

Assuming, therefore, that these social concepts are evoked rather automatically in social construal, the next step is to consider the coordination of shortcut interpretive rules with fuzzy concepts. The argument is that shortcut rules "make sense" (even though they may not be optimally useful in prediction) because they highlight or match well with the fuzzy structure of social concepts. In particular, they make use of the prototypicality structure of the concepts, highlighting "good" and "poor" conceptual fits on the basis of either exemplar or summary prototype comparisons. Judgments of fit with conceptual expectations seem to underlie many of these shortcut procedures. This comparison process also facilitates further inferences, attributions, and gap-filling elaborations when a clear fit is observed, and consideration of the source of incongruence when expectations are violated. In either case, both the filling-in process and the process of disambiguating inconsistencies are eased by the variety and number of related person, situation, and episode concepts that people are able to bring to bear in any given construal effort. These associative links allow a person to focus on personality dispositions, social characteristics, strategic goals, action sequences, contextual constraints, and rules of the situation, all at once, in the process of disambiguation. The rich set of interconcept associations is particularly helpful in the case of apparent incongruities, when invoking another set of concepts can facilitate making sense of violations of the expectancies set up by one particular person, situation, or episode concept.

In the following discussion, we will consider a few selected examples of this procedural and declarative knowledge coordination, beginning with some instances of shortcuts that derive from observations of good conceptual fits and then turning to procedures invoked in the face of violations of expectations.

1. "Schema-triggered affect." Fiske (1981; Fiske & Pavelchak, 1986) has proposed a shortcut procedure for affective evaluation of persons that seems well-suited to a repertoire of person concepts (either caricatures or dispositional or biological categories) structured as "hot prototypes." In her model, when a target person provides a clear fit to a person prototype—on the basis of similarity to a prototypical exemplar or to the summary prototype—it is relatively easy to associate the affective evaluation of the concept as a whole to the target instance, rather than go through a laborious "piecemeal" process of attribute evaluation and information integration (cf. Anderson, 1974). Schema-triggered affect fits the fuzzy structure of person concepts, utilizing both the gist of a concept and information about the continuum of category fit of exemplar instances.

2. "Representativeness heuristic." A similar judgmental shortcut—the "representativeness heuristic" (Kahneman & Tversky, 1974)—also relies on knowledge of the prototypicality continuum in person concepts in the service of making quick and dirty predictions about a target person's future behavior and current social group status (for example, Dave is an engineer because he fits the engineer prototype, even though there are very few engineers in the sample; Dave will be likely to do engineer-like things in the future, even though he has only demonstrated a very few engineer-like features up to this point). Again, these judgmental shortcuts are taken rather automatically; they are likely to cause inconvenience only to the extent that a loose criterion of category-fit was used, the prototype information (summary evaluative tag and gist features) is a fairly gross abstraction from actual data about human behavior, and/or the observer cannot coerce the target to conform to the shortcut impression in the course of future interactions.

3. Social analogies and exemplar-matching. Gilovitch (1981) and Read (1983, 1984) have suggested that one easy way to make social predictions is on the basis of an analogy between a current instance and the behavior or outcomes observed in the case of a concrete example that matches that instance on some critical dimensions. For example, Gilovitch (1981) observed professional sportswriters making predictions about the likelihood for success in the pros for hypothetical college athletes on the basis of feature-similarity to great pro stars of the past. Similarly, as Read (1984) points out, foreign policy episodes often take on crisis proportion simply by virtue of similarity (even on relatively superficial dimensions) to prior world strategic crises (e.g., "Bay of Pigs," "Vietnam War"). Again, the predictive risk involved in analogical reasoning by exemplar-matching is increased to the extent that similarity is measured on relatively undiagnostic dimensions, and the risk is decreased when apparently more diagnostic dimensions of causal relevance are assessed for instance-exemplar similarity (e.g., Read, 1984).

4. Prototype-matching and situation choice. In a very similar procedure, people frequently make use of associative links in quickly leaping to the conclusion that "He's just not the kind of person who would be comfortable in that type of situation" (Cantor, Mischel, & Schwartz, 1982a). In admissions or personnel selection interviewing, the intuitive judgment of person-situation fit is often made on the basis of summary-stereotypic assessments of both persons and situations (Abelson, 1976; Feldman, 1980; Bem & Funder, 1978). Some people even go so far as to choose their dates, college housing, or game-tasks on the basis of an apparently compatible prototype-match (Snyder & Simpson, 1984; Niedenthal, Cantor, & Kihlstrom, 1985; Cantor, Mackie, & Lord, 1984). While these assessments are usually assumed to involve a match to a person or situation stereotype (e.g., the prototypical "Stanford student"), exemplar matches may also be involved, as when a potential student reminds an admissions interviewer of his favorite undergraduate student of the past (Abelson, 1976).

5. "Salience bias" and unexpected events.   When observers attempt to make sense of the activity in a social situation or episode they frequently turn attention to "salient" figures or events in the behavioral ground (Taylor & Fiske, 1978). As Fiske & Taylor (1984) note, salience can be created in numerous ways: by perceptual highlighting, by social novelty, or by violations of scripts. Frequently, these salience-based perceptions derive from violations of expectations based on comparisons with the prototypes for such situations or episodes. For example, Fiske & Taylor (1984) comment on the degree to which attention is grabbed when one observes a young person in an old-age home.

Once noted, salient persons or actions tend to evoke a quick and dirty rule for making causal attributions—the salient figure is inferred to have control over the situation and personal dispositions are ascribed, regardless of the strength of the actual behavioral data. Accordingly, the young person in the old-age home, for example, quickly takes on the virtues and efficacy of the "good samaritan" even though the observer knows little about the target person's prosocial behavior.

Of course, the extent to which this is then a useful shortcut depends on the validity of the attributions and inferences with regard to the particulars of the target person or events in the situation. In some cases, the extra attention accorded to these unusual, salient events may be unfortunate if, at the same time, occurrences that are more typical are ignored: Landman (1984) found, for example, that people exhibit more regret over unusual actions which ended in bad outcomes than over comparably unfortunate actions that were more typical. As always, there is a good and a bad side to these procedural shortcuts.

6. "Schematic memory" and attention to incongruency.   White & Carlston (1983) demonstrated the operation of a similar set of attentional and memory procedures in which individuals focus attention on people's incongruent actions and then jump to some all too hasty conclusions on the basis of scant attention to the schema-congruent behaviors. They asked subjects to watch and listen to a tape of a complex social interaction in which a number of people engaged in conversations at once. Subjects had been primed with personality descriptions of one of the actors, descriptions which created a clear set of social expectations for behavior in the inter-action. First, it was clear that subjects quickly shifted attention away from the activities of the "primed actor" as soon as they were sure that he was behaving in the expected manner; they shifted attention back to him in the face of incongruent behaviors. This pattern of focus on incongruency had clear implications for the accuracy of their memory and inferences about the "primed actor." Subjects were much more likely to rely on gap-filling (and, often, inaccurate) inferences in recalling the actor's behavior the less attention they had accorded him during the interaction episode (i.e., when he fulfilled their schematic expectations). Thus, again, we see that while attention to unexpected events *may* result in a careful analysis of those occurrences, it is often at the expense of accuracy in memory for schema-congruent material.

Consideration of these examples of shortcut interpretive procedures suggests that they are conceptually guided in a direction that may make sense given the structure of the accessible concepts and the processing overload in complex social interactions. For example, in the face of a continuously shifting social episode, it may be quite adaptive to engage in gap-filling inferences and analogical predictions when a "good" conceptual fit is observed, presumably freeing attention and processing capacity in the event of surprise occurrences (White & Carlston, 1983). The value of this approach is increased in the context of a dynamic social interaction in which the observer-actor may well be able behaviorally to confirm those gap-filling inferences-predictions and, simultaneously, update and correct the remaining errors in construal (Snyder, 1981b; Hogarth, 1981).

Of course, this claim for "intelligence" in shortcut processing depends upon evidence of people's sensitivity to critical features of the social context—i.e., their ability to control the target's behavior, the existence of corrective feedback—and their appreciation of the predictive validity (or lack thereof) of the conceptual prototypes. Since it seems clear that most people do not engage in extensive validity checks on their social concepts (cf. Lingle et al., 1983), the safeguards in shortcut processing are more likely to exist in the sensitivity of people to contextual constraints and feedback opportunities. There is some evidence suggestive of that sensitivity: Erber & Fiske (1984) demonstrated that people are less likely simply to discount schema-inconsistent behavior of an interaction partner, and more likely to engage in an effortful search for reconciling meaning, when their outcomes depend on the partner rather than vice versa; Locksley et al. (1980) have shown that people will use diagnostic case data rather than prototype inferences to make predictions about a target person who seems to violate the assumptions of the concept representing his or her social group.

These lines of research (see Hastie, 1984, for other examples) are certainly suggestive of "good processing sense," though they are hardly decisive proof of that wisdom. Another, perhaps more readily available, database for judging the intelligence with which shortcut procedures are used exists in the study of individual differences in social knowledge expertise. Thus, we turn now to the individual differences side of this issue, asking whether people use their shortcut procedures more wisely in domains in which they have declarative knowledge expertise, familiarity with the situation, and motivation.

Individual Differences in Construal

In keeping with the approach to individual differences illustrated earlier, the present discussion begins not with *styles* of procedural knowledge but rather with domains of *expertise* in declarative and procedural knowledge (Nasby & Kihlstrom, 1985). There is already a growing literature suggestive of stylistic regularities in the ways in which individuals process social information—e.g., attributional styles (Metalsky & Abramson, 1981; Peterson & Seligman, 1984); evaluative styles (Pietramonico, 1983; Ostrom & Davis, 1979); styles of attentional focus (Carver & Scheier, 1981); coping styles (e.g., Byrne, 1964; Miller & Mangan, 1983). However, concern with more domain-specific individual differences in procedural knowledge, that derive from differences in declarative expertise in particular domains of social life, is only now beginning to emerge (e.g., Fiske, Kinder, & Larter, 1983). It is to these expertise differences that we turn for evidence of the flexible and controlled (i.e., intelligent) use of shortcut procedures in social construal (Showers & Cantor, 1985).

As we noted earlier, declarative knowledge expertise in a particular domain usually implies: extensive concepts in that domain; well-organized associative networks of domain-relevant concepts; easy access to relevant concepts via well-frequented paths in the concept network/web. Nasby & Kihlstrom (1985) describe the virtues of declarative expertise as follows:

> By definition, of course, experts in a particular domain have acquired more "factual" knowledge, semantic and episodic, than novices. Moreover, experts may organize declarative knowledge differently than novices, establishing more associative links between the cognitive elements that define the domain, and perhaps also structuring the elements according to more complex and efficient hierarchies (e.g., Chase & Simon, 1973; Chi & Koeske, 1983). As a consequence of greater organization, areas of expertise should become more accessible, facilitating retrieval of relevant concepts and episodes to comprehend and interpret new information. (pp. 11-12)

The virtues of social knowledge expertise are relatively easy to see; for example, the expert in a domain should be relatively free (in terms of processing capacity) to take note of unexpected events, violations of expectations, and novel stimuli, given his or her easy access to well-organized declarative knowledge (e.g., Fiske et al., 1983). However, expertise is also a "double-edged sword" (Nasby & Kihlstrom, 1985; Showers & Cantor, 1985). For example, the expert's access to a relatively wide array of domain-relevant concepts may also lead to overly facile reconciliations or assimilations of novel or unexpected or incongruent events (e.g., Langer & Abelson, 1974). The expert may unintentionally hang on to favorite concepts and preferred ways of interpreting events, rather than updating them in the face of new or discrepant information (Nasby & Kihlstrom, 1985; Crocker, Fiske, & Taylor, 1985). Additionally, the highly practiced nature of procedural expertise may render favorite ways of "seeing things" readily available, but not easily articulatable (Chanowitz & Langer, 1980; Nisbett & Wilson, 1977). This characteristic of expertise suggests that "mindless" or automatic forms of processing, such as priming without awareness or schematic assimilation, may occur spontaneously for people in their expert domains. Together, these features of declarative and procedural expertise illustrate the risks that accompany the advantages of knowing a great deal about a particular domain.

These cognitive characteristics of social knowledge expertise are linked to motivational aspects of expertise which typically derive from personal involvement and experience in a domain, and the relevance of a domain or situation to current life plans (Showers & Cantor, 1985; Little, 1983; Klinger, 1975). It is these motivational features of expertise that may hold the key to the "intelligent" (i.e., flexible and controlled) use of procedural shortcuts by experts in their expert domains. As Showers & Cantor (1985) suggested: "The expert's advantage may be that he can intervene and check the progress of automatic interpretations. He may be able to recognize and generate other ways of reading a situation *when motivated to do so*. In this way, the expert has the flexibility to take advantage of automaticity without losing control" (pp. 292–93). Moreover, if the expert does indeed "take control" in important situations, then he of all people is in the best position to engage in constructive alternativism (with a rich repertoire of concepts, multiple paths of conceptual associations, knowledge of exemplar variability, and so forth). Ultimately, it is this potential for controlled processing in important situations that is most suggestive of the wise use of expertise. Let us look then at a few examples of the modulation of procedural shortcuts as a function of personal motivation and expertise.

1. Ingroup bias and social inference.   Social knowledge expertise often derives from membership in specific social groups—groups based upon age, gender, ethnicity, nationality, and so on. Whether simply as a function of experience or in a self-protective motivated fashion, individuals exhibit far less of the simplistic patterns of schema-based inferences for members of their own in-groups than for people in related out-groups (Fiske & Taylor, 1984). Individuals take greater note of the variability of exemplars of their own in-groups and, perhaps as a consequence, seem to make far less hasty inferences about specific in-group target persons on the basis of group stereotypes (Quattrone & Jones, 1980). Moreover, "in-group experts" have more complex, richly elaborated conceptions of in-group members' characteristics than out-group members, and the complexity of their knowledge is reflected in their impressions of specific in-group or out-group target persons (Linville & Jones, 1980). In fact, experts curb their tendencies to ascribe characteristics from their in-group peers to nonpeers (Higgins & Bryant, 1982). Hence, one optimistic way to view the results of the literature on in-group–out-group "biases" is in terms of the expert's proclivity to utilize diagnostic information when available (i.e., for in-group members), to curb hasty generalizations to the out-group from in-group expertise, and to rely on shortcut inference strategies under conditions of impoverished information and/or low motivation for precision (i.e., for out-group members).

2. Personal involvement and systematic processing.   In both the literature on persuasive communication (e.g., Chaiken & Baldwin, 1981) and social inference heuristics (e.g., Borgida & Brekke, 1981), motivational factors, like the potential impact of an issue on the listener or personal involvement in the general attitude-domain in question, have been found to influence the use of "top of the head" judgmental strategies. Borgida & Howard-Pitney (1983), for example, found that subjects who were personally involved in the topic of a social conversation were not as amenable to perceptual salience biases in their judgments of perceived influence and likability as less involved (less "expert") subjects. Highly motivated "expert" subjects engage generally in more systematic, elaborative encoding of topic-relevant information, taking note of inconsistencies (Fiske, Kinder, & Larter, 1983) and processing the material more deeply (Nasby & Kihlstrom, 1985) than do less personally engaged observers.

3. Expertise and affective responses.   Several theorists, most notably Linville (1982a, 1982b), have suggested that expertise, in the form of complexity of social concepts, prepares individuals to be less offhandedly extreme in their affective evaluations of other people (see Tesser, 1978, for a cogent counterexample). For example, one's top-of-the-head evaluative reaction to a mathematician may well depend on the complexity of one's "mathematician prototype" and the variety of exemplars of this group that come to mind when one first meets the target person: to a novice observer of mathematicians the new exemplar may seem especially nice or especially obnoxious as a result of the good/poor fit to a rather simple image of mathematicians. By contrast, the expert observer of mathematicians may well be more moderate in evaluative reaction because he or she spends time considering and integrating information on a number of different aspects of the typical mathematician's character, perhaps also bringing to mind a variety of specific exemplars who differ in degree of pleasantness. In terms of our earlier discussion of schema-triggered affect (Fiske, 1982), there are at least two ways that these more moderate (and, presumably, more fair and representative) evaluations of a new acquaintance could result from social knowledge expertise. First, the expert might save processing time and energy by engaging in schema-triggered evaluations of the mathematician, but the complexity of his or her knowledge of mathematicians in general might be reflected in a more moderate summary evaluative tag for the category. Or, in cases in which the expert observer is a highly-involved participant (e.g., an in-group member herself), she might well take more care in noticing that the target acquaintance does not really fit the category prototype exactly, and a more systematic (piecemeal) analysis and integration of evaluative information might precede the summary affective reaction. In either case, expertise would result in more thorough or careful generalizations from evaluative reactions associated with a social group to evaluative reactions of new acquaintances from that group.

Albeit brief, these illustrations suggest ways in which personal motivation coordinated with complexity of knowledge in a domain can have a moderating influence on social inference processes. When experts are motivated to make full use of their knowledge they are more likely to see the many sides that characterize most social stimuli, to take control of their construals and systematically process new information, and to curb the apparently "natural" tendency for quick and dirty schematic generalizations (Showers & Cantor, 1985). In other words, the advantages of social knowledge expertise may not reside so much in the absence of shortcut procedural tricks, but rather in the potential for vigilant monitoring of the situation, such that the expert is adept at changing from heuristic to systematic processing when the stakes for precision are raised by virtue of personal involvement.

In answer, then, to the earlier question of whether some people are less prone to shortcut procedures in social construal: the response is both yes and no. No, there probably are not across-the-board differences in reliance on complex vs. simple procedural rules for social construal (cf. Cacioppo & Petty, 1982, on "need for cognition"; Sommers, 1981, on cognitive complexity in person perception). Yes, people are probably more systematic in their own expert domains; at least in those domains they have the potential to see many sides to a single event, to take control of the proclivity towards quick and dirty inferences, and to work more cautiously through all the available data.

Of course, there is also the "double-edged" aspect of personal expertise: to the extent that the "self" is invested in the outcome of social construal in a particularly involving domain, there may also be a strong pull toward familiar concepts and procedures (Higgins & King, 1981; Bargh, 1982); a strong (perhaps defensive) tendency to "see" what one wants to or even needs to see (Bruner, 1957; Lewicki, 1985). In that sense, the expert may well be a vigilant, systematic processor in expertise-relevant domains; but the vigilance may ultimately be directed more towards self-preservation (of beliefs, rules-of-thought, routines) than towards the precision and anticipatory accuracy of which Kelly wrote (Kelly, 1955). Therefore, to better judge the potential for flexible and controlled thinking in expert domains it is critical that we consider the full repertoire of *self-knowledge* that quickly and even automatically becomes relevant during the construal process in domains of social expertise (Lewicki, 1985; Bargh, 1982; Markus et al., 1985). Social construal and self-reflection typically go hand in hand, especially in domains of current concern to the individual (Bandura, 1986; Klinger, 1975).

CONSTRUCTIVE ALTERNATIVISM AND SOCIAL KNOWLEDGE

This chapter has presented a portrait of the content and structure of social declarative knowledge, and its coordination with procedural rules, in the service of accounting for *constructive alternativism* in social construal. The social concept repertoire is rich with different units of organization of social knowledge—chunking the world of people and places and events into concepts that differentially highlight features of people's personalities and social affiliations, of their goals, action strategies and intentions, and of the sometimes subtle and sometimes obvious contextual cues and constraints shaping behavior. The mental representations of these concepts are structured so as to emphasize both gist and variability, with the potential for mixed exemplar-summary prototype representations in order to capture both ideal instances and the full continuum of typicality. A multiplicity of associative paths linking concepts, and varying degrees of strength and directionality in those interconcept associations, characterize the fuzzy hierarchies and tangled webs of social concepts. Together, these features of the social concept repertoire encourage individuals to access different bundles of concepts, which highlight different slices of content in the rich patchwork of social knowledge, and, thereby, allow for flexibility in social construal.

Additionally, the content and structural variety of the concept repertoire leads quite nicely to an *expertise* model of individual differences. Individuals, as a function of their unique social learning histories and current concerns in particular domains of social life, may become "experts" about certain *content* in the social world. In this model, that expertise would be represented in the elaboration of content, complexity of organization, and heightened accessibility of concepts that speak in some way to domain-relevant concerns. Moreover, since declarative and procedural knowledge are used in tandem, the accessing of domain-relevant concepts may evoke a different, more systematic set of inference and memory and judgment rules in a person's expert as opposed to novice domains. The expert may spend more processing time and energy making sense of events in his or her expert domain, though such "systematic" processing may not always lead to more objectively "accurate" construals. For it is the very richness of the expert's conceptual base that may make it all too easy to direct that systematic processing towards reconciliations that "smooth out" the jagged edges of the social stimulus field, opening the way to schematic biases in encoding and inferences. Individual differences in domain-specific expertise provide a theoretical mechanism that facilitates richness and variety of construal and systematic and flexible processing of social data; in practice, however, individuals may not always make full use of this potential for intelligent thought. At the least, however, analysis of patterns of thinking across expert and novice domains is a fruitful avenue in the search for wisdom and pragmatic intelligence (Baltes, 1986).

In turn, consideration of social knowledge expertise brings us to the very heart of the cognitive basis of personality adaptation—the repertoire of *self-knowledge*. We have seen that the test case for individual differences in this model is a comparison of patterns of construal across a person's expert and novice domains of social knowledge. Expertise, in turn, tends to be marked by complexity of concepts and proclivity for systematic processing that derive from personal familiarity and concern with a particular aspect of social life. Personal familiarity and involvement in a domain, then, suggest a comparably rich body of self-concepts and personal memories brought to bear in the course of social construal. In making sense of events in these all-important expert domains the observer may become actor and engage in self-reflection in the service of achieving a deeper grasp of the situation.

In other words, the distinctions between self- and social-concepts and social construal and self-reflection that provided a convenient organizational structure at the outset of this chapter must ultimately be revoked for the sake of a more precise characterization of social intelligence. We will complete that bringing together process in two stages: First we will look at the self-knowledge repertoire in the next chapter, and then we will consider, in a subsequent chapter, how the social intelligence repertoire operates as a full system when people work to solve current life tasks.

5

Self-Knowledge and Self-Reflection

The social intelligence repertoire is rich in social concepts and rules for social construal; it is also rich in concepts and memories of self and in rules of self-reflection. There is, of course, a certain paradox surrounding the repertoire of self-knowledge: while individuals theoretically have access to a privileged database from which to construct self-concepts and personal memories and with which to operate in the process of self-reflection, the self is also a particularly difficult *object* of introspection (Wilson & Stone, 1985). As Allport (1961, p. 128) said: "It is much easier to *feel* the self than to *define* the self." It is especially difficult to "know" all that we know about our self, to somehow get outside of the self and see that we see our self in a particular light and that we have arrived at that perception through particular rules of self-inference. Yet is is precisely each individual's *cognitive definition of self* and his or her *rules of self-reflection* that concern us in the present chapter.

DECLARATIVE AND PROCEDURAL SELF-KNOWLEDGE

In keeping with our discussion of the social concept and rule repertoire, a distinction can be entertained between *declarative* self-knowledge—concepts about our characteristic selves and memories of personal events—and *procedural* self-knowledge—rules of inference, memory, evaluation of the self. From the perspective of declarative knowledge, the cognitive self can be defined as one's mental representation of oneself (Markus & Smith, 1981), not different, at least in principle, from concepts of persons, situations, and social episodes (Kihlstrom & Cantor, 1984; Gara, 1986). In this regard, the mental representation of self is not monolithic, for just as there are concepts of different types of persons, situations, and episodes, people know about their different characteristic selves—self as "that kind of *person*" and self "in that kind of *context.*" Moreover, knowledge of the self in different life *episodes* has special status in the repertoire of declarative self-knowledge; people keep a running account or *narrative* of their life episodes in autobiographical memory (Cohler, 1982; Kihlstrom, 1981).

These concepts and narrative memories operate, of course, in tandem with a full repertoire of procedural rules for thinking about the self (Greenwald & Pratkanis, 1985). Interestingly, self-concepts and autobiographical memories also surface quite readily in the course of social construal (Lewicki, 1983; Bargh, 1982). Procedural rules for self-reflection often invoke shortcuts similar to the cognitive heuristics considered earlier (Nasby & Kihlstrom, 1985), though sometimes people reflect upon the self in particularly systematic ways (Rogers, 1981; Kuiper & Derry, 1981). The expertise model of individual differences works especially well in characterizing variations in self-knowledge (Markus, 1977, 1979, 1983). Individuals, in their domains of self-expertise, have particularly rich and well-organized self-concepts and narrative memories, and while they reflect long and hard on those cherished aspects of self, they also run the expert's risk of being overly-conservative in portraying the self in these domains (Swann & Ely, 1984; Swann, 1984).

In all of these ways there is considerable continuity—in content, structure, and function—of self-knowledge and social knowledge. Yet, as one can not help but note (Posner, 1981), there are many unique aspects to the cognitive self, both in terms of declarative richness and procedural facility. Despite the difficulties in taking the self as an object of reflection, once having done so, people have potential access to a privileged database of personal feelings, thoughts, and intentions, experienced across a wide array of situations and over considerable spans of time (Andersen, 1984). Hence, the self-concepts and narrative memories of personal episodes can constitute uniquely elaborate, well-integrated and affectively-charged declarative knowledge. This store of declarative self-knowledge is also likely to be easily accessed precisely because so much detail of temporal-spatio context and subjective phenomenology is preserved in these abstractions about characteristic selves and life events. Moreover, the set of procedural rules of self-inference, self-evaluation, and self-memory frequently serve to protect and defend the definition of self reflected in the concepts and narrative record (Greenwald, 1980, 1982). Hedonic biases may well permeate *self-reflection* and guide the course of *social construal* when the cognitive self is activated.

In other words, while it seems that models of declarative and procedural knowledge and expertise models of individual differences can be applied in characterizing the cognitive self, there is always the fear that the special content and dynamic function of self-knowledge will get lost in these rather "cold" models (Markus, 1983; Cantor, Markus, Niedenthal, & Nurius, 1986). This is precisely the fear that prompted close consideration of the *content* of social concepts in the previous chapter. Hence, before considering structure and expertise in the domain of self-knowledge, we will take a closer look at the (special) content of individuals' subjective definitions of self and records of personal experience.

CONCEPTS AND MEMORIES OF SELF

It is important to note that "the self," as an object of study, has been conceptualized in many ways. Many theorists look to *the self* as the core, unified, central structure in personality, assumed to be stable and independent of the changing contexts in an individual's life (James, 1890; Snygg & Combs, 1949; Rogers, 1951; Allport, 1955). For example, Snygg and Combs (1949) describe the self as the set of characteristics of an individual that are *stable* rather than *changeable,* while Rogers (1951) points to those characteristics over which the individual has *control.* Allport (1955) spoke quite forcefully about the central, core personality characteristics which are independent of context and true for all times and in all places. These approaches to *the self* suggest, in turn, a very specialized and narrow *self-conception:* the self-concept captures the true, stable essence of the self, which people carry with them through life. This view of the self-concept as a unitary and coherent mental structure is intended to highlight the obvious but nontrivial fact that the self belongs to *one* individual.

By contrast, other approaches to a study of the self have stressed the existence of *many selves* within each individual: those selves which operate differently in different social contexts, with different significant others, as people assume different social roles and responsibilities (Cooley, 1902; Mead, 1934; Sarbin, 1952; Gergen, 1971). According to the "fragmentary self" approach, individuals have multifaceted, changeable and quite contextualized selves, in part, because they respond adaptively to the social environment. For example, Mead (1934) argued that a person has as many selves as he has social roles to assume, though some of those selves may be less central in his self-conception. Just as the "unified self" approach conceived of an internally consistent self, the "fragmentary self" approach emphasized the multiplicity of selves. According to this view, even apparently inconsistent selves could peacefully coexist within one person. In other words, the extreme pathological cases of multiple personalities have an everyday analogy in the different sides of self that all individuals present in different contexts for different purposes (Goffman, 1959). For these theorists *the self-conception,* in turn, represents the *many persons* lurking within each individual.

Consideration of these two traditions in the study of the self raises a very important issue to be resolved: The cognitive definition of self must represent, simultaneously, the phenomenal experience of a single, core self and the multiplicity of selves (even inconsistent selves) as experienced in different settings and at different times. Sarbin (1952), for example, foreshadowed the need for a resolution of these apparently conflicting depictions of self; he spoke of each individual having a variety of "empirical selves" corresponding to different social roles, as well as *a* unitary "pure ego" representing the cross-section of all of these empirical selves.

Perhaps another answer resides in viewing *the self* as a *family of selves:* a fuzzy set. Individuals may not possess (or at least as observers, may not focus upon), a core set of necessary and sufficient features which unequivocally *define* one essential *self*. Instead, the meaning of the self is given in the family of selves. The unity of self comes from the many overlapping resemblances among the different selves: as one's "work self," one is caring to students; as one's "self-as-parent," one is loving to one's children; in both selves there is the tendency for impatience, exasperation, and so on. However, all of these selves do not share all of a select few characteristics that comprise *you:* as the "play self" you are neither loving nor impatient, but carefree and self-focused, though your "play self" shares with your "self-as-parent" the attention to athletics and skills at games. You are *yourself* because of this network of overlapping features which are characteristic of the family of selves (Wittgenstein, 1953). And, you are many things in many places with many people. Of course, just as with any fuzzy concept, some of these selves are more central, more important to "who you are" than are others (Markus, 1977). These central selves are more representative of one's self than are the peripheral selves because they exhibit many features shared by other selves in the family of selves—they are closer, then, to the meaning of who you are (Rosenberg & Gara, 1985; Gara, 1986). Additionally, these central selves are representative because they more clearly differentiate self from others (Kihlstrom & Cantor, 1984).

The self-concept, therefore, must represent both the *variety* and the *unity* within each person's family of selves. In that respect, recent theorists have likened the self-concept to an implicit theory (Epstein, 1973) or a network of linked concepts of self (Kuiper & Derry, 1981; Markus & Smith, 1981; T.B. Rogers, 1981). As such, the cognitive definition of self can be varied, encompassing more aspects of self than would a representation of a core self, yet still serving as a unified mental structure. *The* self-concept is, in actuality, many self-concepts interrelated within networks in the concept repertoire.

Further unity in the subjective definition of self is provided by the autobiographical narrative record which preserves specific memories of the temporal and spatial transitions from one self to another—from the "play self" to the "work self"; from the "child self" to the "adolescent self." The autobiographical record provides a running (though selective) diary of events in which the individual has been involved—from feeding the dog this morning to having pneumonia in second grade; and, like other knowledge structures, it is a record not of "objective" events, but of the events as subjectively construed and continuously reconstructed through the filter of the individual's current state of mind (Linton, 1978; Cohler, 1982).

The record keeps track of the sequence of actions in the episode, its spatiotemporal context, and the individual's subjective impression of success and failure and other affective reactions. The autobiographical record can also serve as a procedural action guide, as do social scripts, building present behavior to fit past episodes. Individuals know when to avoid or approach particular people and situations, in part because the record provides information about successes and failures in similar events in the past. Similarly, a person can hold herself in high esteem in some circumstances and feel incompetent in others because of the variety of affect associated with events in her past. Hence, the autobiographical record provides a data base for the acquisition of different positive and negative self-concepts. Yet it also serves to provide a sense of unity and coherence in this multifaceted cognitive self.

In part, this sense of integrity derives from the simple fact that the autobiographical record is all about one person who is there in every instance, even though a slightly different self in each event. Additionally, as Cohler (1982) states: "The sense of stability and consistency which is experienced over time results primarily from continuing *reconstructive activity* leading to the maintenance of a particular narrative of the life course . . ." (p. 205). The narrative record, then, is often a smoothed-over story, with beginning, middle, and projected end: a story that "makes current sense" to the storyteller. In other words, this record is part fact and part fantasy, but all subjective truth.

Together, the concepts of self and the autobiographical record provide a very complex, multifaceted subjective self-definition, but one for which there is a core gist (provided by the continuity of the narrative and the overlapping resemblances between the different selves). Additionally, this self-definition is a dynamic one, incorporating new visions of self and revising old ones to fit the present definition.

In order to get a clearer picture of the gist and the variability, the continuity and the dynamics, of the cognitive self, it is helpful to look directly at the features of self and of personal experience that are represented in the concepts and narrative record. In so doing we lay the groundwork for an analysis of structure and organization in the cognitive self, as well as for consideration of dimensions of individual differences in self-knowledge expertise.

Concepts of Self

What do we know about different characteristic selves? What aspects of self are noted when people draw inferences about the co-occurrence of personal attributes? First, as with other social concepts, there are many schemes for characterizing important selves—from physical appearance (e.g., "my fat self" and "my alluring self") to evaluative assessment (e.g., "my competent self" and "my test anxious self") to social roles (e.g., "my teacher self" and "my student self"). The self as an object of subjective definition is really many selves; constructive alternativism applied to the self.

The multifaceted content of self-concepts has been demonstrated repeatedly in analyses of the self-descriptions which individuals provide in answer to the question "Who am I?" For example, Jones, Sensenig and Haley (1974) asked 150 male and 150 female college students to spend twenty minutes describing "the most significant characteristics of yourself." Jones et al. used these free descriptions in order to derive a measure of the most frequently occurring trait characteristics in self-descriptions; they found ninety-seven such trait characteristics which emerged repeatedly in the students' self-descriptions. Interestingly, though the students tended to list positive self-statements first, they did include a variety of positive *and* negative self-statements. Moreover, apparently contradictory traits—for example, adventurous and cautious or compassionate and critical—occurred quite commonly within the same self-description.

The students' self-descriptions clearly supported the variability of descriptive content within the cognitive self. A multidimensional scaling solution revealed four dimensions of meaning upon which individuals seemed to focus in describing themselves: *evaluation, impulsiveness-inhibition, stereotyped masculinity-femininity,* and *communality with others.* These dimensions reflect the evaluative connotations of self characteristics, the semantic denotations, the "social" side of self, and the similarity of self-to-others. Clearly, therefore, the self-as-object provides a rich stimulus for cognitive definition.

An extensive line of research by McGuire and his colleagues (e.g., McGuire & McGuire, 1981, 1982) demonstrates that this multifaceted cognitive self is acquired quite early on in development. For example, in one study with 252 sixth-graders using the same self-description task ("tell me about yourself"), McGuire and Padawer-Singer (1976) observed the following distribution of content in the self-descriptions: habitual activities, 24%; attitudes, preferences and hopes, 17%; school status, 15%; demographic information, 12%; self-evaluation, 7%; physical descriptions, 5%; miscellaneous, 1%. Even the "spontaneous self-concepts" of sixth-grade children reveal many selves: there are physical, social, emotional, and behavioral sides to the self, and all of these aspects are noted in the cognitive self.

Also of note in this study was the children's tendency to concentrate on aspects of themselves that were relatively unique or distinctive in their environment. For example, a black child in a predominantly white school would mention race; a girl in a family of male siblings would mention gender; a short child with tall friends would mention height, and so on. This attention to *socially distinctive* characteristics on the part of sixth-graders is similar to the attention paid to social comparisons in adult self-descriptions (Jones et al., 1972). Both children and adults appear to focus on the perceived distinctiveness of their personal characteristics within the social environment. Another dimension is also of interest to both young and old: the *evaluation* dimension emerges repeatedly in analyses of self-descriptions as an important component of self-definition.

These analyses of the cognitive self already point to quite a rich and varied repertoire. In fact, the cognitive self may be even more complicated: Individuals also take note of the changes in self apparent across different life contexts—i.e., of "contextualized selves" (Higgins et al., 1986; McGuire, 1984; Kihlstrom, 1985). The "work self" is serious, scholarly, committed; the "home self" is nurturing, giving, loving; the "play self" is relaxed, carefree, self-centered. Often, these contextualized selves simply summarize independent aspects of the "well-functioning" person. At other times, the different contextualized selves represent the potential conflicts between the different "kinds of persons" coexisting within the same self (Rosenberg & Gara, 1985). In this regard, what at first appear to be independent aspects of the self may actually be somewhat contradictory: The "work self" is serious but the "play self" is carefree; the "home self" is nurturing but the "play self" is self-centered; and so on. Through these contextualized selves, the individual can cognitively compartmentalize the different sides of self, establishing a delicate equilibrium in the face of potential role-identity conflicts. In fact, some have argued that by recognizing the complexity of self (in a contextualized cognitive self) individuals can actually enhance self-satisfaction (Linville, 1982a).

These contextualized selves can be elicited with the same methods used by Pervin (1976) when he studied individuals' perceptions of the situations in their lives. For example, after listing the important contexts in which he or she spends time, a person can describe himself or herself in each context and then rate the relevance of each self-descriptor in each context (Kihlstrom, 1985). This procedure elicits a self-by-situation matrix which nicely portrays the different contextualized selves; not only are some self-descriptors irrelevant in some contexts, but others are true-of-self in one context and contradicted-by-self in another life situation. For example, one individual sees himself as compassionate and easy-going at home, while being fairly hard-nosed and individualistic at work. Moreover, these contextualized selves should not be dismissed as simply descriptions of transient, unstable roles assumed to fit the requirements of the moment. These individuals are describing aspects of self which they have repeatedly noted in situations in which they frequently find themselves.

Rosenberg & Gara (1985), using an interview technique in which individuals describe the *features* associated with various personal identities, illustrate very clearly the pattern of "family resemblances" between an individual's different contextualized selves. In the interview, individuals are encouraged to examine a variety of sources of self-identity, including identities derived from social roles, group affiliations, and personal relationships, as well as to consider both liked (positive) and disliked (negative) identities. From these interviews, they derive a matrix of feature-by-identity combinations that concretely portrays the points of overlap and discontinuity between the different self-identities. Often, a set of "basic self-categories" emerge in this analysis; those are the features of self—such as "I am a curious person"—that subsume a number of different self-identities (e.g., researcher, athlete, parent). Hence, a number of different context-specific identities are subjectively organized as different instantiations of a basic self-category (see, also, Gara, 1986). Each self-identity is also typically associated with concrete actions that characterize the person acting out that identity; i.e., features that serve as "blueprints for action." Therefore, collectively, these different identities represent the variety of action patterns through which a person expresses a particular self-category.

In addition to this contextual dimension, there is also an important *temporal dimension* to self-knowledge (Gordon, 1968, Schulz, 1964). As Markus and Nurius (1986) have shown, individuals have quite elaborate concepts about themselves-in-the-past; these "past selves" reveal different facets of the development of a contextualized self (e.g., "the fat child self" and "the young married self"). Moreover, these past selves may be particularly salient when the individual perceives himself or herself to have changed a great deal in a particular domain, i.e., when the past and present selves diverge. Similarly, past selves may be important when the individual wishes to effect a change— that is, when the present self is still *too much like* the past self (Markus, 1983). So, the individual with the nurturing, giving, loving "home self" may know quite well that that is a relatively recent "home self" precipitated by a threat of divorce from a spouse. That same individual may also recognize that his or her past and present "play self" are much alike; he or she has *always* "played alone" and wishes, now, to work towards a new, more mutual and sharing "play self."

Markus and her colleagues (see Markus, 1983; Markus & Nurius, 1986) have demonstrated that a very significant part of the "hot" and dynamic quality of the cognitive self resides in these concepts about past selves and future or "possible selves" in different domains and life contexts. For example, in a questionnaire study with over two hundred undergraduates, Markus and Nurius (1986) observed a great deal of attention being accorded to *past* and *future selves*. Fully one-third of the sample reported "thinking about past selves a great deal" and sixty-five percent of the students reported "thinking about future possible selves a great deal." These students clearly believed in the potential for the development of new self-concepts: sixty percent of them believed that "the majority of their self-concept was still to be developed." Ninety-five percent of these students had very definite ideas about the domains in which they would be likely to acquire new "possible selves." These domains of possibility tend to emphasize *positive* possible selves over *negative* ones, though students are clearly aware of their feared possibilities for future selves, just as they can articulate negative past and present selves.

As Markus & Nurius note, "These students imagine an extremely heterogeneous set of possibilities for themselves, and these possibilities do not appear to be particularly constrained by their current or now selves, even in domains such as personality, others' feelings toward them, and physical characteristics. On the contrary, they seem to believe that they are quite likely to change, often quite dramatically" (p. 959). Clearly, people accord a great deal of attention to past and future selves, as well as to their current "actual" selves (Kelly, 1955; Rogers, 1951). The research of Markus and her colleagues is beginning to document the dynamic potential for growth in the cognitive self.

The temporal dimension to the cognitive self (or selves) is terribly important not only because individuals seem to keep careful note of past, present, and even future potentials for the self, but also because there is a *motivational dimension* associated with these different selves (Markus, 1983; Cantor et al., 1986). There is, of course, a long history of theorizing about the "incentive value" of positive (and negative) ideal (and feared) potential selves (Freud, 1925; Rogers, 1951). However, recent empirical attempts to chart the content and structure of these "ideal" or "ought" or "possible" selves have taken a critical step; these studies have demonstrated that such potential selves are rich and accessible and well-organized enough to serve as standards for self-regulation (Markus & Nurius, 1986; McGuire & Padawer-Singer, 1976; Higgins et al., 1986). In fact, it seems that "ideal" and "ought" and "possible" selves—especially when compared to a discrepant "now" self—figure prominently in regression equations predicting to current affective-mood state (Higgins et al., 1986; Markus & Nurius, 1986). These elaborated potentials for self provide powerful conceptual benchmarks, as individuals reflect on "now selves," work to overcome "past selves," and plan for desired "possible selves."

These past and future possibilities for self vividly portray the multi-faceted contents of people's repertoire of self-concepts. In fact, the utility of these possible selves as guides to behavior depends largely on the *many* potential selves upon which they shed light. Therefore, though past, present, and future selves do provide a temporal perspective in the self-concept repertoire, it is not from these possible selves that a sense of personal coherence and historical continuity is likely to be obtained. Rather, it may be better to look to the autobiographical record of life episodes for a narrative that provides a cognitive basis for the perception of temporal coherence of self. The autobiographical narrative emphasizes the coherence that people see in their life stories (Cohler, 1982; Kihlstrom, 1981). Therefore, in the service of completing the picture of the diversity and the coherence in the cognitive self, we will look briefly at the contents of people's autobiographical narratives.

Contents of the Autobiographical Narrative

The autobiographical record of personal events and experiences may be a key to some of the mystery of perceived coherence and diversity in the cognitive self. The perceived coherence may come from reconstructive "updating" of life events in the service of a sensible story line (Cohler, 1982), while the diversity of self is conveyed by substantial detail about behavior across different life contexts. The record keeps track of the unfolding, *continuous stream* of personal life episodes. It also preserves a wealth of *concrete, context-specific* information about events, involving the self either directly or vicariously: what happened, where it happened, when it happened, how I felt, how you felt, what the outcome was of our interaction, what happened next (Crovitz & Quina-Holland, 1976; Robinson, 1976). These events are typically placed in a *temporal, spatial* and *social context,* such that, at least in principle, the individual has available information about personal reactions and feelings and intentions across a variety of life contexts (Andersen, 1984). People's reports of the recent and even the remote past include a great deal of *vivid imagery*—it looked like this—and *subjective affect*—it felt like this—as well as the more "objective" details of *action* and *context.*

Though these are primarily personal memories, they may include events in the lives of other people when those events impact upon the individual. Moreover, the autobiographical record will mark many private or subjective events in an individual's life: "the moment when I knew that I loved him," "the time that I decided that I *was* fat," "the day that I recognized exactly how manipulative parents can be," and so forth. In fact, these sorts of autobiographical memories undoubtedly help us to "know" that we know something, by marking the moment of acquisition of a concept or the perception of change from before the event to after it (Kihlstrom, 1984).

This data base, therefore, provides a good resource for information about the self over time. First of all, it is temporally organized so as to provide *continuity* of knowledge about the self. In fact, people have clear and rich memories as far back as age seven or eight, though the earlier years are typically obscured by infantile amnesia (Kihlstrom & Harackiewicz, 1982; White & Pillemer, 1979). Retrieval of these episodic memories is also facilitated by the abundance of information about the surrounding context in which the event took place. The individual can retrieve details about the past event by first recalling the context (Tulving, 1972). Furthermore, the intense affect associated with personal experiences serves as an additional aid to memory. These episodes are also very vivid because we are constantly drawing on them, thinking over the past in order to make sense of the present. Such cognitive work solidifies autobiographical memories, although each time we retrieve a personal memory we probably reinterpret and revise it in the light of new experiences (Linton, 1978) and current life themes (Barclay & Wellman, 1984). In fact, the self-reflective process of working on old memories in the context of recent events probably serves to bolster the phenomenological impression of continuity of selfhood.

The record is especially vivid about *unusual* life events which presumably capture a great deal of ongoing and retrospective attention. For example, Brown and Kulik (1977) demonstrated that people have remarkably vivid and detailed "flashbulb" memories of unexpected events of high personal relevance, even events such as a national political crisis, in which the individual is only *vicariously* involved. The salience and elaboration of unusual life events in the autobiographical record may well derive from people's ongoing proclivity to make sense of their life story, to keep the narrative intelligible (Brim & Ryff, 1980).

While it is convenient to consider the content of self-concepts and personal narratives separately, in actuality there are obvious resemblances across these records of self. Information about the temporal unfolding of events contributes to a process of updating current selves; information about the context of events and actions contributes to the articulation of contextual selves; and the record of subjective reactions provides a basis for positive and negative evaluations of self. Moreover, once self-concepts are solidified, individuals tend to recollect past experiences which bolster their current beliefs. All of the techniques used to reveal the content of salient autobiographical memories—diary keeping and subsequent recall of the events, word-cuing to prime memories, and (clinical) interviews—reveal a correspondence between the individual's present concepts of self and the focus of his or her recollections. For example, when Kihlstrom and Harackiewicz (1982) interviewed 164 Harvard University students about their very earliest childhood memories, they found substantial correspondence between the content of current conceptions of self and the early memories. One "very feminine" undergraduate, who was struggling over premedical ambitions, recalled a memory from age three of sitting in her very girlish room with frilly curtains and pink wallpaper and listening to a recording of the story "The Little Engine that Could"; the correspondence between her current conflicts over gender role and profession and the content of her earliest personal memory was striking. In most cases, it seems best to think of the self-concepts and personal narrative as highly interlocking sources of declarative self-knowledge.

STRUCTURE IN THE COGNITIVE SELF

We began the present chapter by remarking upon the apparently heightened accessibility of self-concepts and personal memories in social construal and, of course, in self-reflection. Having now considered the variety and complexity of content of concepts and memories of self, it seems that the rather routine way in which self-knowledge is brought to bear in making sense of life events is actually quite a feat. Given the many contextualized selves (past, present, and possible), and the record of personal and vicarious experience preserved over many temporal epochs, the automatic access which people demonstrate for some self-relevant material is impressive (Bargh, 1982; Lewicki, 1984). Moreover, individuals, as we have seen, do quite a bit of reflective reworking of possible selves and autobiographical episodes; they seem to enter and update the repertoire of self-knowledge rather painlessly, moving back and forth across their episodic and semantic self-knowledge systems (Tulving, 1972).

The facility with which individuals acquire, utilize, and transform a complex self-knowledge repertoire suggests that this knowledge is well-organized and structured to provide easy access. In the following discussion, we will consider some structural assumptions about self-concepts and autobiographical memories in the light of the need for quick accessibility. Additionally, since people demonstrate quite a bit of flexibility and variability in their self-descriptions and self-reflections from moment to moment and context to context (Nurius, 1984; Markus & Nurius, 1986; Higgins & King, 1981), we will also consider structural assumptions that facilitate constructive alternativism for self-construal.

The Family of Selves

The central structural assumption in the present account of the self-concept is that *the* self-concept is really many self-concepts organized as a *family of selves* with overlapping resemblances and interlocking associations (Kihlstrom & Cantor, 1984). This structure is intended to incorporate the variety of contextualized selves, even contradictory selves, without sacrificing organization and integrity in the cognitive self. While there is no presumption of *a* core self, the different selves share resemblances that mark the uniqueness of the individual; some selves are more representative of the person's self-definition than are other more peripheral selves; those *central* selves are quite likely to serve as the focus of self-reflection and to initiate a chain of thoughts involving the other related selves in the family.

As in the case of social concepts, we can consider the structure of the family of self-concepts both at the level of internal concept structure and in terms of organization of these interlocking selves in fuzzy hierarchies and tangled webs. Moreover, concepts of "self-as-kind-of-person" and "self-in-kind-of-context" (in past, present, and future) most certainly are linked at several levels of abstraction to concepts in the tangled web of social concepts and, of course, to pieces of the autobiographical narrative. Hence, we will consider these different aspects of structure in turn.

Internal Concept Structure

As we have repeatedly noted here, the family of selves contains a multiplicity of self-concepts organized around different aspects of the person. For example, Rosenberg & Gara (1985) describe the variety as follows: "Identities are assumed to be tagged with a potpourri of concepts such as the person's physical and psychological traits ('handsome person,' 'smart person'), activities and habits ('gourmet cook,' 'heavy smoker'), achievements ('college graduate'), and ideals or fantasies ('I am going to be a great artist') . . ." (p. 97). To this list one might also add the many context-specific selves, selves which, even after the fact, are closely linked with particular social situations or episodes ("self in interviews," "self at surprise parties").

Each of these self-concepts can be represented by a summary prototype of characteristic features; by a set of typical exemplars of self as that person or in that context; or, as suggested for some social concepts, by a mixed representation. Consider, for example, Jack, who describes himself as a "well-socialized male of the 1950s genre." Jack has a quite well-elaborated "professional self," replete with a summary abstraction of characteristic features, such as "compulsive," "in charge," "tired, frazzled," and "productive." He also refers to a related concept of "self at the office" with remarks about specific self-exemplars of this contextualized self—e.g., "self in a tense meeting," "self with secretary," "self cooling off on the squash court." The content of these two self-concepts is highly overlapping, though the "office self" is more thoroughly associated in his mind with the specifics of the work context, while the "professional person self" has become somewhat more abstracted from that context over the course of his life.

As in the case of social concepts, it is important to note that individuals may structure self-concepts differently at different times in life and according to increasing life experience in a particular domain. For example, initially a self-concept may simply be represented as one exemplar in a social concept of a kind of person. At first, as a fledgling lawyer, Jack was just another entry—and not a very secure one at that—in his concept of "professional men." With experience and increasing personal investment in a domain, a person may come to abstract the central tendency of a self-concept in that life arena and to form a summary prototype of that particular self (Markus, 1979); in fact, the elaboration of a cherished self-concept may be accompanied, or even prompted, by recognition of some possible selves in that domain (Markus, 1983). As time and experience accumulate, the person may also note the variability inherent in his self in that domain; perhaps articulating a set of variable self-exemplars that together represent that self in its many instantiations. Jack, for example, is all too painfully aware that his "professional self" is now frequently exemplified by "a lost-in-thought self" and a "quick-tempered boss self," even as he bolsters self-esteem by reflecting on the "eager-beaver young lawyer" of his past and the "wise mentor self" of the near future. Moreover, with this expertise in a self-relevant domain comes the recognition of a continuum of selves for any given self-concept; from selves that clearly fit the concept (e.g., Jack's "wise mentor self") to those that border on meaning something very different about one's self (e.g., Jack's "quick temper self" is as much about his "emotional self" as about his "professional self"). Self-concepts, thus, conform to a "fuzzy set" structure with a continuum of prototypicality.

Both in the case of his "summary professional person self" and his exemplars of "self at the office," Jack's concepts are quite "hot" in this domain, reflecting his considerable personal investment in his work, his overall satisfaction with these selves, and the specific ups and downs associated with different instantiations of his self in the work world. There is also a clearly articulated temporal dimension to these particular selves, well-illustrated by a comparison of the exemplars for the "novice young lawyer self" of the past; the present "upwardly mobile mid-life lawyer self," and the "burnt-out old lawyer self" that looms as a quite possible future self. Of course, not all of Jack's self-concepts will be equivalently rich in dynamic content or as well-specified along the temporal dimension.

One of the structural features of the family of self-concepts that greatly eases the process of accessing self-knowledge is the organization of selves according to degree of *centrality* (or importance) in the current self-definition (Markus & Smith, 1981; Rogers, 1977; Kuiper & Derry, 1981). While individuals can surely describe themselves in many different ways, not all of these self-concepts are viewed by them as important at a given point in time (Rosenberg & Gara, 1985). For example, Jack is "schematic" (Markus, 1977) in the professional domain, and the self-concepts that relate to this important identity will be far more elaborated, well-organized, and readily accessible for him than will be less central self-concepts (e.g., "self as neighbor"). A person's particular domains of self-expertise are quite likely to have many possibilities for self and to figure heavily in the person's action plans (Markus, 1983). Moreover, as in the realm of social-concept expertise, while everyone has schematic and aschematic self-domains, the distribution across content areas will surely differ from one person to the next.

Interconcept Organization

The organization of self-concepts into fuzzy hierarchies, with aspects of the self characterized at different levels of abstraction and interrelated according to degrees of superset-subset relations, serves to streamline the process of accessing self-knowledge (Kihlstrom & Cantor, 1984; Rosenberg & Gara, 1985). As in the fuzzy hierarchies of social concepts, such self-concept hierarchies are likely to be imperfect in several respects: some of the class-inclusion relations between concepts at different levels of abstraction will be only partially true (e.g., Jack's "self cooling off on the court" concept is only partially a subset of his "self at the office" concept); some self-concepts at the same level of abstraction in a hierarchy that ought to be disjunctive will overlap somewhat in characteristic features of self (e.g., Jack's "wise mentor self" and his "hard-nosed boss self" share more than the odd feature in common). Similarly, associative links between concepts (within a hierarchy) will be based upon more than just these class inclusion relations; different selves will come to be conceptually linked for a person as a function of purely idiosyncratic shared meaning and experiences (e.g., Jack strongly identifies his "hard-nosed boss self" with his "compassionate colleague self" because both selves are necessary sides of a "successful professional self" in his belief system). However, despite imperfections and idiosyncracies in organization, these fuzzy self-hierarchies should facilitate ready access to collections of interrelated aspects of a person's self-definition (Greenwald, 1981). Figure 5-1 traces a line of self-reflective thought which Jack might be prone to experiencing regularly as a function of the organization of his hierarchy of "achieving selves".

FIGURE 5-1 An Illustrative Self-Representation.

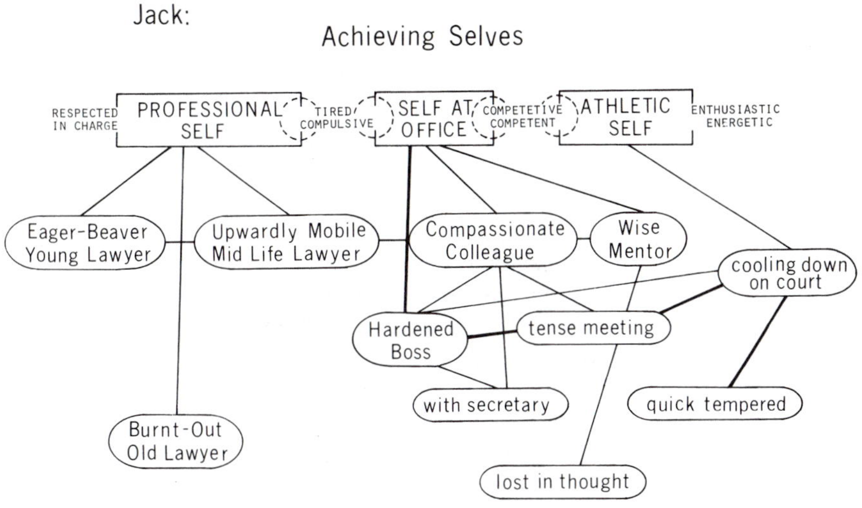

Jack:
Achieving Selves

Consideration of the ways in which individuals might come to routinely access certain subsets of their self-concepts, as a consequence of hierarchical organization and interconcept links within hierarchies, raises once again, the notion of preferred units of construal—in this case, basic or prominant or chronically accessible *self*-concepts (Higgins & King, 1981). There are several plausible ways that a particular self-concept could become the preferred point of entry for a self-reflective chain of associations. For example, Rosenberg & Gara (1985) suggest that concepts (identities in their language) that subsume many self-exemplars in a self-hierarchy would be especially prominent; they also point to self-concepts which are especially elaborated (with many prototypic features) and highly distinctive (with regard to a natural *contrast identity*) as candidates for heightened accessibility (see also Rosch, 1978, on cue validity). Moreover, these authors demonstrate that the hierarchical prominence and prototype elaboration of a self-concept do not always coincide with perceived *importance* of the identity in the person's current self-definition; the implication being that importance might well overwhelm prominence and elaboration in the accessibility chain. For example, as they note, a person might be currently reflecting a great deal on a new possible self, one for which there is hope of attainment, but not a lot of currently available self-instantiation (Wurf & Markus, 1986). Hence, while it is likely that people will favor their currently prominent or elaborated selves in both self- and social construal (Lewicki, 1984), there may be times when as yet unelaborated possibilities for self-definition take center stage (Markus, 1983).

In other words, as in the case of social construal, constructive alternativism in self-construal is very much the rule, not the exception. Although people certainly have their favorite, preferred concepts for self-definition—Gordon (1968) calls these special selves "factual self-conceptions," and Stryker (1986) refers to "salient identities"—there are multiple routes for entering the self-concept repertoire in a nonstereotyped fashion. In fact, Markus and her colleagues (Markus & Nurius, 1986), emphasizing the mutability of individuals' "on-line" self-definitions, distinguish a *working self-concept* from the full pool of self-concepts that could potentially be brought to the forefront of conscious reflection. As they note, "The content of the working self-concept depends on what self-conceptions have been active just before, on what has been elicited or made dominant by the particular social environment, and on what has been more purposefully invoked by the individual" (Markus & Nurius, 1986, p. 957). The preferred units for self-construal will vary, therefore, as a function of contextual demands and personal processing goals, as well as in line with the most chronically salient or prominent self-identities.

Features of the immediate social context will prime certain self-concepts, shaping the contents of the "spontaneous self" (McGuire & McGuire, 1982). For example, aspects of self may be brought into focus simply because they are distinctive in a particular social enviornment; to the extent that the person then experiences that self-distinctiveness repeatedly, those special selves may come to be chronically activated, highly elaborate, even centrally important aspects of self-definition (McGuire, 1984). Or, a more transient contextual prime may serve to make a particular feature of self especially salient only for the moment. For example, individuals with elaborate conceptions of personal competence and achievement can come to describe the self in rather deprecating terms in the face of subtle contextual cues that prime a negative working self-concept (Nurius, 1984). Similarly, when individuals purposefully reflect on the self from the standpoint of a significant other person, thinking about what they "ought" to be like as compared with what they "are" actually like, a rather hopeless picture of self can result. In fact, Higgins et al. (1986) argue that for some people repeated "perspective-taking" of this sort—often engaged in unintentionally—can result in a chronic state of personal anxiety and distress. In that case, what may start as an occasional chain of self-reflective thought may eventually habitually dominate the working self-concept. In principle, the contents of working memory about one's self flexibly shift with context and goals; in practice, there may be some obsessions with self that are hard to banish from consciousness because they surface so readily and seemingly without in-tentional reflection (Nasby & Kihlstrom, 1985).

Chains of reflective thought—the current contents of the working self-concept (Markus & Nurius, 1986)—spread quickly and often automati-cally through the self-concept repertoire, in part because of the many interlocking associations between concepts across different hierarchies. We called this interlocking network structure a tangled web in the discussion of social concepts; the description is perhaps even more appropriate in this instance. First, while the different contextualized selves may well capture slightly different aspects of self, there is likely to be considerable overlap in features across self-concepts (e.g., Jack's "professional self" and "self at office" share many features in common). Rosenberg & Gara (1985) refer to *equivalence* relations between self-identities that share many, if not all, self-features in common. It may well be that equivalence relations between self-concepts vary in strength—based upon amount of feature overlap—and in directionality—based upon the degree to which the common features are central to the prototype of each concept (Tversky, 1977). For example, Jack's "professional self" and "self at office" probably have a great deal in common for Jack; though the strength of the associative path linking these two concepts in the web across hierarchies may be asymmetric in directionality, with a somewhat greater likelihood of Jack's moving from thoughts about his "self at office" to those about his more varied and elaborate "professional self" concept, than vice versa. Again, there is both complexity and order within the tangled web of self-concepts.

Another aspect of the structural complexity in these tangled webs is that the basis for interconcept associations across hierarchies (and within them for that matter) may be quite diverse and idiosyncratic, going beyond mere feature overlap between self-concepts (Kelly, 1955). Self-concepts of very different content may become *psychologically equivalent* by virtue of a person's unique associations to those aspects of self: one might connect them with a particular temporal epoch of his or her life (one emphasized in his or her personal narrative); or connect them in a dynamic sense because these different selves are instantiated in the service of a common current life task or goal. The latter, dynamic equivalences may be especially potent and plentiful if people do indeed focus upon some basic adaptive life tasks (Plutchik, 1980) that permeate different life contexts and temporal epochs, implicitly recruiting different selves in the service of a current concern (Cantor et al., 1986; Klinger, 1978).

When people simultaneously access different self-concepts because they all relate to experiences in one temporal epoch of life, or because a unifying personal concern or life theme is evoked, then they are quite likely to also draw upon a set of relevant personal memories and social concepts. The chain of interconcept associations extends, therefore, beyond the (imaginary) confines of the self-concept repertoire—people seem to move rather easily from self-reflection to social construal and back again; from comparatively abstract aspects of self to concrete vivid personal memories and vice versa.

It is relatively easy to imagine a vast array of associative links between self-concepts and social concepts; in the present account the structures of the two repertoires are highly parallel. There will be natural avenues of overlap between generic person, situation and episode concepts, and the concepts that characterize the self as such a person or in such a context or episode (Markus, Smith, & Moreland, 1985; Holyoak & Gordon, 1983). At a very abstract level, both repertoires probably focus on some basic adaptive task domains—domains such as achievement and affiliation and power and loss; while at a more concrete level, there will be relations between concepts that characterize how the self plays out those abstract tasks in everyday life and social concepts that epitomize the people and places and episodes of which such tasks are made. In some instances, for example, when a person is "trying out a new identity" (Rosenberg & Gara, 1985), the directionality of the self-social concept links will favor a process of *social comparison* in which the generic social prototypes serve as a model for self-instantiation (Snyder, 1979; Niedenthal et al., 1985). Many forms of cognitive therapy operate on the assumption of such a modeling effect, encouraging clients to try out a social concept for the self (Kihlstrom & Nasby, 1981). More typically, when a favorite self-concept is evoked, social construal will follow from that self-construal (Higgins, King, & Marvin, 1982); with the self serving as a strong and vivid *reference point* in social judgment (Markus et al., 1985; Greenwald, 1981). In either case, though self- and social concepts are rarely isomorphic in content, there is an inevitable cognitive pull from one to the other in any given domain of social life activity (e.g., see Linville & Jones, 1980, on polarization of impressions of out-group members).

Structure in the Personal Narrative

Self-reflections are clearly enriched by associations to the broader repertoire of social concepts; another source of elaboration and specification of self-concepts is the autobiographical record of life episodes. In fact, the idiosyncratic associative links between ostensibly unrelated self-concepts often suggest that the different self-concepts have a common place in the personal narrative (e.g., derived from a single episode; related to a common life theme emphasized in a particular temporal epoch in the narrative). As we discuss below, the personal narrative is structured in such a fashion as to allow easy interface with the self-concept repertoire. Of course, the chain of influence also works the other way as well; for people frequently update (and concurrently, revise and reconstruct) the narrative record in the light of their currently important cognitive definitions of self.

Similar to the structure of the self-concept repertoire, these records of personal events are probably structured as associative networks. However, the networks of autobiographical memories presumably are organized according to principles of temporal and spatial contiguity, as well as, perhaps, class inclusion or idiosyncratic meaning similarity (Kihlstrom & Evans, 1979; Mandler, 1979). That is, events will be closely linked if they took place in similar contexts at similar times in the person's life. This narrative organization can be considered to be hierarchical, if *temporal epoch* is the organizing principle. This seems quite likely as Chew (1979) found that personal memories were retrieved more quickly, using a word-cuing technique, the nearer to the present that they took place. So, for example, Jack's record of personal memories might begin in childhood, with only sketchy detail of his very earliest years, and then increasing detail about the elementary and secondary school years, college and law school, marriage and job. These general temporal epochs would be subdivided into narrower time periods—first and second grade, college graduation and first-year law school, marriage right after school, entry level position in the firm—with each narrower time frame encompassing innumerable specific events. The closer a time frame is to the present, the more dense the set of specific events represented within it.

Several theorists have argued on the basis of clinical interview data (Cohler, 1982; Vaillant & McArthur, 1972) and studies of reconstructive memory (Neisser, 1982) that the autobiographical record is structured and restructured to preserve narrative integrity. That is, people seem to see a clear beginning, middle, and potential ending to their story; and within each segment, there is considerable retrospective continuity to personal events, more and more so as time passes. Subjectively, this "smoothing-over" and "continuity-enhancing" process is captured in the intuition that one sees the roots to adult behavior in early experience and that events that once seemed unusual for the self, make good sense *in retrospect*. Cohler (1982) even goes so far as to say that the life course is actually full of discontinuities that, in turn, spark narrative reconstruction: "These transformations are characteristically dramatic and require considerable self-interpretive activity in order to preserve a sense of continuity in the personal narrative which fosters cohesiveness and congruence" (p. 215). He points to three temporal epochs—"the '5-7' shift in cognitive-social development," "the transformation of adolescence and young adulthood," and "the shift from adulthood to middle age"—as particularly critical and active points of narrative-building and self-interpretive activity. Interestingly, his argument rests on the notion that these critical transformation periods make salient particular constellations of personal life tasks and that these tasks, in turn, constitute themes around which to structure the interpretation of personal experience and the threads of self-continuity in the narrative story (see also Levinson, 1978).

These speculations about narrative structure—that it is organized to highlight themes of temporal continuity and growth and the ascendence and recession of different life tasks (Erickson, 1950)—dovetail quite nicely with the recent emphasis in the self-concept literature on a dynamic and mutable cognitive self (Markus, 1983; McGuire, 1984; Higgins et al., 1986). Such a narrative structure would provide experiential data for the development and elaboration of "temporal selves," "contextualized selves," and "task-oriented selves." As people focus on new possible selves, the narrative record would surely provide hints from the past that support those current motivations for self-development.

In other words, the narrative record is closely interwoven with the web of self-concepts that also define the cognitive self. For example, Jack's "self as achiever" concept has many associations to specific events in his life, from as far back as "winning a third-grade spelling bee" to as recent as "winning a big case last week." These connections provide a temporal perspective to the self-concepts and highlight the developmental roots of current life tasks in those of past temporal epochs.

Moreover, perceptions of current life tasks may color, in retrospect, subjective evaluations of the centrality and satisfaction of similar efforts in the past. Vaillant & McArthur (1972) found that high-achieving midlife males tended to portray the achievement struggles of adolescence in a much more positive light in retrospect than in their reports from earlier college years. Hence, Jack, for example, might well imagine now that he has always enjoyed competition and power struggles, reworking that spelling bee competition into a rather more exhilarating experience than it was at the time. Of course, people do not always dwell on continuities in positive self-experience, though reflections about self-change are usually structured so as to emphasize an improvement, not a decline in development (cf. Beck, 1967).

Since the autobiographical narrative keeps track of the person's subjective impressions of success and failure and affective reactions in an event, it also serves to indicate what the person currently sees as important or trivial and what his or her preferences and aversions of the past have been. It would not be surprising, for example, to hear Jack's wife reflect rather negatively on her "lawyer's wife self," given that she still recalls some very negative experiences after college, trying to put Jack through law school. The narrative record serves as a bridge linking specific social learning experiences of the past to currently articulated goals, plans, preferences, and aversions. Such "hot" personal memories, especially those associated with important self-domains, can also provide the experiential basis for specific feelings of self-efficacy or incompetence and, in aggregated form, for more generalized self-esteem. Here again, the subjective definition of self can draw locally upon specialized memories and contextualized selves, or more broadly focus on continuities (imagined or real) in selfhood over time and place.

EXPERTISE AND SELF-KNOWLEDGE

In keeping with the discussion of individual differences in social concepts, we will concentrate here on an expertise model of personality differences in self-knowledge; beginning with self-concept expertise and then turning to narrative memory expertise.

Self-Concept Expertise

Individual differences in expertise with respect to self-concepts—the pattern of domains in which an individual has particular investment with rich and well-organized and highly accessible self-concepts (Markus et. al., 1985)—are especially important in specifying the cognitive basis of personality (Kelly, 1955). After all, we have all had many experiences in many contexts, and therefore our *self-descriptions* are enormously rich. However, only some of these self-descriptions are associated with elaborate *self-concepts* which are also *very important* to an individual's current subjective definition of self (Markus, 1977).

Different methods can be used to isolate an individual's domains of self-concept *expertise:* for example, Markus (1977) finds individuals for whom a particular domain, such as "body weight" or "creativity," is very important to their self-definition and in which they rate themselves as extreme; these "schematics," in turn, have very elaborated self-concepts, with many prototypic self-features and a variety of self-exemplars associated with that domain. McGuire and McGuire (1981) argue that the central attributes in an individual's self-concept will be those generated spontaneously when the individual is asked the "Who am I?" question. In other words, the domains of self-concept expertise will be most salient and "top of the head." Kihlstrom (1985) suggests that *centrality* in the self-concept repertoire is not associated with responses to the context-free question, "Who am I?" but, instead, individuals' important self-concepts will be associated with the recurring situations in their lives.

Regardless of the method used to elicit central self-concepts, it is clear that of all of the self-descriptions which an individual can provide, only a select set will be represented by very elaborate self-concepts. Other descriptions will be associated with self-concepts, but not very rich concepts; still other "facts" about the self will simply be marked by a self-exemplar in a network of person or episode or situation concepts. The individual's expertise is selective, concentrating on domains or contexts which have become particularly important and representative of the self (i.e., these are the prototypical selves within the family of selves).

Consider Jill's self-concept repertoire: She reveals her quite traditional feminine socialization with expertise focused around the abstract domain of *affiliation*. Her nurturing, caring, affiliative self—as represented in self-concepts such as "mother," "self with friends," "self as volunteer," "self in crisis situations"—is of great personal interest and value to Jill. Somewhat less central to her, yet still represented in the repertoire, are Jill's concepts of "self as athlete," "self on vacations," "self as intelligent." Still less self-relevant and, thus, even less elaborated are Jill's representations of self-as-exemplar of the person and situation concepts "professional" (from her teaching job after college), "student" (from experiences in college and earlier), "test situations" (from examination experiences), and so on. Jill can certainly describe "herself-in-test-situations," based upon the association between "herself" and her prototype for test situations. However, that self-description will be less elaborate, less likely to be elicited spontaneously, and less recurrently the focus of her working self-concept, than would Jill's self-descriptions in the much more currently important affiliation domain. These differently elaborated "now selves" constitute a profile of self-concept expertise.

As in the development of all expertise, the attention of individuals is most certainly guided towards certain domains or contexts by both the familial and the broader sociocultural environment. In fact, individuals form expertise in self-relevant domains probably largely in an unconscious effort to *identify* with the norms and values transmitted by role models in their environments (see, for example, Bandura, 1977, 1982, 1986). As Markus and Smith (1981) describe the process, at first the "self-as-x" is simply a poor imitation of "the real thing." But gradually, as more and more time is devoted to activity "of that sort" or "in that context," the "self-as-x" exemplar is both articulated with many characteristic features, and invested with a fair amount of importance, i.e., the transition from novice to expert has begun. This transition is probably especially facilitated if the "past self" in a related domain is a negative one, such that the existence of a new, if only "novice self" in this domain raises the feasibility of attaining the desired "possible self" (Wurf & Markus, 1986; Markus, 1983). Jill, for example, frequently thinks back on the unattractive, socially inept, and squeamish little child of her past; at those times, she is spurred on in her efforts to obtain her possible "self as graceful woman" concept, just like her image of her own mother (however glorified an image that may be).

The impact of the social environment, as a source of cues to normative behavior, appearance, and emotions, is also apparent when individuals form expertise in domains in which they are relatively unique or *distinctive*, given the composition of the social environment (McGuire & McGuire, 1981). The process of developing expertise, in domains or contexts in which one feels *distinctive* is, in some senses, the converse of forming a self-concept via identification. That is, instead of imagining that "you could, if you try hard, be like that person," one develops the self-perception of "being different," often in a quite positive sense, and invests a great deal of attention and affect towards strengthening and bolstering that distinctive self.

Most importantly, "distinctiveness" should be defined *subjectively*. That is, there are many domains in which, whatever the "truth" may be, we perceive ourselves to be different. Despite the protests of parents, a child will say: "I'm just *not* as smart as my brother." Having defined himself or herself as distinctive in that way, that child will undoubtedly cultivate the distinctiveness of self and articulate self-concept expertise in that domain (e.g., he or she may actually cultivate a "self as mediocre" concept). Distinctiveness, as a factor motivating the articulation of self-concepts, must be defined in terms of the individual's own perceptions, regardless of the views of others in the environment.

The identification and differentiation processes described above are probably especially powerful in childhood (Flavell, 1977). However, throughout the lifespan new models are encountered and self-distinctiveness surfaces in new domains. Individuals continue to observe their own behaviors and compare themselves against the normative behaviors of others in the environment (Bem, 1972; Locksley & Lenauer, 1981). These observations of self become data for the articulation of new self-concepts or the revision of old ones. The pattern of self-concept expertise is, therefore, inherently unstable (i.e., dynamic); new possibilities for self are encountered constantly, especially during periods of life transition when the narrative focus may shift as well (Cohler, 1982). Jill, for example, may enter the "empty nest" mid-life years with renewed interest in developing her past "achievement selves." Role changes, like returning to school as an older student, might prompt her to recruit past selves in this recently ignored domain; to articulate relevant new possible selves; and, perhaps slowly, to elaborate her now selves in traditional achievement vs. affiliation domains. Changing the investment in, and content of, central self-concepts is extremely difficult, however, because of the strong associations to related, but unchanged, "expertise" (e.g., Jill's negative view of "self-aggrandizing achievers"). It is especially difficult to "retool" in these central, expert domains because the self-concepts are so tightly organized, such that change precipitates repercussions throughout the repertoire, and so well-integrated with the individual's other congruent social concepts (Nasby & Kihlstrom, 1985).

The particular *organization* of self-concepts (within networks) reflects quite closely the *idiosyncratic* meaning of common concepts for individuals. Individuals also differ tremendously in the actual *content* of their self-concepts. Moreover, differences in the content (or meaning) of obstensibly similar self-concepts are often associated with dramatic variation, from person to person, in individuals' *evaluative assessments* of themselves in a domain. Self-concepts, like all social concepts, can be viewed as "tagged" in memory with summary evaluative associations (Fiske, 1982). These evaluative tags, varying in content and potency, summarize the individual's satisfaction or dissatisfaction with himself or herself in that respect. And, given the variability in people's experiences in a domain, it is no surprise that evaluative assessments differ with respect to superficially comparable self-concepts. Jill, for example, is quite content with her "self as wife" concept (i.e., +++), while Jack is currently suffering a bit over his rather unliberated "self as husband" concept (i.e., −+). Note, as expected, that the intensity or potency of Jill's evaluation is substantially stronger, and the content less ambivalent, than is Jack's. Of course, Jack has an intensely positive evaluative association to his "self as professional" concept (i.e.,++++), while Jill is still a bit wary of her "self as student" (i.e., −+). Both of these individuals would probably be said to have generally "high self-esteem," but this global assessment is averaged over many specific assessments upon which they actually differ considerably.

Individuals will differ, then, in the number of positive and negative self-concepts which they possess, in the intensity of their self-evaluations, and, of course, in the ways in which particular self-concepts are evaluated. In addition, some people may be especially harsh critics of themselves, rather consistently (Beck, 1967). There is a general tendency for individuals to remember more good than bad personal experiences, to attribute personal successes to ability and failures to "bad luck," to exaggerate their own contribution to successful projects, and so on (Greenwald, 1981, on "egocentrism" and "beneffectence"). The repertoire of self-concepts is similarly skewed toward highlighting positive (over negative) selves. However, some individuals, especially those who feel consistently depressed, exhibit *less* tendency towards these self-aggrandizing memory biases and self-enhancing concept descriptions (Kuiper & Derry, 1981; Pietramonaco, 1983). In some cases, individuals keep themselves depressed by setting especially harsh criteria for self-evaluation (Higgins et al, 1986).

Of course even nondepressed individuals articulate and obssess over some self-concepts which are decidedly "negative" in evaluative connotation, which fall short of their "ideal" in a domain, or which suddenly seem dysfunctional in the face of new life tasks. Even Jack, with his generally high level of self-esteem, has some negative self-concepts (e.g., his "fat self"), some less than ideal self-concepts (e.g., his "athlete self"), and some increasingly dysfunctional self-concepts (e.g., his "self as husband"). He regards these aspects of his self-definition as definitely far from the desired end-states.

One further intriguing dimension of individual difference in self-concepts is the degree to which individuals, as observers of themselves, characterize themselves in ways which are consonant with the perceptions that other people have of them. The extent to which an individual shares a *consensual* view of himself or herself is probably another dimension upon which people vary a great deal (Wilson & Stone, 1985). For example, depressed individuals have been found to evaluate their performance on laboratory tasks in much the same way as do outside observers; however, nondepressed individuals rate themselves as having performed much *better* than outside observers' ratings would suggest (Lewinsohn et al., 1980). Of course, in other ways depressed individuals may have very "inaccurate" (harsh) views of themselves (Goldfried & Robins, 1983).

More important than comparisons *between* individuals, though, are comparisons *within* an individual's self-concept repertoire. Suppose, for example, that each person has some self-concepts which are quite "accurate" in that others in the environment also characterize the person in that way; some which are simply idiosyncratic, in that others do not focus upon those aspects of behavior; and finally, some self-concepts with which others would (strongly) disagree, i.e., "inaccurate" or even "delusional" self-concepts. Jack's family, for example, would probably find his self-concept as an achiever (e.g., competitive, workaholic, rising fast, anxious but challenged, sometimes cutthroat) quite an "accurate" reflection of his behavior in that domain. By contrast, they might be surprised to find that he places a great deal of value on his "self as athlete" concept, since they assume that his fluctuating weight, busy work schedule and fast-food habits interfere with his athletic prowess enough to make that domain less than central to his self-image (i.e., an idiosyncratic self-concept). Further, Jack's family would be shocked and amused to learn that he presently viewed himself as "relatively liberated" in the domain of family and marriage (i.e., Jack's "self as father" and "self as husband" concepts are inaccurate, at best, and delusional, at worst, in the eyes of those who know him in these roles). Of course, there is no absolute criterion for truth here, but discrepancies between the concepts which an individual holds about himself and the ways in which he is viewed by others can be quite problematic in social interaction (Kihlstrom & Nasby, 1981).

These problematic discrepanices (between self-concepts and the world's assessment of the individual) can take many forms. For example, frequently an individual will be very insulted in a particular interaction by the simple failure on the part of another person to recognize the importance that the individual places on some past accomplishment, some way of behaving, or some "look" which he or she has cultivated. Most disruptive, though, are the "delusions" which individuals hold about themselves and around which they plan behavior and construct life goals (Goldfried & Robins, 1983; Cantor & Kihlstrom, 1985). Such "differences of opinion" can be very dangerous. The self-concepts summarize a great deal of information about an individual's goals, preferences, and plans in a particular domain or context. Therefore, self-concepts may very strongly influence a person's actions (Markus, 1983). If the self-concept in question is inaccurate or delusional, as is Jack's "self as parent" concept, then the individual's action plans may not meet with others' approval either. Fortunately, inaccurate or delusional self-concepts can be changed, but usually not without a great deal of negative feedback from others and a fair amount of suffering on the individual's part (Goldfried & Robins, 1983; Kihlstrom & Nasby, 1981; Kendall & Hollon, 1981).

There are many factors that make it difficult to change or revise well-articulated self-concepts, even when they are not extremely "delusional." We will discuss the processes involved in concept revision (and behavior change) in a later chapter (see Chapter 8). At this point, however, a few comments are in order. First, individuals tend to pay most attention to, and elicit, feedback from others which *confirms,* not contradicts, their beliefs about themselves. Swann and Read (1981) refer to this process as one of "self-verification." Second, even when we do encounter feedback which contradicts our cherished self-concepts, that feedback can usually be discounted. Markus (1977) found that her schematic subjects discounted, rationalized, or quite simply ignored any feedback from the experimenter which was contradictory to their centrally-held self-concepts (e.g., feedback which told a person who believed himself or herself to be very independent that he or she was actually quite suggestible). These schematic subjects were far more resistant to accepting such contradictory feedback than were aschematic subjects with less well-formed self-concept expertise in the relevant domain (e.g., individuals who saw themselves as only moderately independent and for whom this was not a central self-concept domain).

This "resistance" to information or feedback which contradicts a central self-concept may come from many sources. The feedback is only one bit of evidence, while the individual has many observations in the autobiographical record which *are* (apparently) consistent with that self-concept (Ross, Lepper, & Hubbard, 1975). The self-concept is, presumably, interconnected with many other related self-concepts and it would be difficult, and maybe not wise, to change *them,* as well. The self-concept is very functional in that it describes the individual's goals and preferences quite well in that domain; it would be cumbersome to learn a whole new behavioral repertoire (Markus, 1983). And, or so we reason, "Who knows me better than I do?" (Andersen, 1984; cf. Wilson & Stone, 1985).

These conservative tendencies do not altogether prevent individuals from developing new self-concepts or from becoming dissatisfied with old ones and working towards a more "ideal" self in a domain. Rather, it is simply that self-concepts, especially very central ones, are quite well entrenched within the individual's social intelligence repertoire; it takes a great deal of feedback to penetrate the "defenses" of conservation and self-verification. One suspects that people would need to be very convinced that they had badly "misread" themselves or had developed a very dysfunctional view of themselves, in order to want to *work* to change a self-concept (as well as its associates). Becoming so convinced is a very gradual process and one that eventually requires conscious effort (Kihlstrom, 1984).

A major part of the change process involves coming to believe in the *feasibility* of "being different" in a domain. Despite the variety of selves in the concept repertoire, there is often a strong conviction about a central self-concept that one has "always been this way" and that new selves in this particular domain are not possible, at least *not now.* This conviction is bolstered by the organization of expertise in the personal narrative that emphasizes *continuity* of personal experience. Individual differences in the domains of "self-entrenchment" and the corresponding avenues for self-change are also apparent in that narrative record, to which we now turn.

Narrative Expertise

Individuals may differ markedly in the richness, vividness and cohesiveness of their personal memories in particular temporal epochs (Kihlstrom & Harackiewicz, 1982). Some people remember many early childhood events, while others have almost complete amnesia about their early years. The particular periods of richest self-recollections often vary considerably from person to person. Jill, for example, has a richer set of "early teenage" recollections than does Jack. These differences in the distribution of autobiographical memories across the life span help to define differences in *narrative expertise.*

Individuals will undoubtedly have richer sets of episodic memories relevant to domains in which they are "self-experts," or for past events that now map in some way onto current life tasks. For example, Jack has very elaborate memories associated with episodes at work, while Jill's autobiographical record is more frequently tied to episodes at home, with children, when she enacts her "mother or wife self." Their respective records of more remote personal memories differ in similar ways: Jack recalls a great deal about life at school as a child, while Jill remembers quite vividly the family events of her childhood. It is also likely that, even though individuals' negative personal memories generally fade more quickly than their positive ones (Holmes, 1974), people have quite rich recollections of events in their lives that symbolize aspects of themselves which are "less than ideal." So, while Jack would like to forget about those days early on in their marriage, he is currently aware of a need for change and can use those memories of earlier days as a baseline of comparison, as he now works toward a more acceptable "self as husband" concept. These differences in *content* and *emphasis* in individuals' autobiographical records will usually complement similar differences in the profile of self-concept expertise.

As can be seen in Jack's and Jill's recollections of events during any given week, individuals also differ in the *evaluative connotations* which they associate with shared events. Jack typically recalls Sunday nights as times of anxiety and excitement; he has intense, but mixed evaluative associations with those memories. Jill, by contrast, is more likely to be quite relaxed, and feel more prepared for her Monday activities. While they may have shared the same weekend events, the personal *meaning* of the events—represented by the place of such events within each one's narrative record—will differ. For each person, the events will be experienced within the context established by his or her own constellation of salient self-concepts, narrative memories, and currently pressing life tasks. As we have noted before, the self-concept repertoire and the autobiographical record are intimately related, each, in a sense, enriching and strengthening the other.

An intriguing way in which individuals may differ in self-knowledge is in the *cohesiveness* of their personal memories and self-concepts (Cohler, 1982); or in their proclivity for *retrospective updating* and "smoothing out" of the story line in the personal narrative (Greenwald, 1981). According to most clinical lore, these differences in narrative cohesiveness and retrospective "insight" are generalized stylistic differences in self-reflectiveness, ego-strength, or self-stability. Yet another model, one more in keeping with the expertise analysis, would suggest that individuals will differ in the cohesiveness of memories from different temporal epochs, perhaps as a function of the content of the life tasks emphasized in each period (e.g., Jill may experience young parenthood and grandparenting as periods of particular personal cohesiveness). When a person is able to easily "make sense" of life events in a particular period, perhaps because they fit well with self-concept expertise at the time, then he or she may work to elaborate the narrative and, consequently, achieve cohesiveness in self-recollections *for that period*.

People may be especially likely to "see" continuity and stability of experience over time and place when domains of self-concept expertise are involved. As often happens, the biasing impact of self-concept expertise—in this case, on perceptions of continuity in the personal narrative—may be reflected in the "veridicality" of self-inferences (Wilson & Stone, 1985). This possiblity reminds us, once again, of the interweaving of procedural and declarative knowledge, for the self-concept and narrative expertise together influence the direction that future self-construals take.

INTERPRETIVE RULES FOR SELF-REFLECTION

Having considered in some detail the content and structure of self-knowledge expertise, it is appropriate to turn to the other side of the cognitive self—the *procedural* rules for self-reflection. As always, it is only for convenience that we separate declarative and procedural knowledge, for the self-concepts and personal narrative are acquired, transformed, and accessed via interpretive rules of self-inference, self-memory, and self-evaluation (Kihlstrom & Cantor, 1984). It is through the application of these rules that the special features of content and structure of declarative self-knowledge are acquired in the first place and then preserved and bolstered over time.

The rules of self-inference, memory, and evaluation are a paradox (with regard to accuracy and thoroughness criteria), as are the declarative concepts and narratives with which they operate. That is, while the data base for self-reflection is in many ways a privileged one, and people do make use of the depth and breadth of data about subjective experience (Andersen, 1984), the rules of self-construal are also quite selective, and often self-protective, in the use of those data (Greenwald, 1980; Wilson & Stone, 1985). A brief tour through literature on procedural self-knowledge reveals a pattern that is now common in the social cognition literature more generally: systematic cognitive focus on the self and personal experience and yet pervasive shortcuts and biases in the portrayal of self, both to the self and to others (see Markus & Zajonc, 1985; Showers & Cantor, 1985, for more extensive treatments).

Privileges and Problems in Self-Inference

Individuals potentially have access to a privileged data base about their own experiences. Not only can they observe the covariation of their overt actions with different stimulus factors in specific contexts, as might an observer (Bem, 1972; Locksley & Lenauer, 1981), but they can add to their computations information about the typicality of their present response and the privileged special factors in their personal past that might constrain present behavior (e.g., "idiosyncratic causal theories," Wilson & Stone, 1985). And perhaps most important, actors have access to privileged information about their subjective experiences—the feelings, thoughts, and intentions that provide a rich interpretive context for overt actions (Andersen, 1984).

There is growing evidence that individuals make use of this privileged data base in the self-inference process; as reflected in the dynamic content of self-concepts and the narrative record. For example, as Andersen & Ross (1984) observed, individuals regard their (private) feelings and thoughts as more diagnostic in the self-inference process than they do overt actions taken in the public domain. In that study, subjects were more willing to make extreme dispositional attributions about the self on the basis of subjective data than from objective actions, perhaps because they view their feelings and intentions as closer to the true self, and less constrained by contextual forces than would be their public behavior (Swann, 1984). As Andersen & Ross (1984) note, the relative reluctance to use contextually-constrained behavioral samples as evidence of underlying self-dispositions fits well with the commonly observed "actor-observer" difference in attributional reasoning (Jones & Nisbett, 1972; Albright & Kihlstrom, 1986). Hence, actors apparently take much more care in evaluating the data for self-inferences than for social construals.

While it is clear that people do indeed make use of privileged information in the self-inference process, and that they are relatively careful about drawing inferences about self-dispositions on the basis of context-dependent behavior, less clear is whether the privileged data actually contribute to greater *accuracy* (or predictive utility) in actors' (as compared with observers') conclusions about the self (Wilson & Stone, 1985). For example, when Wilson, Laser, & Stone (1982) asked undergraduates to retrospect about the predictors of their own (or others') mood states over a five-week period, the actor-subjects used their idiosyncratic theories—frequently derived from subjective experience, and different from those of naive observer-subjects. However, since Wilson et al. also had diary records of mood and several potential causal agents of mood (e.g., sleep patterns; success/failure experiences; weather, etc.) from the actor-subjects, they were able to show that, at least in retrospect, the actor-subjects were no more accurate than the observer-subjects in predicting the pattern of covariation between these predictor variables and actual mood over the five-week period.

Thus, as with many analyses of expertise and social inference, it is frequently the case that the privilege of expert insight does not insure against experts being misled in the inference process by a personal preference for certain kinds of explanations over others (e.g., Nisbett & Ross, 1980). Of course, in the long run, the actor-expert may be right because he or she may be able to insure the predictive validity of those private theories by controlling future behavior in line with preferred self-inferences (Swann & Read, 1981). This kind of active self-verification process is, in fact, especially likely to occur in domains of self-investment and expertise—i.e., precisely in those domains for which private theories will be particularly abundant—thus protecting the expert against the debunking of cherished self-inferences (Swann & Ely, 1984). Hence, the dynamics of social interaction, with multiple opportunities for self-validation, may blunt the double-edge sword of self-expertise; while also keeping us from "growing out" of these favored action patterns (Nasby & Kihlstrom, 1985).

Individuals may also be more accurate (than observers) in their causal accounts of personal action when they engage in on-line introspections as compared with retrospective analyses (Ericsson & Simon, 1980) and attempt to explain relatively small samples of behavior in terms of relatively few predictor variables (Swann, 1984; Wilson & Stone, 1985). For example, Funder & Sherrod (1983) observed that actors, but not observers, become more attached to initial causal theories (either dispositional or situational explanations) with the passage of time. The "smoothing-out" process in the personal narrative supports this observation as well (Linton, 1975, 1978). Therefore, it seems that the self-expert makes the best use of privileged data for self-inference when he or she focuses immediately on causal analysis about specific actions (i.e., under conditions of "circumscribed accuracy," Swann, 1984). Interestingly, those are probably also the conditions conducive to accurate predictions by highly trained observers of personality (Shweder, 1980; Nisbett, 1980).

Depth and Selectivity in Self-Memory

Analysis of encoding and retrieval rules, both with regard to self-descriptive material in the abstract and specific memories of personal experience, reveals the same mixture of depth (enhancement) and yet selectivity (biases) observed for self-inference rules (Kihlstrom & Cantor, 1984; Greenwald, 1981). For example, in the now well-researched self-reference effect (Keenan & Baillet, 1980), individuals are observed to retain material better when they evaluate it for self-relevance (as opposed to other encoding tasks) (e.g., Klein & Kihlstrom, 1986; Rogers et al., 1979; Bower & Gilligan, 1979). The self-reference effect on enhanced retention seems to derive from the opportunity to sort the material into two categories: self-descriptive and nonself-descriptive. A similar enhancement occurs when people think about *familiar* others (as compared with nonfamiliar acquaintances), people for whom there presumably also would be a rich encoding context and set of retrieval cues (Chew & Kihlstrom, 1986).

While all material evaluated for self-relevance seems to be highly memorable, there is also evidence that people are quite selective in their recollections of self (Greenwald, 1980). We have already noted several times that individuals reconstruct the personal memory narrative according to currently plausible self-theories. Another very pervasive principle of self-memory selectivity seems to be the preference (at encoding, retrieval, and reconstruction) towards positively evaluated personal experiences and self-descriptions (Kihlstrom, 1981). For example, in the depth of processing self-reference paradigms, nondepressed subjects selectively elaborate and retain positive personal material as opposed to negative self-relevant material (Nasby & Kihlstrom, 1985). This evaluative selectivity in encoding is not completely constrained by the preponderance of positive as compared with negative self-concepts and memories, for these same nondepressed individuals will show enhanced encoding of *negative* as compared with positive self-relevant material when they are in a bad mood or have experienced failure recently (Nasby & Kihlstrom, 1985; Ingram, Smith, & Brehm, 1983). Moreover, this reversal of the typical selectivity pattern is not simply a global mood-congruency effect; Nasby & Kihlstrom (1985) did not report mood "spillover" effects for memory for information about significant other persons. However, despite the existence of negative selves and memories of unpleasant experiences which could well provide rich encoding contexts, the typical encoding bias selects for *positive* self-relevant material.

People are similarly selective in their retrieval of autobiographical experiences, showing a clear proclivity to retrieve pleasant as compared with unpleasant personal memories (Teasdale & Taylor, 1981). This pattern also reverses for depressed individuals. Moreover, current mood state has an asymmetric effect on retrieval of positively and negatively evaluated personal memories: good moods can enhance selectivity for positive past experiences, while bad moods have less impact in establishing a retrieval set for negative memories (Bower, 1981; cf. Snyder & White, 1982). Again, the selectivity bias seems to favor positive over negative material about the self, presumably bolstering a somewhat "illusory glow" in self-evaluation (Bandura, 1986).

Debilitating and Motivating Self-Evaluation

Individuals also draw upon self-concepts and personal memories in the course of evaluating personal performance and motivating themselves for forthcoming tasks (Norem & Cantor, 1986b; Scheier & Carver, 1981). Here, too, in the rules of self-evaluation, there is a mixture of "thorough realism" and yet "protective maneuvering." For example, sometimes people evaluate the "now self" in a domain by comparison to as-yet-unachieved "ideal selves," leaving themselves open to feelings of hopelessness and even depression (Higgins et al., 1986). Of course, thinking about *positive* ideal selves can also be motivating, if a person feels that it is possible to attain the ideal (Markus & Nurius, 1986); in fact, thinking about negative possible selves can motivate activity to avoid that outcome for some people (Norem & Cantor, 1986a, 1986b; Showers, 1986).

However, self-evaluation of current performance often seems to involve some fairly selective and protective self-other comparisons by nondepressed individuals (Bandura, 1986). Typically, people evaluate their performance in a more positive light than do observers (e.g., the "illusory glow" effect, Lewinsohn et al., 1980); they also compare themselves frequently to people who are most likely to perform at a *worse* level than themselves (e.g., "downward social comparison") (Taylor, Lichtman, & Wood, 1984; Wills, 1981). Similarly, nondepressed individuals rate themselves in a generally more positive light than they do a "typical" member of their reference group ("self-enhancement effect," Tabachnik, Crocker, & Alloy, 1983). Tesser and Campbell (1983) refer to a general "self-evaluation maintenance" process, whereby individuals see themselves as comparing favorably to others in domains of positive self-evaluation and see others as more like the self in less favored domains. Moreover, when something is going wrong in a cherished self-domain, it is sometimes possible to dull the impact of a negative life event or poor performance by recruiting other currently more positive images of self (Linville, 1982a). Again, people have potential access to a multifaceted repertoire of cognitive selves; they often use this expertise selectively, in a manner that is functional—in that it motivates rather than debilitates—though not altogether balanced (Snyder, Stephan, & Rosenfeld, 1976).

Not surprisingly, these rules of self-inference, memory, and evaluation provide a picture of processes of self-reflection that is quite congruent with that given by studies of the content and structure of declarative self-knowledge. The depth of processing of self-information and access to a privileged data base of subjective experience fits well with characterizations of declarative self-knowledge as richly elaborated, tightly-organized, and easily accessed (Markus, 1977; Rogers, 1981; Kuiper & Derry, 1981; Higgins & King, 1981). The selectivity biases in self-reflection match the impression garnered from descriptive work on the self-concepts and autobiographical memory—there is a tendency to dwell on the positive side of self and to see personal experience as fitting together a bit more tightly and continuously than perhaps it really does (Matlin & Stang, 1978; Cohler, 1982). Together, both the depth and selectivity of self-reflective thought coincide with one's intuitions that no object of construal is more "worthy of attention" than the self, and yet neither is there an object more worth protecting from the ravages of social life than the self (Freud, 1925; James, 1890).

SELF-EXPERTISE AND CONSTRUCTIVE ALTERNATIVISM

In the previous chapter we argued that *expertise* in a domain of social life, while typically associated with elaborate, well-organized, and easily accessible declarative knowledge, does not in and of itself assure open-minded and flexible construal. Rather, as Nasby & Kihlstrom (1985) note:

> The automatic and unconscious quality of procedural knowledge, ironically enough, means that experts run the risk of applying rules uncritically, even

"mindlessly" (Chanowitz & Langer, 1980), and cannot easily articulate what they are doing or why (Nisbett & Wilson, 1977). If the procedural rules become inappropriate or maladaptive (e.g., because the "rules of the game" have changed), expertise can pose special problems (p. 12).

This double-edged quality of procedural expertise—creating construal "ruts" or routines—is especially likely to occur in the "chronically accessible" domains of self-knowledge expertise (Bargh, 1982). Does this preclude constructive alternativism in domains of self-expertise? Can self-experts monitor their cognitive work in expert domains such that they can interrupt the routine and engage in "alternative thinking" when the context demands flexibility (Showers & Cantor, 1985)?

As one might well expect, the answers to these questions about self-expertise and constructive alternativism are not straightforward—in some contexts, particularly when those cherished selves and procedural routines are *not* threatened, people are really quite good at being flexible; but it may be that self-experts dig in their heels most fervently (though probably unintentionally) when cognitive flexibility would be most valuable (i.e., when the "rules of the game" have changed). Though the data are still quite incomplete on this question, there are several recent studies that reflect the complexity of the relationship between self-expertise and constructive alternativism.

On the side of flexibility, Markus et al. (1985) have shown that, while individuals are quite ready to "read" a great deal of schema-congruent meaning in the behavior of people whom they know little about, but whose surface actions prime a domain of self-expertise, experts can also control their inferences when set to do so. They asked a group of male undergraduates for whom "masculinity" was a domain of self-expertise ("masculine schematics"), and a group for whom this was not an especially important self-domain, to watch a videotape of a male undergraduate performing some masculinity-relevant and some masculinity-neutral acts. The students were asked to unitize the film sequence into meaningful units of action (Newtson, 1976) and then to reconstruct from memory their impressions of the actor. In this case, the masculinity *self*-experts apparently used their self-knowledge as an interpretive framework for processing information about this unfamiliar target person: they organized the stream of masculinity-relevant behavior into larger units than did the aschematic subjects; and, correspondingly, they inferred more global masculinity-relevant personality attributes in their reconstructive impressions than did the aschematics. (There were no group differences in unitizing or impressions from the masculinity-neutral film segments.)

This pattern of construal on the part of self-experts is suggestive of relatively automatic "top-of-the-head" responses based upon their own favored self-concepts (see also Dornbusch et al., 1956; Shrauger & Patterson, 1974; Lewicki, 1983). Yet, these same self-experts were able to control the use of "self as an interpretive framework" (Markus et al., 1985) when motivated (by instructions) to remember the details of the target person's behavior—under those conditions, they unitized with greater detail and maintained their conjectures about the target person at the level of concrete behaviors. Interestingly, the "nonexpert" aschematics were relatively insensitive to processing goals in their unitizing activity or reconstructive impressions. Hence, under relatively commonplace conditions of social construal, both sides of the relation between self-expertise and constructive alternativism emerge: self-experts tend to rely first on favored concepts in social construal; then, when motivated to do so, they can rather successfully control their interpretive behavior and be guided in construal to a greater than usual extent by the target stimulus.

Of course, these were relatively benign conditions for the self-expert; there were no threats to self-definition or self-esteem. By contrast, when an individual is somehow threatened in his or her expert domain with a global assault on self-esteem, then social construal becomes more clearly an avenue for "self-esteem maintenance" (Tesser & Campbell, 1983), and the self-expert becomes less open to data-driven alternative construals. For example, Lewicki (1984) has very cleverly demonstrated the unintentional, but defensively motivated, tendency of people who have been insulted with negative feedback to bolster self-esteem. He showed that "insulted subjects" reaffirmed their status in a person perception task by increasing the general perceived desirability of possessing attributes like their own strong points and, correspondingly, decreasing the perceived negative impact of "bad" attributes which they also possessed. While these cognitive tricks come quite naturally to self-experts, and reflect a fair degree of "quick-thinking," they are not suggestive of a particularly *open-minded* attitude towards social construal.

Individuals' tendencies to "dig in their heels" when aspects of self-expertise are threatened are even more obvious in the context of direct *confrontations* in the course of social interaction. For example, Swann & Ely (1984) found that individuals did everything in their power to provide self-validating evidence when another person challenged their beliefs in a domain of self-expertise. When individuals who were certain that they were highly extroverted interacted with others who thought (with certainty) that the subject was in fact highly introverted, the self-experts presented themselves in an especially extroverted manner (as rated by naive judges). Their efforts at "self-verification" were particularly striking by comparison to other self-described extroverts who were less certain of their beliefs in this domain: the nonexperts tended to confirm the expectancies of the confrontive partner, presenting themselves in a presumably uncharacteristic introverted manner (i.e.,"behavioral confirmation" conditions). However, even the nonexperts did not change their self-descriptions in the extroversion-introversion domain after this apparently "nondiagnostic" performance. Hence, experts in particular, but nonexperts in some sense as well, cling to their (cherished) self-concepts and find ways, in social construal and in self-presentation, to discount challenges and validate their worthiness (Tesser, 1980). Again, while this self-protective proclivity may not result in the most balanced data-driven construal activity, it is certainly understandable and probably even wise for self-experts to be conservative in relinquishing their expertise. After all, those self-concepts are elaborate, tightly linked to many other self-concepts, and interwoven with material from the personal narrative—changes in a domain of self-knowledge expertise can have considerable repurcussions for the entire cognitive self.

Yet, there are certainly times when even self-experts want to *change* their self-definition in a domain of expertise (Kihlstrom & Nasby, 1981; Turk & Salovey, 1985). People do have negative self-concepts and sometimes there is motivation to change those negative selves even when they are central parts of a person's current self-definition (Wurf & Markus, 1986). These occasions provide, in many respects, a test of the limits of flexibility in self-expertise, because the motivation to change conflicts with the natural proclivity to fall back on (or even to actively protect) well-worn habits of self-reflection and social construal.

There is some evidence beginning to accumulate that suggests a less conservative and protective posture in domains of self-expertise when there is heightened motivation for self-change. For example, Wurf & Markus (1986) show a reversal in the typical pattern of self-enhancing self-evaluations on the part of self-experts who strongly desire to be different. They found that "lazy schematics" with high motivation to achieve viewed other people in their college student reference group as especially "conscientious," in contrast to those nonmotivated "lazy schematics" who apparently found comfort in numbers, rating the other students as "lazy" like themselves. These data suggest that self-experts who are motivated to effect change in their domain of expertise may recruit images of "comparison others" to prod themselves to work to achieve their more preferred possible selves (Markus & Nurius, 1986). When the motivation for change is salient, people may well be able to reorient their habitually self-protective rules of construal so as to support the change efforts (Showers & Cantor, 1985), thus turning the "double-edge" of expertise to work for themselves in a novel way (Nasby & Kihlstrom, 1985).

EXPERTISE AND CURRENT LIFE TASKS

This chapter presents a portrait that emphasizes the coexistence of *variety* and *selectivity* in declarative and procedural self-knowledge. The repertoire of self-concepts represents the many sides of the cognitive self—contextual selves; past, present, and possible selves; positive and negative selves—though only some of those selves will be important, elaborated, and frequently activated in the working self-concept of the moment. The personal narrative is a rich history of subjective experience, reflecting the natural mixture of successful and unsuccessful outcomes to everyday life episodes. Yet there is also enormous selectivity in the elaboration of some selves over others and the "smoothing out" of the narrative in such a way as to preserve a picture of continuity and progression in self-development.

This somewhat odd combination of depth and selectivity in declarative self-knowledge is mirrored in the procedural rules for self-reflection. Individuals are at once highly likely to process self-relevant information very deeply, seeing the many sides to the self and bringing to bear extensive data on subjective experience, and also very likely to rely on favorite explanations for personal behavior. Recollections about the self tend to selectively emphasize positive past events, even though self-relevant material is in general more elaborately encoded and more easily retrieved than nonself-relevant material. Similarly, procedures for self-evaluation typically show the self in an especially glowing light (by comparison to others); though, again, the depth or breadth of self-knowledge does allow for emphasis on less-than-ideal selves, and less favorable social comparisons, in the service of motivating self-change or performance effort.

Furthermore, there is no place in which the coexistence of depth and selectivity (in declarative and procedural knowledge) shows up more clearly than in individuals' domains of self-expertise. In those domains, individuals are most sensitive to processing goals and regulating their efforts accordingly, while at the same time most apt to protectively guard cherished beliefs and familiar routines in the face of potential threats of disconfirmation. Yet, in those same expert domains, when people desire to change, there is sometimes a much reduced level of self-protectiveness in construals and more openness to alternative models for behavior.

Once again, the content and structure of self-knowledge certainly allow for considerable constructive alternativism in the construal of social events, in perceptions of others, and in reflections on the self. However, the elaboration of expert domains (of self-definition) sometimes leads to conservatism and protectionism, sometimes to flexibility and openness to revision. In order to see the functioning of this social intelligence more closely it is critical to consider the *life tasks* on which individuals work and the expertise—about the self and the world—brought to bear in solving those current concerns. For it is in the context of problem solving about life tasks that the recurrent pattern of protectionism and of openness (characteristic of social intelligence) may be most functional and, perhaps, even wise. At this juncture it is time to dispense with somewhat artificial boundaries between self-expertise and social expertise and to consider the fully-coordinated repertoire as it is acquired, used, and revised in the service of goal-directed social life activity.

6

Life Tasks and Problem-Solving Strategies

As a first step toward investigating the ways in which people face life situations, it is critical to find a set of contexts or tasks which are especially informative about those individual differences. We need to delineate a set of tasks in which groups of people are habitually involved, yet one in which people work on the tasks in different ways, i.e., use their uniquely organized social intelligence. When the sample of informative life tasks has been defined, then it is possible to begin to look for individuals' characteristic patterns of problem solving. It may also be possible to trace those individual differences in problem solving back to a person's concepts and beliefs about the self and others.

In the present chapter, therefore, we will engage in a step-by-step analysis of people at work on life tasks in which we will lay out: (a) a definition of the life tasks of interest here; (b) an analysis of characteristic problem-solving strategies; and (c) a discussion of the personal concepts and goals that may influence the selection of favorite ways of solving problems.

I. LIFE TASKS: DELINEATING
THE SAMPLE SPACE OF PROBLEMS

Clearly, people work on numerous problems in their everyday lives, from those involving familiar routines to those that constitute the rare emergencies of social life. Therefore, the first step in a problem-solving analysis is to delineate the set of problems expected to be most revealing and informative about personality. Then, one has to find a way of ensuring content validity (Goldfried & D'Zurilla, 1969)—in this case, of ensuring comprehensive sampling of the events which constitute that set of problems for the people under study.

How to limit the problem set? Since the goal in limiting the set of relevant problems is to find an arena in which people naturally draw on their repertoire of social intelligence, it is critical to find problems that truly engage and demand attention and resources. One way to ensure selection of problems which are personally relevant to the people being studied is to adopt the *task* as the unit of analysis (see McFall, 1982; Goldfried, 1983); in other words, we are interested, as are many personologists, in the tasks that consume individuals, rather than the problems which confront them. How do *tasks* differ from *problems*? This is clearly a difficult distinction to make, but it seems to hinge on the extent to which a person's behavior is devoted to solving and, hence, is guided by, a problem. Environments present people with the opportunity to work on numerous problems, from baking a cake to explicating the laws of relativity; individuals define tasks for themselves from this array of problem-solving opportunities.

The Features of Life Tasks

As a first step, then, towards limiting the sample space of relevant problems for study, a focus on the *task* as the unit of analysis places emphasis on the person-by-environment interaction. The interesting problems are those which people make their own in their current life space: those environmental presses (Murray, 1938) or demands which have become salient desires (Reich & Zautra, 1983) at that time and place, those problems which hold motivating force for individuals (Klinger, 1975) and organize their activity towards a specified end-state (Cantor et al., 1986).

Assuming that there are multiple problem-solving opportunities for people, and that the individual plays an active, though not necessarily conscious role in constructing a set of tasks, it is now possible to consider different schemes for describing or classifying individuals' important life tasks. Life tasks can be arrayed or defined with respect to a number of descriptive features.

1. Explicit or implicit? Although the task analysis argues that individuals select the meaningful problems on which they work, it does not follow that people are always *aware* of their tasks at any given moment. For example, it could be argued that Freud described the tasks of different people in terms of the specific instinctual conflicts arising over aggressive and sexual desires as manifest in the particular life environment of each individual (Freud, 1960). He certainly did not, however, characterize the individual as being aware of his or her life tasks; quite the contrary.

In contrast, others have argued that the best way to delimit the sample of meaningful, motivating life tasks for study is to concentrate, first, on those tasks which consume the thoughts and concerns of individuals, i.e., the tasks which the *person* articulates as a central project at that point in time. Along these lines McFall (1982) argues, from the point of view of behavior prediction, that: "It may prove useful to select task units that correspond to the size of unit that ordinary people use to organize their own behaviors (e.g., when describing how they spent time during the day, or when making a 'to do' list)" (p. 15). In other words, as a first pass at identifying the meaningful life tasks, McFall and others suggest concentrating on those projects that people themselves espouse as important in their current lives.

The Freudian position, and the McFall position, seem to fall at ends of a continuum with regard to this aspect of life tasks, i.e., the awareness continuum. A position that falls somewhere in between is one in which the theorist infers the "current concerns" (Klinger, 1977) of an individual from the themes that emerge in the person's stories and fantasy protocols (Atkinson, 1964). From this approach, unlike Freud, the theorist takes the protocol material to be a direct indication of concerns and goals; but, unlike McFall, there is no assumption of real awareness of those same themes or goals on the person's part.

2. Abstract or circumscribed?   Many have noted that people work on tasks which vary tremendously in breadth or abstractness (McFall, 1982; Little, 1983), from the global task of "finding intimacy" to the specific one of "finding company for Saturday night." Hence, in an analysis of individuals' problem-solving activity, it is critical to settle on the size of the task unit. There are in fact many solutions to this problem: for example, concentrating on a theme, such as achievement tasks or affiliation tasks, and then attempting to specify the daily activities that map onto this theme (e.g., trying to get good grades) and building larger and more global task units which characterize a substantial chunk of the person's work in that domain (e.g., competitive school activities) (Veroff, 1983). From this view it is as if the theorist were describing a vertical section of the hierarchical "life-task tree" for the individual, with the global theme or task unit at the top and the more and more specific subtasks stacked below. The subtasks are, of course, the units which comprise the global task for that person. Another slice of tasks in the tree might proceed horizontally at one specified vertical level. In this case, the objective would be to compare an individual's problem-solving approach across two or more life task domains, e.g., studying and dating.

Whichever slice is taken, the aim is to limit the tasks under study so as to be able to superimpose those tasks onto units of activity for the person.

As McFall (1982) points out: "Thus, for example, it would be difficult to analyze social competence in relation to such vague and global tasks as 'becoming famous' or 'enjoying life.' The most meaningful task unit is one that can be translated into 'how to do it terms'" (p. 15). However, the objective is also to find a scheme that allows one to be relatively *complete* in the sampling of relevant tasks for the person in one domain or at one level in the hierarchy. Therefore, it is important not to become too specific in defining the task unit, so as to avoid the necessity of sampling activity in thousands of little subtasks that comprise the more global one (e.g., picking up the phone; shaking hands with your date; drinking a beer with your date, and so on). Limiting the sample of tasks by choosing an appropriately sized unit and a thorough array within that size sample is a very tricky, but critical pursuit.

3. Universal or unique?   A related question in limiting the sample of relevant tasks concerns the search for universally central life tasks. That is, some begin their analysis of personality with a finite set of basic or universal life tasks, such as the search for intimacy, power, and identity (Plutchik, 1980; Adler, 1929, 1931; Erikson, 1950). Typically these tasks are derived from an evolutionary perspective and, hence, are descriptive of other nonhuman species as well (Smuts, 1985). Moreover, while in principle such basic life tasks could be quite circumscribed and specific, as in the case of the drive to satisfy a particular hunger, more commonly the universal task units are quite global. Starting from this framework is convenient, for it affords some sense of completeness in sampling, while also reducing the number of task domains to a manageable, finite collection of central human concerns. However, the uniqueness in the ways in which these universal problems become specific tasks in the actual lives of real people makes the analysis less simple and more taxing in practice than in theory.

4. Enduring or stage-specific?   Another way to limit the set of relevant tasks for study is to make them time-linked, as in "stage" theories of life tasks (e.g., Erikson, 1950; Neugarten, 1976; Veroff, 1983; Levinson, 1978). For example, one could imagine that each problem in the core set of universal problems becomes a task for individuals only at a certain stage in their growth; so, adolescents search for identity and mid-life adults search for power and control. The stage-specific approach has an advantage in that the demands of the environment—including the person's physiological and maturational states as well as the social-institutional context—are relatively uniform for all of those individuals in a common stage or life period. Hence, against this backdrop of common demands, it may be easier to see the variations from person to person in the manifestation of a universal problem in a unique personal task. By contrast, another limiting scheme would involve the study of one "basic" life problem as manifest in different life tasks across the developmental life span of the individual. Freud, for instance, presented a scheme with an enduring need for gratification and defense of sexual and aggressive instincts, though the tasks were different at different life periods (Freud, 1925).

   5. Rare or commonplace?   Another way in which to limit the sampling of tasks is by selecting for study only those tasks which are quite rare and, hence, monumental for the person. Some have argued that in the face of personal crises, individuals' true style of facing problems and working on tasks can be seen most clearly and vividly (Adler, 1931; Haan, 1982). In the difficult crises of life, the individual has a heightened commitment to solving tasks. At such times, the everyday problems fade and the important and taxing life tasks come into focus. Of course, the risk involved with the study of crises as life tasks is that they obscure from view the daily tasks to which individuals are also directing attention. For example, if, as McFall argued, we should select task units that can easily be translated into "how to do it" terms (1982; p. 15), crises may not be the right unit of analysis— after all, people's everyday activities are not organized by or given motivating force by a crisis task, almost by definition. In this light, others have purposely selected tasks so as to represent the full array of commonplace activities in people's lives (Little, 1983). From this approach, tasks are typically defined in terms of the "personal projects" on which people see themselves as struggling and for which they can point to specific events or situations that commonly occur as evidence of those struggles.

   6. Ill-defined or well-defined solutions?   A very important and general feature that seems to differentiate life tasks is the extent to which the task presents a *clearly agreed upon problem* and, correspondingly, a single *scripted or preferred solution.* Some tasks are so well defined, with clear agreement on the problem at hand and the goal in sight, that practically everyone will use the same procedure for working towards a solution; ordering food in a restaurant, for example, is a problem in social life that is *relatively* well defined or scripted (Abelson, 1981), while properly greeting a new neighbor presents a somewhat less well-defined problem which could be construed by different people as part of different "tasks," e.g., winning friends or requesting help (Cantor & Kihlstrom, 1985).
   The extent to which a task is well defined (and carries a scripted solution) varies with the other features of life tasks which we have discussed. For example, global or universal or rare tasks tend to present quite ill-defined problems with much leeway in the preferred or relevant solutions. By contrast, the more explicit, commonplace, or circumscribed tasks, in which the task is clearly linked to specific life situations or events or even actions, come very close to being so well defined that they may not represent problems at all; in those instances, the rules of the game are clear

to all, the position of the players is ritualized, and there is no doubt when a successful solution is near (Argyle, 1981).

The choice of more or less well-defined tasks presents a true dilemma in the study of individual differences in problem-solving behavior: If the chosen tasks are too global, so as to be quite ill defined, then the observed behavior may not be representative of people's typical responses or "personalities"; however, to the extent that the tasks present well-defined problems and little freedom in the relevant solutions, then few informative individual differences are likely to emerge. As is frequently the case, a proper middle ground must be found in sampling life tasks so as to maximize the observation of *meaningful* patterns of variation across individuals or within an individual across the life span. Before we specify the present approach to life tasks, therefore, it may be useful to review a few examples of other perspectives.

Adler's "Style of Life"

For Alfred Adler, the most basic or global task for all human beings is to overcome the inevitable feelings of *inferiority* that accompany infancy and childhood. However, despite the universality of our precarious beginnings, Adler (1929, 1931) emphasized in his "individual psychology" the essential differences between people. People differ in the special *meaning* they give to their inferior state—i.e., in their "opinion of life"—and in the "style of life" or pattern of striving and meeting problems that they develop. Interestingly, it is the young child, before the age of five, who creates and constructs the personal meaning of superiority-inferiority, based on a strong sense of experiencing the vicissitudes of early inferiority and dependency.

In other words, in Adler's theory the young child constructs, prelinguistically and without explicit awareness, an opinion of his or her strengths and weaknesses that, in turn, shapes the individual's own form of striving for superiority and security. In so doing, the universal task of overcoming inferiority has become the individual's unique task, manifest in every sphere of life activities—the task of working to "turn a minus situation into a plus one." Of course, the actual *style of life* or way of facing problems and striving for that special brand of superiority takes time and training to develop, but the initial themes around which the individual's life tasks will pivot are established quite early on and persist thereafter. It is these early themes that give coherence to the person's varied behavior. So, the concrete avenues for striving may change and the style of striving may vary, but the underlying goals remain relatively fixed for each individual, once his or her "opinion of life" is set.

For Adler, then, activities or events in life become part of an individual's set of life tasks because somehow the early themes of inferiority are evident in them and the person can strive to overcome similar feelings by working on those activities. The variety of adult activities which recruit basic strivings or goals is tremendous. Adler suggests, however, that three arenas of life most clearly reflect an individual's style of life: occupational activity, friendship patterns, and pursuit of intimacy and love. To see an individual's style of life, it is best to watch the ways in which he or she faces obstacles and difficult situations within these three key arenas of life activity. In the face of difficulty, not in the everyday commonplace occurrences of life, the early experiences of inferiority are most closely recreated. And the style of life that emerges may serve the individual's own needs for "superiority" best when the group or social needs or interests are met. In fact, the most "healthy" style of life involves striving for cooperation and the social good, being freed from the lower needs of personal, selfish power or physical security. So, the altruistic physician who strives to circumvent another's pain may also serve his own goals. For the physician the current situation of the patient may tap into early experiences of her own personal or interpersonal injury or insecurity and this occupation may allow for fulfillment of the feeling of inferiority that is uniquely hers (p. 181).

The individual's style of life is only implicit, derived as it is from early, preverbal experiences, but it organizes the goal-directed activity in these three basic domains of social life. To Adler, there is coherence in the individual's behavior in those arenas, because he or she sees problems through a single lens—the opinion of life—and works on them in a consistent manner—the style of life.

Klinger's "Current Concerns"

In a more recent discussion of the organizing role of *incentives* in human behavior, Eric Klinger (1977) joins Adler in arguing that the *meaning* in an individual's life is defined by the set of goals to which he or she has become *committed*— his or her collection of "current concerns." According to Klinger, individuals place negative and positive value on many potential end-states in life—everything from finishing a sandwich to achieving fame. Through innate mechanisms or various forms of learning, certain states, events, and objects acquire value for a particular person. However, in order to really understand and predict a person's goal-striving behavior, it is necessary to find those incentives to which he or she has a *current commitment*; those incentives that provide meaning in the person's life at this moment.

For Klinger, the key to uncovering central life tasks is not to ask an individual "What are you doing?" or even "What do you want?" directly, but rather to question the person about the things in his or her life that *give meaning* to life; things without which a *void* would exist. For example, when Klinger interviewed college students about the meaningful parts of their lives, the following classes of incentives emerged repeatedly:

personal relationships/friendships; "being on my own"; future job goals; recreational activities. While these are the general categories of incentives for all students, Klinger suggests that for a given individual the important incentives will be those connected to the concerns to which the student is currently committed. Within the domains of current concern the student's actions, thoughts (including fantasy material and dreams), affective reactions, and focus of attention will reveal the ways in which particular incentives have become *tasks* then and there.

Just as the attractiveness of an incentive shifts for an individual over time and exposure, so too does the status of current concerns fluctuate. These changes are in themselves revealing. In fact, for Klinger the most interesting studies are those that chart the individual's cycle of commitment/striving/battling obstacles and then his or her attainment or disengagement from a current concern. For Klinger, as for Adler, the important life tasks are quite uniquely constructed by the thinking individual. Unlike Adler, however, Klinger argues that individuals' current concerns shift and vary without a presumption about an underlying core theme.

Little's "Personal Projects"

An even more recent task analysis approach that also emphasizes personal incentives and plans and goals is that of Brian Little. Little (1985) is interested in individuals' choices of *personal projects* around which to organize their daily life activities. Building upon Henry Murray's (1951) earlier notion of "serials" in people's lives, Little defines his task unit as follows: "a personal project is a set of interrelated acts extending over time, which is intended to maintain or attain a state of affairs foreseen by the individual" (1983; p. 276). These projects, ranging for college students from finishing a term paper to finding a best friend, are *explicitly* articulated and framed by the individual, and the individual organizes everyday commonplace activities according to these special projects. In contrast to Adler's beliefs, and perhaps even more directly than in Klinger's scheme, Little suggests that the plans and projects on which individuals say they are working at any given time are, in fact, the central organizing forces in their behavior.

Of course, individuals' projects are constrained and afforded by the opportunities in their environment; however, people differ significantly in their choices of projects, the size and difficulty and consuming nature of those projects, the length of time encompassed by a project, and the number of projects potentially demanding attention at any given time. In other words, everyone in a given life environment has a system of personal projects; however, the content of their goals and plans differs, as do the structure and elaborateness of their collection of projects.

Little makes the intriguing suggestion of including in the task analysis an entire family or social group's set of consuming personal projects. The assumption here is that one of the main determinants of a smoothly functioning group is the compatability—with respect to time and resources and values—of the projects of individuals in the group. For example, one can imagine a smooth-running roommate relationship between two first-year college students, one of whom is focused on the project of "overcoming my shyness" while the other plans to "stop being so bossy and assertive." While Little assumes that these personal projects are quite idiosyncratic and dependent upon a person's prior experiences, people can and do communicate about their projects and work on adapting their plans to fit the needs and resources in their current life environment. Personal projects are typically quite flexible and fluid, they are embedded in people's daily activity, and they emerge, in part, to give that activity a future-directed and cohesive structure.

In these three descriptions of important life tasks, the critical feature emphasized is the personal incentive associated with working on the task for the individual. Although each theorist provides examples of life tasks and the ways in which they emerge for particular people at particular times, there is relatively little focus on the universality of certain incentives or the stage-of-development at which some tasks become specially meaningful to many individuals. In delineating a set of informative tasks, other theorists, by contrast, have entered the large sample of potentially relevant tasks via a search for more universally applicable, though often stage-linked human needs or goals or tasks (e.g., Maslow, 1970; Erikson, 1950). Next, we will sample a few such schemes for studying *basic life tasks*.

Universal Needs or Tasks

Several theorists have suggested that there exists a hierarchy of basic (universally experienced) needs which motivate goal-directed human behavior (e.g., Rotter, 1954; Rogers, 1951; Murray, 1938). One prominent proponent of this position, Abraham Maslow (1968), went so far as to construct a hierarchy of basic needs which individuals work to fulfill, beginning with the common physiological drives, moving to the more complex safety needs and needs for belongingness and love, and gradually ascending to much more complex needs for esteem and self-actualization. These basic needs, then, define the goals that motivate human striving, as well as the order in which these goals become salient. Of course, each individual works at these tasks somewhat differently, but Maslow emphasized more strongly than Adler the common components in goal-directed striving, going so far as to characterize the traits and attributes common to the very few people who reach full self-actualization. While the basic needs serve as common benchmarks for individuals, the potential for human *growth* is ample, as people make their way towards fulfilling higher and higher basic goals, further and further from the lower, primary drives.

Working from an evolutionary, functionalist perspective, others have come to stress also the finite set of basic problems of survival which become tasks for animals at all levels of phylogenetic development. In fact, Plutchik (1980) derives a set of eight basic emotions (defined as cycles of activity involving cognition, feeling, and behavior) which correspond to people's efforts to work on eight basic survival tasks (see also Chapter 4). According to Plutchik, species confront these problems in different forms; interesting comparisons are then possible with regard to the form in which a basic task is manifest. Moreover, in this scheme, "emotions are reflections of the adaptations that animals make to universal problems" (p. 32); the emotion cycle, say one of *fear* for example, signals the animal's effort to establish equilibrium in a life-task domain, the domain of hierarchy/ dominance in that case. The fear cycle includes cognitions, such as the interpretation of a threat, feelings of fear that accompany that interpretation, and efforts to reestablish a balance, including running for protection or, in the more assertive anger cycle, attacking to attain dominance.

In the case of Maslow and Plutchik, basic life tasks provide global guides to human problem-solving activity. In order to narrow the description of these tasks (and the associated problem-solving behavior) a bit more, others have worked with the developmental life cycle, attaching certain basic needs and tasks to critical periods of development. Two such examples are described briefly below.

Stage-Linked Basic Tasks

Certainly the most well-known and comprehensive stage theory of basic social life tasks is that of Erik Erikson. In *Childhood and Society* (1950), Erikson presents a scheme of eight basic stages of ego development across the life cycle, in which each stage is associated with a special life task for the individual to negotiate (however successfully). According to Erikson, as the individual matures he or she becomes ready for a new task, the solution of which is facilitated by exposure and practice in social institutions appropriately geared to that stage of life. So, for example, the child entering school for the first time approaches the task of "industry vs. inferiority" by building on the successful solution of earlier life tasks— trust, autonomy and initiative—and by working away at this new task in the context of the rituals of school-life. In Erikson's scheme, there is room for variation in the solutions to these tasks, since the tasks are structured somewhat differently by different cultures' rituals. There is variation, too, in the smoothness with which individuals, given their own particular experiences and growth patterns, traverse the life stages and accomplish successful solutions to each basic task.

In a recent "take-off" on Erikson's stages of ego development, Levinson and his colleagues have presented an in-depth look at the basic tasks of adult men as they transit from parental home and adolescence to the perils of independent mid-life (Levinson, 1978). Based on biographies of forty men, interviewed at ages 35–45, Levinson suggests five relatively universal transition points or stages between the ages of 18 and 45; at each stage a particular set of tasks becomes the focal point for personal growth. Although these tasks are often quite general, as in the case of the task of "making it" during the settling down stage in the early thirties, frequently there are specific patterns of activities that mark the emergence of task-directed goals; for example, in "making it," the male in his early thirties articulates a deeper commitment to work and to family.

The tasks are linked to the demands that the social environment places on an individual during each stage of life, as when the adolescent goes to college or the military and is burdened with becoming financially independent. However, even in the context of these age-linked and socially-prescribed transitions in life tasks, Levinson and his colleagues leave some room for the personal articulation and construal of appropriate "dreams" and values and incentives. That is, by the time the twenty-year-old has really embarked on "getting into the adult world," his dreams and values begin to be seen clearly in the "life structure"—the roles, memberships, style of living and fantasies—that he creates and reconstructs over the next few stages of personal definition. Once again, though, it is assumed that there are relatively universal and age-linked adult developmental periods within which variations take place.

LIFE TASKS: AN INTEGRATION AND EXAMPLE

At the outset of this chapter we argued that if the cognitive basis of personality is to be revealed in individuals' problem-solving behavior, then it is critical to find a set of problems which will be informative about those individual differences. In the subsequent discussion, we have pointed to a number of features that differentiate types of tasks, and provided examples of different theorists' schemes for choosing a set of important life tasks for analysis. Now it is time to settle on a working definition or description of *life tasks* so that we may proceed to analyze the dynamics of individuals at work on problem solving. In so doing, we will pick and choose from the schemes of others in an effort to generate a set of tasks that are at once of general applicability, embedded within the daily lives of many, and yet ill-defined enough to allow for considerable variation in the *meaning* of the task and the preferred forms of problem-solving *solutions.*

Loose Definition

In this spirit, we loosely define an individual's *current life tasks* as the set of tasks which the person sees himself or herself as working on and devoting energy to solving during a specified period in life. These are the tasks which individuals perceive to be central and important in their lives during a stated period of time. These are the tasks, as articulated by several colleagues, of "getting tenure," "handling a two-career marriage," and "staying fit and trim." In Klinger's terms, these are the incentives for which an individual is currently committed to striving, the tasks that give meaning to an individual's life at that point in time. Life tasks organize a significant number of a person's activities over a substantial period of time and imbue them with specific meaning. Consequently, considering the life task as a unit of analysis facilitates an understanding of (everyday) problem-solving activity as future-oriented and goal-directed.

Life tasks, then, suggest end-states which, when accomplished, would imply a significant change for the person. In that sense, life tasks reflect the major goals or dreams or style of life that individuals shape for themselves (Adler, 1931; Levinson, 1978). Still, life tasks are played out in the arena of daily life as they are embedded in ongoing activities. Indeed, people can point easily to the situations or problems or events that reside within the scope of a life task (Little, 1983). And, when major transitions in life take place, the focus of attention often shifts to new life tasks or back to old ones now in new forms (Levinson, 1978; Veroff, 1983).

Critical Features

What, then, are the critical features of life tasks so defined? First, and most importantly, these are tasks which the individual articulates through his or her own eyes as being self-relevant, time-consuming, and meaningful. These are the "demands" in the environment which a person has construed as "desires" (both negative and positive incentives) for himself or herself (Reich & Zautra, 1983). While people certainly do not have conscious awareness of all of the tasks on which they work, we join McFall, Klinger, & Little in promoting the heuristic value of allowing individuals to define for us the central tasks for themselves; at the least, those tasks will be ones on which people are motivated to work. These self-generated life tasks should provide a kind of map or organizing scheme for the consuming activities of the individual (including those that are never successfully negotiated). As in the case of Little's (1983) personal projects, these life tasks are embedded in the ongoing daily life of the individual—in the situations, events and thoughts which fill days and nights. In specifying a life task, an individual ought to be able to enumerate his or her task-relevant activities. However, the concept of life task itself is a more molar unit than the single project, as it is intended to encompass a related set of goal-directed activities over a substantial period of time. It is assumed, moreover, that the activities that serve a single goal, or life task, change in content over the life span (see also Veroff, 1983, on this point).

Because we believe that the important tasks are those which people construct for themselves, it is critical that life tasks capture the personal meaning of daily life activity for each individual. However, individuals live in *social* environments and construct their self-relevant life tasks in that social context. Therefore, another feature of life tasks is that they are assumed to be responsive to the demands, structure, and constraints of the social environment, that is, the culture in which the person has grown and learned to adapt. It seems quite likely, for example, that there will be common themes within the central life tasks of people embarking on a shared transition in life (Levinson, 1978). In order to reveal that commonality, life tasks should really be defined by the individual for a particular and fairly substantial "chunk" of time in life. Group comparisons are most profitably made within the context of an obvious life period, i.e., one which makes sense to the participant as a specified unit.

In fact, we agree with Erikson and others in that tradition, in arguing for the special value of the study of *transition* periods, those times of entrance into new institutions. The value of the transition period is not that all individuals' life tasks and problem-solving styles will then look uniform and well-defined; rather, it is that during these times the demands and constraints in the social environment are often made (painfully) clear. In the face of clear social demands the individual becomes especially aware of his or her role in shaping personal life tasks. Life transitions, then, are good times to see the constructive activity of the motivated individual.

Yet, there is no necessary reason to believe that there is a fixed order or universal content to the life tasks that individuals shape for themselves in any particular period in life. Unlike Erikson (1950), or even the more contemporary stage theorists (Levinson, 1978), we assume that individuals flexibly construct appropriate tasks for themselves, given their unique history and values and needs. Certain tasks may be encouraged by the social institutions or maturational patterns characteristic of certain times in life, but the presence of an incentive does not ensure its meaning for an individual (Klinger, 1975). There is little reason to assume that people are locked into an inevitable unfolding sequence of universal life tasks. Indeed, as patterns of socially acceptable life "schedules" are relaxed (e.g., timing of marriage, childbearing, career changes) within certain biological limits, the timing of life transitions and the kinds of tasks that are associated with them become more and more unique across individuals.

Hence, in defining and measuring life tasks, the personologist walks a very tricky tightrope between the search for universal, common themes and presentation of an accurate vision of the life tasks of real individuals—a dilemma common to all such endeavors (Allport, 1937). Life tasks are constructed within constraints emanating from structured social environments (Stokols, 1982) and they are shaped by individuals who are subject to common evolutionary pressures and problems (Plutchik, 1980). Common themes of intimacy, control, identity, and power do characterize our strivings, at some level of generality. However, what is interesting and distinctly creative about people are the infinite variations on those common themes as manifest in the actual tasks which people make their own. As much as we may want to be sensitive, as researchers, to capturing those more basic themes, we do well to recall that life tasks are interesting largely because they are *ill-defined*. Individuals, even within common life periods and environments, differ in their interpretations of what the actual "problem" to be solved is and in their preferred means of attacking the task. Each person shapes a set of current life tasks in response to his or her own history of social experiences and the particular concepts and goals made salient by those experiences. The individual's social intelligence guides interpretations and solutions for life tasks. There are neither definitive solutions nor even single definitions of the life tasks for any given group of people. Life tasks are *pressing* and *engaging*, but *ill-defined*.

College Life Tasks

In our attempts to find an optimal task unit of analysis, it is helpful to turn from the theoretical drawing-board to the practical testing ground. For this purpose Cantor et al. (1985) chose the transition from high school and home to college life as a particularly informative period in which to investigate life tasks. First-year college students clearly feel quite motivated to tackle the demands of a new environment; they speak explicitly of "taking personal control" over their new lives by working on new problems energetically or learning to face old ones in different, more productive, ways. The transition itself naturally encourages some uniformity in the salient life tasks because similar pressures are encountered by most beginning students—increasing academic and social pressures and the need to define changing relationships with family and friends. Against this backdrop of uniformity, however, the individual first-year student has his or her uniquely construed life tasks and problem-solving strategies.

In the context of this sometimes difficult, but always challenging transition, Cantor et al. (1985) asked students in the middle of their first year in the Honors College at the University of Michigan to describe their experiences in terms of ". . . the areas to which you have been, and expect to be directing your energies; your thoughts about what will make this both a good and bad year for you; and the plans you have made for accomplishing some of your goals during your time here. . . ." These instructions were intended to orient the students toward the time-consuming and important activities in their ongoing school life which they construed as *goal-directed* and personally *demanding*.

As expected, these students found it easy and even helpful to think about their time-consuming and pressing life tasks. On average they each listed eight or nine life tasks that currently held their attention. Moreover, when asked to code their own tasks into six "normative" task categories, the students were able to fit over 80 percent of their personal concerns into these commonly-held task categories: Social life concerns of "making friends" or "being on my own" and "establishing an identity"; and academic concerns of "getting good grades" and "establishing a future direction" and "managing my time and getting organized." Hence, at a general level of description, the life task themes for these students centered on issues of intimacy, achievement, and self-control (see Klinger, 1977; Little, 1983 for similar reports).

The role of these life tasks in providing (personally-construed) meaning and organization to the students' ongoing daily activities could be seen quite clearly in these protocols. In mapping the meaning of a life task for a student, differences were evident in the students' construal of these six important life tasks (measured by ratings on scales such as: stress, challenge, difficulty, absorption, enjoyment) and in the *intricacy of the plans* for handling the situations that comprise the tasks (measured by coding the complexity of their plans according to the number of alternative actions being considered and the extent to which a full action sequence was anticipated for each outcome).

Generally, the students found their important academic tasks, such as "getting good grades" and "carving a future direction," more demanding and stressful than was the case for social life tasks, such as "making friends" and "being on my own." The situations associated with "getting good grades," for example, were seen as difficult to handle, likely to end in "worst-case outcomes." Meanwhile the students were much more optimistic about "making friends": They had well-specified but highly scripted and simple plans for coping with social life situations. By contrast, they typically felt "at sea" in "getting good grades" and, perhaps as a consequence, were likely to experiment with multiple, alternative plans for these task-situations. The academic life tasks (e.g., "getting good grades") were perceived as far more of an "unknown" challenge for these students than were the equivalently central social life tasks (e.g., "making friends"). Perhaps the latter type of task provides the students with a natural cushioning device to help alleviate the stresses and strains of the transition to college life, so that when "things get rough" in the academic sphere, these students may turn their psychological attention to the more "under control" and therefore rewarding social domain (Klinger, 1975, hypothesized a similar interaction between different "current concerns"). Interestingly, by their second year of college life, these students have come to view their social life tasks with more trepidation. Accordingly, their strategies for coping with social life tasks are now more intricate and time-consuming. The interplay between the students' two key task domains seems to change as they turn from first-year college "novices" to seasoned "experts" in this life environment (Cantor, Brower, & Korn, 1984).

When these students were asked to provide details about their activities, plans, and feelings in each central life-task domain, the *unique construals* of common themes also emerged quite readily. Students' "readings" of the *activities* involved in a task varied considerably. So, while one student believed the task of "being on my own" involved learning to handle the stress of personal failures without "dad's hugs," another concentrated on the more practical side of independence—"managing money," "eating well." Students with similar activities in mind for common life tasks, such as "preparing for a difficult exam" as part of "getting good grades," anticipated using very different *strategies of action* in these situations, such as "cramming until the end" vs. "going out drinking to relax before the exam" (Jones & Berglas, 1978; Snyder, 1985). Even within the commonly feared academic domain, there were clear differences in plans for handling the stress: some students imagined "best-case scenarios" and avoided any intricate planning, while others worked through their fears about the likelihood of "worst-case" outcomes in generating extremely intricate plans (Norem & Cantor, 1986c). These different interpretations of common life tasks translated into very different ways of addressing these "problems." Most important, the personal construal of normatively salient life tasks initiated a chain of cognitive-behavioral activity with repercussions for these students' future performance (Cantor et al., 1985). For example, students with equivalently good prior academic records (SAT, high school GPA), diverged significantly on measures of *Winter term GPA* and of *perceived stress*, in line with the amount of detailed reflective thinking demonstrated in their plans (from Fall term) for handling life-task situations. Those students who experimented with more alternatives in their plans generally had better academic records and felt less stressed in their daily life activities (Cohen et al., 1983). Interestingly though, individual difference analyses revealed some striking exceptions to the "plan reflectivity"–"good outcomes" relationship. Students who characteristically construe the difficult academic tasks with confidence and optimism, did far better in GPA (and stress) when they *avoided* reflective planning ahead of time. By contrast, students with an unexpectedly pessimistic attitude towards academic tasks (despite excellent achievement records), performed much better on GPA when they *confronted* their fears with a reflective planning strategy. These "defensive pessimists" (Norem & Cantor, 1986c) fit the overall pattern in which it helps to reflect in detail about potentially risky life-task events, though their level of perceived stress remains quite high. The "optimists," who do just as well in the end, arrive at positive outcomes through their own idiosyncratic means. These results, and several other similar construal-planning patterns, begin to highlight the *motivating* function of life-task construals; individuals find unique strategies for solving their unique version of a normative life task.

APPRAISING THE VALUE OF THE LIFE-TASK ANALYSIS

Even preliminary attempts to develop an integrated, albeit loose, definition of the life-task unit and to test this approach in the context of students making the transition to college life, suggest the potential for a rich analysis of individuals' problem-solving strategies within life-task domains. Individuals seem to have little difficulty delineating the tasks which consume them. The concept of life tasks provides a useful framework on which to map daily life activity, while simultaneously highlighting the engaging and demanding problems which engender highly-charged emotions and motivate intricate plans. By concentrating the analysis within a well-circumscribed life period, it is also possible to see common life tasks, even as individuals go about "solving" them in different ways. Additionally, looking across the different important life tasks for a single individual reveals the complexity of the life-task system as a functioning whole at any given time (see Little, 1983 on project *systems*).

The life-task construct serves as a convenient theoretical tool in the analysis of the cognitive bases of personality, i.e., social intelligence. Taking this approach, a *unit of analysis* is specified: one studies the person at work in a personally-articulated life task domain over a period of life announced by entrance into a new social institution, such as a new job, marriage, or school experience. The life task provides a *frame* for the individual's activity, revealing a relatively coherent package of motivated problem solving. Life tasks also specify a focus for *assessment* efforts: the focus is on the cognitive-behavioral strategies used and reused and reshaped by individuals as they gain experience within a life-task domain. Looking across domains and over time, it may be possible to see the dynamics of personality at work, as people negotiate a social environment, construct new strategies for action, shape new life tasks for themselves, and seek out new ways to give their lives *meaning* and their activities *direction*. Finally, as more insight is gained into the different strategies that people use in working on life tasks, it may then be possible to link the choice of a particular problem-solving approach to aspects of the person's declarative and procedural knowledge and episode memories in that life-task domain. In so doing, we come full circle, back to the social intelligence expertise that makes the person distinctive and special.

II. STRATEGIES: PROBLEM SOLVING ON LIFE TASKS

Having arrived at a somewhat sharper definition of life tasks, we are now in a position to begin to ask about the ways in which individuals go about working on these pressing personal concerns (projects, agendas). The ultimate objective, then, is to characterize differences in problem-solving strategies, which, in turn, seem to derive from variations in the knowledge—concepts, goals, memories, rules—which people bring to bear on a life task. First, as was the case for life tasks, it is necessary to arrive at a working definition and description of a *problem-solving strategy* that is flexible enough to be applicable in the complex social life domains at issue here (see Gagne, 1984; Anderson, 1981, for discussions of problem-solving strategies broadly defined).

Adopting the person by life-task unit helps somewhat in the difficult job of simplifying the social interaction sequence so as to be able to observe problem-solving strategies. For the purposes of a life-task analysis, the interaction is considered from the perspective—through the eyes, so to speak—of one actor, who is known to "see" a specific life task embedded within the situation. The analysis, then, begins with the knowledge of that person's *goals* in this life-task situation. The aim is to describe the set of procedures—a *strategy*—that he or she uses in an effort to achieve those goals.

Strategies for working on life tasks are complex because everything about the interaction is in flux: the situation changes as the actors interact; the target person's goals and agendas shift during the unfolding interaction; sometimes the person even turns to work on another life task, as his or her goals change, and a new strategy surfaces. So, even with the simplifying assumptions of a life-task analysis, it is still the case that only a frozen slice of the full interaction sequence is captured in any one analysis.

Loose Definition

With these caveats on the table, it is time to provide a loose working definition of a problem-solving *strategy* in the context of complex life-task domains. We refer to a strategy as the set of cognitive processes that link a person's goals to his or her subsequent behavior in a life-task situation. That is, the strategy involves the ways in which the person interprets the "problem" and plans a "solution" so as to be consistent with his or her prevalent goals in that "task." Borrowing from Bruner et al. (1956), one might say that a strategy is "a pattern of decisions in the acquisition, retention, and utilization of information that serves to meet certain objectives, i.e., to insure certain forms of outcomes and insure against certain others" (p. 54).

Strategies are "strategic" only in the sense of being goal-directed or initiated in the service of personal goals; not in the lay sense of the term, as in manipulative or false or deceptive. Frequently individuals are unaware of their strategies in the course of an interaction, often because they have become "second nature" through practice (Smith, 1984). At other times, when faced with particularly agonizing or especially important task situations, the need for a coherent strategy is painfully obvious, though one is not always easy to find; such is often the case in the midst of a life crisis of illness or bereavement or injury (Wortman, 1983). More typically, individuals are somewhat aware of their goals ("I've got to get over my panic") and occasionally in tune with favorite strategies ("If I prepare for the worst it won't seem so bad after all"), though still, actions seem to unfold quite automatically and without too much effort.

Regardless of the performer's level of awareness as the strategy is translated into action, the central notion in a cognitive strategy is one of "executive control" (see Gagne, 1984), implying that the person has taken control of interpretations, plans, and actions in the service of a pressing goal (Showers & Cantor, 1985). In that sense, the strategy reflects the striving toward the goal in the form of a coherent, though diverse set of reactions that "make sense" for that person in that life-task situation at that time.

THE COMPONENTS OF STRATEGIES

Problem-solving strategies involve fine-tuned coordination of declarative and procedural knowledge. A strategy draws on a variety of rules for interpreting actions and events and problems, for planning and monitoring behavior, for evaluating progress towards a goal, and for understanding the causes of an outcome. The strategy is composed of select elements from the wide array of declarative and procedural knowledge—the concepts and rules in the repertoire—so as to guide problem-solving activity in a direction consistent with the person's current life-task goals. As Gagne notes: "In many studies of learning and of human problem solving, it has been repeatedly shown that learners bring to new tasks not only previously learned declarative knowledge and procedural knowledge but also some skills of *when* and *how* to use this knowledge" (1984, p. 381).

A *strategy* is involved when the problem-solver makes a concerted effort (whether consciously or not) to pull together different aspects of knowledge in the service of shaping a plan of action well suited to some pressing goals. Therefore, in order to understand the complexity and power of cognitive strategies, and to see the variations in preferred ones, it is important to unpack the components in the problem-solving cycle, i.e., to see the different rules that underlie each component. Frequently it seems as if the interpreting and planning and evaluating just run off effortlessly as people work on life tasks. But smoothness of production should not be confused with true "mindlessness" (cf. Langer, 1978); at each point in the problem-solving cycle an impressive array of knowledge is being brought to bear in the service of action. This point is best illustrated by considering the basic concepts and rules that comprise the structure of strategies.

Playing Through Outcomes

One of the most common ways in which people begin working on a problem is to "get a sense of the problem" by playing through or "simulating" a number of possible outcomes or end-states (Kahneman & Tversky, 1982). We say to ourselves, "Well, this could happen and the result would be awful, or that could occur and I'd be thrilled." The simulation takes no time at all, but the cognitive procedures involved are considerable. For example, as the simulation unfolds, various hypotheses or hunches about the likelihood of different plausible outcomes are tested by scanning through autobiographical memory for similar episodes or by comparing this situation to others about which something is known.

Fortunately, while people probably do run-through or simulate *multiple* plausible outcomes in preparation for an important task, the sample of outcomes is reduced greatly by prior beliefs and expectations (see Langer, 1970; Gilovitch, 1983, on gamblers' beliefs about outcomes in games of "chance"). Most people assume that "things will turn out well" in a "just world" (Lerner, 1970). Everyone, for example, underestimates the potential for personal misfortune (see Weinstein, 1980; Slovic, Fischoff, & Lichtenstein, 1976 on the underestimation of the likelihood of personal injury, disease, or accidents). However, once the risk in a situation has been emphasized, even if only slightly by the wording of an instruction, the potential for worst-case outcomes becomes the natural and feared hypothesis to test (Kahneman & Tversky, 1982). In other words, there are many different shortcut paths that delimit the simulation process.

Planning and Monitoring

In the midst of forming impressions in a situation and generating plausible outcomes, people also formulate specific *plans,* carry them into action and *monitor* the results. Often multiple plans are considered and discarded, even as first impressions are being coalesced—the social interaction problem-solving cycle is indeed complex. At the basis of the planning activity is procedural knowledge that allows for a "means-end analysis" in which a goal(s) is formulated and different action sequences or *tactics* are constructed as means to that goal or end-state (Baron, 1982; Spivak et al., 1976). This analysis requires people to think in cause-effect terms about very intricate social interactions, negotiations, or confrontations (see Klos et al., 1983, on strategic problem solving in negotiations). In this process of playing through, *ordering* principles of temporal-spatial action and reaction relations are particularly important (see Crockett, 1984, on the universality of linear ordering schemes in human thought).

The cognitive challenge posed by most social interaction planning is increased by awareness of the tendency of others *not* to "cooperate" with exact expectations and plans (Hilton & Darley, 1985). For example, Klos et al. (1983) asked college students to "negotiate" with roommates about sleeping schedules and other potential conflicts. Those students who attempted strategically to plan reported "a dual level of experiencing: carrying on a dialogue with the other person, while simultaneously making tactical decisions and evaluating progress toward the interaction goal of conflict resolution" (p.14).

The nice thing about many life-task situations is that they often unfold in familiar circumstances for which there *is* interindividual agreement about some basic scripts or "rules of the game" (Argyle, 1981; Forgas, 1982). Of course, the existence of some well-defined scripts for behavior is no guarantee that things will unfold *as planned*. Social scripts are frequently violated, as when the unknowing hostess becomes the target for a game of pin the tail on the donkey. The individual, even as he or she obeys the common scripts and rules of conversation has to construct new and innovative ways to "get his or her message across" (see Higgins & McCann, 1982, on the "communication game").

Throughout the problem-solving cycle there is constant *monitoring* taking place. In order to negotiate a task effectively, each person has to monitor the success of his or her plans, the discrepancy between his or her intention and achieved outcome, the feelings and reactions of the others in the interaction, and more (Meichenbaum, 1977; Miller, Galanter, & Pribram, 1960). Monitoring in an ongoing interaction involves some fairly complicated "mental calculus." First, the discrepancy between "where you are now" and "where you want to be" (i.e., the goal standard of comparison) has to be updated constantly (see Carver & Scheier, 1981 on the feedback-monitoring process). If that discrepancy is too great it may not be worth the effort to persist in the present direction, i.e., either a new tactic or altered goal is needed or the performer may just withdraw from the task. If the discrepancy is very small, the performer may choose to increase effort in a final burst of activity.

Typically, the discrepancy is anything but clearcut, and further mental calculations are necessary. For example, many researchers have suggested that persistence in a task is a function of the performer's *expectancy* for a successful outcome multiplied by the *value* placed on achieving that outcome (Rotter, 1954; Atkinson, 1981). This calculation becomes more complicated if the *price* or cost of performing the actions necessary to reach the goal is included (Klinger, 1977). Also, as Bandura (1977) has pointed out, the expectancy for a successful outcome often involves two calculations—the expectancy that if you perform the planned action then you will really reach your goal (outcome expectancy), and, more importantly, the expectancy that you will actually be able to perform that action (self-efficacy expectation).

The monitoring procedures are even more intricate when the comparison process includes others' performance at the same task, as it frequently does (see Nicholls, 1984, on achievement motivation as a function of social comparison information). In some tasks the impact of feedback about the discrepancy between current performance and the desired end-state is moderated by social comparison information of others' standings at the same moment (Darley & Goethals, 1980). Another factor to figure into this monitoring equation is the fluctuation of the perceived value of reaching a particular goal over the course of involvement in the task. Klinger (1975) points out that the incentive to attain a goal varies as a function of the obstacles that arise, the success of related goal-directed efforts, the mood state of the person at the time, and simple experience at the task. Moreover, the paradox of goal-setting is that people are often less intrigued or impressed with an end-state the closer they come actually to achieving it. That is, people frequently adjust goals "upwards" as they update their expectations based on the current achievements (see Lewin et al., 1944; Heckhausen, Schmalt, & Schneider, 1984). These factors make it all the more impressive that people execute the procedures of performance monitoring at all (Kuhl, 1985).

People do develop different patterns of monitoring as a function of experiences in a situation (see Swann, Stephenson, & Pittman, 1981, on learned helplessness and information-seeking behavior). For example, in the face of some stressful events, such as an impending operation or an unfolding serious illness, some people choose to increase their information-seeking and monitoring behavior, while others choose to "blunt" the stress by avoidance (Miller & Mangan, 1983; Baum et al., 1982; Wortman, 1983). Some people may even develop habitual patterns of "repressing" or "sensitizing" in the face of risk, conflict, anxiety (see Bell & Byrne, 1977).

Finally, the target of one's monitoring may shift as a function of the nature of one's involvement in a particular task (Greenwald, 1982). In certain tasks a person may be very "task-involved," focusing on personal standards of performance and learning, while in other tasks that same person may be very "ego-involved," monitoring personal performance in comparison to others' behavior and simultaneously striving to "do well" and to "leave the right impression" (Nicholls, 1984; Schlenker, 1980). There are multiple ways to "be involved" in an important task and correspondingly many ways to monitor the success of one's efforts at the task.

Attributions and Retrospections

A great deal of the cognitive activity that occurs in the midst of a task, and that follows the resolution of the performance, involves attempts to understand the causes of an outcome (e.g., attributions about one's own or another person's behavior), to evaluate the inevitability of that outcome (e.g., decisions about personal control over the outcome), and to retrospect about similar past events or (re)construct alternative scenarios for how things could have gone differently. In other words, a great deal of cognitive energy is expended "making sense" of past events and establishing some degree of "control" over the outcomes via this deeper understanding (Harvey & Weary, 1984). Accounts of why and how things happened are constructed in the service, presumably, of gaining a sense of cognitive control and order and of learning how to do it differently (or the same) in future encounters (see, for example, Harvey et al., 1983, on accounts after the breakup of intimate relationships).

Frequently the mental calculus for attributions is simplified greatly by cues in the situation that suggest the plausibility of a particular interpretation (Taylor & Fiske, 1978), by prior beliefs about the likely causes of certain types of performances (Reeder & Brewer, 1979), and by "self-serving" or "self-protecting" intentions (Harvey & Weary, 1984; Tetlock & Levi, 1982). Thus, when a joint project goes well, for example, each participant suddenly claims to be the major contributor, a pattern that is exactly reversed in the face of undesired outcomes (see Ross & Sicoly, 1979, on the "contribution bias").

As noted previously, most of these shortcut procedures serve people well in the course of their everyday problem-solving efforts. When the goal is efficiency these heuristics provide for enormous "cognitive economy"; when the aim is to motivate continued effort at a difficult task, self-enhancing cognitive "tricks" may be quite effective (Norem & Cantor, 1986b). Moreover, when it is critical that attributions or interpretations be "defensible" people modulate their use of self-serving rules of judgment (see Weary et al., 1982). Whether these shortcuts arise from simple necessity in a complex cognitive system or from "deeper" motives of self-protection and enhancement (see Tetlock & Levi, 1982), it is wise to remember that they facilitate social problem solving, and keep people motivated and working hard on demanding life tasks (Bandura, 1986).

When it is all over and done with, at least for the moment, people still engage in strategic reworking and reviewing of past events, putting things in order and planning ahead for the future (see Greenwald, 1980 on "revisionist personal history"). The retrospective process involves memory retrieval, reevaluation, and interpretive procedures. Again, many shortcuts are used in this process of "putting it all in order." For example, in making sense of outcomes there often is a "biased scanning" of selective past experience. For most of us, the past looks rosier from this reconstructed view and more consistent with present attitudes and beliefs (e.g., Ross, McFarland, Conway, & Zanna, 1983). An interesting reversal of this typical pattern occurs when people have put effort into *changing* their habitual behavior. For example, when Conway & Ross (1984) convinced students to take part in an (actually ineffective) study skills improvement program, the students reevaluated their initial skills in a more negative light *after* engaging in the program of change as compared with those students who did not take part but performed just as (in)efficiently on both occasions.

In a similar vein, when an event occurs that patently violates expectations, individuals spend a great deal of cognitive effort explaining the causes of this unanticipated outcome (Hastie, 1981, 1984). The process is particularly painful in the case of regret for undesired outcomes, in which case people often try to mentally "undo" the event (see Landman, 1984, on regret and undoing). Interestingly, just as prospective "simulation" of possible future outcomes is often quite selective, retrospective "undoing" often involves imagining a change in some action that was "unusual," even though the action itself doesn't appear to have been causally related to the negative outcome in question (Kahneman & Miller, 1986). In a related phenomenon, people feel more regret when an undesirable outcome accompanies some overt action as compared with the same event in the absence of that action. This is so even when the action in question seems to be unrelated to the outcome being regretted (Landman, 1984).

However selective these retrospections might be, they seem to serve well in motivating future problem-solving behavior. For example, Ross et al. (1983) found that when asked to describe past behavior in an attitude domain such as health prevention efforts, people selectively retrieved examples of actions *consistent* with their present attitudes. Most importantly, having recalled that (biased) sample of past behavior, the subjects were even more *committed* than ever to engaging in new, attitude-consistent efforts. This effect provides a good example of the way in which a perfectly "unintentional" cognitive error, such as retrieving a selective sample of past behaviors because they are made cognitively available by focusing on a present attitude or behavior (Tversky & Kahneman, 1974), can serve to *motivate* future activity. It may be difficult to tease apart the cognitive and motivational underpinnings of social problem solving activity; yet, cognitive strategies for working on life tasks serve people well, regardless of the origin of each component procedure.

III. INDIVIDUAL DIFFERENCES IN PREFERRED STRATEGIES

It is easy to lose sight of the goal-directed nature and coherence of problem-solving strategies when they are decomposed into their components and the underlying procedural and declarative knowledge. However, we assume that when people are aroused and invested in life-task situations, the repertoire of procedural and declarative knowledge is used in a coherent fashion to serve the personal goals that are operative (though not necessarily consciously invoked) in that context. Therefore, in putting the pieces back together, we need to consider a situation(s) that fits within a salient life-task domain, identify different strategies that seem to serve different goals, and then consider the reasons that individuals may invoke or construct different goals and strategies in ostensibly similar situations.

Achievement Strategies

One domain in which it is possible to observe easily a wide variety of cognitive strategies is the set of achievement situations that tap personal concerns of competence or aptitude (Klinger, 1977; Weiner, 1985; Nicholls, 1984). As Cantor et al. (1985) observed, many college students find their academic tasks—facing exams, handling competition, setting reasonable performance standards, maintaining motivation—extremely absorbing, stressful, and demanding of intricate planning and monitoring. The academic life-task domain is quite challenging, even for the best of students. Thus, situations relating to concerns in this domain, such as the classic "test anxiety situation," are ideal settings in which to observe individual differences in the use of problem-solving strategies (Baumeister, 1985; Carver & Scheier, 1985).

In most achievement situations there are competing goals invoked, e.g., as Nicholls explains: "the goal is to develop or demonstrate—to self or to others—high ability, or to avoid demonstrating low ability" (1984, p. 328). There is the desire to avoid "failure," (subjectively defined), the need to prepare for "failure" should it occur, and the desire to achieve success. One needs to simultaneously protect self-esteem, and attempt to take advantage of an opportunity to enhance it. According to the present position, these goals are constructed by people as they engage in the particular task at hand; people construct a variety of goals depending on past experience and the knowledge brought to bear in the situation. Hence, there is little reason to expect that individuals will be very consistent in the goals invoked across different achievement situations (see Atkinson, 1981 for a somewhat different perspective). What is interesting, however, is the extent to which a given goal, once invoked within a particular situation, can call up a coherent pattern of activity—a problem-solving strategy—which serves to "insure certain outcomes and insure against others" (Bruner et al., 1956). In the following discussion we will look at a few such goal-directed achievement strategies (see Nicholls, 1984; Dweck, 1983, for more comprehensive treatments).

1. Embracing "success." Perhaps the most commonly described achievement strategy is the "optimistic" one (Norem & Cantor, 1986a; Showers & Cantor, 1984). The goal for the person using this strategy involves a straightforward striving for success based on high expectations derived from positive past experience, and a desire to enhance an already strong image of competence. However, as might be expected, given the complexity of achievement situations and the wealth of procedural knowledge at hand, this is not a "mindless," or effortless strategy. The confident optimist needs to select "tests" carefully so as to maximize the probability of "success," with the desired outcome defined not simply by the score on the test but rather by its diagnosticity with regard to true ability (Trope, 1979, 1986; Jones & Pittman, 1982). If he or she exerted effort on an "easy" task and succeeded, the success would reveal little about true ability; similarly, there is little point in working too hard at an "impossible" task, so just the right level of difficulty must be found (Nicholls, 1984).

Having selected a task by playing through these attributional consequences and considering past performances in similar situations, the optimist must still continue to monitor performance as a particular episode unfolds. He or she needs to increase effort if too little progress is being made and decrease "unnecessary" effort if the goal is coming too easily (in order to avoid an attribution of success to effort after the fact). If the desired success is achieved, the optimist may work to enhance the value of his or her performance by engaging in "downward social comparison" with those who did not fare as well, thereby increasing the sense of personal responsibility for an apparently rare successful performance (Wills, 1982; Alloy & Abramson, 1979). Perhaps more importantly, in the event of failure, the optimist must work to construe the situation in ways that protect self-esteem, for example, by denying having had control over a negative outcome (Norem & Cantor, 1986a). In the case of either apparent failure or apparent success, the optimist's strategy has served to "embrace success," in ways that are motivating during the task, and has served to enhance or protect his or her competence image after the performance is completed.

2. Preparing for "failure."   In many contexts, the desire to protect a sense of competence may overwhelm the goal of pursuing success when one confronts a stressful performance situation. Sometimes the need to prepare for failure stems from a faint distrust of prior successes, even though the secret hope for success is as strong as ever (Jones & Pittman, 1982). In these instances, multiple self-protective strategies are available for cushioning blows to self-esteem before the fact (Showers & Cantor, 1985). For example, Jones & Berglas (1978) refer to a "self- handicapping" strategy in which the person works to avoid any unequivocal feedback about low ability at an important task. The self-handicapping individual works to set up a protective "attributional environment" before any outcome is known. He or she places obstacles in the way of success, such as "drinking all night before an exam," or withdrawing preparatory effort in a test situation (Snyder, 1985). If failure occurs, the self-handicapper has a protective attributional "cover" or excuse already in place. If success is achieved, he or she appears exceptionally able, having done well against all odds.

Self-handicapping as a protective strategy for achievement situations can be contrasted to another anticipatory strategy called "defensive pessimism" (Norem & Cantor, 1986a, 1986b; Showers & Cantor, 1984). Using this strategy, individuals emphasize to themselves the possibility of failure by setting low expectations for their performance, despite successful past performances. That is, instead of withdrawing preparatory effort, the performer deals with the threat of failure by playing through a "worst-case" scenario in advance, and then working very hard to avoid that salient worst case. Pessimists cope with failure before it occurs by preparing themselves and potential audiences for the possibility beforehand, thus releasing some of the pressure of high expectations. Emphasizing negative possibilities may thus also serve to motivate increased effort by moderating the inhibitory effects of anxiety (Norem & Cantor, 1986b). The pessimist's defensive maneuver also works to neutralize any negative implications of hard work and effort—after all, it was never a question of whether hard work was necessary, given that the situation was structured a priori as one in which failure was all but inevitable. There is little need, when the situation is set up this way, for the defensive pessimist to resort to cognitive restructuring after the fact: a bad outcome and its implications have already been worked through (Norem & Cantor, 1986a). In fact, few outcomes will measure up to the "worst case" anticipated by the pessimist, since prior records of success and the hard work motivated by the strategy make failure very unlikely.

Neither the self-handicapping strategy nor the defensive pessimist strategy is likely to lead people to be happy with a "failure" performance. Both strategies, however, do serve to prepare individuals for the psychological consequences of potential failure. In addition, the self-handicapping strategy may enhance the self-esteem–boosting effects of success, and the defensive pessimist strategy may increase the potential for achieving success by motivating increased effort and reducing anxiety. Thus, both strategies can be seen as "intelligent" approaches to the "problem" of preparing for failure.

The Selection of Achievement Strategies

These achievement strategies serve to illustrate the *systematic* nature of cognitive processing as people work in situations which tap important life tasks (Nicholls, 1984). The procedural and declarative knowledge that underlies such strategic behavior can be combined and transformed so as to serve many different goals. Individuals draw on concepts and rules creatively to work towards a particular goal as it becomes predominant in a life task situation. While in practice it is common to get stuck in a particular problem-solving mode, in principle at least people exhibit considerable diversity in their favored strategies for handling different tasks. Hence, the "risk-taker" in one achievement situation is the "self-handicapper" in another testing context (Norem & Cantor, 1986b). Further, the differences in strategic achievement behavior rarely depend on obvious differences in performance ability per se. Instead, *perceived ability*

in the eyes of the performer seems to be the more critical variable underlying choice of strategy (Bandura, 1977, 1986).

1. Evaluative content.   The evaluative associations that a person has
formed from direct experience and indirect observation in achievement
situations will be absolutely critical as he or she faces each new testing
situation. Probably most influential in the goal-setting process will be the
feelings of self-efficacy and self-concept of ability derived from specific
autobiographical memories (Bandura, 1977; Harter, 1983). When we enter
new testing situations it is almost as if we are flooded by the affect
associated with memories of events in similar situations in the past. That
affective atmosphere is set up by specific feelings recalled in those situations and by a general evaluative association with "succeeding" or "failing" (or something in between) at that task. In fact, the evaluative tone
that characterizes self-concept of ability in a domain is likely to be based
on an aggregate (perhaps even an average) of evaluative reactions to past
life events in similar settings (Kihlstrom & Cantor, 1984). While the
defensive pessimist, for example, may "know" (intellectually) that he or
she has succeeded in the past in these kinds of tests of ability, the
evaluative associations to such situations may be negatively tinged by
memories of the anxiety and fatigue and worry that accompanied those
"winning" performances (Showers & Cantor, 1984). Those evaluative associations, in turn, may result in the construction of self-protective goals
in a new testing situation, though the potential for self-enhancement is
simultaneously acknowledged.

2. Personal potential.   As we discussed in earlier chapters, people's
self-concepts are complex and diverse in content (see Chapter 5). One
dimension of self-knowledge that is likely to be very influential as a person
considers different goals in an achievement situation is that of "potential,"
as studied by Markus and her colleagues (see Markus, 1983). On the basis
of past experience, and probably very much in line with the evaluative
tone of relevant autobiographical memories, people elaborate images of
themselves as they might ultimately become in an achievement domain;
e.g., the desired "star self" or the feared "stupid fool self." These possible
selves are as well-articulated as are concepts of "current" achievement
selves. That is, we may know as much about the feared "stupid self" as
about the currently precarious "achiever self." These are very vivid and
salient end-states because they are continuously elaborated in the course of
life's ongoing fantasy activity. Moreover, as some have argued, these
possible selves, and not the "validated" current self-concepts, may be the
key motivators of behavior (Markus, 1983; Cantor et al., 1986): Possible
selves can set up end-states to avoid, or attain, goals to achieve.

Most important for our analysis, the content of possible selves may
help to explain the divergent goals that people with similar past perfor-

mance records seem to pursue in achievement situations. For example, while the self-handicapper may have the same current self-concept of ability in a particular area as does an optimist, the spectre of a feared possible self—perhaps the "unloved failure"—may be stronger for one person than for the other. Jones & Berglas (1978) speculated that the self-handicapper's need for self-protection at all costs stemmed from a sort of "conditional love experiment" played by significant others in his or her life environment. It might be better to risk a failure that did not reflect on personal ability than to end up verifying the feared "stupid self" who would then truly be unworthy of attention and support.

3. Standard of comparison.   In the process of assessing the subjective probability of "looking good" in a situation, the performer has to compare himself or herself to some standard of comparison or ideal (Carver & Scheier, 1981). Individuals differ considerably in the content and extremity of those ideal standards (Beck, 1976). The optimist may make himself or herself feel good by adopting a "realistic" standard of peer performance, while the test-anxious person may contribute to his or her anxiety by making comparisons to highly accomplished experts in the task domain. Similarly, there are some domains of life in which a person feels very close to where "he or she wants to be"—the self-concept and prototype ideal are not too discrepant—and other contexts in which he or she feels far from the standard, despite a reasonable record of performance. When a person feels very distant from an ideal standard, the discrepancy can be overwhelming and debilitating (Rogers, 1951). Recently, the self-ideal discrepancy has been found to be associated with considerable negative affect (Higgins et al., 1986) and it sometimes leads to withdrawal and lethargy. Variations in the nature of the standard of comparison and the amount of self-ideal discrepancy could well account for differences in the strength of anxiety about failure (generated in an achievement situation by similarly "capable" individuals.

4. Expertise and involvement.   Individuals differ considerably in the centrality or predominance of a particular life-task domain within their set of relevant tasks, that is, the extent to which that task absorbs their cognitive and behavioral attention over and above other pressing tasks. Moreover, as we observed in the data of Cantor et al. (1985) on college life tasks, predominance of a life task is often associated with intricacy of plans for handling the task and extremity of affect about the task. This kind of "task expertise" can be very helpful, as long as it doesn't immobilize the performer in a state of anxiety and indecision. That is, expertise—defined as elaborate and accessible concepts about the task—can be a mixed blessing. For example, in the context of a life transition, such as the one from high school to college, when new demands in familiar task domains are being encountered, the "novice" may be better off engaging in cautious observation than in plowing ahead with well-worn, expert routines. In those cases, initial optimism engendered by expertise from *prior* experiences may quickly degenerate into demoralizing anxiety and withdrawal to avoid failure in the new and strange test situations.

A similar argument has been made with regard to task involvement and investment: Linville (1982a), for example, argues that individuals with a great deal of self-concept identification in a particular role may be quite devastated by even small "failures" in that arena (see Klinger, 1975, for a related point on depression-disengagement). She operationalizes this (over)investment in terms of the complexity of the person's self-concept system. In this view, low complexity means that one's self-concepts are highly interwoven and centralized around a few domains of life (or social roles), such that "failure" in one domain generalizes to feelings about the self in other domains as well. In other words, the person is not cushioned against the impact of even minor blows to self-esteem (see Thoits, 1983, for data on the self-protecting function of multiple social roles).

In the present context, we might speculate that such centralized investment in the achievement life-task domain may place an exceptional burden on the performer. This burden may translate into a strategy that opts for self-protection over self-enhancement in "risky" situations, even when the potential gains of direct effort are great and the likelihood of success is reasonable given past performance.

Once again it seems likely that the performer's goals and strategies in specific achievement situations will be a complex function of his or her feelings about the self, the situation, and past experiences in similar contexts—feelings derived from knowledge that is itself an interpretation and not a direct reflection of the "objective" facts about ability, past record, or current odds of success. The concepts and interpretive rules set the general stage for life-task goal-setting and strategic problem solving in specific situations.

INDIVIDUALS AND THEIR LIFE-TASK STRATEGIES

In this chapter we have argued for a very "intentional" view of the ways in which individuals work on life tasks (see Nicholls, 1984, on intentional problem solving). By "intentional" we mean that the strategies which people select (from a varied social intelligence repertoire) are preferred because they are appropriate for their life-task goals at a given point in time (Showers & Cantor, 1985). Individuals interpret situations in light of salient life-task goals; the strategies of action are coordinated with those goals. And, since the life-task goals, both in the abstract and in a concrete situation, reflect the person's concepts, rules, and memories, the strategies serve to *translate* his or her world view into specific action in a pressing task domain. It is in this sense that the strategies are *intentional* and *appropriate*.

In other words, there is a model implicit in this description in which links are made between the declarative and procedural knowledge used to interpret situations, the goals set by individuals in particular contexts, and the action strategies developed to work on those task goals. Figure 6-1 illustrates the basic scheme for this model. There are a number of points to note about this schematic model of intentional social problem solving. First, as we go from left to right the set of knowledge implicated in the problem-solving behavior gets more and more specific to the particular situation at hand. It is as if underlying very concrete actions in a circumscribed situation is a more general set of goals relevant to a life task and an even wider collection of concepts pertaining to the self and others, now and in the past, in similar situations, or across the span of related contexts. The more general, abstract knowledge provides the framework for the emergence of concrete strategies of action. It is therefore convenient to think of this scheme as portraying a chain of influence from an abstract world view to more particularized rules of action.

Of course, it is critical not to get too attached to the left-to-right progression; quite frequently people are induced to perform a strategy which in turn leads them to develop appropriate goals and to make certain inferences about their own attitudes and talents (Vallacher & Wegner, 1985). Another complicating factor is the tendency to simplify the chain of influence by imagining that each situation taps nicely into only *one* set of life-task goals and relevant declarative knowledge. In fact, most social situations are complex precisely because competing goals are engaged and different aspects of the self are being played out in an "overdetermined" set of actions or intentions. Finally, while it is convenient to look through the eyes of one target person in analyzing problem-solving behavior, most life tasks are worked on in the course of social interactions in which the situation itself is constantly changing shape (Darley & Fazio, 1980). Therefore, the target persons can not always control the direction that an interaction takes; in fact, typically, their problem-solving strategies unfold in fits and starts, often interrupted by the necessity to attend to new problems as they arise.

FIGURE 6-1   Intentional Problem-Solving Cycle

The objective in the next chapter is to approach the flow chart scheme of an individual's intentional problem solving (Figure 6-1) from many directions. In so doing we hope to capture some of this complexity and flexibility in the social interaction cycle. First, starting from the leftmost portion of Figure 6-1, we will consider the general body of declarative and procedural knowledge and the factors which shape an individual's world view over the course of *development*. Here we will highlight general principles of learning and development as manifest in the specifics of a person's repertoire of concepts and memories about the self and his or her world. Then, we will turn to the rightmost portion of Figure 6-1 and consider the specific factors in a social interaction setting that contribute to a person's selection of a strategy of action. Here we will try to outline some of the *dynamics* of the social situation that make problem-solving behavior complex and not merely a straightforward translation of favorite concepts and rules in the service of life-task goals.

7

Developments and Dynamics

The intentional problem-solving scheme depicted in Figure 6-1 suggests that people favor strategies for life tasks which translate personal world views into congruent action in specific social contexts. In the present chapter, we will take that problem-solving scheme apart in an effort to understand the *development* of a personal world view and the *dynamics* of the translation of intentions into actions. The aim here is to capture flexibility in social intelligence. The problem-solving scheme is not a rigid one; there is room for continuous development over the life span, for dynamic responsiveness to the specifics of a current life situation, and for fundamental change in world view during a particular life period. Individuals can construct appropriate ways of adapting to life situations without necessarily becoming inextricably locked into particular world views or life-task goals or action strategies. Yet, clearly, there are also powerful factors which *constrain* the development of social intelligence, or *impede* the translation of beliefs into action, or *prevent* personality change. In fact, often it seems that the smoothly unfolding intentional problem-solving scheme serves mainly as a theoretical ideal towards which people strive, rather than a practical representation of social reality. In principle, social intelligence is used in a flexible, optional, and creative way; in practice we may all fall somewhat short of that intelligent action control (Kuhl & Beckmann, 1985).

I. DEVELOPMENT OF SOCIAL INTELLIGENCE

The present discussion of the development of social intelligence will be necessarily selective and abbreviated. The conditions of social learning which facilitate and guide the acquisition of culturally-meaningful declarative knowledge are, themselves, the topic of many important works (e.g., Bandura, 1977, 1986). Similarly, there has been substantial progress in recent years in charting the development of procedural social knowledge (Keil, 1984; Fischer, 1980) and the metaknowledge that contributes to strategic self-regulation (e.g., Flavell, 1979; Flavell & Wellman, 1977; Mischel, 1983). We will not attempt to comprehensively review that material.

Rather, our intention is to draw selectively from the developmental literature on infancy, early childhood, and adolescence in the service of highlighting some key points in the acquisition of social intelligence. The emphasis will be on the emergence of the child's personal world view and life task intentions in the context of social interaction. Social intelligence is acquired through interactions with the family in infancy, the slightly broader school and social environment in childhood, and the even wider culture-at-large in adolescence.

Analysis of events in the acquisition of declarative social knowledge must also be coordinated with consideration of the social events that serve as preconditions for the awakening of procedural skills underlying the intentional problem-solving model. In both instances, the child (even infant) engages in the construction of social intelligence in the light of experiences with his or her personal-biological, interpersonal, and cultural environments (Hay, 1986; Lewis & Brooks-Gunn, 1979). It is that process of active construction, based upon direct tutelage and more indirect observational and incidental learning, that seems to us to set the stage for intentional problem solving over the life span (Lewis & Feiring, 1981; Bruner, 1981).

INFANCY: SETTING THE STAGE FOR INTENTIONALITY

From the present perspective, social interactions, even of the most basic sort between parent and infant, provide the context for the development of intentional problem solving (Hay, 1986). As Bruner (1981) elegantly outlined in a recent paper on the pragmatics of mother-child speech exchanges, the social negotiations that take place in these most primitive problem-solving interactions set the stage for the development of three vital components of intentionality: (1) goal-directedness; (2) self-awareness and sensitivity to means; and (3) mechanisms for corrective reactions. Contrary to the traditional view of egocentricity in early "social" interactions, there is growing evidence that the beginnings of social responsiveness   and self-agency are evoked in the context of early attempts at communication (Bruner, 1981), exploration (Hay, 1986), cooperative interaction (Rheingold, 1982), and self-regulation (Kopp, 1982). These experiences may well constitute the preconditions for intentionality of social behavior.

Analyses of these early forms of social interaction have been expanded in recent years to portray a complex set of *bidirectional influences,* with the infant evoking parental reaction as well as the parent shaping the infant's behavior (Hay, 1986). In this context of reciprocal interactionism, the genetic contribution is also conceived as a dynamic regulator of developmental change open to modification with experience over the lifespan (see Plomin, 1983; Mayr, 1974). Similarly, the environmental contributions extend beyond the obvious "direct effects" of tutelage to quite "indirect" influences, as when one parent makes the other feel good and the child benefits in later interactions with the target parent; or when the toddler learns the "rules of conversation" by observation of adult exchanges (Lewis & Feiring, 1981). Even the direct effects of parental behavior towards children increasingly are seen as distinctly tuned to each child; hence, the notion of "unshared environmental variance" in analyses of family influences on personality development (Plomin, 1983; Goldsmith, 1983). There is tremendous richness and information value in the rudimentary interactions of infants and their immediate social environments.

1. Infant temperament. Individual differences in activity level and tempo and in primitive forms of sociability and emotional reactivity, often labeled as temperament style, are believed by many to be critical in setting the tone for future social interactions (Goldsmith, 1983). For example, in the pioneering work of Thomas & Chess (1968), behavioral observations of mothers and young infants and maternal reports about their infants suggested that the heightened reactivity, apparent "moodiness" and irregularity in eating and sleeping of some infants constitute a "difficult temperament style." These researchers set the trend for later work on temperament differences by associating "constitutional disturbances" in infancy with stable patterns of intense and frequent negative outbursts and behavioral problems in later life.

While this early work tended to focus on extremes of placidity and heightened reactivity, more recent work in the behavior genetics tradition searches for early precursors to adult temperament differences within more "normal" ranges of intensity and duration of expressive behavior (Buss & Plomin, 1975; Goldsmith, 1983). As Goldsmith (1983) indicates in a review of this literature, "these theories alert us to expect that temperamental dimensions will appear early in development, be relatively stable over time, and show some evidence of heritability"(p. 341).

In pursuit of such differences, genetic studies of infant temperament typically utilize the twin study methodology (or adoption study methods):

estimating heritability coefficients at different ages on factors concerned with task-orientation (attention span, impulsivity, persistence), activity level, and sociability/emotionality (fearfulness, interactive behavior, cooperativeness) (e.g., Matheny, 1980; Torgersen & Kringlen, 1978). Most of these studies report moderate level heritability coefficients on global temperament dimensions, though the coefficients are much larger for aggregated verbal report measures than for more molecular behavior recordings (Plomin & Foch, 1980). The most promising findings in many of these studies, somewhat ironically, concern differences in personality and behavior among biologically-related siblings that seem to derive from differences in the ways in which siblings *within* families are treated—from "unshared environmental variance" (see Plomin, 1983; Goldsmith, 1983).

This mixed pattern of results is, of course, not surprising given the difficulties encountered in conducting such research, such as small sample size restrictions in twin studies, the heterogeneity of measures and assessment situations across studies, and the familiar problem of reconciling "objective" behavioral assessments with more "subjective" observer report measures. Such common problems are exacerbated in the context of infant temperament studies because the parents, who often serve as assessors of temperament, have their own theories of the child's "nature" which they show by reacting differently to each child (see Goldsmith, 1983). Additionally, it is difficult to assess cross-situational temperament patterns reliably with objective behavior measures *on infants* (Plomin & Foch, 1980).

Taking these difficulties into account, most researchers in the behavior genetics tradition still consider early temperament differences to be very promising candidates for heritability analysis. They expect to find *moderate* levels of genetic effects on *broad dimensions* of sociability, emotionality, and activity (Buss & Plomin, 1975) and simultaneously significant amounts of variation associated with the differential treatment of children within families (Plomin, 1983).

Regardless of one's opinion about the conclusiveness of the heritability data to date (or, for that matter, the appropriateness of even attempting to tease apart *separate* effects, see Lewontin, Rose, & Kamin, 1984), these data on infant temperament are still important. This is especially true to the extent that these theorists are correct in proposing that: "temperament may be conceptualized as the foundation for later personality (Willerman, 1979)" (Goldsmith, 1983, p. 341). Thus, while we strongly agree with Lewontin et al. (1984) in questioning the utility of these nature-nurture debates, we are also convinced that patterns of temperament—*whatever their sources*—are significant precursors to the patterning of self-regulatory activity later in life.

Early patterns of reactivity, though consistently elicited only in specific situations such as encountering a stranger or working alone on a frustrating "problem," may come to set the tone for these social interactions in the future. Reactions to novel, unfamiliar events or persons or problems—often used as a measure of "behavioral inhibition" and temperament (Kagan et al., 1984)—may become established as temporally stable patterns of social reactivity in the infant-child's repertoire, thus biasing the child's openness to future explorations in his or her environment that, in turn, are critical to the development of intentionality in many spheres of life (Hay, 1986).

Most critically, the patterning of the infant's "social openness" will certainly be encouraged and channeled (perhaps even created) by the distinctive reactions that parents and other significant figures in the social environment have to infants with specific "temperamental styles" (Lewis & Feiring, 1981). The behavior genetics research described above makes very clear the strength of parental reactions to the different temperaments which they *see* in their infants' reactions to strangers or to frustrations of various sorts or to socializing and cuddling in familiar settings. Quite quickly, patterns of reciprocal interaction between infant and parent become set in motion in certain prototypical social situations. These interaction patterns influence the child's habitual form of responding *and* the very nature of the environments in which he or she typically comes to operate. What may begin as *specific* patterns of reactivity come, through both direct and indirect socialization (Lewis & Feiring, 1981), to take on increasing importance as the infant makes increasingly bolder forays into the wider social environment.

Therefore, the impact of temperament differences, once solidified and extended in the context of recurrent parent-child interactions, is to set the tone with regard to the child's *openness* to new experiences in his or her widening social environment (Hay, 1986; Rheingold, 1985). As Hay (1986) points out, this emphasis on the fine-tuning of attitudes toward unfamiliar experience, brings together a diverse literature on infancy: organizing work on behavioral inhibition and temperament (Kagan et al., 1984), attachment security (Ainsworth et al., 1978; Antonucci & Levitt, 1984), and observational learning of novel actions (Hay et al., 1985; Meltzoff, 1985). Degree of openness to assimilating new experience has traditionally been seen as a fundamental component in the development of intentionality, both as a basis for accomodation to the structure of existing social rituals (Piaget, 1952) and for more self-generated attempts at manipulation of the environment (Bruner, 1981).

2. Infant explorations.   Increasingly, infants are found to engage in exploratory activity that constitutes rudimentary forms of intentional problem solving (Hay, 1986). For example, classic Piagetian object permanence tasks can be interpreted as evidence of *search* missions, such that behavior that once seemed misguided—such as returning to a familiar hiding place—may now be interpreted in the light of the infant's motivation to learn everything possible about each environmental niche (e.g., Hunter et al., 1982). These search problems are prototypical examples of early intentional exploration (Rheingold, 1985); attempts to master that environment (Yarrow et al., 1984). As such, Hay (1986) characterizes them as "developmental strands" in "the emergence of self as effective agent" (p. 145).

3. *Environmental facilitation.* Adults can encourage these earliest attempts at intentional exploration and problem solving in numerous direct and indirect ways: by explicitly directing the child to attempt solutions just beyond his or her current skill level (Vygotsky, 1962); or, somewhat more subtly, in the very way in which the child's environment is set up to present "problems" of ever-increasing difficulty; or, even more indirectly, in the manner in which attitudes are modeled (Bandura, 1973; Lewis & Feiring, 1981). These environmental effects are enormously rich and complex; a few selective examples will suffice to make this clear.

In the nature of *direct effects,* Bruner (1981) presents an elegant analysis of the assistance that mothers give their young children, as the youngsters attempt with progressively more *intentional demands* to negotiate the social ritual of "requests." He argues that mothers seem to have a "natural" sense of how to slowly increase the ante in order to lead the child to become more and more "goal-directed" and "means-sensitive" in their request behavior.

Adults also *indirectly* push children towards intentionality in the course of routine daily activities. Sometimes this happens without any direct tutelage, as when two-year-old children simply start "assisting" parents with common household chores, even exhibiting goal-relevant behaviors not being modeled at the time by the adults in the situation (e.g., Rheingold, 1982). Rheingold (1982) labeled such interactions as "nascent prosocial behavior" (p. 114).

Feiring, Lewis, & Starr (1981) present an even more indirect effect of parental modeling on very young children's "intentional" cooperative acts. In an analysis of "social transitivity" in the social behavior of fifteen-month-old children, they observed significantly more openly cooperative acts between infants and strangers when the infants' mothers had interacted previously in a positive manner with the stranger. In both direct and indirect ways, adults (sometimes) encourage children to explore their environments, to try out different means to an "intended" goal, and to become engaged in important social rituals.

It seems, then, that the recurrent and routine social interactions of the child's first two years of life often provide the context for the development of early forms of self-regulation. Of course, the internalization of social rules for conduct and self-control, as well as complicated forms of intentional self-monitoring of thought and behavior, emerge against a background of maturation in basic cognitive skills (see Kopp, 1982; Mischel, 1983). The phases of cognitive growth of particular interest in the fine-tuning of self-regulatory patterns are nicely outlined in a recent paper by Claire Kopp. She outlines critical points of transition and associated cognitive requisites, as summarized in Table 7-1.

In keeping with this discussion, it is important to note that at each point in the development of self-regulation, the emergence of a *cognitive requisite* can be strongly facilitated or inhibited as a function of the *social experiences* of the infant-child. For example, in the earliest phases of neurophysiological and sensory modulation, infant reactivity patterns and the sensitivity of caregivers' responses impact considerably on the fine-tuning of voluntary motor control and the regularization of action patterns. These achievements, in turn, are necessary precursors to *self-awareness of actions.*

Later, as the child begins to engage in ritualized forms of communication with the caregiver, such as the interactions around "labeling" and "requesting" that Bruner described, the patterns of reciprocal turn-taking and action-initiation in these episodes help to cement advances in *self-initiated monitoring* (Hubley & Trevarthen, 1979). As Kopp points

TABLE 7-1 Precursors to Self-Regulation

PHASES	APPROXIMATE AGES	COGNITIVE REQUISITES	SOCIAL MEDIATORS
Neuro-physiological modulation of arousal	Birth to 2–3 months		Caretaker routines and interactions
Sensorimotor modulation of action	3 months–9 months		Proclivity for social behavior
Control & compliance	12 months–18+ months	Intentionality, goal-directed action, self-agency	Bidirectional social inter-actions
Self-control	24+ months	Representational thinking & recall, continuity of self	Communication & language episodes
Self-regulation (flexible self-control)	36+ months	Strategy production, conscious introspection, plans	Social class factors

After: From *Antecedents of self-regulation: A developmental perspective,* by C. B. Kopp (Tables 1 and 2). Copyright 1982 by the American Psychological Association. Adapted by permission of the publisher and author.

out: "It is likely that caregiver sensitivity to a child's preferred style of interacting with the world of objects and people is a crucial facilitator or deterrent to growth of control. Given a child with very high energy levels and great enthusiasm for movement, verbal communications that specify acts for the child to do or that focus child activity into specific channels of play (Schaffer & Crook, 1978) should also foster control" (1982, p. 206). Similarly, Kopp reports that the language and techniques utilized by caregivers to communicate expectations to their preschoolers affect the level of skill at self-control as well as the child's proclivity to comply with social demands (e.g., Lytton, 1976; Golden et al., 1977).

As children develop even more complicated forms of *strategic self-regulation*—with techniques of distraction and goal-focus and self-instruction and the like (Mischel, 1983)—these early experiences in the context of recurrent parent-child interactions will set the tone for developments to come (Mischel, 1984). Far from contributing to an egocentric view of the world, the young child's social activities in the first few years of life seem to present opportunities for social negotiation which, in turn, aid in the recognition of "self-as-agent" in those interactions (Hay, 1986).

In sum, the two-year-old emerges from these early attempts at exploration and communication and compliance (or defiance, as the case may be) with a much sharpened recognition of an "existential self" (Brooks-Gunn & Lewis, 1984) and a generalized "will" to independently carry forth his or her intentions (Bruner, 1981). At the same time, the child now grasps better and better the demands and limits imposed by the immediate social environment (Kopp, 1982). The stage is set for the fine-tuning of *intentionality* with increasing definition of self in different domains and further exploration of different environments to master the art of self-regulation.

EARLY CHILDHOOD: DEFINING THE INTENTIONAL SELF

Adults know an enormous amount about themselves, their social world, the people and situations of importance to them. It should come as no surprise, however, that this repertoire of declarative knowledge is accumulated in pieces, shaped over a considerable time period, and unevenly embellished across different domains of expertise. A close analogy for repertoire building is map-making following explorations in a new world. The explorers first fill in a vision of the familiar parts of their world. With that anchor in hand, they then voyage to find new treasures and frequently end up in unexpected places. Then, upon returning to home ground the old map looks wrong in the light of new discoveries, so the process starts again in another entirely new direction.

In other words, the map is not built in a neat orderly fashion with areas progressively being filled in along a nice straight path. Areas close together on the map do not always reach the same level of articulation at similar times. The explorers go where the opportunities are available in the order in which they emerge as potential places for discovery. Each explorer's map ultimately looks just slightly different and unique, in part because of the order in which the parts were discovered, the amount of time spent exploring different regions, and the kinds of reconstructions of older visions necessitated by recent journeys.

Until recently (Fischer, 1980; Keil, 1984) the dominant portrait of cognitive growth presented a substantially more orderly, logical sequence of stages and progressive accumulation of knowledge than that suggested by the map-makers analogy (Piaget, 1952; Werner, 1957). With maturation and experience the child "got smarter" in much the same way in which he or she "got taller" with passing years and more and more nutriments encouraging growth. However, the orderly picture is too neat in many respects.

First, the role of social experience and selective exposure to certain aspects of the world at certain times is underplayed in the neat picture (Keil, 1984). The young child works selectively, sharpening his or her knowledge of the objects and events *most familiar and regularly encountered* in his or her world (Rheingold, 1985). Mervis (1984), for example, tells the story of her ten-and-one-half-month-old son, Ari, who had a very restrictive concept of "duckie" with sharp boundaries of membership (e.g., an eagle, vulture, and various songbirds did not fit), while having a very vague, overgeneralized category for "kitty-cat" (including, for example, panthers, lions, tigers). Ari, like the explorers, eventually loosened the boundaries on his concept of "duckie" to include a picture of ducks as ducks, while still leaving the "kitty-cat" category very overgeneralized. This child would appear relatively unsophisticated about the objects in his world if we measured his conceptual "stage" by taking an average of his performance across a variety of different domains in his world. However, as Keil (1984) points out, the "average stage" description is unrealistic because there is always tremendous unevenness in the development of declarative knowledge across domains as a function of selectivity in social experience.

The process of building a repertoire has other irregularities reminiscent of map-making as well. For example, just as the child is sharpening one skill or filling in the facts about one area of social activity, another totally different arena becomes the focus of rapt attention. The school-age child, having mastered the arrangement of the planets, doesn't necessarily build on that skill by attending to information about lunar eclipses; instead, he or she may shift entirely to concerns about the physics of light. In part, these discontinuities in the accumulation of declarative knowledge may arise because of age limits on the procedural sophistication of the child—he or she may simply have gone as far as possible in that domain at that time. However, as Higgins and Parsons (1983) point out, different interests and skills are also "demanded" and "encouraged" by parents, teachers, and peers for different age-groups. Given the age-demands and norms of each period, the child may go on to some other arena simply because he or she has all that is needed at that time in that domain for *that* age, and a different opportunity has arisen to be explored.

The reader may be wondering at this juncture why we are emphasizing the irregularities, discontinuities and domain-specificity of cognitive growth, when it is clear that there are some basic trends, and most children get there in the end in one form or another. There is no doubt that most two-year-olds cannot "role-take" the perspective of others, and almost all adolescents perform this feat quite naturally; school-age children concentrate on the concrete observable features of their self-attributes, while adults prefer to characterize the self with dispositional concepts of a more abstract nature (see Harter, 1983). Why then emphasize the variability in trends when the communality is so evident?

We emphasize the lack of order in cognitive growth because the *process* of acquisition of knowledge about the self and the social world—the special sequence in which discoveries are made, the different time spent in different regions, the personal reworking of prior visions—is key to the idiosyncratic content and structure of each person's current map. Because there are basic trends along the way and commonalities in the end results, it is all too easy to overemphasize the *inevitability* of cognitive development and to forget that growth occurs in the context of an active and selective child operating in a reactive and opinionated social world.

Selective Experience and Active Construction

As early as two to three years of age children are actively engaged by the effort to learn how to be "competent" and "in charge" in different domains of social life (White, 1959; Kohlberg, 1966; Lewis & Brooks-Gunn, 1979). Their "efforts after meaning" move at different rates in different domains, as a function of the distinctiveness of the behavior patterns which they observe *and* perform (McGuire, 1984) and the clarity of social and self-reinforcements (Bandura, 1977, 1986). In some domains, such as aggression and sociability and emotional reactivity, very young children will be generating quite distinct cues and receiving rather clear social responses of discouragement or reinforcement (Buss & Plomin, 1975; Lewis & Feiring, 1981). Some physical characteristics, such as those associated with gender, will serve as salient cues around which to organize an awakening definition of self and self-efficacy (Kohlberg, 1966). Here too, the social environment explicitly trains the child by providing rather clear patterns of gender-differentiated reinforcements and models (Mischel, 1970; Money & Ehrhardt, 1972).

The process of constructing a clear sense of "who I am" and "how the world works" begins quite early. The child uses a variety of self-generated and socially-presented data in the process of sharpening a cognitive self-definition and feelings of specific self-worth that are critical to effective self-regulation (Harter, 1983). In the following discussion we will touch briefly on a number of avenues of influence in this fine-tuning of self-awareness and intentionality.

1. Directive social learning.   From quite an early age and at an accelerated pace during the elementary school years, members of the child's social world shower the perceptive child with evaluative feedback about various displays of behavior. Adults communicate pleasure and displeasure freely and directly through both verbal and nonverbal channels. Moreover, the pattern of reinforcements and punishments provided by adults corresponds to the cultural demands for children at each major age-phase across the life span. As Higgins and Parsons (1983) point out, a parent may scream at a ten-year-old for an act for which a five-year-old would not evoke even a grimace. Therefore, these contingencies for behavior not only help to train or untrain a specific response, but also serve as information to the child about the expectations for children in his or her "age subculture."

Additionally, social cues from parental or peer reactions help to provide the child with further input about self-worth (Rosenberg, 1977) and self-efficacy (Bandura, 1977). Minton (1979), for example, found that by early elementary school age, children come to derive a sense of self-worth from the reflected appraisals of parents and peers. Parental and social acceptance were key issues of concern among the children in her sample. Similarly, Bandura (1977) notes the importance of reinforcements from teachers and peers in "cultivating" a sense of mastery or self-efficacy in various domains of achievement and competence (see also Harter, 1983). Coopersmith (1967), in an early study of the child-rearing antecedents of self-esteem, also notes the importance of feedback from parent to child in communicating both positive regard and the limits of "appropriate" behavior. Hence, through some rather directive means, the social world continues to shape the (verbal) child's self-perceptions of esteem and competence, much as parents do earlier in infancy with "temperamental babies."

Some of the most interesting things that the young child learns about his or her social world are, of course, unintentionally communicated. Social learning theorists have noted that children learn an enormous amount about the way the social world works in general and about their own role in that world by simply watching the behaviors, gestures, and reactions of others (Bandura & Walters, 1963). Children are constantly faced with the adult world's *interpretations* and *opinions* of events, either through direct tutelage or indirect modeling of behavior. If we assume that the child is actively seeking information about the kind of person he or she is and the ways in which such a person should act so as to be rewarded and deemed competent, then where better to look than at the faces and in the words and actions of familiar adults, similar peers and siblings, idolized figures from television and books. With hindsight, one wonders why researchers were surprised to find that children learned an enormous amount of novel aggressive behavior from simply observing the antics of a "harmless" cartoon cat on television (Bandura & Walters, 1963).

Children probably learn more about aggression, altruism, conformity, social roles, and stereotypic behaviors by *watching* than from *listening* to adults (Staub, 1978). Of course, when they watch the behaviors and reactions of others, children learn more than simply a set of novel behaviors. Values and goals are formed by observing the positive and negative outcomes associated with different actions (Bandura, 1977). Actions that are habitually modeled become reinforcing as a function of their "mere familiarity" (Rheingold, 1985; Klinger, 1977; Zajonc, 1980). The regularity with which certain behaviors are rewarded and others punished allows the child to build expectations about the likely outcomes of his or her own actions. Then, by watching peers with similar ability perform those actions it is possible to vicariously achieve a sense of *self*-efficacy at the task (Bandura, 1977).

The "simple" process of observation is a means by which a wealth of data is added to the child's repertoire of self- and social concepts, memories of successes and failures, values and goals and desires. The social world provides the child with numerous hypothesis-testing experiences; it "teaches" about the characteristic behaviors of different types of people, provides information about the likely outcomes associated with those actions, and indirectly communicates a set of values about social interaction patterns.

2. Subtle environmental influence.   Many subtle features of the social environment itself (and the experiences to which a child is exposed) also have impact on the form and content of the world views being developed in these early school-age years. For example, McGuire (1984) argues that school-age children (from the first to the sixth grades) form self-conceptions that are centered around the features of self that are *distinctive* in the context of their social environment (see Chapter 5). Although most of his research has focused on distinctive physical attributes (e.g., gender, height, hair color), McGuire's hypothesis can certainly be extended to apply in other domains of personality and social behavior. Imagine, for example, the one "uncoordinated" infant in a family of athletes; the "easily aroused" two-year-old in a group of placid siblings; the "self-confident" first-born child who encounters a set of cliques in grade-school. These distinctive cues provide information for the child in his or her quest to be "competent" and "in control" and to gain a clear sense of differentiation from others. Additionally, the social world itself will undoubtedly react more strongly to the child in areas of personality, ability, and physique in which he or she seems to "stand out" and "demand" attention.

This is not to say that the social environment always positively evaluates distinctiveness: parents and peers frequently attempt to shape the child in a direction more in line with modal behaviors or interests. However, simply by according differential attention to the features that distinguish the child from that environment, the socializers may ensure a special place for those atypical preferences in the child's memories and self-conceptions. As a result, the actively observant child develops a set of values and self-attributes not directly in accord with those modeled in the environment, but rather, directly at odds with the typical or implicitly promoted world view. As McGuire (1984) and others (Higgins & Parsons, 1983) have argued, children are sometimes quite perverse in their reactions to the values modeled in their social environment. Children do a great deal of *self-socializing* and the results are not always in line with normative expectations.

Perhaps the clearest example of the active control of children over their own tastes, preferences, and beliefs occurs daily in the classroom, as teachers attempt to use rewards in the service of shaping behavior (see Deci, Nezlek, & Sheinman, 1981). As many have noted, one way to squelch a child's "intrinsic" interest in a task is to attempt to control behavior with extrinsic rewards for performance on an attractive activity (Lepper & Greene, 1978; Harackiewicz, 1979). Similarly, consider the number of times that a child interprets the message behind an adult's actions in a way quite discrepant with what was "really" intended. Parents will go to great lengths to disabuse a younger child of the belief that he or she gets less attention than the "better" older sibling. It is rarely parents' overt actions that *directly* shape a child's self-concept—children are as selective in *their interpretations* of the meaning and import of adults' actions and words as are adults themselves (Greenwald, 1981).

3. Self-socialization of a cognitive self.

How, then, does the child come to distill, abstract, and infer from these data his or her own quite unique collection of concepts and intentions and preferences? By adolescence, the cognitive self is represented in memory as a complicated network of concepts which vary in degree of abstraction and elaboration, in their evaluative and semantic content, and with regard to their associations with other aspects of world knowledge. What is the nature of these changes that allow the personal repertoire to "grow" over the childhood years from first grade to adolescence?

Susan Harter (1983) has recently presented a model of self-concept development which is quite compatible with the present discussion. In reviewing the available data on this topic, derived from studies in which children answer the question, Who am I? (e.g., Rosenberg, 1979), Harter suggests that it is easy to oversimplify the developmental process as one that goes from simple to complex evenly in all domains. To be sure, in general the features of self around which self-knowledge is focused seem to change with age; so, the first-grader is interested in concrete physical attributes and possessions and skills, the middle school child emphasizes social traits, and the adolescent reflects on characteristic thoughts, emotions, and motives (Montemayor & Eisen, 1977). However, as Harter points out, quite *elaborate,* abstract concepts can be formed around even the most concrete and *obvious* physical attributes of self (e.g., "femininity" formed around a concept of physical petiteness).

According to Harter, the main "advance" in self-knowledge over the years from six to eighteen consists of building abstract concepts about the self that unite multiple specific attributes (see also Peevers & Secord, 1973, on social perceptions). Table 7-2 presents a schematic version of Harter's four "stages" of structural development in one content domain—the development of a self-concept network in the general content domain of behavioral (versus social) skills. This scheme is intended to be representative of the developmental progression in many content domains of importance to children and adults.

TABLE 7-2   Schematic Example of Harter's Self-Concept Model in Domain of Behavioral Competences

STAGE I: SIMPLE DESCRIPTIONS		
GLOBAL	DIFFERENTIATED	
"Good at drawing, puzzles, alphabet, numbers, colors . . . "	"Good at drawing, puzzles"	"Not good at alphabet, numbers"
STAGE II: TRAIT LABELS		
GLOBAL	DIFFERENTIATED	
"All dumb because bad at math, science, geography"	"Smart in writing, art, music"	"Dumb in math, science, geography"
STAGE III: SINGLE ABSTRACTIONS		
GLOBAL	DIFFERENTIATED	
"Low intelligence since dumb at standardized tests"	"Artistic, creative, poetry"	"Modest conventional intelligence"
STAGE IV: HIGHER ORDER ABSTRACTIONS		
GLOBAL	DIFFERENTIATED	
"Bohemian who rejects conventional values"	"Bohemian"	"Political radical"

Children's early self-assessments are somewhat primitive in that they tend to focus rather disjointedly on a number of skills across a range of domains of social life. However they must be viewed from the perspective of the "age-culture" or "tasks" of the child (Higgins & Parsons, 1983; Erikson, 1950). The job for these young map-makers is to get a sense of the "lay of the land," and then to spread out in all directions and test their skills. The parents and teachers in their world are most likely presenting them with a continuously changing set of tasks, emphasizing a range of opportunities versus depth of experience in any one domain. Initially the adults' feedback refers to "good" performances more than to "poor" showings, since no one can expect a child to master everything at once. In fact, in many cases adults emphasize tasks that seem to fit a child's particular temperament and style, thereby increasing the chances of "success" while also consolidating experiences in line with early "constitutional strengths." Gradually children encounter tasks for which they are "ill-suited" and begin to construct conceptions of self-deficits, along with skills. The developments in this early stage not only set the process in motion, but also clear the way for the construction of quite an idiosyncratic collection of self-conceptions from one child to the next.

By the time children have mastered and failed at a variety of tasks at school and at home (age seven or so) they begin to see some connections between skill domains and to consolidate a broader self-conception of competence or skill (see stage II in Table 7-2). However, in making this "advance" rather than forming a conception based on an average of these skills and deficits, they typically return to the early form of all-or-none thinking and decide that they are altogether "dumb" (because of an inability to master math, geography, *and* shop). In the face of some particularly salient successes or failures, a child may shift the tone of the assessment altogether, without giving a thought to previous experiences (Nicholls, 1984).

By age seven to nine, children begin to notice that adults and peers give *discriminative feedback* about competence (for example, "You're great at math.") and openly discourage an all-or-none assessment of competence ("Oh come on, you're not *all that* smart!"). Seemingly in recognition of the variety of experiences, youngsters soon come to view themselves as "smart" in some areas and "dumb" in others. The particular configuration of "smart areas" and "dumb areas," as well as the actual content of the autobiographical memories behind each assessment, varies from child to child. In other words, the network already looks quite different in content and organization for different children.

The self-concept network in the ability/competence domain takes clear shape by adolescence with the burgeoning skill at "social comparison" (Nicholls, 1984) and the cultural-cohort message to "form a clear identity" (Higgins & Parsons, 1983). The variety of self-assessments of "smarts" and "stupidity" is first consolidated into an overrepresentative and often quite unfair all-or-none concept of self-intelligence; later the adolescent differentiates that conception into more domain-specific ones of, for example, "superior analytic intelligence" and "modest spatial IQ" (see stage III, Table 7-2). However, as Harter suggests, these differentiated conceptions promote a sense of self-fragmentation in an arena of life in which the culture-at-large encourages consolidation (for example, in standardized admissions assessments). Therefore, late adolescents may form a "higher-order abstraction," presenting themselves perhaps, as the "classic legal-mind type." In so doing, they make sense of their earlier assessments, probably reconstructing some (e.g., being good at the alphabet was the first sign of an orderly mind) and discarding as naive other "childish" self-conceptions (e.g., "How could I have thought that I was good at drawing, when you consider how good Johnny was at it?"). The self-conceptions have now been ordered, consolidated, and integrated into an idiosyncratic network of the "budding Oliver Wendell Holmes."

These "stages" of structural development allow for considerable flexibility in the shape that a child's self-conceptions take within different content domains of social life. Harter argues that a child may be at different states of consolidation of self-knowledge in different content domains. To illustrate, a quite abstract and full network in the behavioral skills domain may be accompanied by a very under-developed set of disparate self-conceptions with regard to characteristics of emotional life. The child undoubtedly eventually forms some higher-order self-assessments in the once less well-developed areas (e.g., the adolescent "learns about love"). However, the more fully articulated "early selves" may remain quite salient even in the face of adult efforts to go beyond them and achieve new possibilities (Guidano & Liotti, 1983).

In addition to age-trends in the *structure* of self-conceptions, there are also shifts with age in the content domains which capture "center stage" in self-descriptions (Rosenberg, 1979; McGuire, 1984). In fact, there are really two age-shifts in the *content* of self-descriptions: (1) children focus on concrete observable aspects of self, while by adolescence the more phenomenological domains are of primary interest; and (2) over time different broad content domains of social life, such as gender roles, social relationships, and behavioral skills, become the primary focus of self-reflections. The first shift is somewhat intertwined with the development of more and more abstract representations of the self, as when the young boy considers his self-categorization of gender to revolve around the workings of his external genitalia and the adolescent articulates a more encompassing gender role of the "macho man" (Money & Ehrhardt, 1972; Tavris & Wade, 1984).

The second shift often derives from changes in the child's physical maturation and in the expectations communicated by the social environment. For example, young children are encouraged to master the differences between "boys and girls" as they become increasingly aware of their own bodies and when their environment starts to point out anatomical gender differences. Gender becomes a somewhat less important domain during the middle years at school and then emerges as a central category, but in a different light, with pubescence and the "chores" of adolescent sexuality. Once again, there is a merging of biological and social input that serves to highlight a particular content domain as the growing child works on establishing a definition of self.

While different aspects of the self become the normative focus of reflection during different periods of development, individual children also work on those age-specific self-concepts to different degrees. When young children are sorting through their behavioral skills and adolescents are trying to determine their value identities, there will be differences in the amount of cognitive elaboration of individuals' self-concepts in those content domains. As McGuire (1984) suggests, some domains will be especially intriguing to a child because of his or her distinctive status relative to others around them; by contrast, the significance accorded to a domain by models in the home and school environment may determine the level of a child's interest in that arena of life (Bandura, 1977). Some domains may become persistently important to a child because of the difficulties experienced in feeling competent in them. So, for example, the "weak" child may devote himself or herself to athletics with a passion equal to none. In other domains it may be the continuity of successful experiences that makes the domains very special for that child, as when a temperamentally "active" infant fosters an athletic orientation as a school child. Regardless of the antecedent motivating force, quite naturally and quickly the child or adolescent or adult becomes an "expert" with a highly articulated and specific sense of self in certain domains (Markus, 1977, 1979, 1983).

The Intentional Adolescent

An enormous advance in understanding with respect to the "intentional self" occurs in the context of social interactions during childhood, both within and outside the family environment. If infancy prepares the child for working intentionally towards self-understanding, then childhood prepares the late adolescent for actual attempts at life-task problem solving. In other words, with the sharpened and differentiated self-awareness of adolescence comes increased sensitivity to the intricacies of turning intentions into actions in social situations (Duval & Wicklund, 1972).

Adolescents' expanded awareness of self in environment, relative to their sophistication at earlier times, is apparent in both the content and form of their thoughts about social life. When they think about events and the behavior of others and themselves, they are able to "control themselves" from projecting the self on others and yet also use the self as a special point of reference (Higgins, 1981; Bannister & Agnew, 1977). In appraising the self, they are able to see the self as others might (Nicholls, 1984) and to criticize and praise the self more as one might evaluate another person (Ruble & Rholes, 1981). Their assessments of competence or self-efficacy are highly differentiated and derived with others' performances in mind (using social comparison information). Most importantly, they can introspect about the logic and appropriateness of their own thought processes (Flavell & Wellman, 1977; Flavell & Ross, 1981). These advances in procedural knowledge bring adolescents closely in tune with their own perceived abilities (Harter, 1983), feelings of self-worth and control (Rosenberg, 1979), and personal goals (Markus, 1983), setting them off into the world of "action control" (Kuhl, 1985).

The culmination of childhood development in the heightened self-awareness and intentionality of late adolescence fits beautifully (presumably, not by chance) with the age-graded normative tasks of this period in life (Baltes et al., 1984). As Erikson (1950) and other life-span theorists suggest, the late adolescent is moving from the safety of home to the freedom of the social-occupational-educational world with a strong desire and implied cultural demand to forge a very personal identity and a set of driving values and goals (Levinson, 1978). Given the broadly consensual life task goals of this age period, the specific declarative and procedural knowledge constructed at prior times should serve quite well.

First, late adolescents are exceptionally well-versed in the "demands" of their peer, family, and school cultures, having just spent many years observing models, contemplating the reinforcement contingencies surrounding social behavior, and sharpening skills of social comparison and self-appraisal. Second, late adolescents know enough about themselves and others, and have survived enough victories and defeats, to have acquired a taste for "being themselves," i.e., for uniquely defining pressing life tasks. By this time the intense pressures of early adolescent conformity and fear of social stigma have been relegated to the private miseries of autobiographical memory. The late adolescent is cognitively and socially ready to be the intentional problem-solver that most people expect and perhaps indirectly encourage, ready to construct and to work on personal "dreams" (Levinson, 1978) and achieve new "possible selves" (Markus, 1983). Probably more than any other life period, late adolescence is marked by intense awareness of that mission. Accordingly, we turn now to a fuller consideration of the self-regulatory tasks of late adolescence and adulthood.

II. THE DYNAMICS OF SELF-REGULATION

Facilitating Intentionality

The adolescent is a model of an *intentional problem-solver,* determined to carry into action the "identity" recently consolidated. The task of self-consistency is facilitated from within by a new facility with introspection and from without by the cultural demand for articulation of a sense of purpose, a personal dream. But conditions do not remain conducive to self-regulation for long. The tasks of (young) adulthood are considerably less directly focused on self-consistency than before. Instead, the tasks the adult faces operate to pull the individual "out of him/herself" and into the social group of family, occupational organization, community clubs, and the like (Levinson, 1978; Veroff, 1983). In these group-oriented contexts, maintaining a self-focused attitude gets increasingly more difficult. As Levinson (1978) argues, social pressures on the adult make fulfillment of personal goals (the "dream") a more complex, "social" enterprise. In other words, while the adolescent could worry about finding a way to "be him/herself" in every situation, the more socially-conscious adult has to construct goals for self that also reflect the likely appraisal from others (Schlenker, 1985). These social demands considerably constrain the translation of personal intentions into action. In the next section we will consider some of the conditions that make the translation process easier to accomplish.

1. Involving the self.   As intentional self-regulation gets more difficult with the increasingly diverse demands of adult social life, maintaining a "self-aware" stance in social contexts becomes all the more critical to achieving personal intentions (Duval & Wicklund, 1972). For some individuals, a self-focus of attention on their currently pressing internal states, goals, and attributes is a characteristic stance towards social interaction (Fenigstein, Scheier & Buss, 1975; Snyder, 1974). For others, a recent salient experience may serve to *clarify* a relevant self-goal and strengthen the intention to behave consistently (Abelson, 1982; Fazio & Zanna, 1978). In any case, heightened self-awareness as to personal goals and attitudes, whether characteristically achieved or adopted in response to specific situations and experiences, seems to be conducive to intentional self-regulation.

There are many contexts of daily life that are conducive to self-focus of attention and ego-involvement (Greenwald, 1982)—situations in which one finds oneself "watching the self" and "trying to *be* the self" even as one behaves. For example, Markus (1983) has suggested that when people enter domains of activity which reflect on their most "cherished" self-images (i.e., schematic domains), they regulate behavior with more vigilance than is typically the case. The "weight schematic" monitors calories like a hawk, while the "comic ham" perks up when a receptive audience appears. Moreover, these conditions of self-focus can be simulated in a laboratory by the simple manipulations of placing a mirror in front of one person (i.e., making them privately self-aware) and an audience behind the other (i.e., encouraging public self-awareness) (Carver & Scheier, 1978).

Although we do not typically encounter mirrors or cameras or specially-attentive audiences, we do frequently create our own "private audiences" (Baldwin & Holmes, 1985) for the purpose of regulating behavior. Baldwin & Holmes (1985) suggest that in a state of heightened self-focus, individuals regulate their behavior by imagining the reaction of a private audience of their own selection. The "weight schematic" imagines the frowning face of the Weight Watchers official, while the "perpetual performer" conjures up the appreciative applause of a welcoming crowd in order to get beyond stage fright and motivate joke-telling behavior.

Whether by simply entering a cherished domain of life or encountering a vigilant audience, or even by calling up one's own private audience, the self-aware individual makes him/herself ready to intentionally regulate behavior in line with now-salient images of self. In such contexts, the individual is not only aware of *current* self-definitions, but also often sees the potential for achieving new possibilities for self (Markus & Nurius, 1986). Heightened self-focus brings these special selves forward, to be actualized in the here and now (Rogers, 1951).

These conditions of heightened self-awareness that promote self-consistency are prevalent even in routine social activities. Individuals often encounter domains of central importance in which they readily "see" the potential for self-definitional activity (Gollwitzer & Wicklund, 1985). Social audiences make frequent demands for "accountability" (Tetlock, 1986), even when they operate more in our minds than in reality (Baldwin & Holmes, 1985). Less commonplace but equally powerful inducements to self-consistency occur when cherished self-definitions are somehow threatened in the course of social interaction. In that vein, Swann and Ely (1984) suggest that people are particularly vigilant and self-aware when another person acts towards them in such a way as to threaten the validity of a central self-conception.

Individuals frequently engage in intentional self-regulation so as to present themselves in an "accurate" light and generate self-confirming social feedback (Swann & Read, 1981). One very intriguing version of this effort at self-verification is examined by Gollwitzer & Wicklund (1985) in the context of a theory of "symbolic self-completion." They argue for the remarkable ingenuity and drive that people demonstrate in finding alternative symbolic substitutes when an act of self-definition has been thwarted. In their studies, individuals strive most concertedly and intentionally to find an avenue for self-verification in the face of negative social feedback or an obvious failure to meet a self-goal.

The theme which seems to permeate all of these examples of successful self-regulation is one of *active self-definition:* the intention is to take control of behavior so as to present "the self" (to others and to oneself) in an accurate, if not always positive light. We note also the seeming self-demeaning intentions behind some self-presentation strategies (Jones & Pittman, 1982; Lewinsohn et al., 1980). Hence, conditions conducive to self-regulation are those which prompt the individual to see that central self-definitions are at issue and thus to work to find a comfortable outlet for "the self" in a situation. Of course, once having achieved a state of self-focus, it then becomes necessary to monitor behavior vigilantly in order to keep on track towards those goals.

2. Controlling the self. In order to effectively keep on target towards a goal, individuals have to continuously bolster the strength of current intentions and control the urge to direct attention and action into alternative purposes (Kuhl, 1985). Unfortunately it is typically the case that conditions which are conducive to working on life-task goals are also likely to be highly charged with potentially disruptive emotions, require substantial self-focused effort, and demand that immediate rewards be sacrificed in the service of long-term objectives. The college student studying for a final exam knows well the temptations of sleep, the "excuses" provided by a hangover, or the disruption caused by panic that overwhelms at unexpected moments (see Snyder, 1985). Strategies for self-control require fairly intensive effort, though even young children manage to find ways to keep on-target (Mischel, 1983).

In his recent analysis of mechanisms for "action control," Julius Kuhl outlines five categories of procedures for maintaining intentions in the face of obstacles and/or competing interests. These strategies are summarized in Table 7-3. Interestingly, many of these procedures are precisely those cultivated by children as they "work", on self-control and social compliance. Both children and adults, for example, know the value of maintaining a "good feeling" and "optimistic outlook" (cf. Norem & Cantor, 1986b), of making public commitments which keep up the level of social pressure, of self-instructions about the importance of reaching *that* goal at *that* time, and finally, of knowing when to stop thinking and start acting (Kuhl, 1983). As Kuhl (1985) notes, however, children seem to be less actively "in charge" when they use such metacognitive strategies, demonstrating somewhat less persistence in the face of tantalizing diversions and less flexibility in the face of obstacles than do adults.

3. Evaluating the self. The process of self-regulation involves constant monitoring of performance, evaluation of goals, and adjustment of

TABLE 7-3 Kuhl's Categories of Self-Regulatory Controls

I.	*Selective Attention*—Keep intention in forefront of attention
II.	*Selective Encoding*—Focus on intention-relevant stimuli
III.	*Motivation Control*—Self-instruct on importance of achieving goal
IV.	*Emotion Control*—Keep check on distracting or debilitating emotional reactions
V.	*Environmental Control*—Enlist social support and pressure for the goal
VI.	*Rumination-Action Control*—Activate stop rules for deliberation; evoke action

After: *From Action control from cognition to behavior,* by J. Kuhl & J. Beckmann. Copyright 1985 by Springer-Verlag. Used by permission.

behavior to reach a desired goal (Miller, Galanter, & Pribram, 1960; Kanfer, 1970). Because this is a constantly evolving process, we refer to it as one of *dynamic* self-regulation (Carver & Scheier, 1981).

Bandura (1978, 1982) argues, for example, for a complicated *self-evaluative process* in the context of achievement performance: the performer judges his or her current position by integrating information about past performance, level of mastery at the task (self-efficacy) and expectations for reward upon completion of the task. Assessing self-efficacy itself involves the weighing of multiple cues: personal success at similar tasks, social comparison information, level of arousal (which might disrupt performance if too high), and social feedback (about the likelihood of task-specific success).

Frequently, the affect aroused in the course of such a self-evaluative judgment can serve a valuable motivating function. Pride, as compared with disgust or anxiety, may encourage the performer in new exciting directions (Weiner, 1985). A set of particularly positive subjective evaluations can stimulate increased effort at a *potentially* rewarding but currently difficult task (Carver, Blaney, & Scheier, 1979; Scheier & Carver, 1982). In fact, Harter (1983) argues that it is the *affect* generated in the course of competence judgments that then mediates an adolescent's motivation and decision to pursue challenging tasks in a school setting. By contrast, negative evaluative reactions may prime feelings of threat to self-esteem, making quite likely a strategy of effort withdrawal, especially under conditions of self-focused attention (see Carver & Scheier, 1981, 1985).

Self-evaluative efforts provide both immediate cues to strategy selection (e.g., increasing or withdrawing effort at an achievement task), and feedback for long-term assessments of perceived competence and efficacy. The child who refuses to believe in his or her ability, and who then unexpectedly experiences "good luck" at an important test and increases effort in the course of monitoring that performance, may come to see him/herself as slightly more competent as a function of that experience. This will happen only if he or she can resist discounting the feedback as nondiagnostic of ability (due to luck and effort) and "go with the flow" of positive affect for a time; then he or she may set the future goals in achievement settings a bit higher—more realistically in line with the actual performance record. Self-evaluative processes are critical to problem-solving behavior not only because they enable the person to translate intentions into strategies of action that protect the current self-definitions but also because they provide feedback as to the feasibility of setting new goals.

Disrupting Intentionality

Thus far we have been implying that people do an exceptionally good job at systematic self-regulation in the service of consistency with personal goals and standards of performance. This clearly is only one side of a complicated picture—under many circumstances people fail to regulate their behavior either because of perceived inability to control outcomes (Miller, 1979) or the absence of motivation for pursuit of self-goals (Peterson & Seligman, 1984). Unusual negative life events can induce a state of helplessness and pessimism that disrupts active attempts at goal-striving (Herrmann & Wortman, 1985). In many routine tasks of everyday living people passively stop regulating behavior, when they rely on familiar scripts without being especially careful to monitor and evaluate the results (Chanowitz & Langer, 1980).

1. Mindless scripts. Often, in the course of a familiar interaction, individuals fall back into old scripts. The trip back home for an adult sometimes can be disconcerting precisely because of the old patterns that get reestablished so effortlessly. At those times it feels as if the situation has somehow pulled out an "old self" and a set of "old goals and habits" long since laid to rest. Those past selves and old strategies of interaction which were thought to be long since gone are likely never lost from the repertoire, but simply from conscious awareness (Erdelyi, 1985; Kihlstrom, 1984; Anderson, 1978). The social situation elicits those "forgotten" memories and routines as if they were just used yesterday. This is one example of a breakdown in intentional self-control.

2. Mindful ruminations. In other contexts, it is the person's own mood or emotions or ruminations that interfere with self-regulation and performance. We have already noted how disruptive negative mood states and negative emotions of anger and frustration can be in the course of performance evaluation and monitoring (Carver & Scheier, 1985). Once a person begins to focus on anxiety or anger or frustration it often becomes increasingly difficult to rid the mind of these performance-debilitating feelings (Salovey & Rodin, 1985). This is partly a function of the tendency to (rather automatically) retrieve from memory a host of other personal episodes with negative affective connotations that provide data for, and thus reinforce, a currently negative view of self (Nurius, 1984; Clark & Isen, 1982; Bower, 1981). It is also a function of the self-fulfilling nature of such negative ruminations: the negative affect associated with negative thoughts may disrupt attention, interfere with self-monitoring efforts, and result in a less-than-perfect performance. Alternatively, the flooding of negative emotion may become overwhelming in itself, resulting in lethargy and effort withdrawal. Individuals may develop what Kuhl (1985) calls a "failure-oriented state orientation" (p. 108), ruminating endlessly on the *causes* of past failures, rather than actively embracing new *means* for pursuing success. Of course, as Herrmann & Wortman (1985) point out, it is not necessarily wise to quickly adopt an action-orientation if the circumstances of life have genuinely changed dramatically. Some amount of state-oriented rumination may also serve to provide a necessary rejuvenative respite in the face of life crises.

3. Overly-extrinsic motivation.   A less dramatic, but more commonly experienced impairment in self-regulatory motivation occurs when people become too involved in pursuing an *extrinsic* reward, or too worried about future *performance evaluation,* in a task on which they are already *intrinsically* motivated to work (Deci & Ryan, 1980; Harackiewicz et al., 1984). In Kuhl's (1985) language, the former is an instance of negative state orientation and the latter, one of positive action orientation. Deci et al. (1981) found considerable impairment in the achievement performance of school children whose teachers used threats and inducements of rewards as a means of "controlling" the children's classroom behavior. These children seemed to adopt an "extrinsic motivational orientation," losing the intrinsic interest in schoolwork and the drive to meet personal standards of excellence. Most disturbing, the children's perceived level of personal competence (as measured on the Harter self-esteem scale, Harter, 1981) was also diminished.

Conditions which encourage an extrinsic orientation to performance evaluation also impact negatively on individuals' perceptions of competence and self-efficacy. Children (and adults) who find themselves engaging in a task primarily in the hopes of "pleasing the teacher" or "avoiding criticism" may ultimately come to feel less confident about the likelihood of a good outcome and find less reason to pursue the challenge altogether. It is as if their motivation to engage in the rigorous self-regulation necessary to complete a difficult task has also been undermined.

4. Helplessness and withdrawal.   The effort involved in intentional self-regulation demands a high degree of motivation (to reach a goal) on the part of the target individual. This motivation can be impaired when people begin to perceive a lack of *control* over the outcome of an event (Seligman & Maier, 1967). A state of "learned helplessness" may prevail to the extent that a person perceives little or no control over the occurrence of an aversive event (Hiroto & Seligman, 1975), when he or she focuses endlessly on this "negative state" (Kuhl, 1985), or feels hopeless in the face of strong expectations of impending failure (Carver & Scheier, 1985). The perception of lack of control and/or efficacy often impairs performance on an unrelated task that the person may previously have found rewarding. The effects on performance and self-regulatory functioning are particularly severe when the person attributes the lack of control over the failure outcome to his or her own "incompetence" (Abramson et al., 1978). The tendency to make such stable, internal attributions for uncontrollable negative life events may ultimately put a person "at risk" for depression (Peterson & Seligman, 1984).

In sum, there are many conditions under which normal activity is disrupted and motivation to work hard at challenging tasks falters. In some cases, people simply get drawn off track in the process of responding to signals from others (Darley & Fazio, 1980). At other times, the task itself does not challenge the person sufficiently to warrant self-awareness or an ego-involved attitude (Greenwald, 1982). More discouraging yet, are the occasions when the person desperately attempts to regulate behavior, but can not overcome the flooding of negative emotion (Meichenbaum, 1977). Debilitating states of negative rumination may sometimes accompany life crisis events, though in those cases some form of "time-out" from action control may be beneficial in the long run (Herrmann & Wortman, 1985). More subtle though equally devastating disruption of self-regulation occurs when intrinsic motivation to pursue a task becomes undermined because of extrinsic controls (Deci et al., 1981), or when the person simply "gives up" after perceiving success to be hopeless and negative outcomes unavoidable (Peterson & Seligman, 1984). These are the times when one feels most pessimistic about accomplishing even a small step towards a life task goal.

INTENTIONALITY AND CORRECTIVE CHANGE

In the present chapter we have emphasized, perhaps a bit too optimistically, the power of individuals—even infants—to act intentionally in striving for life-task goals. We have argued that over the course of development, children fine-tune their skills of intentionality through a constant process of social negotiation that makes both personal and interpersonal objectives clear. As Bruner (1981) noted, the familial environment seems to come quite naturally to the aid of the developing infant, sometimes inducing a certain mode of intentional action to fit the infant's "temperament and style" (Plomin, 1983). Once in the broader school environment, the child eagerly builds on this nascent sense of self-agency, paying special attention to those dimensions of self-definition that make him or her unique in that environment (McGuire & McGuire, 1981). The adolescent, with newly refined skills of self-reflection and appraisal, demonstrates strong intentionality in the pursuit of a "personal dream" within the culture's normative demands (Levinson, 1978). Primitive self-awareness has turned into strong self-agency and the adolescent has the cognitive-social skills to translate those life-task intentions into action.

Unfortunately, the dynamics of translation are never really as simple or straightforward as one would like (Gollwitzer & Wicklund, 1985). The vigilance required to effect self-consistent action in complex and sometimes antagonistic social contexts can be quite overwhelming. The individual has to be sensitive to "the self," taking note of opportunities for self-realization, of potentially disruptive emotional states or distracting intentions, and of the conditions that elicit "old habits" with bad outcomes (Kuhl, 1985). There has to be a "coordinated act of will" on the part of person and environment—much as occurs in the reciprocal interactions of parent and child—in order to direct action towards self-fulfilling ends.

8

Assessment and Change

In considering the dynamics of intentionality, one focuses on individuals' proclivity for *anticipating* difficulties in problem solving and guiding behavior towards desired goals. By contrast, in the context of cognitive-behavior change, value is placed on *corrective mechanisms* that allow the individual to recognize and correct recurrent failures in achieving pleasurable end-states (Bruner, 1981; Miller, Galanter, & Pribram, 1960). These corrective mechanisms are considered by most theorists of intentionality to be critical components of adaptive problem solving, precisely because it is so very difficult to *accurately* translate intentions into action in the midst of social interactions—the organism needs to know, at least in retrospect, why reality has fallen short of intentions (Einhorn, 1982; Hogarth, 1981).

SELF-AWARENESS AND CORRECTIVE CHANGE

Corrective change—whether naturally evoked in the course of social negotiations or more consciously elicited in a therapeutic encounter—first requires bringing to the surface underlying assumptions and habitual rules of interpretation that guide behavior in important life-task domains. It is perhaps one of the cruel facts of daily life that individuals feel the pain of missed opportunities, degenerated intentions, and self-defeating strategies much more clearly than they can articulate the reasons for distress (Guidano & Liotti, 1983; Arnkoff, 1980). The censure of negative social feedback often seems as if it came from "left field," since it is frequently the automatized routines of which we are unaware that others find most annoying (Kelley, 1979). Uncovering the roots of distress or acknowledging dysfunctional routines requires an effort of its own, which Freud called the insight process, independent of procedures to effect actual and longlasting changes in habitual patterns of thought and action (Meichenbaum & Cameron, 1982).

While the insight process is well worth an effort by itself, it takes on special importance in the context of effecting change. Conscious intentions to change, derived from insight into dysfunctional routines, may be easier to accomplish because the process of verbalization itself signifies an act of commitment to that change. In this regard, Bruner (1981) argued that when people announce an intention (for example, "I am going to cross the street"), as compared with stating a "caused action" ("I am going to be sick"), the framing of the action as such communicates a willingness to take personal responsibility (or not) for the outcome. He also suggests that intentional announcements of that sort serve to elicit social feedback and even to enlist social support that can be vital to the success of the (change) effort (see also Kuhl, 1985). Following this line of thought, some conscious self-awareness may be very beneficial in the process of self-change.

The objective of the "awareness" part of the correction process is to provide insight into personal expertise—favored concepts and rules of interpretation—in central life-task domains. Just as self-focused attention and ego-involvement aid in the *prospective* translation of intentions to actions (Carver & Scheier, 1981), so too do efforts at *corrective change* stand on a foundation of insight into the self, one's declarative and procedural expertise (Cantor & Kihlstrom, 1985).

The need to uncover such expertise is apparent in problems as diverse as the self-defeating cognitions associated with some global depressions (Dobson & Shaw, 1986), the more specific disturbances of distressed couples, or the anxiety of underachieving students (Snyder, 1985). Across these diverse problem areas, analyses reveal distinct patterns of dysfunctional cognitions associated with feelings of distress (Turk & Salovey, 1985; Heppner & Anderson, 1985).

Debilitating cognitions emerge in both the declarative and procedural domains. Depressed individuals not only have chronically accessible negative self-schemas that fall far short of their ideal expectations (e.g., Higgins et al., 1986; Dobson & Shaw, 1986), but a self-defeating "explanatory style" puts them at risk for depression episodes (Peterson & Seligman, 1984). Similarly, distressed couples often reveal quite discrepant "relationship prototypes" (Ruhrold, 1986) and demonstrate divergent patterns of attributions for aspects of conflict in the relationship (Holtzworth-Munroe &

Jacobson, 1985; Kelley, 1979). Underachieving students sometimes rely on non-functional strategies of self-handicapping to avoid a diagnostic test of an "insecure" competence image in achievement domains (Jones & Berglas, 1978). In all of these cases, dysfunctional interaction patterns are associated with habitual ways of thinking about the self and others, and of interpreting social experience, that are somehow incompatible with the long-term happiness and adjustment of the individual.

It is important to note that the patterns of dysfunctional cognitions outlined above are quite consistent with the "expertise" model of social intelligence presented earlier (Chapters 4-6). For example, assessments of declarative social knowledge often focus on dimensions of self-ideal discrepancy, prototype consensuality, and perceived self-efficacy in presenting a profile of an individual's "expertise and ignorance" (Cantor & Kihlstrom, 1985). These declarative profiles are coordinated with procedural knowledge assessments that stress the individual's preferred ways of attributing causality, making decisions, and managing mood states.

The emphasis in such assessments usually is positive in thrust, explicating the ways in which these favorite procedures protect the self and motivate performance in important life-task contexts (e.g., Showers & Cantor, 1985). However, there are many instances, as noted in earlier chapters, when the "double edge" of expertise is apparent—as when the individual "protects" a negative view of self or, by contrast, clings to an unrealistically positive self-schema, ignoring negative social feedback (Markus & Wurf, 1987). In other words, patterns of dysfunctional cognition fit well within our expertise model, though in these cases, the individual's expertise is often the problem itself.

Of course, researchers continue to debate the causal status of these dysfunctional cognitions in the etiology of personal problems (e.g., Coyne, 1982; Coyne & Gotlib, 1983; vs. Hammen & Mayol, 1982; Miller, Klee, & Norman, 1982). Even so, there is general agreement that cognitive self-awareness is beneficial in precipitating efforts at corrective change (Kendall & Hollon, 1981; Hollon, DeRubeis, & Evans, 1986).

Assessing Problematic Expertise

In this vein, in a series of recent papers, Kihlstrom and Nasby (1981; Nasby & Kihlstrom, 1985) and Cantor and Kihlstrom (1982, 1985) have presented the outlines of an assessment technology for bringing (distressed) individuals' declarative and procedural expertise to the surface by extending the laboratory methods used to document normative patterns of social intelligence to the case of individual clients (Kelly, 1955). In their assessment suggestions, Kihlstrom and Nasby draw on methods familiar to the laboratory study of social and nonsocial cognition. Some of these techniques are intended to tap consciously accessible mental representations. Essentially, they are means of inducing clients to reflect on their concepts of themselves and others and on everyday life episodes. In so doing they may learn something surprising about themselves that is so familiar it is taken for granted in routine interactions—but this is not the same as gaining access to unconscious mental representations. Other techniques, however, seem able to tap preconscious and subconscious declarative mental structures, as well as unconscious procedural knowledge (Kihlstrom, 1984, 1985). Through a variety of these methods a profile of an individual's construct system and favorite ways of interpreting experience—their social intelligence expertise—emerges, making some assumptions and habits of thought clear that routinely guide behavior without *conscious* intention.

1. Measuring life tasks.   A first step in assessing expertise is to "un-pack" (or "unearth") the person's current life-task intentions and then to place them in two important contexts: the historical context of the personal narrative and the contemporary context of the everyday social world. These life-task intentions provide a map of the individual's own idiosyncratic reading of normative age-graded demands. By placing current intentions in a historical context, the individual is encouraged to articulate those implicit personal themes that give temporal continuity to his or her life-task activities. By contrast, embedding life-task themes in the reality of current life situations provides data about the diversity of social demands that actually shape day to day life. Ultimately, the combination of continuity of themes or goals and flexibility of behavior probably conveys an accurate picture of the individual's "life-task space."

As noted in earlier chapters, people seem to find it quite easy to talk about their current life-task intentions—the goals that they find self-absorbing, motivating, and time-consuming (Cantor et al., 1985). In most cases simple and direct self-reports about life tasks, personal projects, or current concerns are very informative (Little, 1983; Klinger, 1977). This seems to be especially true when individuals embark in new directions in a life transition or, conversely, find themselves distressed and tired of familiar life contexts. From such self-reports it is often possible to get a fairly clear sense of how much and in what ways the person's idiosyncratic life tasks diverge from, or converge with, those of relevant peer or family reference groups (i.e., the *consensuality* of personal life tasks).

In considering current life tasks it is useful to evaluate progress on the system of tasks as a whole, in addition to focusing on a few especially absorbing problem areas. For this purpose, Little (1983) suggests a "conflict grid" in which individuals assess the degree to which each current personal project facilitates or inhibits progress on every other project in the system. An average measure of life-task system *conflict* can be derived from such a method; or, attention more simply could be accorded to points of particular conflict in the system. Little (1983) also suggests extending this conflict grid tool to measurements of project conflict *between* individuals, such as might well occur within a family. Although this might be a very labor intensive project, it does seem important to at least find out something about the tasks of others in the person's current social world—for the change process will always involve extensive social negotiations.

Placing these current (consciously articulated) life tasks within a *historical perspective* of the person's narrative story may well require more indirect projective methods (see McAdams, 1985, for an interesting methodology). Since the aim is to have the person narrate a story by embedding the current life tasks in the context of past events, it may be possible to adapt assessment techniques from the autobiographical memory literature for this purpose (Kihlstrom, 1981). For example, current life-task intentions could be used as probes in a cued recall task (Robinson, 1976). There is now a great deal of interest in analyzing people's narrative memories, and this interest should generate many novel procedures of value in this particular enterprise (Nasby & Kihlstrom, 1985). Similarly, we expect that many investigators will put forth interesting indices of *self-continuity* that could be used to provide a temporal perspective on a person's current life tasks (Carlson, 1981).

Several fruitful methods are available for embedding a person's tasks within *everyday life activity*. One easy method is to ask participants to list the situations in their lives which map onto their current life tasks, and to describe their feelings in each situation (Pervin, 1976). Extensions of that method can probe for the prototypical scripts or episodes that give form to the social activity in those life-task contexts (Abelson, 1981) or, similarly, ask about the person's own plans for handling those situations (Cantor et al., 1985).

Because there may be some reasonable qualms about the validity or representativeness of self-reports of task intentions and task situations, additional, more direct measures of life-task activity may be useful. For example, Norem and Cantor (1986c) used an experiential time-sampling method to obtain an "on-line" picture of the activities of college students engaged in the transition from high school to college (Diener & Larsen, 1984; Nezlek, Wheeler, & Reis, 1983). These students carried electronic beepers and responded to randomly programmed "beeps" during a two-week period by writing descriptions of task-relevant details of their current activities (e.g., "What are you doing?" "What are you working on?" "Who's there with you?"). These on-line measures actually converged quite well with the students' self-reports about their life tasks, even though the latter were obtained at least six months earlier in the year. Together with the self-generated lists of life task–situation pairings, these on-line activity data provide for interesting individual difference comparisons on dimensions tapping the richness and diversity of life-task *opportunities* in the person's current environment.

In general, the process of life-task assessment, in coordination with analysis of personal narratives and current life contexts, should serve an invaluable function, clarifying some already conscious intentions and bringing other more preconscious ones to the surface for inspection. In turn, inspection of one's life-task priorities can be extremely enlightening, precipitating questions of the following sort: "Is this task worth my effort (task value)? Is it feasible to imagine myself reaching these goals (task efficacy)? Is my immediate social environment helping me achieve this task (task support)?" Initial answers to these critical questions may then come from analysis of the content and structure of the person's current life-task system. For example, task value, efficacy, and support should be positively related to the degree of self-continuity, life-task opportunities, and social consensuality in the task system, and negatively related to task system conflict. Table 8-1 presents a summary of methods and individual difference dimensions described here for life-task assessments.

Self-evaluation with respect to current life-task intentions, their feasibility and importance, can only be fully accomplished with further examination of the underlying concepts and rules of interpretation that direct the translation of intentions into actions in everyday life contexts. That is, the life-task assessment provides the motivational framework for making sense of the person's declarative and procedural expertise as it is manifest in daily life. In order to know whether it is wise for a person to continue to pursue current life tasks—perhaps in new contexts or with new means—or better to redirect energy elsewhere, it is essential to know more about the ways in which the person typically construes the self and others in task-relevant domains.

2. Measuring declarative expertise. Many of the common methods for measuring individuals' preferred concepts about the self, other people, and social episodes and situations rely on a computerized version of Kelly's REP Test or Rosch's prototype feature-listing procedure (see Chapters 4, 5). These methods capitalize on individuals' ability to bring easily to mind the attributes they associate with common experiences in their everyday life. Variations in the instructions can guide clients to consider the character-

TABLE 8-1 Assessing Life Tasks

SAMPLE TECHNIQUES	SAMPLE INDIVIDUAL DIFFERENCE DIMENSIONS
Life-Task Listings	Consensuality (Idiosyncracy)
Conflict Grid	System Conflict
Narrative Memory	Self-Continuity
Experiential Time-Sampling	Life-Task Opportunities

istics of different people or selves or events, from different people's perspectives, with regard to different content characteristics.

If the aim is to assess an individual's most "natural" construal of his or her life situations, then client-generated stimuli are in order. By contrast, many of the interesting concepts of clinical significance might be just those ones that the client "contrives" to leave out or "inadvertently" fails to mention. In those cases, the client can be asked to fill in the features of a set of common categories of persons, roles, and situations. While it is usually nice to keep the method as idiographic as possible, there is much to be gained also from analysis of the degree of *consensuality* between the client's and others' construals of common social categories.

This reporting method is a completely straightforward one, yet analyses of the descriptions can provide a rich stimulus for self-reflection. For example, Rosenberg & Gara (1985; Gara, 1986) ask their subjects to generate descriptions of the features of their different self-identities and to rate the relevance of each feature for each identity. When the final identity by attribute matrix is submitted to hierarchical cluster analysis, grouping identities together on the basis of similarity of features, a graphic display emerges of how the person conceptually organizes his or her multifaceted self-concept. This display can be an end in itself, stimulating self-reflection about personal roles and relationships.

Further content analyses also can highlight individual difference comparisons on a number of theoretically relevant dimensions. For example, measures of cognitive *complexity* based upon the depth of elaboration of features of particular identities (e.g., Markus, 1977) or the breadth of elaboration of distinct identities within the full system (e.g., Linville, 1982a; 1985) can be obtained. Similarly, an assessment of the overlap between the individual's portrayal of his or her identities and the descriptions generated by significant others (Ruhrold, 1986) or peer reference group members (Niedenthal et al., 1985) can provide a measure of *consensuality* of expertise.

The *evaluative content* of the identity features can also be considered as part of an assessment of the positiveness of self-definition (Beck, 1976; Dobson & Shaw, 1986). While comparisons between the content of identities generated for the "now self" and for the "ideal self" can fill out this portrait of dominant affective state (Higgins et al., 1986), it is critical to note, though, that sometimes *self-ideal discrepancy* in moderation can be motivating, rather than self-debilitating (Ruffins et al., 1986). Analyses can also focus on the dynamic self-definition (Markus & Wurf, 1987): assessing the nature of the *possibilities* for self envisioned by the individual (Markus & Nurius, 1986) or probing for the person's *flexibility* about self in terms of the number of "symbolic alternatives for self-completion" (Gollwitzer & Wicklund, 1985).

There are multiple avenues for individual difference assessment that follow naturally from this quite simple self-report methodology. Table 8-2 lists some of the dimensions of special relevance here. These dimensions of individual difference characterize aspects of people's social intelligence that are presumed (and, in some cases, already shown) to have significance for many "problems in everyday living" (e.g., Higgins et al., 1986).

These self-report methods are attractive because they are simple and yet they yield rich data for self-reflection and analysis. Nevertheless, there are times when less directive or intrusive measures of expertise are desirable. Here, too, laboratory techniques of cognitive assessment can be adapted to the measurement of individual differences in preconscious or subconscious concepts about the self and others. For example, several researchers have turned to nonintrusive priming tasks—sometimes making use of subliminal primes (Silverman, 1983)—or divided attention tasks in the service of demonstrating the automatic activation of chronically accessible self-concepts (Bargh, 1982; Lewicki, 1985; Higgins, King, & Marvin, 1982). Similarly, analyses of clustering in free recall or memory for violations of expectations (e.g., Bower, Black, & Turner, 1979) can unobtrusively reveal individuals' preferred, but not always consciously reported ways of organizing events.

In many instances a relatively simple measure of the latency to respond to a question about the self or one's life may be as good an index as any of the prevalent set of (preconscious) beliefs and assumptions that frequently guide social behavior. Relatively unobtrusive methods (e.g., priming) combined with indirect measures of accessibility (e.g., latency), can also provide confirmation of the validity of individuals' introspective reports about their more consciously accessible concepts (e.g., Markus, 1977; 1983).

Once again, examination of the results of such tasks can serve as valuable stimuli for further self-reflection and insight into the nature of the world view that may well be causing trouble at the current time. The data

TABLE 8-2 Assessing Declarative Expertise

SAMPLE TECHNIQUES	SAMPLE INDIVIDUAL DIFFERENCE DIMENSIONS
Feature-Listing Descriptions:	
Self-Identities	Complexity
Social Prototypes	Consensuality
Actual and Ideal Selves	Discrepancy
Self-Attributes	Evaluative Content
Possibilities for Self	Flexibility
Indirect Assessments:	
Priming	Accessibility
Divided Attention	Automaticity
Clustering in Recall and Latency	Schematicity

gathered in such tasks are not altogether different from those favored by Freud and his disciples for gaining self-insight (Erdelyi, 1985)—the data are valuable, regardless of the theoretical framework from which they are derived.

3. Measuring procedural expertise.

Although it is sometimes necessary to use quite subtle methods for assessing preconscious and subconscious declarative knowledge (Shevrin, 1986), the task of uncovering procedural expertise poses special problems. As Nasby & Kihlstrom (1985) note: "Procedures are by their very nature largely unconscious, inaccessible to introspective awareness. Therefore, self-report methodologies of the sort proposed for assessing the individual's fund of ostensible facts will have limited utility when it comes to his or her rules or skills" (p. 15). Because most of the procedures that individuals use to interpret events and plan behavior are so well practiced and long since dissociated from awareness, these elements of expertise are especially difficult to articulate (Nisbett & Wilson, 1977) and, of course, even more arduous to change. Yet it is critical to attempt to bring these automated procedures to the surface, even if it requires rather indirect means and a fair amount of observation and inference to arrive at a conclusion about the "mindless" (but not thoughtless) undercurrent in social construal and interactions (Chanowitz & Langer, 1980). In the following, we will consider only a few examples of methods to uncover unconscious procedures, illustrating at the same time the relevance of that procedural expertise to clinical concerns.

As Kuhl (1985) noted in his theory of *Action Control*, people develop strategies of selective attention which usually serve to bolster current intentions and plans and prevent diversionary activity. As always, however, these same attentional strategies can work to the detriment of the individual under some conditions, perpetuating a negative mood state and directing attention so selectively as to miss the recognition of potentially mood-altering social feedback (e.g., Nasby & Yando, 1980, 1982).

Mischel et al. (1972) devised a simple but clever method for assessing *selectivity* in attention to self-relevant feedback among subjects who had been induced to experience a positive or negative mood state. During one part of the experiment, subjects were allowed to freely examine booklets with personality feedback about their "positive assets" or their "negative liabilities"; the amount of time spent looking at each booklet served as an index of selective attention. As it turned out, subjects who had previously experienced success bolstered their positive mood state by selectively attending to their assets for a relatively long period of time. In this case, with a population of "normal" subjects, patterns of overattention to personal liabilities, such that a negative mood state induced by a failure experience might be unintentionally perpetuated, were not observed. Yet, it might well be that just such negative selectivity would be typical for depressed individuals (Beck, 1976) or individuals facing depressing life crises (Herrmann & Wortman, 1985) or less traumatic but more frequent failure experiences in important life-task domains (Kuhl, 1985; Salovey & Rodin, 1985). The simple method devised by Mischel et al. (1972) could well be extended to the clinical laboratory, perhaps including measurements of order of information search preferences among a variety of sources of personal feedback.

Related to the selectivity biases in attentional strategies is a preference for expectancy-confirming evidence in some interpersonal interaction settings in which individuals attempt to test hypotheses about other people and themselves (Snyder, 1981b; Swann & Read, 1981; but see also Trope & Bassock, 1983). Here again the "biases" in hypothesis testing are "unintentional," though they may have substantial effects in setting the tone of a social interaction (Skov & Sherman, 1986). For example, Fong and Markus (1982) found that "extravert schematics" questioned unknown partners in such a way as to reveal the partners' extraversion; while "introverted schematics" focused their questioning around the introvert hypothesis— not surprisingly, these different perceivers see different sides of their target partners' personalities (Snyder & Swann, 1978). Riggs and Cantor (1982) brought the confirmatory hypothesis-testing strategy closer to the clinical domain in demonstrating the same pattern of confirmatory questioning on the part of "anxious" students prior to a competitive dyadic game.

As Nasby & Kihlstrom (1985) note: "Preferentially applying rules to understand others that draw from some areas of personal 'expertise' about the self (e.g., hostility, suspicion) may cause serious problems and interpersonal difficulties" (p. 34–35). They go on to ask the reader to imagine responding to the seemingly naive and harmless probings of a "self-expert" about hostility, which if confirmed would confirm the reader's malice, but which if disconfirmed, would serve the same end. Analyses of habitual forms of "hypothesis testing" with significant others in everyday social interactions can be both revealing and disturbing, pointing out just how easy it is to confirm a personal world view and how rarely it is apparent at the time that such a view is not consensually held (Kelley, 1979).

Methods for assessing commonplace hypothesis-testing strategies can suggest much about the nature of people's interpersonal habits: their proclivity for *confirming* already held views and the degree of *consensual* support in their significant social world for those views. Table 8-3 lists these dimensions of individual difference in procedural expertise, along with several other ways in which people differ in their habits of construal about important life events.

Another arena of procedural expertise, one already known to have significant clinical implications, concerns the ways in which individuals attribute causality for positive and negative experiences in their social

TABLE 8-3   Assessing Procedural Expertise

SAMPLE PROCEDURAL DOMAINS	SAMPLE INDIVIDUAL DIFFERENCE DIMENSIONS
Attention	Selectivity
Hypothesis Testing	Confirmatory
Attribution	Motivating/Defeating
Social Judgment	Consensuality

world (Metalsky & Abramson, 1981). Clinical researchers have studied attributional rules in a variety of problem domains—from learned helplessness in adults (e.g., Abramson, Seligman, & Teasdale, 1978) to problems of aggression control in children (e.g., Nasby, Hayden, & DePaulo, 1980) and insomnia in adults (e.g., Davison, Tsujimoto, & Glaros, 1973). Typically, the methods have relied perhaps a bit too much on individuals' awareness of where their characteristic attributional rules fall out on a three-dimensional scheme of internality, globality, and stability of causal agents for outcomes (see Nasby & Kihlstrom, 1985, for a critique).

More recent innovations in content analysis make use of freely generated attributional responses (Elig & Frieze, 1979), even permitting the analysis of material from natural discourse, newspapers, and dream reports (see Peterson & Seligman, 1984). Moreover, as Nasby & Kihlstrom (1985) suggest, incorporating some nonobtrusive latency and memory measures when individuals provide attributions for "causally ambiguous" life events, might help greatly in the process of uncovering the attribution rules that have become *proceduralized* for a particular person in a particular life domain. Convergence between content measures and these accessibility measures would provide powerful support for the suggestion that both *self-defeating* and *self-protective* attributional rules are often embraced automatically and without awareness.

An especially pleasing analysis would be one that pinpointed the use of self-defeating attributional rules—such as global, internal, stable attributions for failure (Weiner, 1985)—to occasions when individuals encounter their problematic life contexts. C.R. Snyder (1985) has elegantly demonstrated the flexible use of self-protective attributional maneuvers in his analysis of the ways in which students resort to excuses about test anxiety only when the context is right for others to make the "correct" attribution for poor performance. There is little doubt that in most settings in which attributions are naturally made, either in a self-defeating or self-protective manner, the strategies have become proceduralized with repeated practice *in specific social contexts.*

These automatized procedures need, therefore, to be uncovered within familiar contexts, occasionally enabling the individual to arrive at a strategy that works to alleviate "bad habits" of thought—as when a defensive pessimist turns test anxiety into a positive motivator for successful performance (Norem & Cantor, 1986b). Of course, more frequently, we all persist in making attributions and interpretations that can only serve to debilitate (rather than motivate) precisely because the eliciting conditions in those familiar contexts do remain unnervingly consistent—it takes an act of will or an "experiment of nature" such as occurs in a major life transition to force a change in proceduralized knowledge and routines. We turn now to a brief consideration of some of the extraordinary circumstances and/or (therapeutic) acts of will that take individuals beyond awareness *towards* corrective change.

EFFECTING CHANGE

The process of life-task and expertise assessment culminates in a profile of the individual's motivated cognitive strategies for that life period (Showers & Cantor, 1985). The process of corrective change begins then, with an evaluation of the feasibility of reaching current life-task intentions and the effectiveness of the relevant expertise. This evaluation process takes place, of course, repeatedly over time, either explicitly in concert with a therapist or social partner, or implicitly in private internal dialogues. The client seems to have at least three avenues of change to pursue, usually embracing some combination of the three for different life-task domains.

Depending on the particular strengths and weaknesses of the profile, the change effort may be variously directed at: (1) developing new life-task intentions in particularly troublesome domains for which the old intentions are unrealistic or self-defeating in some basic way; or (2) continuing to pursue current task intentions, but with the hopes of finding new solutions—i.e., developing new expertise; or (3) in the case of missed opportunities, "simply" enriching the life-task system by embracing new possibilities for the self, without acquiring new expertise. None of these approaches is easy and rarely will a person find the need to use one exclusively across all life-task domains. In particular, though, the most formidable effort would seem to be entailed by the desire to effect substantial change directly within a domain of personal expertise.

One of the disconcerting implications of the social intelligence analysis is that the (problematic) expertise, which one becomes aware of in the course of defining personal problems from this point of view, is quite likely to be unamenable to direct efforts at corrective change. As we noted in earlier chapters, the repertoire seems to be organized so as to resist major changes in domains of personal expertise—this is especially true for unconscious procedural knowledge, but also probably is true for central self- and social concepts. For example, understanding that one has acquired a negative self-concept in the "physical attractiveness" domain which is out of line with consensual opinion may help to raise the possibility of a future "glamorous possible self" (Markus & Nurius, 1986), but it will take an act of concentration to deny the immediacy of the flood of painful personal memories of "adolescent ugliness" that rather automatically surface in the face of a bathroom mirror on a "bad mood" day (Salovey & Rodin, 1985). Declarative knowledge expertise is intricately elaborated; a few cogent counterexamples or some particularly pointed consensus information can help a person to disavow one concept without coming anywhere near abolishing the "evidence base" in the full concept and narrative repertoire (Nisbett & Ross, 1980).

The situation is even bleaker for procedural expertise. As Nasby & Kihlstrom (1985) note: "The process of replacing inappropriate, maladaptive procedures with more appropriate, adaptive ones is probably arduous and time-consuming, if only because 'old' rules, once automatized, may not be truly lost from the repertoire, and hence may continue to intrude upon 'new' ones" (p. 13).

Interactions in familiar settings and with well-known partners will be especially hard to resist as stimuli for the application of well-worn interpretive rules and action strategies; even when the best of intentions for change are present and there is an awareness on the part of all concerned about the self-defeating nature of these routines. In fact, the most natural conditions for actually effecting change will, disappointingly, probably not be those closest to the problems at issue.

There seems to be some folk wisdom about the advisability of avoiding a "frontal assault" on well-entrenched expertise. Students, for example, who are worried about their "shy high school self" spoiling heterosexual interactions at college, frequently try out new assertiveness routines in less threatening domains, such as with roommates or with teaching assistants after class (Cantor, Brower, & Korn, 1984). They appear rather naturally to know that it is best to work on *old* life tasks in *new* life contexts, in order to avoid falling back on past, disappointing solutions. Still, the hope is that these "new" concepts and rules formed in nonthreatening, novel contexts, will eventually generalize to familiar contexts and overwhelm the problematic expertise.

Correcting Problematic Expertise

This discussion, thus far, suggests that the most rewarding efforts at change will be those that start "at the periphery" of both the familiar life task contexts and the relevant social intelligence expertise and cautiously work towards the problematic center. At the same time, such a conservative approach is not always feasible; nor do we know much about the strength of generalization of new routines learned in novel settings back to highly familiar life-task situations. Sometimes, corrective change has to take place in precisely those settings most likely to elicit exactly the expertise which is hardest to ignore and most problematic in nature.

Individuals are rarely faced with the nonthreatening opportunities for change afforded by major shifts in social environment and roles—life transitions by their very definition only occur infrequently. In any case, eventually "new selves" have to be tested with old friends and family, in which contexts the risks for "regression" are paramount. It takes a special presence of mind not to falter in the resolve to do something differently or to be a different person when confronted with the skepticism or, worse yet, oblivious reactions of significant people in important life contexts. It is hard enough to change one's own expertise; changing the favorite interpretations of others is exceptionally difficult (Petty & Cacioppo, 1981) and adds a special burden to the change process.

Consequently, if the desire is to work on new tasks (and embrace new possible selves) in old settings, or even more problematically, to work on old tasks in new ways in those same familiar settings, then it is never sufficient to work on change only outside of the realm of the familiar. In this vein, cognitively-oriented behavior therapists have developed techniques of change explicitly directed at making the transition from "old scripts" to "new selves" in familiar settings, and for eliciting social support in the process (Wilson & Franks, 1982)—that is, for negotiating the *pragmatics* of change effectively.

While a full treatment of these techniques is beyond the scope of this discussion, we will consider briefly some of them in the hopes of conveying a bit of optimism about the enacting of change in patterns of behavior in familiar settings. We draw mainly from the description of cognitive-behavior modification (usually abbreviated as CBM) presented by Meichenbaum and Cameron (1982).

1. Avoiding old scripts. As a start toward building new expertise and action strategies, individuals have to learn to "catch themselves" when they are about to begin familiar, but maladaptive behavior routines. Initially, maladaptive cycles get set in action so swiftly that there is little sense of conscious control: "Something in her tone or her face just makes me defensive and I react, almost without knowing it, by getting louder and screwing up my face, and it's all over then . . ." There is growing evidence in favor of just such immediate and basic affective states, presumably elicited by some innate or well-learned releasing signals of danger or comfort or pleasure to come, communicated without much awareness in the person's facial gestures (Izard, 1977; Tomkins, 1980). While these primary affective reactions may sometimes precede conscious control and cognitive mediation (Zajonc, 1980), the self-regulatory processes of *emotion work* also can go into action quite quickly.

It is the activation of these regulatory procedures that a client must learn if the debilitating effects of many social communications of primary affect are to be controlled and redirected. It is somewhat of a myth that emotion cannot be bridled (Lazarus, 1966). Singer (1974) and Izard (1971) have discussed techniques for working with emotions that have been useful in psychotherapy and behavior change programs. Singer (1974), for example, has shown that imagery-induced positive emotion can be utilized effectively to heighten feelings of self-control and overcome maladaptive negative emotions (Izard, 1977).

According to Hochschild (1979), individuals embrace this kind of emotion work quite readily—i.e., work comprised of cognitive, bodily and facial-expressive efforts to "psych oneself up" into feeling a different way, to evoke an absent feeling state, or to suppress an unwanted state. Emotion work is involved when people try to get themselves to see a situation differently, use self-instructions, monitor for the signs of inappropriate affect, and communicate desired affect to others in the hopes of making it real. To be sure, it does not always work, for often unwanted affect is leaked via facial grimaces or body gestures (Goffman, 1959). Yet it is part of the repertoire of self-control procedures through which behavioral change can be accomplished. Emotion work takes the emotion problem-solving cycle (Plutchik, 1980) one more conscious step forward toward behavior change by redirecting a feeling state (Salovey & Rodin, 1985).

Emotion work thus provides an example of the (highly contested) value of seeing the self in a new light or trying out a new self in precipitating behavior change (Hochschild, 1979). Wilson (1983), for example, argues that the bride who convinces herself that she is happy on the morning of her wedding is engaging in self-deception, not self-change. If we analyze emotion work as a simple act of social conformity—getting oneself to feel the "right" feelings—then it fits well in the realm of self-deception. As Wilson also points out, such efforts of self-deception are not likely to work for long.

However, we are not sure that the self-deception argument quite captures the dynamics of emotion work. In many uncertain and risky social situations, when a person has not established a comfortable sense of self or role yet, the aim of emotion work is to "try on a different face," to test a hypothesis about self in this new situation. The bride knows, at some "deeper" level of awareness, that she isn't fully or "naturally" happy, at least not yet. She also knows that it is worth trying, at least on this day.

Precisely because others will expect her to be happy, they will treat her as such and this "uncertain" self-conception ("I can rise to an occasion and overcome fear") may obtain some momentary support (Swann & Ely, 1984). The support is not for a long-term self-conception as the "happy bride." That will take more time and more testing. However, the incident has demonstrated something new about the self to this bride, i.e., that she can psych herself up to have a good time and that effort brings some positive feedback. This is only self-deception if the bride generalizes beyond the circumscribed inference to an unwarranted inference about her global emotional state or status as a bride (Swann, 1984). Instead, we believe that people learn a great deal about themselves by "trying on new faces," without, at the same time, "forgetting the old faces."

In the end, we suspect that every person experiences a more or less constant tug-of-war between the tendency to fall back on well-worn, but sometimes self-defeating routines and the challenge of making an active attempt to operate differently. Familiar cues and social expectations and the effortless quality of well-practiced routines serve to lock us in to old ways. Life transitions with new roles and new demands may encourage the battle for a "new self," or the painful critique from a significant other may shake us into action even in an old familiar context. Ironically, we all look for "real" changes in our central, and probably most recalcitrant life domains. In those arenas of expertise, it may be very difficult to effect immediate change. The prospect of striking out and trying on a new self in a less important arena of life may well be an effective first step. There is nothing quite equal to practice—from in vivo experience or observational learning—in the building and correcting of social intelligence.

2. *Learning new scripts.* The metacognitive (and metaemotional) skills of self-regulation are perfected in the process of learning new behaviors for old situations and new cognitions about those events. A substantial component of the therapeutic change process involves the teaching of new interpretive and behavioral skills for the particular problem situations at issue (Meichenbaum & Cameron, 1982). The hope here is that the person will come to feel better about him- or herself and the situation in part by observing an improvement in the interaction itself. Indeed, according to Mahoney (1979), "modifying behavior is the best way to modify cognitions" (Meichenbaum & Cameron, 1982, p. 330).

In particular, it is terribly important that, through the observation of even small successes, the perception of self-efficacy and mastery in a problem context is built up anew (Bandura, 1977). The feedback from such events can serve, slowly, as input in the modification of a relevant self-concept (of ability) in the problem domain (Bem, 1972; Locksley & Lenauer, 1981). Simply hearing oneself make positive self-reinforcement statements after a "good" performance or attributing a "poor" showing to bad luck can aid a person in building a more encouraging self-concept of ability (Harter, 1983; Bandura, 1986). The hope, then, is that these new insights and skills will provide the person with an altered perspective so that future encounters with similar stressful situations are less threatening (Lazarus & Launier, 1982).

A variety of behavioral and observational techniques can be employed to strengthen the repertoire. Modeling and guided participation, for example, have been used very effectively with phobics (Bandura, Blanchard, & Ritter, 1969). In addition, anticipatory playing through of an event, along with self-regulatory relaxation techniques, serves well to minimize incapacitating anxiety before tests or performances or heterosocial interactions (Goldfried & Goldfried, 1980; Bruch, Kaflowitz, & Kuethe, 1986; D'Zurilla & Nezu, 1980).

In other contexts, where a more diffuse problem has been identified, perfecting a satisfactory repertoire may involve more labor intensive in vivo practice. For example, in marital conflict situations, it is often very important to begin to work on new skills of interacting face to face (Jacobson, 1984). Often the two partners do not see eye to eye (so to speak) on the interpretation of events and the difficulties begin at that stage. Typically, one partner sees the other's actions as more "intentionally" aimed at hurting or angering than does the other partner (Kelley, 1979). It is extremely important to bring them together, at least to communicate the different perspectives and begin to negotiate common interpretations (Sager et al., 1971).

However, part of the problem of in vivo practice sessions is that the negative affect likely to be communicated or aroused in the course of trial and error confrontation may do more current harm than cathartic good. Therefore, some cognitive therapists suggest a "video reconstruction training" technique (e.g., Meichenbaum, 1977; Klos et al., 1983), in which problematic interpersonal communications can be *observed* but in a less confrontive context. Klos et al. (1983) report that individuals are quite surprised, in this "safe" context, to see how much contempt they actually do communicate to a spouse in the course of a "routine argument."

In this context, we would argue that the material about self and social interaction patterns revealed in the protected confines of the cognitive laboratory or therapist's office, can have enormous value in the change process. The self-reflections that such material precipitates may feed back into the social interaction cycle at some later point and, simultaneously, serve as input to the construction of new self-concepts, memories, and goals. By working over the insights gained in this process, individuals are more likely to communicate "new" selves, either directly or implicitly in their actions, in the course of future daily life events. When this happens with enough regularity the communication itself begins to turn hypothesis into fact.

There is social communication value in these messages, though it may take quite an assault to change the expectations of familiar others about the "recalcitrant" target person (Swann & Ely, 1984). Similarly, there is subjective communication value in feedback to the "cognitive self"; though, here too, past selves will not be discarded in favor of newer present selves without a substantial struggle (Markus, 1983). There is nothing better as an agent of change than to learn that one has the ability to control actions and reactions in a difficult setting, i.e., to learn *not* to do what one always did and then regretted; to learn *to* do what one never could do but always envied in others' behavior. The aim in CBM is for a client to learn new things about the self that are possible *to control*.

3. Persisting in change efforts. While it is certainly the case that gaining some insight into the precipitating causes of a negative interaction or learning new social skills and ways to regulate emotion and arousal contribute much to reducing psychological distress, it is also the case that the corrective process is never over. In their description of the final phase of therapy, Meichenbaum and Cameron (1982) maintain that the critical communication between therapist and client concerns the inevitability of "relapses" into self-defeating patterns and the necessity of conscientious attention to self-regulation and self-appraisal. The client has to learn to be "open" to social feedback, to read the danger signals and not to panic (Haan, 1982). The hope, of course, is that the experience of self-control perfected during the therapeutic efforts will serve to enhance the perception of mastery even in the face of renewed anxiety about "relapse."

To be sure, it is not easy to make substantial changes in declarative expertise and procedural habits of interaction without experiencing many such relapses into "old ways." Yet, a good part of the battle is simply coming to believe that cognitive-behavioral change *is possible*. Establishing a belief in change is, in turn, made especially difficult by the disbelievers that one encounters in the familiar social world. Not infrequently, those who care most about the person are also most prone to the "fundamental attribution error" (Ross, 1977), believing that "true change" would be nearly impossible to effect. It takes a fair share of faith on the target person's part not to falter in the face of implicitly nonsupportive, but explicitly encouraging environmental feedback.

Once again, as Meichenbaum and Cameron (1982) remind us: "What therapy aims to change are clients' responses to problems *as they arise;* the goal is to have clients acquire ways of thinking and behaving that help them cope productively with issues on an *ongoing basis*" (p. 332, our italics); to which we would add, individuals must also learn to negotiate change with the important people in their lives, because new intentions and new expertise can only be effective in a relatively receptive social environment.

4. Reflecting on the self. The preceding discussion suggests that to effect cognitive-behavioral *change* in currently self-defeating expertise, one has to retrace the steps reviewed earlier in the *development* of intentionality (see Freud, 1925, for an elaborated statement of this point). If, as Bruner (1981) demonstrated, children learn from social negotiations to be intention-directed, self-aware and sensitive to the means towards their goals, and, most critically, to be open to social feedback and corrective action, then clients involved in a self-change process must learn the same. The process of change, whether in the formal context of therapy or the natural context of social dialogue, serves to heighten individuals' awareness of those critical components of intentional problem solving in difficult life-task domains.

While it is tempting to conclude, therefore, that if the child can do it, so can the cognitively and socially more sophisticated adult, this is probably not always the case. In fact, as we have argued above, it may be precisely that very sophistication, comprised of automatic routines, well-entrenched concepts, and a significant social environment with clear expectations for consistency, that makes it difficult to remain vigilantly intent on enacting new and different self-definitions and rules of interaction. The change process itself constitutes a very taxing problem-solving endeavor.

COGNITION AND EMOTIONAL LIFE

In the present chapter we have put considerable stress on the role of *cognitive change* in behavior modification. However, this cognitive emphasis does not necessitate a disregard for human emotions and motivation as forces in personality change, as some have assumed (e.g., Hogan, 1982). Such assumptions about a "cold" cognitive enterprise tend to divide researchers unnecessarily, diverting attention from efforts to fully capture the workings of human personality. While it is beyond the scope of the present book to provide a detailed treatment of these issues, it does seem appropriate to provide at least a general statement of our position on the place of cognitions in individuals' emotional life.

Most important, cognitivists are not uninterested in emotional experience. Rather, the declarative knowledge and interpretive processes that constitute social intelligence are at the very heart of the complex emotions experienced in the context of life-task problem solving (Lazarus, 1984). As Plutchik (1980) noted, when organisms experience *fear* in the context of a threatening stimulus, the feeling state is one aspect of a complex problem-solving event; the "affective" state is intimately intertwined with "cognitive" processes of interpretation. Similarly, when individuals work to tame *anxiety* in the context of working on an achievement life task, their "thoughts" and "feelings" and "motives" interact within a *hot* interpretive process. Life-task problem solving has significant implications for self-definition, for self-evaluations, and for motivational states (Klinger, 1975, 1977). As a consequence, the study of social intelligence and life task problem solving is directly concerned with the emotional life of individuals.

The reciprocal interaction of affect and cognition in life-task problem solving is apparent in a diverse set of literatures, from those concerned with social cognition per se, to those that focus primarily on individuals' affective states and coping skills. The experience of emotion is manifest in multiple (affective and cognitive) response channels—including mood states, articulated sentiments and beliefs, and psychophysiological arousal (Clore & Ortony, 1984; Mandler, 1975). These products of emotional life, in turn, influence each other in the process of social problem solving. For example, Isen and her colleagues (see Isen, 1984) have repeatedly demonstrated the powerful role that mood states play in shaping social cognition as well as social behavior. Positive moods not only enhance prosocial behavior—a domain of behavior typically identified with the study of emotions—but also facilitate performance on "cognitive" tasks of category learning and creative thinking. Similarly, the prospective studies of depression reviewed by Peterson & Seligman (1984) clearly demonstrate the role of cognitive explanations and attributions for performance as risk factors for some forms of depressive affect. Hence, while emotional and motivational processes frequently influence social cognition, it is also important to underscore the reciprocal role of cognition in the *construction* and *control* of emotional states (Schachter & Singer, 1962).

From our perspective, therefore, there is heuristic value to be gained in identifying the experiences of emotion with the ongoing and multifaceted problem-solving efforts of people and other nonhuman species (Plutchik, 1980). The potential power of this integrative approach is well illustrated by the work of Bandura and his colleagues (see Bandura et al., 1985) in charting the complex interactions of cognitive, motivational, and physiological processes in human coping. For example, fluctuations in levels of perceived control and efficacy can set off a host of accompanying changes in autonomic system arousal, providing "cognitive" and "affective" cues to emotional experience and motivational state. In order to understand the coping and change process it is critical that these interactions not be ignored.

Accordingly, this position focuses researchers' attention away from debates about the primacy of either affect or cognition in social behavior and towards investigation of the *reciprocal interaction* of affect and cognition in social problem solving. As some have argued, it may well be useful sometimes to consider *affect without cognition* (Zajonc, 1980b). However, as Norem and Cantor (1986c) recently argued, to consider *cognition without affect* in a discussion of social intelligence and life tasks is virtually impossible; analogous, perhaps, to the study of "flavorless jelly beans" or "motionless tornados." As is clear from our choice of examples in previous chapters of "hot" self-concepts and "motivating" strategies, social intelligence can not be accurately portrayed as strictly (and "coldly") cognitive in nature, devoid of affect and motivation. Nor can the influence of this "hot" social intelligence on noncognitive response channels be underestimated in capturing the "flavor" of social behavior and coping.

Consistency and Intelligence

> Because he can represent his environment, he can place alternative constructions upon it, and, indeed, do something about it if it doesn't suit him. To the living creature, then, the universe is real, but it is not inexorable unless he chooses to construe it that way. (George Kelly, 1963, p.8)

It seems fitting to have begun this book with Jerome Bruner, and now to end it with George Kelly. For we began with individuals' expertise and life-task motivation—their readiness to see life situations and life events in a certain light—and want to end by raising the possibility of constructive alternativism in construal and action. We began with an emphasis on personality consistency. Individuals bring to bear their social intelligence in working to enact their life-task goals. We want to end with questions for the future about the potential for individuals actually to generate creative solutions to life-task problems; solutions that would facilitate their personal adjustment to the normative demands of social life. Ultimately, the study of personality must address concerns about both consistency and intelligence in social behavior.

CONSISTENCY AND EXPERTISE

It would seem almost heretical these days to end a book about personality without reference to issues of consistency. Of course, there are numerous ways to define and to search for consistency; the ubiquitous cross-situational personality coefficient is certainly not the only relevant measure, though it may be an important one (Allport, 1937). Consistency—or at least personal coherence—can be construed in a variety of additional ways that provide useful insights into the patterning of individuals' behavior. To name just a few old and new suggestions: there is *depth consistency* between unconscious drives and thoughts and the manifest behavior that provides some (albeit partial) gratification of those basic human needs (e.g., Freud, 1925), and the *dynamic consistency* of the social motive tradition (Murray, 1938; Atkinson, 1981). More recently, there is *prototype consistency*, in which the configuration of acts forms a coherent, though not well-defined category (e.g., Buss & Craik, 1983; Mischel & Peake, 1982), or *narrative consistency*, where the coherence in the self-story emerges over the life span (e.g., Epstein, 1973; Block, 1971). Finally, there is also *competence consistency*, elicited, ironically, by overstepping the person's ability to respond flexibly in taxing situations (e.g., Wright & Mischel, 1985). These are very promising directions, some well-tread and others newly explored, in the search for personality coherence.

In looking back over this book, we see elements of each of these consistencies in people's thoughts and feelings and actions in important life-task domains. Frequently, for example, we noted the cognitive and behavioral work that individuals go through in maintaining coherence in their personal narrative, and the dynamics that follow as they then play out life-task intentions in unusual ways at "odd times." Similarly, the number of cognitive-behavioral means to a common life-task outcome, as those illustrated in the achievement strategies that students ingeniously devise for handling those risky situations, is very suggestive of the fuzzy structure of act categories. Conversely, individuals' competence limits are equally apparent when their cognitive responses turn to static ruminations and their behavior is inflexible and immobilized, as in extreme instances of test anxiety or learned helplessness. Consistency of the configural and/or deep sort may be quite functional, though repetitive, specific consistency can result in pain rather than pleasure in difficult social life contexts.

Additionally, this perspective has a natural affinity for other definitions of personality consistency that place special emphasis on the ways in which individuals see themselves in situations and then bring to bear cognitive-behavioral strategies in order to reach those goals. This form of consistency, which directs attention to the cognitive representation of possible selves and life tasks and motivational intentions and their translation into action (Markus, 1983; Cantor et al., 1986; Kuhl, 1985), has, unfortunately, all of the complex manifestations of those other forms and little of the simplicity of the traditional cross-situational coefficient—but then we never have gotten all that far with simplicity.

Instead, the *intentional consistency* to which we refer here is apparent in the anticipatory intentions of individuals as they articulate personal projects or life tasks and attempt to work towards them (Little, 1983), or in the retrospective intentions embraced in the "emergence of action" (Vallacher & Wegner, 1985), as new meaning is associated after the fact with once "accidental" action. Intentional consistency is very complexly patterned, including as it does the "defensive" work of the cushioning pessimist or the protective self-handicapper (Norem & Cantor, 1986a; Snyder, 1985) and the clever substitutions arrived at by the "symbolic self-completer" (Gollwitzer & Wicklund, 1985). Furthermore, the intentions toward which the activity (cognitive, as well as behavioral) is aimed, frequently reside in the realm of "possibility" (Markus & Nurius, 1986), sometimes a bit too far from reality, as in the "degenerated intentions" of which Kuhl (1985) writes. These are all domains of intentional consistency that occur often in the context of life-task problem solving, even though the mapping between a single intention and a straightforward solution is rarely apparent at first. More frequently, there are multiple competing intentions complemented by multiple solutions to the ill-defined problems of social life (Kuhl & Beckman, 1985).

In addition to specifying the form that consistency takes, personality theories also attempt to relate structure to form—linking aspects of individuals (dispositions or motives or learning histories) to the patterning of their social behavior. With this objective in mind, we have concentrated attention on the cognitive basis of personality structure—the social intelligence expertise—as it determines the form that life-task problem solving takes in everyday situations. We assume that individuals gravitate (consciously or "mindlessly") towards life-task goals and interaction strategies that are consistent with their concepts, memories, and interpretive rules in relevant domains of expertise. This is the unabashedly mentalist position that places concepts and rules at the center of personality (Chapters 4 and 5).

Accordingly, the prediction of an individual's behavior within a normative life-task domain is expected to follow, at least in part, from knowledge of the self-concepts and personal memories and social concepts, along with habitual rules of interpretation that shape his or her intentions in the domain (Chapter 6). When students, for example, make the transition from high school to college and face the normative pressures of academic and social life on their own, they very quickly make those tasks their own (Cantor, Niedenthal, & Brower, 1985). In so doing, the construals they give to those normative tasks and the elaboration of their plans for handling task-relevant situations comes in time to influence the success of their adjustment to college life. As we would expect, the patterning of this consistency is complex. In general, those students who ultimately do the best in their academic tasks at the end of the first year are individuals who initially construe these tasks in positive terms (such as, likely to be enjoyable and not impossibly difficult) and exert effort to plan for the details of task-relevant situations. However, there is considerable flexibility and individuality in the "good solutions" to these achievement problems. Some of these students, with characteristically "optimistic" outlooks in academic domains, do best when they construe the tasks in positive terms, but explicitly avoid reflective thinking in advance of tackling each academic situation (Norem & Cantor, 1986c). Others of them, the academic "defensive pessimists" emphasize the potential for failure and engage in extensive reflection before the fact, doing very well by the end of the first year (though not without the price of relatively high perceived life stress). The pattern of intention-action consistency is indeed complicated, though the strategy that works for each student is predictable from knowledge of their self-concepts and social prototypes and rules for construing similar situations in their past.

There are, to be sure, many ways to compare individuals with respect to their social intelligence expertise in life-task domains that have been made normatively important by a life transition (Chapter 8). Some of the simplest comparisons often prove the most useful, as when a relatively straightforward measure of self-ideal discrepancy is related to affective mood state (Higgins et al., 1986) and satisfaction and behavior in specific social situations (Ruffins, Niedenthal, & Cantor, 1986). Other individual difference dimensions that follow from an expertise analysis, such as elaboration of concepts, consensuality of social prototypes, complexity of self-definition in relevant domains, also prove valuable as guides to the patterning of behavior and satisfaction at the tasks (e.g., Niedenthal et al., 1985; Linville, 1982a, 1985).

From the standpoint of *intentional consistency*, the more expertise the better. That is, to the extent that individuals have elaborate, well-integrated, relatively consensually-validated and self-relevant expertise in a life-task domain, they should be able to find creative ways to pursue their goals with ease and be somewhat buffered from the impact of initial failures to enact those goals. The positive side of expertise is that it provides a knowledge base for flexibility (Showers & Cantor, 1985; Borgida & Howard-Pitney, 1983), while simultaneously motivating people to persist in difficult tasks and ignore the distractions of competing intentions, disruptive emotions, or discrediting negative feedback (Markus, 1983; Swann & Ely, 1984). Further, when individuals have elaborate self-concepts in a particular domain they are much more likely to see "possible selves" in their futures in that arena, again serving to motivate activity—i.e., ensuring some form of intentional consistency (Markus & Wurf, 1987).

However, as we often noted in this book, intentional consistency is not the only relevant criterion measure of adjustment. Expertise can also contribute to distressingly self-defeating patterns of social interaction, as when an individual persists in playing out an unnecessarily harsh view of self or clings to old routines in the face of dramatic shifts in the rules of the social game (Nasby & Kihlstrom, 1985). The parents, for example, who fail to see their "child" grow into an independent adult, run the risk of alienating that son or daughter with inappropriately intrusive or patronizing advice-giving routines—they may persist all too long in operating from old prototypes and interaction strategies that no longer fit the task at hand. Social intelligence is developed through a process of social negotiation (Chapter 7). Similarly, it must be renegotiated fairly frequently as life contexts and roles and interaction partners evolve and transform with time and experience. The proclivity for self-awareness and for corrective change, undertaken to get rid of self-defeating routines and/or to fit the needs of a changing social environment, is another criterion measure of an effective personality. Unfortunately, this other measure may sometimes reveal the negative side of expertise.

INTELLIGENCE AND EXPERTISE

The analysis of social intelligence expertise inevitably raises questions about the qualities that make social intelligence functional or dysfunctional, adaptive or maladaptive for a particular life task: What configuration of concepts and rules is best for coping with life tasks? Are some people especially good at translating that cognitive expertise into comfortable social interactions? What fosters the proclivity for corrective action and social negotiation? These are the questions about adaptation and coping that follow from taking an *intelligence* perspective on issues in personality (Chapter 3).

For these are the features of intelligent behavior that comprise the core of the lay conception of intelligence on which such an analysis is primarily based (Sternberg et al., 1981). When people talk about the characteristics of individuals whom they see as especially intelligent, it is often their special wealth of knowledge in an area, their pragmatic ability to get things done, and their self-reflective and socially sensitive attitude that emerge as distinctive (see Table 3-1). Accordingly, we have emphasized declarative and procedural expertise, strategies of action and self-regulation, and mechanisms for effecting change in a social context, as central features of social intelligence; all the while attempting to remain relatively value-free and to avoid "good coper" vs. "bad coper" distinctions as much as possible. Yet, given the intelligence context in which we have placed this approach, it seems only fitting to turn attention for the future more explicitly to these questions of adjustment that have been central to the mandate of personologists for quite some time (Murray, 1938). In fact, we hope that the intelligence perspective on personality will eventually shed new light on these old questions of adaptation.

First, at a general level, we join other "social cognitivists"—Kelly, Mischel, Rotter, and Bandura—in placing the value on individuals' ability to find creative solutions to challenging life problems and on their openness to self-reflection and corrective change when things are not going well. In every life-task context there are numerous ways to frame a problem and a variety of comparably fulfilling goals to pursue; the intelligent individual tries to avoid dependence on a favorite "cognitive style" of problem solving (Chapter 2). Therefore, if there is such a thing as a "good coper"—and we doubt there is such a generalized phenomenon—then it is more likely that the skill resides in a (metacognitive) attitude rather than in the specific content of a good problem-solving style (see Baltes, 1986, on wisdom in the pragmatics of life planning and life review).

More specifically, the social intelligence analysis guides one away from generalized assessments of "coping status" or global adjustment, towards more particular conclusions about the individual's profile of expertise (and ignorance) in the life-task domains of central concern at that point in time (Chapters 6 and 8). Within a life-task domain—one as broad as interpersonal intimacy or as specific as finding a spouse (depending on the person's construal of his or her life situations)—it is possible to say that the more the person is an "expert" in that life domain the better. Expertise implies the potential for creative solutions to difficult problems and multiple avenues for self-definition. Expertise (usually) implies elaborate concepts that represent a diversity of experience and self-identities in the domain and that highlight positive possibilities for the self which are relatively in line with others' expectations. In turn, this declarative knowledge base typically maps onto flexible routines for construing situations and events and for finding comfortable patterns of social interaction. In that sense, expertise can be very motivating, allowing people reasonably to see themselves working productively on their special life tasks in many current life contexts, with the implicit approval of meaningful private audiences (Baldwin & Holmes, 1985), and perhaps the explicit support of relevant public audiences.

Consider, as one hypothetical illustration, the fate of "experts" at assertive confrontation who like to face interpersonal conflict directly, working in even the most emotionally difficult situations until all concerns are aired (see Nasby & Kihlstrom, 1985). These are people who seem to regulate and control their expertise at conflict resolution quite naturally in accordance with the messages from social partners in different life-task contexts. When working on long-term intimacy with a spouse who can tolerate "only so much commotion," they learn new routines, mixing the heavy with the light, the confrontive with the comic gesture (Klos, Loomis, & Ruhrold, 1983). By contrast, when "dealing" with recalcitrant colleagues, and mixing interpersonal and achievement tasks, they find that it works best just to get it over with quickly and go on about their business, at least enabling themselves not to ruminate too long and too hard (Kuhl, 1985). In this case, as in most examples of functional expertise, intelligence for a life task means "knowing a lot about the task" and "knowing what it is that one can do" and "with whom to do what"—it means that one's expertise is well-suited to the pragmatic realities of the current life-task contexts (Chapters 2, 6 and 7).

Yet there is another side to intelligence which does not follow automatically from the presence of a special expertise in a life-task domain. This is the proclivity for "knowing when to stop, look, and change" the thrust of life-task activity in the face of disappointing results or negative social feedback. This is the self-critical side of intelligence that is much less apparent in routine social interactions and, therefore, less likely to receive attention in the literature. In fact, much more is known about the conservative aspects of declarative and procedural expertise, than about individuals' willingness to relinquish preferred concepts and strategies of interaction that present impediments to social adjustment.

Perhaps this self-critical side to intelligent behavior is less well-developed, or the potential for constructive self-change less realized, because the motivation to change often is not sufficient to counteract reliance on automatized routines in familiar life settings (Chapter 8). Even the most well-intentioned adult finds himself or herself acting in exactly the way that he or she most wanted to avoid, when a familiar script surfaces in the context of a well-practiced task.

Sometimes, of course, those verbalized intentions to change actually mask an underlying belief in the correctness of one's actions; a belief that inhibits any real movement towards change. For example, it is often extremely hard for one partner in a relationship to truly believe that the other partner would not be better off conforming to his or her suggestions. The "truth-value" in one's own expertise is so self-evident that others appear to be perversely resistant when they fail to conform to those optimal patterns of interaction.

Nevertheless, if one person's solutions to interpersonal problems are not sufficiently negotiated with the plans and desires of others, then new problems will inevitably arise. It is not adaptive or intelligent to contribute one's own delusions in an effort to solve a life task—as every parent who has tried to hang on to the "good old days" of family togetherness knows all too well. The same concepts and rules that made it "easy" to solve a life task at one point in time, in one environment, can all of a sudden present major stumbling blocks to progess in a new life-task environment. Expertise for life tasks that is not properly negotiated with the reality of changing life contexts and interaction partners inevitably creates more problems than it solves.

Clearly, then, we know a great deal about the impediments to effective coping presented by individuals' reluctance, sometimes motivated by conviction and sometimes simply reflecting the persistence of well-practiced habits, to embrace new solutions to old problems. By contrast, far less is known about the many ways in which people successfully negotiate compromises in everyday social interactions—i.e., socially construct their expertise in the midst of working on joint life tasks (Little, 1983). The prototype for this kind of intelligent interchange is quite apparent in parent-child communications (Bruner, 1981); the "communication game" also provides an adult analogue (Higgins, 1981). Similarly, "group think" tasks certainly require those skills at negotiated solutions (Janis, 1982), as do most "family systems" (Sager, 1976). In all these contexts, people develop ways of intelligently leaving their own expertise behind, at least for the moment.

In this regard, it is important, on a more optimistic note, to recognize that people sometimes do demonstrate another side to social intelligence: the proclivity for compromising or even disregarding their own expertise. Unfortunately, the instances of such change are hard to observe in laboratory contexts because they are fostered in truly *social* interactions (Goffman, 1959). Moreover, the change process is likely to be very subtle for a good long time—as are all such negotiated compromises—and may even be missed initially by the key actors in the event. It is rare that individuals verbally announce their intentions to change old habits, although, as Kuhl (1985) noted, such announcements are very effective motivators of social support for change. There is something very intelligent about expressing the knowledge of personal limitations so as to enlist social support in the change process. This is the other side of individuals' *social* intelligence, a side to which we anticipate much attention will be given in future analyses of the promise and the limits of that intelligence.

As Kelly and Bruner recognized, people confront life situations with a readiness to see in them what they want to be there; but human intelligence also allows recognition that things are not always as anticipated or desired. In our language, individuals develop characteristic ways of problem solving about specific life tasks. These favorite situation readings and preferred strategies of action reflect the relatively unique collection of concepts and rules in each individual's social intelligence repertoire. However, those life tasks and strategies also can change in the face of new learning and new experiences. Of course, what we do not know is just how frequently and in what circumstances people actually do develop a readiness to see something new—to engage in constructive alternativism in social construal and action.

References

Abelson, R. (1976). Script processing in attitude formation and decision making. In J. S. Carroll & J. W. Payne (Eds.), *Cognition and social behavior*. Hillsdale, NJ: Erlbaum.
—— (1981). Psychological status of the script concept. *American Psychologist, 36*, 715-29.
—— (1982). Three modes of attitude-behavior consistency. In M. P. Zanna, E. T. Higgins, & C. P. Herman (Eds.), *Consistency in social behavior: The Ontario symposium* (Vol. 2). Hillsdale, NJ: Erlbaum.
——, Kinder, D., & Peters, M. (1982). Affective and semantic components in political person perception. *Journal of Personality and Social Psychology, 42*(4), 619-30.
Abramson, L. Y., Seligman, M. E. P., & Teasdale, J. D. (1978). Learned helplessness in humans: Critique and reformulation. *Journal of Abnormal Psychology, 87*, 49-74.
Acredolo, L. P., Adams, A., & Goodwyn, S. W. (1984). The role of self-produced movement and visual tracking in infant spatial orientation. *Journal of Experimental Child Psychology, 38*, 312-27.
Adler, A. (1929). *The science of living*. New York: Greenberg.
—— (1931). *What life should mean to you*. Boston: Little, Brown.
Ainsworth, M. D. S., Blehar, M., Waters, E., & Wall, S. (1978). *Patterns of attachment*. Hillsdale, NJ: Erlbaum.
Albright, J. S., & Kihlstrom, J. F. (1986). *Motivation, visual perspective, and the self-other difference in causal attribution*. Unpublished manuscript, Northwestern University.
Alloy, L. B., & Abramson, L. Y. (1979). Judgment of contingency in depressed and non-depressed students: Sadder but wiser? *Journal of Experimental Psychology, 108*, 441-87.
—— (1982). Learned helplessness, depression, and the illusion of control. *Journal of Personality and Social Psychology, 42*, 1114-26.
Allport, G. W. (1937). *Personality: A psychological interpretation*. New York: Holt.
—— (1955). *Becoming*. New Haven: Yale University Press.
—— (1961). *Pattern and growth in personality*. New York: Holt, Rinehart, & Winston.

REFERENCES

— (1986). *Social foundations of thought and action: A social cognitive theory.* Englewood Cliffs, NJ: Prentice-Hall.

—, Blanchard, E. B., & Ritter, B. (1969). Relative efficacy of desensitization and modeling approaches for inducing behavioral, affective, and attitudinal changes. *Journal of Personality and Social Psychology, 13,* 173–99.

—, Reese, L., & Adams, N. E. (1982). Microanalysis of action and fear arousal as a function of differential levels of perceived self-efficacy. *Journal of Personality and Social Psychology, 43,* 5–21.

—, Taylor, C. B., Williams, S. L., Mefford, I. N., & Barchas, J. D. (1985). Catecholamine secretion as a function of perceived coping self-efficacy. *Journal of Consulting and Clinical Psychology, 53,* 406–14.

—, & Walters, R. H. (1963). *Social learning and personality development.* New York: Holt, Rinehart & Winston.

nister, D., & Agnew, J. (1977). The child's construing of self. In J. Cole (Ed.), *Nebraska Symposium on Motivation.* Lincoln: University of Nebraska Press.

—, & Mair, J. M. M. (1968). *The evaluation of personal constructs.* London: Academic Press.

lay, C., & Wellman, H. (1984). *Autobiographical memory: recognizing, ordering and dating everyday events.* Unpublished manuscript, University of Michigan.

h, J. A. (1982). Attention and automaticity in the processing of self-relevant information. *Journal of Personality and Social Psychology, 43,* 425–36.

—, & Thein, R. D. (1985). Individual construct accessibility, person memory, and the recall-judgment link: The case of information overload. *Journal of Personality and Social Psychology, 49,* 1129–46.

er, R. G. (1968). *Ecological psychology.* Stanford: Stanford University Press.

n, J. (1981). Reflective thinking as a goal of education. *Intelligence, 5,* 291–309.

— (1982). Personality and intelligence. In R. Sternberg (Ed.), *Handbook of human intelligence.* Cambridge: Cambridge University Press.

m, A., Calesnick, L. E., Davis, G. E., & Gatchel, R. J. (1982). Individual differences in coping with crowding: Stimulus screening and social overload. *Journal of Personality and Social Psychology, 43,* 821–30.

meister, R. F. (1985). A self-presentational view of social phenomena. *Psychology Bulletin, 91,* 3–26.

, A. T. (1967). *Depression: Causes and treatment.* Philadelphia: University of Pennsylvania Press.

— (1976). *Cognitive therapy and the emotional disorders.* New York: International University Press.

, P. A., & Byrne, D. (1977). Repression-sensitization. In H. London & J. E. Exner, Jr. (Eds.), *Dimensions of personality.* New York: Wiley.

, D. (1972). Self-perception theory. In L. Berkowitz (Ed.), *Advances in experimental social psychology* (Vol. 6). New York: Academic Press.

—, & Funder, D. (1978). Predicting more of the people more of the time: Assessing the personality of situations. *Psychological Review, 85*(6), 485–501.

glas, S., & Jones, E. E. (1978). Drug choice as an internalization strategy in response to noncontingent success. *Journal of Personality and Social Psychology, 36,* 405–17.

k, J. (1971). *Lives through time.* Berkeley, CA: Bancroft Books.

giano, A., & Ruble, D. (1979). Competence and the overjustification effect: A developmental study. *Journal of Personality and Social Psychology, 37,* 1462–68.

gida, E., & Brekke, N. (1981). The base rate fallacy in attribution and prediction. In J. Harvey, W. Ickes, & R. Kidd (Eds.), *New direction in attribution research* (Vol. 3). Hillsdale, NJ: Erlbaum.

—, & Howard-Pitney, B. (1983) Personality involvement and the robustness of perceptual salience effects. *Journal of Personality and Social Psychology, 45,* 560–70.

nstein, P., & Quevillon, R. (1976). The effects of a self-instructional package on overactive preschool boys. *Journal of Applied Behavior Analysis, 9,* 176–88.

er, G. H. (1981). Mood and memory. *American Psychologist, 36,* 129–48.

—, & Gilligan, S. G. (1979). Remembering information related to one's self. *Journal of Research in Personality, 13,* 404–19.

—, Black, J. B., & Turner, T. J., (1979). Scripts in memory for text. *Cognitive Psychology, 11,* 177–220.

————, & Odbert, H. S. (1937). Trait-names, a psycho-lexical study. *Psychologi graphs, 47* (Whole No. 211).

Andersen, S. M. (1984). Self-knowledge and social inference: II. The diagnosticit tive/affective and behavioral data. *Journal of Personality and Social Psyc* 294–307.

————, & Klatsky, R. L. (in press, 1986). Traits and social caricatures: Levels of cat in person perception. *Journal of Personality and Social Psychology.*

————, Lazowski, L., & Donisi, M. (1986). Salience and self-inference: The rol recollections in self-inference processes. *Social Cognition, 4*(1), 75–95.

————, & Ross, L. (1984). Self-knowledge and social inference: I. The impact o affective and behavioral data. *Journal of Personality and Social Psychology*

Anderson, C. A. (1983). Imagination and expectation: The effect of imagining scripts on personal intentions. *Journal of Personality and Social Psyc* 293–305.

———— (1982). Innoculation and counter-explanation: Debiasing techniques ir verance of social theories. *Social Cognition, 1,* 126–139.

Anderson, J. R. (1976). *Language, memory, and thought.* Hillsdale, NJ: Erlbaum

———— (1978). Arguments concerning representations for mental imagery. *P Review, 85,* 249–77.

———— (1981). *Cognitive psychology and its implications.* San Francisco: W. H.

Anderson, N. H. (1968). Likableness ratings of 555 personality-trait words. *Personality and Social Psychology, 9,* 272–79.

———— (1974). Cognitive algebra: Integration theory applied to social attrib Berkowitz (Ed.), *Advances in experimental social psychology* (Vol. 7) Academic Press.

Antonucci, T. C., & Levitt, M. J. (1984). Early prediction of attachment secur variate approach. *Infant Behavioral Development, 7,* 1–18.

Argyle, M. (1981). The experimental study of the basic features of situations. Ir son (Ed.), *Toward a psychology of situations: An interactional perspecti* NJ: Erlbaum.

Arnkoff, D. (1980). Psychotherapy from the perspective of cognitive theory. In (Ed.), *Psychotherapy process.* New York: Plenum Press.

Asch, S. E. (1946). Forming impressions of personality. *Journal of Abnorm Psychology, 41,* 258–90.

————, & Zukier, H. (1984). Thinking about persons. *Journal of Personali Psychology, 46,* 1230–40.

Ashmore, R. D., & Del Boca, F. K. (1980). Conceptual approaches to st sterotyping. In D. L. Hamilton (Ed.), *Cognitive processes in stereotyp group behavior.* Hillsdale, NJ: Erlbaum.

Athay, M., & Darley, J. M. (1981). Toward an interpersonal action-cente personality. In N. Cantor & J. F. Kihlstrom (Eds.), *Personality, cogniti interaction.* Hillsdale, NJ: Erlbaum.

Atkinson, J. W. (1964). *An introduction to motivation.* Princeton: Van Nostran

———— (1981). Studying personality in the context of an advanced motivation *American Psychologist, 32*(2), 117–29.

Baldwin, M. W., & Holmes, J. G. (1985). *Salient private audiences and awarer* Unpublished manuscript, University of Waterloo.

Baltes, P. B. (in press, 1986). The aging of intelligence: On the dynamics b and decline. *Scientific American.*

————, Dittman-Kohli, F., & Dixon, R. A. (1984). New perspectives on the c intelligence in adulthood: Toward a dual-process conception and a mc optimization with compensation. In P. B. Baltes & O. G. Brim, Jr. (E *development and behavior* (Vol. 6, pp. 33–76). New York: Academic Pre

Bandura, A. (1973). *Aggression: A social learning analysis.* Englewood Cliff Hall.

———— (1977). Self-efficacy: Toward a unifying theory of behavioral change *Review, 84,* 191–215.

———— (1978). The self system in reciprocal determinism. *American Psycholog*

———— (1982). Self-efficacy mechanism in human agency. *American Psycholog*

Brewer, M. B., & Kramer, R. M. (1985). The psychology of intergroup attitudes and behavior. In M. R. Rosenzweig & L. W. Porter (Eds.), *Annual review of psychology* (Vol. 36). Palo Alto, CA: Annual Reviews.

Brim, O. G., Jr., & Ryff, C. D. (1980). On the properties of life events. In P. B. Baltes & O. G. Brim, Jr. (Eds.), *Life-span development and behavior* (Vol. 3). New York: Academic Press.

Brooks-Gunn, J., & Lewis, M. (1984). The development of early visual self-recognition. *Developmental Review, 4*, 215–39.

Brown, R., & Kulik, J. (1977). Flashbulb memories. *Cognition, 5*, 73–99.

Bruch, M. A., Kaflowitz, N. G., & Kuethe, M. (1986). Beliefs and the subjective meaning of thoughts: Analysis of the role of self-statements in academic test performance. *Cognitive Therapy and Research, 10*(1), 51–69.

Bruner, J. S. (1957). On perceptual readiness. *Psychological Review, 64*, 123–52.

———— (1981). Intention in the structure of action and interaction. *Advances in Infancy Research, 1*, 41–56.

———— (1983). *The pragmatics of language and the language of pragmatics.* Paper presented to Katz-Newcomb Lecture, University of Michigan, Ann Arbor, MI.

————, & Goodman, C. (1947). Value and need as organizing factors in perception. *Journal of Abnormal and Social Psychology, 42*, 33–44.

————, Goodnow, J. J., & Austin, G. A. (1956). *A study of thinking.* New York: Wiley.

————, & Tagiuri, R. (1954). Person perception. In G. Lindzey (Ed.), *Handbook of social psychology* (Vol. 2). Reading, MA: Addison-Wesley.

Brunswik, E. (1956). *Perception and the representative design of psychological experiments* (2nd ed.). Berkeley and Los Angeles: University of California Press.

Bugenthal, D., Whalen, C., & Henker, B. (1977). Causal attributions of hyperactive children and motivational assumptions of two behavior-change approaches: Evidence for an interactionist position. *Child Development, 48*, 874–84.

Bulman, R. J., & Wortman, C. B. (1977). Attributions of blame and coping in the "real world": Severe accident victims react to their lot. *Journal of Personality and Social Psychology, 35*, 351–63.

Buss, A. H. (1980). *Self-consciousness and social anxiety.* San Francisco: Freeman.

———— & Plomin, R. (1975). *A temperament theory of personality development.* New York: Wiley.

Buss, D. M., & Craik, K. H. (1983). The act frequency approach to personality. *Psychological Review, 90*, 105–26.

Byrne, D. (1964). Repression-sensitization as a dimension of personality. In B. A. Maher (Ed.), *Progress in experimental personality research.* New York: Academic Press.

Cacioppo, J. T., Glass, C. R., & Merluzzi, T. V. (1979). Self-statement and self-evaluations: A cognitive-response analysis of heterosocial anxiety. *Cognitive Therapy Research, 3*, 249–63.

Cacioppo, J. T., & Petty, R. E. (1982). The need for cognition. *Journal of Personality and Social Psychology, 42*, 116–31.

Campbell, J. D., & Tesser, A. (1983). Motivational interpretations of hindsight bias: An individual-difference analysis. *Journal of Personality, 51*, 605–20.

Cantor, N. (1978). *Prototypicality and personality judgments.* Unpublished doctoral dissertation, Department of Psychology, Stanford University.

————, Brower, A., & Korn, H. (1984). *Cognitive bases of personality in a life transition.* Paper presented at the 23rd International Congress of Psychology, Acapulco.

————, & Genero, N. (1986). Psychiatric diagnosis and natural categorization: A close analogy. In T. Millon & G. Klerman (Eds.), *Contemporary issues in psychopathology.* New York: Guilford Press.

————, & Kihlstrom, J. F. (1981). *Personality, cognition, and social interaction.* Hillsdale, NJ: Erlbaum.

————, & Kihlstrom, J. F. (1982). Cognitive and social processes in personality: Implications for behavior therapy. In E. M. Franks & G. T. Wilson (Eds.), *Handbook of behavior therapy.* New York: Guilford.

————, & Kihlstrom, J. F. (1985). Social intelligence: The cognitive basis of personality. In P. Shaver (Ed.), *Review of personality and social psychology* (Vol 6). Beverly Hills: Sage.

———, Mackie, D., & Lord, C. (1984). Choosing partners and activities: The social perceiver decides to mix it up. *Social Cognition, 2,* 256–72.

———, Markus, H., Niedenthal, P., & Nurius, P. (1986). On motivation and the self-concept. In R. M. Sorrentino & E. T. Higgins (Eds.), *Motivation and cognition: Foundations of social behavior.* New York: Guilford Press.

———, & Mischel, W. (1979). Prototypes in person perception. In L. Berkowitz (Ed.), *Advances in experimental social psychology* (Vol. 12). New York: Academic Press.

———, Mischel, W., & Schwartz, J. (1982a). A prototype analysis of psychological situations. *Cognitive Psychology, 14,* 45–77.

———, Mischel, W., & Schwartz, J. (1982b). Social knowledge: Structure, content, use, and abuse. In A. Hastorf & A. Isen (Eds.), *Cognitive Social Psychology.* New York: Elsevier North-Holland.

———, Niedenthal, P., & Brower, A. (1985). *Life task problem-solving in the transition to college.* Presented at Annual Meeting of the Society of Experimental Social Psychology, Evanston, IL.

———, Smith, E. E., French, R., & Mezzich, J. (1980). Psychiatric diagnosis as prototype categorization. *Journal of Abnormal Psychology, 89,* 191–93.

Carlson, R. (1981). Studies in script theory: 1. Adult analogs of a childhood nuclear scene. *Journal of Personality and Social Psychology, 40,* 501–10.

Carver, C. S., Blaney, P. H., & Scheier, M. F. (1979). Focus of attention, chronic expectancy, and responses to feared stimulus. *Journal of Personality and Social Psychology, 37,* 1186–95.

Carver, C. S., & Scheier, M. F. (1978). Self-focusing effects of dispositional self-consciousness, mirror presence, and audience presence. *Journal of Personality and Social Psychology, 36,* 324–32.

——— (1981). *Attention and self-regulation: A control-theory approach to human behavior.* New York: Springer-Verlag.

——— (1985). A control-systems approach to the self-regulation of action. In J. Kuhl & J. Beckmann (Eds.), *Action Control.* New York: Springer-Verlag.

Cattell, R. B., & Horn, J. L. (1978). A check on the theory of fluid & crystallized intelligence with description of new subtest designs. *Journal of Educational Measurement, 15,* 189–264.

Chaiken, S., & Baldwin, M. W. (1981). Affective-cognitive consistency and the effect of salient behavioral information on the self-perception of attitudes. *Journal of Personality and Social Psychology, 41,* 1–12.

Chanowitz, B., & Langer, E. (1980). Knowing more (or less) than you can show: Understanding control through the mindlessness-mindfulness distinction. In J. Garber & M. Seligman (Eds.), *Human helplessness: Theory and applications.* New York: Academic Press.

——— (1981). Premature cognitive commitment. *Journal of Personality and Social Psychology, 41,* 1051–63.

Chase, W. G., & Simon, H. A. (1973). The mind's eye in chess. In W. G. Chase (Ed.), *Visual information processing.* New York: Academic Press.

Cheney, D., Seyfarth, R., & Smuts, B. (in press, 1986). Social relationships and social cognition in nonhuman primates. *Science.*

Chew, B. R. (1979). *Probing for remote and recent autobiographical memories.* Paper presented at the 87th Annual Meeting of the American Psychological Association, New York.

———, & Kihlstrom, J. F. (1986). *Processing personal information in search of self-other differences.* Unpublished manuscript, University of Wisconsin.

Chi, M. T. (1978). Knowledge structures and memory development. In R. S. Siegler (Ed.), *Children's thinking: What develops?* Hillsdale, NJ: Erlbaum.

———, & Koeske, R. (1983). Network representations of a child's dinosaur knowledge. *Developmental Psychology, 19,* 29–39.

Clark, M., & Isen, A. (1982). Toward understanding the relationship between feeling states and social behavior. In A. Hastorf & A. Isen (Eds.), *Cognitive social psychology.* New York: Elsevier.

Clore, G. L., & Ortony, A. (1984). Some issues for a cognitive theory of emotion. *Cahiers de Psychologie Cognitive, 4*(1), 55–57.

Cohen, C. E. (1981). Goals and schemas in person perception: Making sense out of the stream of behavior. In N. Cantor & J. Kihlstrom (Eds.), *Personality, cognition, and social behavior.* Hillsdale, NJ: Erlbaum.

Cohen, S., Kamarick, T., & Mermelstein, R. (1983). A global measure of perceived stress. *Journal of Health and Social Behavior, 24,* 385-96.

Cohler, B. (1982). Personal narrative and life course. In P. Baltes & O. Brim, Jr. (Eds.), *Life-Span Development and Behavior* (Vol. 4). New York: Academic Press.

Collins, J. L. (1982). *Self-efficacy and ability in achievement behavior.* Paper presented at the annual meeting of the American Educational Research Association, New York.

Conway, M., & Ross, M. (1984). Getting what you want by revising what you had. *Journal of Personality and Social Psychology, 47,* 738-48.

Cooley, C. (1902). *Human nature and the social order.* New York: Scribner.

Coopersmith, S. (1967). *The antecedents of self-esteem.* San Francisco: Freeman.

Coyne, J. C. (1982). A critique of cognitions as causal entities with particular reference to depression. *Cognitive Therapy and Research, 6,* 3-13.

———, & Gotlib, I. H. (1983). The role of cognition in depression: A critical appraisal. *Psychological Bulletin, 94,* 472-505.

Crocker, J., Hannah, D., & Weber, R. (1983). Person memory and causal attributions. *Journal of Personality and Social Psychology, 44,* 55-66.

———, Fiske, S. T., & Taylor, S. E. (1985). Schematic bases of belief change. In R. Eiser (Ed.), *Attitudinal judgment.* New York: Springer-Verlag.

Crockett, W. (1983). *Constructs, impressions, actions, responses, and construct change: A model of processes in impression formation.* Paper presented at the Fifth International Conference of Personal Construct Psychology, Boston, MA.

Cronbach, L. J. (1957). Beyond the two disciplines of scientific psychology. *American Psychologist, 30,* 116-27.

Crovitz, H. F., & Quina-Holland, K. (1976). Proportion of episodic memories from early childhood by years of age. *Bulletin of the Psychonomic Society, 7,* 61-62.

Darley, J. M., & Fazio, R. H. (1980). Expectancy confirmation processes arising in the social interaction sequence. *American Psychologist, 35,* 867-81.

———& Goethals, G. R. (1980). People's analyses of the causes of ability-linked performances. In L. Berkowitz (Ed.), *Advances in experimental social psychology* (Vol. 13). New York: Academic Press.

Dasen, P. R., Berry, J. W., & Witkin, H. A. (1979). The use of developmental theories cross-culturally. In L. Eckensberger, Y. Poortinga, & W. Lonner (Eds.), *Cross-cultural contributions to psychology.* Amsterdam: Swets & Zeitlinger.

Davison, G. C., Tsujimoto, R. N., & Glaros, A. G. (1973). Attribution and the maintenance of behavior change in falling asleep. *Journal of Abnormal Psychology, 82,* 124-33.

Deaux, K. (1985). Sex and gender. In M. Rosenzweig & L. W. Porter (Eds.), *Annual Review of Psychology* (Vol. 36). Palo Alto, CA: Annual Reviews.

———, & Lewis, L. L. (1984). The structue of gender stereotypes: Interrelationships among components and gender label. *Journal of Personality and Social Psychology, 46,* 991-1004.

Deci, E. L., Nezlek, J., & Sheinman, L. (1981). Characteristics of the rewarder and intrinsic motivation of the rewardee. *Journal of Personality and Social Psychology, 40*(1), 1-10.

Deci, E. L. & Ryan, R. M. (1980). The empirical exploration of intrinsic motivational processes. In L. Berkowitz (Ed.), *Advances in experimental social psychology* (Vol. 13). New York: Academic Press.

Denney, N. (1984). A model of cognitive development across the life span. *Developmental Review, 4,* 171-91.

———, Pearce, K. A., & Palmer, A. M. (1982) A developmental study of adults' performance on traditional and practical problem-solving tasks. *Experimental Aging Research, 8,* 115-18.

Devine, P. G., & Ostrom, T. M. (1985). Cognitive mediation of inconsistency discounting. *Journal of Personality and Social Psychology, 49,* 5-21.

Dewey, J. (1933). *How we think: A restatement of the relation of reflective thinking to the educative process.* Boston: Heath.

Diener, E., & Larsen, R. J. (1984). Temporal stability and cross-situational consistency of affective, behavioral, and cognitive responses. *Journal of Personality and Social Psychology, 47*(4), 871-83.

Dobson, K. S., & Shaw, B. F. (1986). Cognitive assessment with major depressive disorders. *Cognitive Therapy and Research, 10*(1), 12–29.

Dornbusch, S. M., Hastorf, A. H., Richardson, S. A., Muzzy, R. E., & Vreeland, R. S. (1956). The perceiver and the perceived: Their relative influence on the categories of interpersonal cognition. *Journal of Personality and Social Psychology, 1,* 434–40.

Duval, S., & Wicklund, R. (1972). *A theory of objective self-awareness.* New York: Academic Press.

Dweck, C. (1983). Achievement motivation. In P. H. Mussen (Ed.), *Handbook of Child Psychology: Ed. 4. Socialization, Personality and Social Development* (Vol. 4). New York: Wiley.

D'Zurilla, T. J., & Goldfried, M. R. (1971). Problem solving and behavior modification. *Journal of Abnormal Psychology, 78,* 107–26.

———, & Nezu, A. (1980). A study of the generation-of-alternatives process in social problem solving. *Cognitive Therapy and Research, 4,* 67–72.

Ebbesen, E. B., & Allen, R. B. (1979). Cognitive processes in implicit personality trait inferences. *Journal of Personality and Social Psychology, 37,* 471–88.

Einhorn, H. J. (1982). Learning from experience and suboptimal rules in decision making. In D. Kahneman, P. Slovic, & A. Tversky (Eds.), *Judgment under uncertainty: Heuristics and biases.* New York: Cambridge University Press.

———, & Hogarth, R. (1986). Judging probable cause. *Psychological Bulletin, 99*(1), 3–19.

Elig, T. W., & Frieze, I. H. (1979). Measuring causal attributions for success and failure. *Journal of Personality and Social Psychology, 37,* 621–34.

Epstein, S. (1973). The self-concept revisited, or a theory of a theory. *American Psychologist, 28,* 404–16.

Erber, R., & Fiske, S. T. (1984). Outcome dependency and attention to inconsistent information. *Journal of Personality and Social Psychology, 47*(4), 709–26.

Erdelyi, M. H. (1985). *Psychoanalysis: Freud's cognitive psychology.* New York: Freeman.

Ericsson, K. A., & Simon, H. A. (1980). Verbal reports as data. *Psychological Review, 87,* 215–51.

Erikson, E. H. (1950). *Childhood and society.* New York: Norton.

Fazio, R., & Zanna, M. (1978). Attitudinal qualities relating to the strength of the attitude-behavior relationship. *Journal of experimental social psychology, 14,* 398–408.

———, (1981). Direct experience and attitude-behavior consistency. *Advanced Experimental Social Psychology, 14,* 161–202.

Fehr, B., & Russell, J. A. (1984). Concept of emotion viewed from a prototype perspective. *Journal of Experimental Psychology: General, 113,* 464–86.

Feiring, C., Lewis, M., & Starr, M. (1981). *Indirect and direct effects on children's reactions to unfamiliar adults.* Unpublished manuscript, Rutgers University.

Feldman, D. H. (1980). *Beyond universals in cognitive development.* Norwood, NJ: Ablex.

Fenigstein, A. (1979). Self-consciousness, self-attention, and social interaction. *Journal of Personality and Social Psychology, 37,* 461–70.

———, Scheier, M. F., & Buss, A. H. (1975). Public and private self-consciousness: Assessment and theory. *Journal of Consulting and Clinical Psychology, 43,* 522–27.

Fischer, K. (1980). A theory of cognitive development: The control and construction of hierarchies of skill. *Psychological Review, 87*(6), 477–531.

Fischhoff, B. (1982). For those condemned to study the past: Heuristics and biases in hindsight. In D. Kahnemen, P. Slovic, & A. Tversky (Eds.), *Judgment under uncertainty: Heuristics and biases.* New York: Cambridge University Press.

Fiske, S. T. (1980). Attention and weight in person perception: The impact of negative and extreme behavior. *Journal of Personality and Social Psychology, 38,* 889–906.

——— (1981). Social cognition and affect. In J. Harvey (Ed.), *Cognition, social behavior, and the environment.* Hillsdale, NJ: Erlbaum.

——— (1982). Schema-triggered affect: Applications to social perception. In M. S. Clark & S. T. Fiske (Eds.), *Affect and cognition: The 17th Annual Carnegie Symposium on Cognition.* Hillsdale, NJ: Erlbaum.

———& Kinder, D. R. (1981). Involvement, expertise, and schema use: Evidence from political cognition. In N. Cantor & H. Kihlstrom (Eds.), *Personality, cognition, and social interaction.* Hillsdale, NJ: Erlbaum.

———, Kinder, D. R., & Larter, W. M. (1983). The novice and the expert: Knowledge-based strategies in political cognition. *Journal of Experimental Social Psychology, 19,* 381-400.

——, & Pavelchak, M. A. (1986). Category-based versus piecemeal-based affective responses: Developments in schema-triggered affect. In R. M. Sorrentino & E. T. Higgins (Eds.), *Handbook of Motivation and Cognition.* New York: Guilford Press.

——, & Taylor, S. E. (1984). *Social Cognition.* Reading, MA: Addison-Wesley.

Flavell, J. H. (1977). *Cognitive development.* Englewood Cliffs, NJ: Prentice-Hall.

—— (1979). Metacognition and cognitive monitoring. *American Psychologist, 34,* 906-11.

——, & Ross, L. (1981). *Social and cognitive development: Frontiers and possible future.* New York: Cambridge University Press.

——, & Wellman, H. (1977). Metamemory. In R. V. Kail, Jr. & J. Hagen (Eds.), *Perspectives on the development of memory and cognition.* Hillsdale, NJ: Erlbaum.

Fong, G. T., & Markus, H. (1982). Self-schemas and judgments about others. *Social Cognition, 1,* 191-205.

Ford, M. E., & Tisak, M. S. (1983). A further search for social intelligence. *Journal of Educational Psychology, 75*(2), 196-206.

Forgas, J. P. (1976). The perception of social episodes: Categorical and dimensional representations in two social milieus. *Journal of Personality and Social Psychology, 33,* 199-209.

—— (1982). Episode cognition: Internal representations of interaction routines. *Advances in experimental Social Psychology, 15,* 59-101.

Frankel, A., & Snyder, M. L. (1978). Poor performance following unsolvable problems: Learned helplessness or egotism? *Journal of Personality and Social Psychology, 36,* 1415-23.

Fredericksen, N. (1972). Toward a taxonomy of situations. *American Psychologist, 27,* 114-23.

Freud, S. (1901) 1960. The psychopathology of everyday life. In J. Strachey (Ed.), *The standard edition of the complete psychological works* (Vol. 6). London: Hogarth.

—— (1925) *Collected papers.* London: Hogarth.

Funder, D., & Sherrod, D. (1983). *Temporal shifts in self-attribution: An information processing approach.* Paper presented at the meetings of APA, Anaheim, CA.

Gagne, R. M. (1984). Learning outcomes and their effects: Useful categories of human performance. *American Psychologist, 39,* 377-86.

Gara, M. (1986). *Personal prototypes and their organization in the perception of self and other.* Unpublished manuscript, Rutgers University Medical School.

Gardner, R. W., Holzman, P. S., Klein, G. S., Linton, H. B., & Spence, D. P. (1959). Cognitive control. *Psychological Issues, 1*(4), (Monograph).

Genero, N., & Cantor, N. (in press, 1986). Exemplar prototypes and clinical diagnosis: Towards a cognitive economy. *Journal of Clinical and Social Psychology.*

Gergen, K. J. (1971). *The concept of self.* New York: Holt, Rinehart, & Winston.

Gilligan, S. G., Bower, G. H. (1984). Cognitive consequences of emotional arousal. In C. E. Izard, J. Kagan, & R. B. Zajonc, (Eds.), *Emotions, cognition, and behavior.* New York: Cambridge University Press.

Gilovich, T. (1981). Seeing the past in the present: The effect of associations to familiar events on judgments and decisions. *Journal of Personality and Social Psychology, 40,* 797-808.

—— (1983). Biased evaluation and persistence in gambling. *Journal of Personality and Social Psychology, 44,* 1110-27.

Goffman, E. (1955). On face work. *Psychiatry, 18,* 213-31.

—— (1959). *The presentation of self in everyday life.* Garden City, NY: Doubleday Anchor Books.

—— (1974). *Frame Analysis.* New York: Harper & Row.

Goldberg, L. R. (1978). Differential attribution of trait-descriptive terms to oneself as compared to well-liked, neutral, and disliked others: A psychometric analysis. *Journal of Personality and Social Psychology, 36,* 1012-28.

Golden, M., Montare, A., & Bridger W. (1977). Verbal control of delay behavior in two-year-old boys as a function of social class. *Child Development, 48,* 1107-11.

Goldfried, M. R. (1983). History of behavioral assessment. In A. E. Kazdin (Chair), *Behavioral assessment: Historical developments, advances, and current status.* Symposium conducted at the meeting of the World Congress on Behavior Therapy, Washington, DC.

————, & D'Zurilla, T. J. (1969). A behavioral-analytic model for assessing competence. In C. D. Spielberger (Ed.), *Current topics in clinical and community psychology (Vol. 1)*, New York: Academic Press.

————, & Goldfried, A. P. (1980). Cognitive change methods. In F. H. Kanfer & A. P. Goldstein (Eds.), *Helping people change* (2nd ed). New York: Pergamon Press.

————, Padawer, W., & Robins, C. (1984). Social anxiety and the semantic structure of heterosocial interactions. *Journal of Abnormal Psychology, 93*, 87–97.

————, & Robins, C. (1983). Self-schema, cognitive bias, and processing of therapeutic experiences. In P. C. Kendall (Ed.), *Advances in cognitive-behavior research and therapy* (Vol. 2). New York: Academic Press.

Goldsmith, H. (1983). Genetic influence on personality from infancy & adulthood. *Child Development, 54*, 331–55.

Gollwitzer, P. M., & Wicklund, R. A. (1985). The pursuit of self-defining goals. In J. Kuhl & J. Beckmann (Eds.), *Action control from cognition to behavior*. Heidelberg: Springer-Verlag.

Gordon, C. (1968). Self-conceptions: Configuration of content. In C. Gordon & K. J. Gergen (Eds.), *The self in social interaction*. New York: Wiley.

Gough, H. (1966). Appraisal of social maturity by means of the CPI. *Journal of Abnormal Psychology, 71*, 189–95.

———— (1968). *Manual for the Chapin Social Insight Test*. Palo Alto, CA: Consulting Psychologists Press.

Gould, S. J. (1981). *The mismeasure of man*. New York: Norton.

Greenwald, A. G. (1980). The totalitarian ego: Fabrication and revision of personal history. *American Psychologist, 35*, 602–18.

———— (1981). Self and memory. In G. H. Bower (Ed.), *The psychology of learning and motivation*. New York: Academic Press.

———— (1982). Ego-task analysis: An integration of research on ego-involvement and self-awareness. In A. Hastoff & A. Isen (Eds.), *Cognitive social psychology*. New York: Elsevier.

————, & Breckler, S. (1984). To whom is the self presented? In B. Schlenker (Ed.), *The self and social life*. New York: McGraw-Hill.

————, & Pratkanis, A. R. (1985). The self. In R. S. Wyer & T. K. Srull (Eds.), *Handbook of social cognition*. Hillsdale, NJ: Erlbaum.

Guidano, V. F., & Liotti, G. (1983). *Cognitive processes and emotional disorders*. New York: Guilford Press.

Guilford, J. (1967) *The nature of human intelligence*. New York: McGraw-Hill.

Haan, N. (1982). The assessment of coping, defense, and stress. In L. Goldberger & S. Breznitz (Eds.), *Handbook of stress: Theoretical and clinical aspects*. New York: Free Press.

Hamilton, D. (1979). A cognitive attributional analysis of stereotyping. In L. Berkowitz (Ed.), *Advances in experimental social psychology* (Vol. 12). New York: Academic Press.

———— (1981). *Cognitive processes in stereotyping and intergroup behavior*. Hillsdale, NJ: Erlbaum.

———— & Zanna, M. P. (1974). Context effects in impression formation: Changes in connotative meaning. *Journal of Personality and Social Psychology, 29*, 649–54.

Hammen, C., & Mayol, A. (1982). Depression and cognitive characteristics of stressful life-event types. *Journal of Abnormal Psychology, 91*, 96–101.

Hampson, S. E. (1982). *The construction of personality: An Introduction*. London: Routledge & Kegan Paul.

———— (1983). Trait ascription and depth of acquaintance: The preference for traits in personality descriptions and its relation to target familiarity. *Journal of Research in Personality, 17*, 398–411.

————, John, O. P., & Goldberg, L. R. (1986). Category breadth and hierarchical structure in personality: Studies of asymmetries in judgments of trait implications. *Journal of Personality and Social Psychology, 51*(1), 37–54.

Hampton, J. A. (1982). A demonstration of intransitivity in natural categories. *Cognition, 12*, 151–64.

Harackiewicz, J. (1979). The effects of reward contingency and performance feedback on intrinsic motivation. *Journal of Personality and Social Psychology, 3*(8), 1352–1363.

————, Manderlink, G., & Sansone, C. (1984). Rewarding pinball wizardry: Effects of evaluation and cue value on intrinsic interest. *Journal of Personality and Social Psychology,* *47*(2), 287-300.

Harré, R., & Secord, P. F. (1973). *The Explanation of Social Behavior.* Blackwell: Oxford.

Harter, S. (1981). A model of mastery motivation in children— Individual differences and developmental change. In W. A. Collins (Ed.), *Aspects of development of competence: Minnesota Symposia on child psychology,* (Vol. 14). Hillsdale, NJ: Erlbaum.

———— (1983). Developmental perspectives on the self-system. In P. H. Mussen (Ed.), *Handbook of Child Psychology: Ed. 4 Socialization, Personality and Social Development* (Vol. 4). New York: Wiley.

Harvey, J. H., Weber, A. L., Huszti, H., Garnick, N., & Galvin, K. S. (1983). Attribution and the termination of close relationships: A special focus on the account. In R. Gilmour, & S. Duck (Eds.), *Personal Relationships.* Hillsdale, NJ: Erlbaum.

Harvey, J. H., & Weary, G. (1984). Current issues in attribution theory and research. In M. Rosenweig & L. W. Porter (Eds.), *Annual Review of Psychology* (Vol. 35). Palo Alto, CA: Annual Reviews.

Hastie, R. (1980). Memory for behavioral information that confirms or contradicts a personality impression. In R. Hastie, T. Ostrom, E. Ebbesen, R. Wyer, D. Hamilton, & D. Carlston (Eds.), *Person memory: The cognitive basis of social perception.* Hillsdale, NJ: Erlbaum.

———— (1981). Schematic principals in human memory. In E. T. Higgins, C. P. Herman, & M. P. Zanna (Eds.), *Social Cognition: The Ontario Symposium* (Vol. 1). Hillsdale, NJ: Erlbaum.

———— (1984). Causes and effects of casual attribution. *Journal of Personality and Social Psychology, 46*(1), 44-56.

————, & Carlston, D. (1980). Theoretical issues in person memory. In R. Hastie, T Ostrom, E. Ebbeson, R. Wyer, D. Hamilton, & D. Carlston (Eds.), *Person memory: The cognitive basis of social perception.* Hillsdale, NJ: Erlbaum.

Hay, D. F. (1977). Following their companions as a form of exploration for human infants. *Child Development, 48,* 1624-1632.

———— (1986). Infancy. In M. Rosenzweig, & L. W. Porter (Eds.), *Annual Reviews of Psychology,* (Vol. 37). Palo Alto, CA: Annual Reviews.

————, Murray, P., Cecire, S. & Nash, A. (1985). Social learning of social behavior in early life. *Child Development, 56,* 43-57.

Heckhausen, H., Schmalt, H. D., & Schneider, K. (1984). *Advances in Achievement Motivation Research.* New York: Academic. Press.

Heppner, P. P., & Anderson, W. P. (1985). The relationship between problem-solving self-appraisal and psychological adjustment. *Cognitive Therapy and Research, 9*(4), 415-427.

Herrmann, C., & Wortman, C. B. (1985). Action control and the coping process. In J. Kuhl & J. Beckmann (Eds), *Action control from cognition to behavior.* New York: Springer-Verlag.

Higgins, E. T. (1981). The "communication game": Implications for social cognition and persuasions. In E. T. Higgins, C. P. Herman, & M. P. Zanna (Eds), *Social Cognition: The Ontario Symposium* (Vol. 1). Hillsdale, NJ: Erlbaum.

————, & Bryant, S. (1982). Consensus information and the fundamental attribution error: The role of development and in-group versus out-group knowledge. *Journal of Personality and Social Psychology, 43*(5), 889-900.

————& King, G. A. (1981). Accessibility of social constructs: Information-processing consequences of individual and contextual variability. In N. Cantor & J. F. Kihlstrom (Eds.), *Personality, cognition, and social interaction.* Hillsdale, NJ: Erlbaum.

————, King, G., & Marvin, G. (1982). Individual construct accessibility and subjective impressions and recall. *Journal of Personality and Social Psychology, 43*(1), 35-47.

————, Klein, R., & Strauman, T. (1985). Self-concept discrepancy theory: A psychological model for distinguishing among different aspects of depression and anxiety. *Social Cognition, 3,* 51-76.

————, McCann, C. D., & Fondacaro, R. (1982). The "communication game": Goal-directed encoding and cognitive consequences. *Social Cognition, 1,* 21-37.

————, & Parsons, J. (1983). Social cognitions and the social life of the child: Stages as subcultures. In E. T. Higgins, D. N. Ruble, & W. W. Hartup (Eds), *Social cognition and social development.* New York: Cambridge University Press.

————, Strauman, T., & Klein, R. (1986). Standards and the process of self-evaluation: Multiple affects from multiple stages. In R. Sorrentino & E. Higgins, *Handbook of motivation and cognition: Foundations of social behavior*. New York: Guilford.

Hilton, J., & Darley, J. (1985). Constructing other persons: A limit on the effect. *Journal of Experimental Social Psychology, 21*, 1–18.

Hiroto, D. S., & Seligman, M. E. P. (1975). Generality of learned helplessness in man. *Journal of Personality and Social Psychology, 31*, 311–27.

Hochschild, A. R. (1979). Emotion work, feeling rules, and social structure. *American Journal of Sociology, 85*, 551–75.

Hoffman, C., Mischel, W., & Mazze, K. (1981). The role of purpose in the organization of information about behavior: Trait-based versus goal-based categories in person cognition. *Journal of Personality and Social Psychology, 40*, 211–25.

Hogan, R. (1982). On adding apples and oranges in personality psychology. *Contemporary Psychology, 27*, 851–52.

Hogarth, R. M. (1981). Beyond discrete biases: Functional and dysfunctional aspects of judgmental heuristics. *Psychological Bulletin, 90*, 197–217.

Hollon, S., DeRubeis, R., & Evans, M. (in press, 1986). Causal mediation of change in treatment for depression: Discriminating between nonspecificity and noncausality. *Psychological Bulletin.*

Holmes, D. S. (1974). Investigations of repression: Differential recall of material experimentally or naturally associated with ego threat. *Psychological Bulletin, 81*, 632–653.

Holtzworth-Munroe, A., & Jacobson, N. S. (1985). Causal attributions of married couples: When do they search for causes? What do they conclude when they do? *Journal of Personality and Social Psychology, 48*(6), 1398–1412.

Holyoak, K. J., & Gordon, P. C. (1983). Social reference points. *Journal of Personality and Social Psychology, 44*, 881–87.

———— (1984). Information processing and social cognition. In R. S. Wyer, Jr., T. K. Srull, & J. Hartwick (Eds.), *Handbook of social cognition*. Hillsdale, NJ: Erlbaum.

Holzman, P. S. (1954). The relation of assimilation tendencies in visual, auditory, and kinesthetic time-error to cognitive attitudes of leveling and sharpening. *Journal of Personality, 22*, 375–94.

————, & Gardner, R. W. (1959). Leveling and repression. *Journal of Abnormal and Social Psychology, 59*, 151–55.

Homa, D., Sterling, S., & Trepel, L. (1981). Limitations of exemplar-based generalizations and the abstraction of categorical information. *Journal of Experimental Psychology: Human Learning and Memory, 7*, 418–39.

Horn, J. L. (1980). Concepts of intellect in relation to learning and adult development. *Intelligence, 4*, 285–317.

Hubley, P., & Trevarthen, C. (1979). Sharing a task in infancy. In I. C. Uzgiris (Ed.), *Social interaction and communication during infancy*. San Francisco: Jossey-Bass.

Hultsch, D. F., & Dixon, R. A. (1984). Memory for text materials in adulthood. In P. B. Baltes & O. G. Brim, Jr. (Eds.), *Life-span development and behavior* (Vol. 6). New York: Academic Press.

Hunter, M. A., Ross, H. S., & Ames, E. W. (1982). Preferences for familiar or novel toys: Effects of familiarization time in 1-year-olds. *Developmental Psychology, 18*, 519–29.

Ingram, R. (Ed.) (1985). *Information processing approaches to psychopathology and clinical psychology*. New York: Academic Press.

————, Smith, T. W., & Brehm, S. S. (1983). Depression and information processing: Self-schemata and the encoding of self-referent information. *Journal of Personality and Social Psychology, 45*, 412–20.

Irwin, M., Engle, P. L., Klein, R. E., & Yarbrough, C. (1976). Traditionalism and field dependence. *Journal of Cross-cultural Psychology, 7*(4), 463–71.

Isen, A. M. (1984). Toward understanding the role of affect in cognition. In R. S. Wyer & T. K. Srull (Ed.), *Handbook of social cognition* (Vol. 3). Hillsdale, NJ: Erlbaum.

Izard, C. E. (1971). *The face of emotion*. New York: Appleton-Century-Crofts.

———— (1977). *Human emotions*. New York: Plenum.

Jacobson, N. S. (1984). The modification of cognitive processes in behavioral marital therapy: Integrating cognitive and behavioral intervention strategies. In K. Hahlweg & N. S. Jacobson (Eds.), *Marital interaction: Analysis and modification*. New York: Guilford Press.

Jahoda, G. (1980). Theoretical and systematic approaches in cross-cultural psychology. In H. C. Triandis & W. W. Lambert (Eds.), *Handbook of cross-cultural psychology* (Vol. 1). Boston: Allyn & Bacon.

James, W. (1890). *The principles of psychology*. New York: Holt.

Janis, I. L. (1972). *Victims of groupthink*. Boston: Houghton Mifflin.

Jones, E. E., & Berglas, S. (1978). Control of attributions about the self through self-handicapping strategies: The appeal of alcohol and the role of underachievement. *Personality and Social Psychology Bulletin, 4,* 200–206.

Jones, E. E., & Davis, K. E. (1965). From acts to dispositions: The attribution process in person perception. In L. Berkowitz (Ed.), *Advances in experimental social psychology* (Vol. 2). New York: Academic Press.

Jones, E. E., & Goethals, G. (1972). Order effects in impression formation: Attribution context and the nature of the entity. In E. E. Jones, D. Kanouse, H. Kelley, R. Nisbett, S. Valins, & B. Weiner (Eds.), *Attribution: Perceiving the causes of behavior*. Morristown, NJ: General Learning Press.

———, & Nisbett, R. E. (1972). The actor and the observer: Divergent perceptions of the causes of behavior. In E. E. Jones, D. E. Kanouse, H. H. Kelley, R. E. Nisbett, S. Valins, & B. Weiner (Eds.), *Attribution: Perceiving the causes of behavior*. Morristown, NJ: General Learning Press.

———, & Pittman, T. S. (1982). Toward a general theory of strategic self-presentation. In J. Suls (Ed.), *Psychological perspectives on the self*. Hillsdale, NJ: Erlbaum.

———, & Wortman, C. (1973). *Ingratiation: An attributional approach*. Morristown, NJ: General Learning Press.

Jones, R. A., Sensenig, J., & Haley, J. V. (1974). Self-descriptions: Configurations of content and order effects. *Journal of Personality and Social Psychology, 30,* 36–45.

Kagan, J. & Kogan, N. (1970). Individual variation in cognitive processes. In P. Mussen (Ed.), *Carmichael's manual of child psychology,* (Vol. 1). New York: Wiley.

Kagan, J., Reznick, S., Clarke, C., Sardenein, N., & Garcia-Coll, C. (1984). Behavioral inhibition to the unfamiliar. *Child Development, 55,* 2212–25.

Kagan, J., Rosman, B. L., Day, D., Albert, J., & Phillips, W. (1964). Information processing in the child: Significance of analytic and reflective attitudes. *Psychological Monographs, 78,* (1, Whole No. 578).

Kahneman, D., & Miller, D. (in press, 1986). Norm theory: Comparing reality to its alternatives. *Psychological Review*.

———, & Tversky, A. (1973). On the psychology of prediction. *Psychological Review, 80,* 237–51.

——— (1982). The stimulation heuristic. In D. Kahneman, P. Slovic, & A. Tversky (Eds.), *Judgement under uncertainty: Heuristics and biases*. New York: Cambridge University Press.

——— (1984). Choices, values, and frames. *American Psychologist, 39*(4), 341–51.

Kanfer, F. H. (1970). Self-regulation: Research issues and speculations. In C. Neuringer & J. L. Michael (Eds.), *Behavior modification in clinical psychology*. New York: Appleton-Century-Crofts.

Keating, D. P. (1978). A search for social intelligence. *Journal of Educational Psychology, 70*(2), 218–23.

Keenan, J. M., & Baillet, S. D. (1980). Memory for personally and socially significant events. In R. S. Nickerson (Ed.), *Attention and performance VIII*. Hillsdale, NJ: Erlbaum.

Keil, F. C. (1984). Transition mechanisms in cognitive development and the structure of knowledge. In R. Sternberg (Ed.), *Mechanisms of cognitive development*. San Francisco: Freeman.

——— (in press, 1986). The acquisition of natural kind and artifact terms. In W. Demopoulos & A. Marras (Eds.), *Language learning and concept acquisition*. Norwood, NJ: Ablex.

Kelley, H. (1967). Attribution theory in social psychology. In D. Levine (Ed.)., *Nebraska symposium on motivation* (Vol. 15). Lincoln: University of Nebraska Press.

——— (1972). Causal schemata and the attribution process. In E. E. Jones, D. Kanouse, H. Kelley, R. Nisbett, S. Valins, & B. Weiner (Eds.), *Attribution: Perceiving the causes of behavior*. Morristown, NJ: General Learning Press.

——— (1979). *Personal relationships*. Hillsdale, NJ: Erlbaum.

———, & Michela, J. L. (1980). Attribution theory and research. In M. Rosenzweig & L. W. Porter (Eds.), *Annual Review of Psychology* (Vol. 31). Palo Alto, CA: Annual Reviews.

————, & Thibaut, J. (1978). *Interpersonal relations: A theory of interdependence.* New York: Wiley.

Kelly, G. (1955, 1963). *The psychology of personal constructs.* New York: Norton.

Kendall, P. C., & Hollon, S. D. (1981). *Cognitive-behavioral interventions: Theory, research, and procedures.* New York: Academic Press.

Kihlstrom, J. F. (1981). On personality and memory. In N. Cantor & J. F. Kihlstrom (Eds.), *Personality, cognition, and social interaction.* Hillsdale, NJ: Erlbaum.

————, (1984). Conscious, subconscious, unconscious: A cognitive perspective. In K. Bowers & D. Meichenbaum (Eds.), *The unconscious reconsidered.* New York: John Wiley.

———— (1985). *Cognitive representations of the self.* Paper presented at American Psychological Association, Los Angeles.

————, & Cantor, N. (1984). Mental representations of the self. In L. Berkowitz (Ed.), *Advances in experimental social psychology* (Vol. 17). New York: Academic Press.

————, & Evans, F. (1979). Memory retrieval processes in posthypnotic amnesia. In J. Kihlstrom & F. Evans (Eds.), *Functional disorders of memory.* Hillsdale, NJ: Erlbaum.

————, & Harackiewicz, J. (1982). The earliest recollections: A new survey. *Journal of Personality, 50,* 134-48.

————, & Nasby, W. (1981). Cognitive tasks in clinical assessment: An exercise in applied psychology. In P. Kendall & S. Hollon (Eds.), *Cognitive-behavioral interventions: Assessment methods.* New York: Academic Press.

Kinder, D., Peters, M., Abelson, R., & Fiske, S. (1980). Presidential prototypes. *Political behavior, 2*(4), 315-35.

Klein, S. B., & Kihlstrom, J. F. (1986). Elaboration, organization, and the self-reference effect in memory. *Journal of Experimental Psychology: General, 115,* 26-38.

Klinger, E. (1975). Consequences of commitment to and disengagement from incentives. *Psychology Review, 82,* 1-25.

———— (1977). *Meaning and void: Inner experience and the incentives in people's lives.* Minneapolis: University of Minnesota Press.

Klos, D., Loomis, J., & Ruhrold, R. (1983). *Anger and strategic thinking during interpersonal conflict.* Presented at American Psychological Association meeting, Anaheim.

Kogan, N., & Wallach, M. A. (1964). *Risk taking: A study in cognition and personality.* New York: Holt, Rinehart, & Winston.

Kohlberg, L. (1966). A cognitive-developmental analysis of children's sex-role concepts and attitudes. In E. E. Maccoby (Ed.), *The development of sex differences.* Stanford, CA: Stanford University Press.

Kopp, C. B. (1982). Antecedents of self-regulation: A developmental perspective. *Developmental Psychology, 18,* 199-214.

Kuhl, J. (1983). *Motivation, Konflikt und Handlungskontrolle.* Heidelberg: Springer.

————, & Beckmann, J. (1985). *Action control from cognition to behavior.* New York: Springer-Verlag.

———— (1985). From cognition to behavior: Perspectives for future research on action control. In J. Kuhl & J. Beckmann (Eds.), *Action control from cognition to behavior.* New York: Springer-Verlag.

Kuiper, N. A., & Derry, P. A. (1981). The self as a cognitive prototype: An application to person perception and to psychopathology. In N. Cantor & J. F. Kihlstrom (Eds.), *Personality, cognition, and social interaction.* Hillsdale, NJ: Erlbaum.

Kunda, Z., & Cantor, N. (1986). *From general belief structures to specific evaluations: A study of belief accessibility.* Unpublished manuscript, Princeton University.

Laboratory of Comparative Human Cognition (1982). Culture and intelligence. In R. Sternberg (Ed.), *Handbook of Human intelligence.* Cambridge: Cambridge University Press.

Labov, W. (1973). The boundaries of words and their meanings. In C. J. N. Bailey & R. W. Shuy (Eds.), *New ways of analyzing variation in English* (Vol. 1). Washington, DC: Georgetown University Press.

Landman, J. (1984). *Regret and undoing.* Unpublished doctoral dissertation, University of Michigan.

Lang, P. J. (1979). Language, image, & emotion. In P. Pliner, K. R. Plankstein, & J. M. Spigel (Eds.), *Perception of Emotion in Self and Others.* (Vol. 5.) New York: Plenum.

Langer, E. J. (1978). Rethinking the role of thought in social interaction. In J. Harvey,

W. Ickes, & R. Kidd (Eds.), *New directions in attribution research* (Vol. 2). Hillsdale, NJ: Erlbaum.

———, & Abelson, R. P. (1974). A patient by any other name . . . : Clinician group difference in labeling bias. *Journal of Consulting and Clinical Psychology, 42,* 4-9.

Larkin, J. H., McDermott, J., Simon, D. P., & Simon, H. A. (1980). Models of competence in solving physics problems. *Science, 200,* 1335-42.

Lazarus, R. S. (1966). *Psychological stress and the coping process.* New York: McGraw-Hill.

——— (1982). Thoughts on the relations between emotion and cognition. *American Psychologist, 37,* 1019-24.

——— (1984). On the primacy of cognition. *American Psychologist, 39,* 124-29.

———, & Launier, R. (1978). Stress-related transactions between person and environment. In L. Pervin & M. Lewis (Eds.), *Internal and external determinants of behavior.* New York: Plenum.

Lepper, M. R., & Greene, D. (1978). *The hidden costs of reward.* Hillsdale, NJ: Erlbaum.

Lerner, M. J. (1970). The desire for justice and reactions to victims. In J. McCauley & L. Berkowitz (Eds.), *Altruism and helping behavior.* New York: Academic Press.

Levenson, H. (1972). Distinction within the concept of internal-external control. Paper presented at the American Psychological Association Convention, Washington, DC.

Leventhal, H. (1984). A perceptual-motor theory of emotion. In L. Berkowitz (Ed.), *Advances in experimental social psychology* (Vol. 17). New York: Academic Press.

Levinson, D. J. (1978). *The seasons of a man's life.* New York: Balantine.

Lewicki, P. (1983). Self-image bias in person perception. *Journal of Personality and Social Psychology, 45,* 384-93.

——— (1984). Self-schema and social information processing. *Journal of Personality and Social Psychology, 47*(6), 1177-90.

——— (1985). Nonconscious biasing effects of single instances on subsequent judgments. *Journal of Personality and Social Psychology, 48*(3), 563-74.

Lewin, K. (1935). *A dynamic theory of personality.* New York: McGraw-Hill.

———, Dembo, T., Festinger, L., & Sears, P. (1944). Level of aspiration. In J. Hunt (Ed.), *Personality and the behavior disorders.* New York: Ronald Press.

Lewinsohn, P., Mischel, W., Chaplain, W., & Barton, R. (1980). Social competence and depression: The role of illusory self-perceptions. *Journal of Abnormal Psychology, 89,* 203-12.

Lewis, M., & Brooks-Gunn, J. (1979). *Social cognition and the acquisition of self.* New York: Plenum Press.

Lewis, M., & Feiring, C. (1981). Direct and indirect interactions in social relationships. *Advances in Infancy Research, 1,* 129-61.

Lewontin, R. C., Rose, S., & Kamin, L. J. (1984). *Not in our genes.* New York: Pantheon.

Lingle, J. H., Altom, M. W., & Medin, D. L. (1983). Of cabbages and kings: Assessing the extendability of natural object concept models to social things. In R. S. Wyer, Jr., T. K. Srull, & J. Hartwick (Eds.), *Handbook of social cognition.* Hillsdale, NJ: Erlbaum.

Linton, M. (1975). Memory for real-world events. In D. A. Norman, D. E. Rummelhart, & the LNR Research Group (Eds.), *Explorations in cognition.* San Francisco: Freeman.

——— (1978). Real world memory after six years: An in vivo study of very long term memory. In M. Gruenberg, P. Morris, & R. Sykes (Eds.), *Practical aspects of memory.* New York: Academic Press.

Linville, P. W. (1982a). Affective consequences of complexity regarding the self and others. In M. Clark & S. Fiske (Eds.), *Affect and cognition: The 17th Annual Carnegie Symposium.* Hillsdale, NJ: Erlbaum.

——— (1982b). The complexity-extremity effect and age-based stereotyping. *Journal of Personality and Social Psychology, 42,* 193-211.

——— (1985). Self-complexity and affective extremity: Don't put all of your eggs in one cognitive basket. *Social Cognition, 3*(1), 94-121.

———, & Jones, E. E. (1980). Polarized appraisals of outgroup members. *Journal of Personality and Social Psychology, 38,* 689-703.

Little, B. (1983). Personal projects—A rationale and methods for investigation. *Environmental Behavior, 15,* 273-309.

Locksley, A., & Lenauer, M. (1981). Considerations for a theory of self-inference processes. In N. Cantor & J. F. Kihlstrom (Eds.), *Personality, cognition, and social interaction.* Hillsdale, NJ: Erlbaum.

Locksley, A., Borgida, E., Brekke, N., & Hepburn, C. (1980). Sex stereotypes and social judgment. *Journal of Personality and Social Psychology, 39*, 821-31.

Locksley, A., Hepburn, C., & Ortiz, V. (1982). Social stereotypes and judgments of individuals: An instance of the base rate fallacy. *Journal of Experimental Social Psychology, 18*, 223-42.

Lytton, H. (1976). The socialization of 2-year-old boys: Ecological findings. *Journal of Child Psychology and Psychiatry, 17*, 287-304.

Magnusson, D. (Ed.). (1981). *Toward a psychology of situations: An interactional perspective.* Hillsdale, NJ: Erlbaum.

———, & Ekehammar, B. (1973). An analysis of situational dimensions: A replication. *Multivariate Behavioral Research, 8*, 331-39.

Mahoney, M. J. (1979). Cognitive skills and athletic performance. In P. C. Kendall & S. D. Hollon (Eds.), *Cognitive-behavioral interventions: Theory, research and procedures.* New York: Academic Press.

Mair, J. M. M. (1977). The community of self. In D. Bannister (Ed.), *New perspectives in personal construct theory.* London: Academic Press.

Mandler, G. (1975). *Mind and emotion.* New York: Wiley.

Mandler, J. M. (1979). Categorical and schematic organization in memory. In C. R. Puff (Ed.), *Memory organization and structure.* New York: Academic Press.

Markus, H. (1977). Self-schemata and processing information about the self. *Journal of Personality and Social Psychology, 35*, 63-78.

——— (1979). The self in thought and memory. In D. Wegner & R. Vallacher (Eds.), *The self in social psychology.* New York: Oxford University Press.

——— (1983). Self-knowledge: An expanded view. *Journal of Personality, 51*, 543-65.

———, & Nurius, P. (1986). Possible selves. *American Psychologist, 41*(9), 954-969.

———, & Smith, J. (1981). The influence of self-schemata on the perception of others. In N. Cantor & J. Kihlstrom (Eds.), *Personality, cognition and social interaction.* Hillsdale, NJ: Erlbaum.

———, Smith, J., & Moreland, R. (1985). Role of the self-concept in the perception of others. *Journal of Personality and Social Psychology, 49*, 1495-1512.

———, & Wurf, E. (in press, 1987). The dynamic self-concept: A social psychological perspective. In M. R. Rosenszweig & L. W. Porter (Eds.), *Annual Review of Psychology* (Vol. 38). Palo Alto, CA: Annual Reviews.

———, & Zajonc, R. B. (1985). The cognitive perspective in social psychology. In G. Lindzey, & E. Aronson (Eds.), *Handbook of Social Psychology* (Vol. 1). New York: Random House.

Maslow, A. (1968). *Toward a psychology of being.* New York: Van Nostrand.

——— (1970). *Motivation and personality.* New York: Harper & Row.

Matheny, A. P. (1980). Bayley's infant behavior record: Behavioral components and twin analyses. *Child Development, 51*, 466-75.

Matlin, M., & Stang, D. (1978). *The Pollyanna principle.* Cambridge, MA: Schenkman.

Mayr, E. (1974). Behavior programs and evolutionary strategies. *American Scientist, 62*, 650-59.

McAdams, D. P. (1985). The "imago": A key narrative component of identity. In P. Shaver (Ed.), *Review of personality and social psychology* (Vol. 6). Beverly Hills: Sage.

McFall, R. (1982). A review and reformulation of the concept of social skills. *Behavioral Assessment, 4*, 1-33.

McGuire, W. J. (1984). Search for the self: Going beyond self-esteem and the reactive self. In R. A. Zucker, J. Arnoff, & A. I. Rubin (Eds.), *Personality and the prediction of behavior.* New York: Academic Press.

———, & McGuire, C. V. (1981). The spontaneous self-concept as affected by personal distinctiveness. In M. D. Lynch, A. A. Norem-Hebeisen, & K. Gergen (Eds.), *Self-concept: Advances in theory and research.* New York: Ballinger.

———, & McGuire, C. V. (1982). Significant others in self-space: Sex differences and developmental trends in the social self. In J. Suls (Ed.), *Psychological perspectives on the self.* Hillsdale, NJ: Erlbaum.

———, & Padawer-Singer, A. (1976). Trait salience in the spontaneous self-concept. *Journal of Personality and Social Psychology, 33*, 743-54.

Mead, G. (1934). *Mind, self, and society.* Chicago: University of Chicago Press.

Meichenbaum, D. (1977). *Cognitive Behavior Modification: An Integrated Approach*. New York: Plenum.

———, & Cameron, R. (1982). Cognitive-behavior therapy. In G. T. Wilson & C. M. Franks (Eds.), *Contemporary behavior therapy: Conceptual and empirical foundations*. New York: Guilford.

Meltzoff, A. N. (1985). Immediate and deferred imitation in fourteen- and twenty-four-month-old infants. *Child Development, 56*, 62–72.

Mervis, C. B. (1984). *The role of cognition and language in early lexical development*. Paper presented at a symposium entitled "Concept development with and without language," at Michigan State University.

Messer, S. (1976). Reflection—impulsivity: A review. *Psychological Bulletin, 83*(6), 1026–52.

Metalsky, G. I., & Abramson, L. Y. (1981). Attributional styles: Toward a framework for conceptualization and assessment. In P. C. Kendall & S. D. Hollon (Eds.), *Cognitive-behavioral interventions: Assessment methods*. New York: Academic Press.

Miller, A., Wattenberg, M., & Malanchuk, O. (1982). *Cognitive representations of candidate assessments*. Paper presented at 1982 Annual Meeting of the American Political Science Association, Denver, CO.

Miller, G., & Cantor, N. (1982). Review of *Human inference: Strategies and shortcomings of social judgment*. *Social Cognition, 1*, 83–93.

Miller, G., Galanter, E., & Pribram, K. (1960). *Plans and the structure of behavior*. New York: Holt, Rinehart, & Winston.

Miller, I. W., Klee, S. H., & Norman, W. H. (1982). Depressed and nondepressed inpatients' cognitions of hypothetical events, experimental tasks, and stressful life events. *Journal of Abnormal Psychology, 91*, 78–81.

Miller, J. G. (1984). Culture and the development of everyday social explanation. *Journal of Personality and Social Psychology, 46*(5), 961–978.

Miller, S. M. (1979). Controllability and human stress: Method, evidence, and theory. *Behavior Research and Therapy, 17*, 287–306.

———, & Mangan, C. (1983). Interacting effects of information and coping style in adapting to gynecologic stress: Should the doctor tell all? *Journal of Personality and Social Psychology, 45*, 223–36.

Minton, B. (1979). Dimensions of information underlying children's judgments of their competence. Unpublished master's thesis, University of Denver.

Mischel, W. (1968). *Personality and assessment*. New York: Wiley.

——— (1970). A social learning view of sex differences in behavior. In P. H. Mussen (Ed.), *Carmichael's manual of child psychology* (Vol. 2). New York: Wiley.

——— (1973). Toward a cognitive social learning reconceptualization of personality. *Psychological Review, 80*, 252–83.

——— (1977). The interaction of person and situation. In D. Magnusson & N. Endler (Eds.), *Personality at the crossroads: Current issues in interactional psychology*. Hillsdale, NJ: Erlbaum.

——— (1979). On the interface of cognition and personality. *American Psychologist, 34*, 740–54.

——— (1981). Metacognition and the rules of delay. In J. Flavell & L. D. Ross (Eds.), *Cognitive social development: Frontiers and possible futures*. New York: Cambridge University Press.

——— (1984). Convergences and challenges in the search for consistency. *American Psychologist, 39*, 351–64.

——— (1985). Delay of gratification as process and as person variable in development. In D. Magnusson & V. P. Allen (Eds.), *Interactions in human development*. New York: Academic Press.

———, Ebbesen, E. B., & Zeiss, A. R. (1972). Cognitive and attentional mechanisms in delay of gratification. *Journal of Personality and Social Psychology, 21*, 204–18.

———, & Peake, P. K. (1982). Beyond déjà vu in the search for cross-situational consistency. *Psychological Review, 89*, 730–55.

Money, J., & Ehrhardt, A. A. (1972). *Man and woman, boy and girl: Differentiation and dimorphism of gender identity from conception to maturity*. Baltimore: Johns Hopkins University Press.

Montemayor, R., & Eisen, M. (1977). The development of self-conceptions from childhood to adolescence. *Developmental Psychology, 13*, 314-19.

Moos, R. H. (1968). Situational analysis of the therapeutic mileau. *Journal of Abnormal Psychology, 73*, 49-61.

—— (1973). Conceptualizations of human environments. *American Psychologist, 28*, 652-65.

Murray, H.A. (1938). *Explorations in personality*. New York: Oxford Press.

—— (1951). Toward a classification of interaction. In T. Parsons & E. A. Shils (Eds.), *Toward a general theory of action*. Cambridge, MA: Harvard University Press.

Nasby, W., Hayden, B., & DePaulo, B. M. (1980). Attributional bias among aggressive boys to interpret unambiguous social stimulus displays of hostility. *Journal of Abnormal Psychology, 89*, 459-68.

——, & Kihlstrom, J. F. (1985). Cognitive assessment of personality and psychopathology. In R. E. Ingram (Ed.), *Information-processing approaches to psychopathology and clinical psychology*. New York: Academic Press.

——, & Yando, R. (1980). Clinical and developmental implications of memory and affect in children. In R. Selman & R. Yando (Eds.), *New directions for child development: Clinical-developmental psychology*. San Francisco: Jossey-Bass.

——, & Yando, R. (1982). Selective encoding and retrieval of affectively-valent information: Two cognitive consequences of mood. *Journal of Personality and Social Psychology, 43*, 1244-53.

Neisser, U. (1976). General, academic, and artificial intelligence. In L. B. Resnick (Ed.), *The nature of intelligence*. Hillsdale, NJ: Erlbaum.

—— (1979). The concept of intelligence. *Intelligence, 3*, 217-27.

—— (1982). *Memory observed*. San Francisco: W. H. Freeman.

Neugarten, B. (1976). Adaptation and the life cycle. *Counseling Psychology, 6*, 16-20.

Newtson, D. (1976). Foundations of attribution: The unit of perception of ongoing behavior. In J. Harvey, W. J. Ickes, & R. F. Kidd (Eds.), *New directions in attribution research*. Hillsdale, NJ: Erlbaum.

Nezlek, J. B., Wheeler, L., & Reis, H. T. (1983). Studies of social participation. *New directions for methodology of social and behavioral science, 15*, 57-73.

Nicholls, J. G. (1984). Achievement motivation: Conceptions of ability, subjective experience, task choice, and performance. *Psychological Review, 91*(3), 328-46.

Niedenthal, P. M. (1985) "Hot" concepts in memory: Speculations and directions. Unpublished manuscript, University of Michigan.

——, Cantor, N., & Kihlstrom, J. F. (1985). Prototype-matching: A strategy for social decision-making. *Journal of Personality and Social Psychology, 48*(3), 575-84.

Nisbett, R. E. (1980). The trait construct in lay and professional psychology. In L. Festinger (Ed.), *Retrospections on social psychology*. New York: Oxford Press.

——, & Wilson, T. (1977). Telling more than we can know: Verbal reports on mental processes. *Psychological Review, 84*, 231-59.

——, & Ross, L. (1980). *Human Inference: Strategies and Shortcomings in Social Judgement*. Englewood Cliffs, NJ: Prentice-Hall.

Norem, J. K., & Cantor, N. (1986a). Anticipatory and post hoc cushioning strategies: Optimism and defensive pessimism in "risky" situations. *Cognitive Therapy and Research, 10*(3), 347-62.

—— (1968b). Defensive pessimism: "Harnessing" anxiety as motivation. *Journal of Personality and Social Psychology, 51*(6).

—— (in press, 1986c). Capturing the "flavor" of behavior: Cognition, affect and interpretation. In A. Isen & B. Moore (Eds.), *Affect and social behavior*. New York: Academic Press.

Norman, W. (1963). Toward an adequate taxonomy of personal attributes: Replicated factor structures in peer nomination personality ratings. *Journal of Abnormal and Social Psychology, 66*, 574-83.

Nurius, P. (1984). *A dynamic view of self-concept and its relation to behavioral self-regulation*. Unpublished doctoral dissertation, University of Michigan.

Nuttin, J. R. (1984). *Motivation, planning, and action: A relational theory of behavior dynamics*. Hillsdale, NJ: Erlbaum.

Osgood, C. E., Suci, G. J., & Tannenbaum, P. H. (1957). *The measurement of meaning*. Urbana: University of Illinois Press.

Ostrom, T., & Davis, D. (1979). Idiosyncratic weighting of trait information in impression formation. *Journal of Personality and Social Psychology, 37*(11), 2025-43.

—— (1984). The sovereignty of social cognition. In R. S. Wyer & T. K. Srull (Eds.), *Handbook of social cognition* (Vol. 1). Hillsdale, NJ: Erlbaum.

Passer, M. W., Kelley, H. H., & Michela, J. L. (1978). Multidimensional scaling of the causes for negative interpersonal behavior. *Journal of Personality and Social Psychology, 36,* 951-62.

Peevers, B., & Secord, P. (1973). Developmental changes in attribution of descriptive concepts to persons. *Journal of Personality and Social Psychology, 27,* 120-128.

Pervin, L. (1976). A free-response description approach to the analysis of person-situation interaction. *Journal of Personality and Social Psychology, 34*(3), 465-74.

—— (1985). Personality: Current controversies, issues, and directions. In M. Rosenzweig & L. W. Porter (Eds.), *Annual Review of Psychology* (Vol. 36). Palo Alto, CA: Annual Reviews.

Peterson, C., & Seligman, M. (1984). Causal explanations as a risk factor for depression: Theory and evidence. *Psychological Review, 91*(3), 347-74.

Pettigrew, T. F. (1958). The measurement and correlates of category width as a cognitive variable. *Journal of Personality, 26,* 532-44.

Petty, R. E., & Cacioppo, J. T. (1981). *Attitudes and persuasion: Classic and contemporary approaches.* Dubuque, IA: W. C. Brown.

Phares, E. J. (1976). *Locus of control in personality.* Morristown, NJ: General Learning Press.

Piaget, J. (1952). *The origins of intelligence in the child.* New York: International Universities Press.

—— (1972). Intellectual evolution from adolescence to adulthood. *Human Development, 15,* 1-12.

Pietramonaco, P. (1983). *The nature of the self-structure in depression.* Unpublished doctoral dissertation. University of Michigan.

Pittman, N. L., & Pittman, T. S. (1979). Effects of amount of helplessness training and internal-external locus of control on mood and performance. *Journal of Personality and Social Psychology, 37,* 39-47.

Plomin, R. (1983). Developmental behavioral genetics. *Child Development, 54,* 253-89.

——, & Foch, T. T. (1980). A twin study of objectively assessed personality in childhood. *Journal of Personality and Social Psychology, 39,* 680-88.

Plutchik, R. (1979). Universal problems of adaptation: Hierarchy, territoriality, identity, and temporality. In J. B. Calhoun (Ed.), *Perspectives on adaptation, environment and population.* New York: Praeger.

—— (1980). A general psychoevolutionary theory of emotion. In R. Plutchik & H. Kellerman (Eds.), *Emotion: Theory, research, and experience.* New York: Academic Press.

——, & Kellerman, H. (Eds.) (1980). *Emotion: Theory, research, and experience.* New York: Academic Press.

Posner, M. I. (1981). Cognition and personality. In N. Cantor & J. F. Kihlstrom (Eds.), *Personality, cognition, and social interaction.* Hillsdale, NJ: Erlbaum.

Price, R. H. (1981). Risky situations. In D. Magnusson (Ed.), *Toward a psychology of situations: An interactional perspective.* Hillsdale, NJ: Erlbaum.

——, & Bouffard, D. L. (1974). Behavioral appropriateness and situational constraint as dimensions of social behavior. *Journal of Personality and Social Psychology, 30,* 579-86.

Quattrone, G. A., & Jones, E. E. (1980). The perception of variability within ingroups and outgroups: Implications for the Law of Small Numbers. *Journal of Personality and Social Psychology, 38,* 141-52.

Read, S. J. (1983). Once is enough: Causal reasoning from a single instance. *Journal of Personality and Social Psychology, 45,* 323-34.

—— (1984). Analogical reasoning in social judgment: The importance of causal theories. *Journal of Personality and Social Psychology, 46*(1), 14-25.

Reeder, G. D., & Brewer, M. B. (1979). A schematic model of dispositional attribution in interpersonal perception. *Psychological Review, 86,* 61-79.

Reich, J. W., & Zautra, A. J. (1983). Demands and desires in daily life: Some influences on well-being. *American Journal of Community Psychology, 1,* 41-58.

Rheingold, H. (1982). Little children's participation in the work of adults: A nascent prosocial behavior. *Child Development, 53,* 114-125.

—— (1985). Development as the aquisition of familiarity. In M. Rosenzweig & L. W. Porter (Eds.), *Annual Review of Psychology,* (Vol. 36) Palo Alto, CA: Annual Reviews.

Riggs, J., & Cantor, N. (1982). Getting acquainted: The role of self-concept and preconceptions. *Personality and Social Psychology Bulletin, 10*(3), 432-46.

Robinson, J. A. (1976). Sampling autobiographical memory. *Cognitive Psychology, 8,* 578-95.

Rogers, C. R. (1951). *Client-centered therapy.* New York: Houghton-Mifflin.

Rogers, T. B. (1977). Self-reference in memory: Recognition of personality items. *Journal of Research in Personality, 11,* 295-305.

—— (1981). A model of the self as an aspect of human information processing. In N. Cantor & J. Kihlstrom (Eds.), *Personality, cognition, and social interaction.* Hillsdale, NJ: Erlbaum.

——, & Rogers, P. J., & Kuiper, N. A. (1979). Evidence for the self as a cognitive prototype: The "false alarms" effect. *Personality and Social Psychology Bulletin, 5,* 53-56.

Rosch, E. (1978). Human Categorization. In N. Warren (Ed.), *Studies in cross-cultural psychology.* London: Academic Press.

——, & Lloyd, E. B. (Eds.). (1978) *Cognition and categorization.* Hillsdale, NJ: Erlbaum.

——, Mervis, C., Gray, W., Johnson, D., & Boyes-Braem, P. (1976). Basic objects in natural categories. *Cognitive Psychology, 8,* 382-439.

Rosenberg, M. (1979). *Conceiving the self.* New York: Basic Books.

Rosenberg, S. (1977). New approaches to the analysis of personal constructs in person perception. In A. W. Landfield (Ed.), *Nebraska symposium on motivation* (Vol. 24). Lincoln: University of Nebraska Press.

——, & Sedlak, A. (1972). Structural representations of implicit personality theory. In L. Berkowitz (Ed.), *Advances in experimental social psychology* (Vol. 6). New York: Academic Press.

——, & Gara, M. A. (1985). The multiplicity of personal identity. In P. Shaver (Ed.), *Review of personality and social psychology* (Vol. 6). Beverly Hills: Sage.

Ross, L. (1977). The intuitive psychologist and his shortcomings: Distortions in the attribution process. In L. Berkowitz (Ed.), *Advances in experimental social psychology* (Vol. 10). New York: Academic Press.

——, Lepper, M. R., & Hubbard, M. (1975). Perseverance in self-perception and social perception: Biased attribution processes in the debriefing paradigm. *Journal of Personality and Social Psychology, 35,* 817-29.

Ross, M., McFarland, C., Conway, M., & Zanna, M. (1983). Reciprocal relations between attitude and behavior recall: Committing people to newly formed attitudes. *Journal of Personality and Social Psychology, 45,* 257-67.

——, & Sicoly, F. (1979). Egocentric biases in availability and attribution. *Journal of Personality and Social Psychology, 37,* 322-37.

Rotter, J. B. (1954). *Social learning and clinical psychology.* Englewood Cliffs, NJ: Prentice-Hall.

—— (1966). Generalized expectancies for internal versus external control of reinforcement. *Psychological Monographs, 80*(1, Whole No. 609).

—— (1971). External control and internal control. *Psychology Today, 5,* 37-42, 58-59.

——, Chance, J. E., & Phares, E. J. (1972). *Applications of a social learning theory of personality.* New York: Holt, Rinehart, & Winston.

Ruble, D. N., & Rholes, W. S. (1981). The development of children's perceptions and attributions about their social world. In J. H. Harvey, W. Ickes, & R. F. Kidd (Eds.), *New directions in attribution research* (Vol. 3). Hillsdale, NJ: Erlbaum.

Ruffins, S., Niedenthal, P., & Cantor, N. (1986). *Flexibility in the use of prototypes to guide behavior in social situations.* Paper presented at Midwestern Psychological Association, Chicago.

Ruhröld, R. (1986). *Differentiation of social knowledge structures and skill in marital problem-solving.* Unpublished doctoral dissertation. University of Michigan.

Russell, J. (1980). A circumplex model of affect. *Journal of Personality and Social Psychology. 39,* 1161-78.

Ryff, C. D. (1982). Successful aging: A developmental approach. *The Gerontologist, 22,* 209-14.

Sager, C. J. (1976). *Marriage contracts and couple therapy.* New York: Brunner/Mazel.
———, Kaplan, H., Grundlack, R., Kremer, M., Lenz, R., & Royce, J. F. (1971). The marriage contract. *Family Process, 10,* 311-26.
Salovey, P. & Rodin, J. (1985). Cognitions about the self: Connecting feeling states and social behavior. In P. Shaver (Ed.), *Review of personality and social psychology* (Vol. 6). Beverly Hills: Sage.
Sarason, I. G. (1975). Anxiety and self-preoccupation. In I. G. Sarason, & C. D. Spielberger (Eds.), *Stress and anxiety* (Vol. 2). New York: Wiley.
Sarbin, T. R. (1952). A preface to a psychological analysis of the self. *Psychological Review, 59,* 11-22.
Schachter, S., & Singer, J. E. (1962). Cognitive, social, and physiological determinants of emotional state. *Psychological Review, 69,* 379-99.
Schaffer, H. R., & Crook, C. K. (1978). The role of the mother in early social development. In H. McGurk (Ed.), *Issues in childhood social development.* London: Methuen.
Schank, R., & Abelson, R. (1977). *Scripts, plans, goals, and understanding.* Hillsdale, NJ: Erlbaum.
Scheier, M. F., & Carver, C. S. (1980). Private and public self-attention, resistance to change, and dissonance reduction. *Journal of Personality and Social Psychology, 39,* 390-405.
——— (1982). Cognition, affect, and self-regulation. In M. S. Clark & S. T. Fiske (Eds.), *Affect and cognition: The 17th Annual Carnegie Symposium.* Hillsdale, NJ: Erlbaum.
Schlenker, B. R. (1980). *Impression management: The self-concept, social identity, and interpersonal relations.* Monterey, CA: Brooks/Cole.
——— (Ed.) (1985). *The self and social life.* New York: McGraw-Hill.
Schneider, D. J. (1973). Implicit personality theory: A review. *Psychological Bulletin, 79,* 294-309.
———, & Blankmeyer, B. L. (1983). Prototype salience and implicit personality theories. *Journal of Personality and Social Psychology, 44,* 712-22.
———, Hastorf, A. H., & Ellsworth, P. C. (1979). *Person perception.* Reading, MA: Addison-Wesley.
Schulz, A. (1964). *Collected papers* (Vol. 2). The Hague: Mouton.
Schwartz, J., & O'Connor, C. (1984). The social ecology of memorable emotional experience. Paper at the Second International Conference on Personal Relationships. Madison, WI.
Scribner, S., & Cole, M. (1973). Cognitive consequences of formal and informal education. *Science, 182,* 553-59.
——— (1978). Literacy without schooling: Testing for intellectual effects. *Harvard Educational Review, 48*(4), 448-61.
Seligman, M. E. P., & Maier, S. F. (1967). Failure to escape traumatic shock. *Journal of Experimental Psychology, 74,* 1-9.
Serpell, R. (1976). *Culture's influence on behaviour.* London: Methuen.
Shapiro, D. (1965). *Neurotic styles.* New York: Basic Books.
Shaver, P., Schwartz, J., O'Connor, C., Kirson, D., Marsh, C., & Fischer, S. (1985). *Emotions and emotion knowledge: A prototype approach.* Unpublished manuscript, University of Denver.
Shevrin, H. (1986). The role of consciousness, motivation, and level of organization in person schemata. Presented at Program on Conscious and Unconscious Mental Processes of the John O. and Katherine T. MacArthur Foundation, Center for the Advanced Study in the Behavioral Sciences, Stanford, CA.
Showers, C. J. (1986). *Anticipatory cognitive strategies: The positive side of negative thinking.* Unpublished doctoral dissertation, Department of Psychology, The University of Michigan.
———, & Cantor, N. (1984). *The effects of best- and worst-case strategies: Making sense of judgment "bias."* Paper presented at Midwestern Psychology Association, Chicago.
———, & Cantor, N. (1985). Social cognition: A look at motivated strategies. In M. Rosenzweig & L. W. Porter (Eds.), *Annual Review of Psychology* (Vol. 36). Palo Alto, CA: Annual Reviews.
Shrauger, J. S., & Patterson, M. B. (1974). Self-evaluation and the selection of dimensions for evaluating others. *Journal of Personality, 42,* 569-85.
Shweder, R. A. (1980). Fallible judgment in behavioral research. In D. W. Fiske (Ed.), *New*

directions for methodology of social and behavioral science (Vol. 4). San Francisco: Jossey-Bass.

——— (1982). Fact & artifact in trait perception: The systematic distortion hypothesis. *Progress in Experimental Personality Research, 11*, 65–100.

Siegler, R. S., & Richards, D. D. (1980). *College students' prototypes of children's intelligence.* Paper presented at American Psychological Association, New York.

——— (1982). The development of intelligence. In R. J. Sternberg (Ed.), *Handbook of human intelligence.* New York: Cambridge University Press.

Silverman, L. H. (1983). The subliminal psychodynamic activation method: Overview and comprehensive listing of studies. In J. Masling (Ed.), *Empirical studies of psychoanalytic theories* (Vol. 1). Hillsdale, NJ: Erlbaum.

Simon, H. (1955). A behavioral model of rational choice. *Quarterly Journal of Economics, 69*, 99–118.

Singer, J. L. (1974). *Imagery and daydream: Methods in psychotherapy and behavior modification.* New York: Academic Press.

Skov, R. B., & Sherman, S. J. (1986). Information-gathering processes: Diagnosticity, hypothesis-confirmatory strategies, and perceived hypothesis confirmation. *Journal of Experimental Social Psychology, 22*, 93–121.

Slovic, P., Fischof, B., & Lichtenstein, S. (1976). Cognitive processes and societal risk taking. In J. S. Carroll, & J. W. Payne (Eds.), *Cognition and social behavior.* Hillsdale, NJ: Erlbaum.

Smith, E. E., & Medin, D. (1981). *Categories and concepts.* Cambridge, MA: Harvard University Press.

Smith, E. (1984). A model of social inference processes. *Psychological Review, 91*(3), 392–413.

Smuts, B. B. (1985). *Sex and Friendship in Baboons.* Hawthorne, NY: Aldine.

Snyder, C. (1985). The excuse: An amazing grace? In B. Schlenker (Ed.), *The self and social life.* New York: McGraw-Hill.

Snyder, M. (1974). The self-monitoring of expressive behavior. *Journal of Personality and Social Psychology, 30*, 526–37.

——— (1979). Self-monitoring processes. In L. Berkowitz (Ed.), *Advances in experimental social psychology* (Vol. 12). New York: Academic Press.

——— (1981a). On the influence of individuals on situations. In N. Cantor & J. Kihlstrom, *Personality, cognition, and social interaction.* Hillsdale, NJ: Erlbaum.

——— (1981b). Seek, and ye shall find: Testing hypotheses about other people. In E. T. Higgins, C. P. Herman, & M. P. Zanna (Eds.), *Social cognition: The Ontario symposium on personality and social psychology* (Vol. 1). Hillsdale, NJ: Erlbaum.

———, & Simpson, J. (1984). Self-monitoring and dating relationships. *Journal of Personality and Social Psychology, 47*, 1281–91.

———, & Swann, W. B., Jr. (1978). Behavioral confirmation in social interaction: From social perception to social reality. *Journal of Personality, 50*, 149–57.

———, & White, P. (1982). Moods and memories: Elation, depression, and the remembering of events of one's life. *Journal of Personality, 50*, 149–57.

Snyder, M. L., Stephan, W. G., & Rosenfield, D. (1976). Egotism and attribution. *Journal of Personality and Social Psychology, 33*, 435–41.

——— (1978). Attributional egotism. In J. Harvey, W. Ickes, & R. Kidd (Eds.), *New directions in attribution research* (Vol. 2), Hillsdale, NJ: Erlbaum.

Snygg, D., & Combs, A. W. (1949). *Individual behavior.* New York: Harper & Row.

Sommers, S. (1981). Emotionality reconsidered: The role of cognition in emotional responsiveness. *Journal of Personality and Social Psychology, 41*, 553–61.

Spivak, G., Platt, J., & Shure, M. (1976). *The problem-solving approach to adjustment.* San Francisco: Jossey-Bass.

Srull, T. K., & Wyer, R. S., Jr. (1980). Category accessibility and social perception: Some implications for the study of person memory and interpersonal judgments. *Journal of Personality and Social Psychology, 38*, 841–56.

Staub, E. (1978). Positive social behavior and morality. *Personal and social influences* (Vol. 1). New York: Academic Press.

Sternberg, R. (1982). The nature of intelligence. *New York University Education Quarterly, 12*, 10–17.

——— (1984). Toward a triarchic theory of human intelligence. *The Behavioral and Brain Sciences, 7*, 269–315.

————, Conway, B., Keton, J., & Bernstein, M. (1981). People's conceptions of intelligence. *Journal of Personality and Social Psychology, 41*(1), 37–55.

————, & Salter, W. (1982). Conceptions of intelligence. In R. Sternberg (Ed.), *Handbook of human intelligence.* Cambridge: Cambridge University Press.

————, & Smith, C. (1985) *Social intelligence and decoding skills in nonverbal communication.* Unpublished manuscript, Yale University.

Stokols, D. (1982). Environmental psychology: A coming of age. In A. Kraut (Ed.), *The G. Stanley Hall Lecture Series* (Vol. 2). Washington DC: American Psychological Association.

Streibel, M. J., & Ebenholtz, S. M. (1982). Construct validity of perceptual style: Role of stimulus size in Embedded Figures Test and the rod-and-frame test. *Perception and Psychophysics, 31,* 128–138.

Stryker, S. (1986). Identity theory: Developments and extensions. In K. Yardley & T. Honess, (Eds.), *Self and identity.* New York: Wiley.

Swann, W. (1984). Quest for accuracy in person perception: A matter of pragmatics. *Psychological Review, 91,* 457–77.

————, & Ely, R. (1984). A battle of wills: Self-verification versus behavioral confirmation. *Journal of Personality and Social Psychology, 46,* 1287–1302.

————, & Read, S. (1981). Acquiring self-knowledge: The search for feedback that fits. *Journal of Personality and Social Psychology, 41,* 1119–28.

————, Stephenson, B., & Pittman, T. S. (1981). Curiosity and control: On the determinants of the search for social knowledge. *Journal of Personality and Social Psychology, 40,* 635–42.

Tabachnik, N., Crocker, J., & Alloy, L. (1983). Depression, social comparison, and the false-consensus effect. *Journal of Personality and Social Psychology, 45,* 688–99.

Tavris, C., & Wade, C. (1984). *The longest war: Sex differences in perspective* (2nd edition). San Diego: Harcourt.

Taylor, S. E., Lichtman, R. R., & Wood, J. V. (1984). Attributions, beliefs about control, and adjustment to breast cancer. *Journal of Personality and Social Psychology, 46,* 489–502.

Taylor, S., & Fiske, S. (1978). Salience, attribution, and attention: Top of the head phenomena. In L. Berkowitz (Ed.), *Advances in experimental social psychology* (Vol. 11). New York: Academic Press.

Teasdale, J. D., & Taylor, R. (1981). Induced mood and accessibility of memories: An effect of mood state or of induction procedure? *British Journal of Clinical Psychology, 20,* 39–48.

Tesser, A. (1978). Self-generated attitude change. In L. Berkowitz (Ed.), *Advances in experimental social psychology* (Vol. 11). New York: Academic Press.

———— (1980). Self-esteem maintenance in family dynamics. *Journal of Personality and Social Psychology, 39,* 77–91.

————, & Campbell, J. (1983). Self-definition and self-evaluation maintenance. In J. Suls, & A. G. Greenwald (Eds.), *Psychological perspectives on the self* (Vol. 2). Hillsdale, NJ: Erlbaum.

Tetlock, P. (1986). Accountability: The forgotten context for social judgment. Paper presented at the University of Michigan.

———— & Levi, A. (1982). Attribution bias: On the inconclusiveness of the cognition-motivation debate. *Journal of Experimental Social Psychology, 18,* 68–88.

Thoits, P. (1983). Multiple identities and psychological well-being: A reformulation and test of the social isolation hypothesis. *American Sociological Review, 48,* 174–87.

Thomas, A., & Chess, S. (1968). *Temperament and behavior disorders in children.* New York: New York University Press.

Thorndike, E. (1920). Intelligence and its uses. *Harper's, 140,* 227–35.

Thurstone, L. L. (1938). *Primary mental abilities.* Chicago: University of Chicago Press.

Tomkins, S. S. (1981). The quest for primary motives: Biography and autobiography of an idea. *Journal of Personality and Social Psychology, 41,* 306–29.

Torgersen, A. M., & Kringlen, E. (1978). Genetic aspects of temperamental differences in twins. *Journal of American Academy of Child Psychiatry, 17,* 433–44.

Trope, Y. (1979). Uncertainty-reducing properties of achievement tasks. *Journal of Personality and Social Psychology, 16,* 116–29.

———— (1983). Self-assessment in achievement behavior. In J. Suls & A. Greenwald (Eds.), *Psychological perspectives on the self* (Vol. 2). Hillsdale, NJ: Erlbaum.

—— (1986). Self-enhancement and self-assessment in achievement behavior. In R. Sorrentino & E. Higgins (Eds.), *Handbook of Motivation and Cognition: Foundations of Social Behavior.* New York: Guilford.

——, & Bassock, M. (1983). Information-gathering strategies in hypothesis-testing. *Journal of Experimental Social Psychology, 19,* 560–576.

Trzebinski, J., McGlynn, R., Gray, G., & Tubbs, D. (1985). The role of categories of an actor's goals in organizing inferences about a person. *Journal of Personality and Social Psychology, 48*(6), 1387–97.

Tulving, E. (1972). Episodic and semantic memory. In E. Tulving & W. Donalson (Eds.), *Organization of memory.* New York: Academic Press.

Turk, D. C., & Salovey, P. (1985). Cognitive structures, cognitive processes, and cognitive behavior modification: I. Client issues. *Cognitive Therapy and Research, 9,* 1–17.

Turkle, S. (1984). *The second self: Computers and the human spirit.* New York: Simon & Shuster.

Tversky, A. (1977). Features of similarity. *Psychological Review, 84,* 327–52.

——, & Kahneman, D. (1974). Judgment under uncertainty: Heuristics and biases. *Science, 185,* 1124–31.

Valliant, G., & McArthur, C. (1972). Natural history of male psychological health. I: The adult life-cycle from 18-50. *Seminars in Psychiatry, 4,* 415–27.

Vallacher, R. R., & Wegner, D. M. (1985). *A theory of action identification.* Hillsdale, NJ: Erlbaum.

Veroff, J. (1983). Contextual determinants of personality. *Personality and Social Psychology Bulletin, 9,* 331–44.

Vygotsky, L. S. (1962). *Thought and language.* Cambridge, MA: MIT Press.

Wagner, R. K., & Sternberg, R. J. (1985). Practical intelligence in real world pursuits: The role of tacit knowledge. *Journal of Personality and Social Psychology, 49*(2), 436–58.

Walker, J. H. (1975). Real-world variability, reasonableness, judgments, and memory representations for concepts. *Journal of Verbal Learning and Verbal Behavior, 14,* 241–52.

Weary, G., Harvey, J. H., Schweiger, P., Olson, C. T., Perloff, R., & Pritchard, S. (1982). Self-presentation and the moderation of the self-serving bias. *Social Cognition, 1,* 140–59.

Weinberg, R. S., Gould, D., & Jackson, A. (1979). Expectations and performance: An empirical test of Bandura's self-efficacy theory. *Journal of Sport Psychology, 1,* 320–31.

Weiner, B. (1985). An attributional theory of achievement motivation and emotion. *Psychological Review, 92*(4), 548–73.

——, Frieze, I., Kukla, A., Reed, L., Rest, S., & Rosenbaum, R. (1972). Perceiving the causes of success and failure. In E. E. Jones, D. Kanouse, H. Kelley, R. Nisbett, S. Valins, & B. Weiner (Eds.), *Attribution: Perceiving the causes of behavior.* Morristown, NJ: General Learning Press.

Weinstein, E. A. (1969). The development of interpersonal competence. In D. A. Goslin (Ed.), *Handbook of socialization theory and research.* Chicago: Rand McNally.

Weinstein, N. (1980). Unrealistic optimism about future life events. *Journal of Personality and Social Psychology, 39,* 806–20.

Werner, E. E. (1979). *Cross-cultural child development.* Monterey, CA: Brooks/Cole.

Werner, H. (1957). The concept of development from a comparative and organismic point of view. In D. B. Harris (Ed.), *The concept of development.* Minneapolis: University of Minnesota Press.

Wheeler, L., Reis, H., & Nezlek, J. B. (1983). Loneliness, social interaction, and sex roles. *Journal of Personality and Social Psychology, 43*(4), 943–53.

White, J., & Carlston, D. (1983). Consequences of schemata for attention, impressions, and recall in complex social interactions. *Journal of Personality and Social Psychology, 45*(3), 538–49.

White, R. W. (1959). Motivation reconsidered: The concept of competence. *Psychological Review, 66,* 297–333.

White, S., & Pillemer, D. (1979). Childhood amnesia and the development of a socially acceptable memory system. In J. Kihlstrom & F. Evans (Eds.), *Functional disorders of memory.* Hillsdale, NJ: Erlbaum.

Wiggins, J. (1979). A psychological taxonomy of trait-descriptive terms: The interpersonal domain. *Journal of Personality and Social Psychology, 37*(3), 395–413.

Willerman, L. (1979). *The psychology of individual and group differences*. San Francisco: W. H. Freeman.

Wills, T. (1981). Downward comparison principles in social psychology. *Psychology Bulletin, 18*, 68–88.

Wilson, G. T., & Franks, C. (Eds.). (1982). *Cognitive behavior therapy*. New York: Guilford.

Wilson, T. (1983). Strangers to ourselves: The origins and accuracy of beliefs about one's own mental states. In J. H. Harvey & G. Weary (Eds.), *Attribution in contemporary psychology*. New York: Academic Press.

———, & Stone, J. I. (1985). Limitations of self-knowledge: More on telling more than we can know. In P. Shaver (Ed.), *Review of personality and social psychology* (Vol. 6). Beverly Hills: Sage.

———, Laser, P., & Stone, J. (1982). Judging the predictors of one's own mood: Accuracy and the use of shared theories. *Journal of Experimental Social Psychology, 18*, 537–56.

Winter, L., Uleman, J., & Cunniff, C. (1985). When are social judgments made? *Journal of Personality and Social Psychology, 49*, 904–17.

Wishner, J. (1960). Reanalysis of "impressions of personality." *Psychological Review, 67*, 96–112.

Witkin, H., & Goodenough, D. (1977). Field dependence and interpersonal behavior. *Psychological Bulletin, 84*(4), 661–89.

———, Dyk, R. B., Faterson, H. F., Goodenough, D. R., & Karp, S. A. (1962). *Psychological differentiation*. Potomac, MD: Erlbaum.

Wittgenstein, L. (1953). *Philosophical investigations*. Oxford: Basil Blackwell.

Wober, M. (1966). Sensotypes. *Journal of Social Psychology, 70*, 181–89.

Wortman, C. (1983). Coping with victimization. *Journal of Social Issues, 39*, 197–223.

Wright, J., & Mischel, W. (1982). Influence of affect on cognitive social learning person variables. *Journal of Personality and Social Psychology, 43*, 901–14.

——— (1985). *Predicting cross-situational consistency: The role of person competencies and situation requirements*. Unpublished manuscript, Columbia University.

Wurf, E., & Markus, H. (1986). *Self-schemas and self-definition: The importance of being different*. Unpublished manuscript, University of Michigan.

Wyer, R. S., & Srull, T. K. (1981). Category accessibility: Some theoretical and empirical issues concerning the processing of social stimulus information. In E. T. Higgins, C. P. Herman, & M. P. Zanna (Eds.), *Social cognition. The Ontario symposium* (Vol. 1). Hillsdale, NJ: Erlbaum.

Yarrow, L. J., MacTurk, R. H., Vietze, P. M., McCarthy, M. E., & Klein, R. P. (1984). Developmental course of parental stimulation and its relationship to mastery motivation during infancy. *Developmental Psychology, 20*, 492–503.

Zajonc, R. B. (1980a). Cognition and social cognition: A historical perspective. In L. Festinger (Ed.), *Four decades of social psychology*. Oxford: Oxford University Press.

——— (1980b). Feeling and thinking: Preferences need no inferences. *American Psychologist, 35*, 151–75.

——— (1984). On the primacy of affect. *American Psychologist, 39*, 117–23.

———, & Markus, H. (1985). Must all affect be mediated by cognition? *Journal of consumer research, 12*, 363–64.

Zigler, E. (1963). A measure in search of a theory. *Contemporary Psychology, 8*, 133–35.

Zuroff, D. C. (1982). Person, situation, and person-by-situation interaction components in person perception. *Journal of Personality, 50*, 1–14.

Index

Holmes, J. G., 89, 209, 241
Holtzworth-Munroe, A., 217–18
Holyoak, K. J., 90, 93, 94, 95, 97, 98,
103, 138
Holzman, P. S., 12
Homa, D., 92
Horn, J. L., 48, 49, 50, 54, 55, 56
Howard-Pitney, B., 117, 239
Hubbard, M., 147
Hubley, P., 196
Hultsch, D. F., 56
Hunter, M. A., 195
Huszti, H. 180

I
Ingram, R. E., 6, 152
Irwin, M., 16
Isen, A. M., 104, 212, 235
Izard, C. E., 229, 230

J
Jackson, A., 37
Jacobson, N. S., 217–18, 232
Jahoda, G., 16
James, W., 123, 153
Janis, I. L., 243
John, O. P., 94, 95, 96, 99, 100,
102, 104
Johnson, D., 103, 104, 105
Jones, E. E., 5, 87, 88, 106, 108, 116,
117, 127, 139, 150, 173,
183, 186, 209, 218
Jones, R. A., 126

K
Kaflowitz, N. G., 232
Kagan, J., 12, 14, 16, 18, 21, 27, 194
Kahneman, D., 61, 111, 176–77, 181
Kamarick, T., 173
Kamin, L. J., 193
Kanfer, F. H., 211
Kaplan, H., 232

Keating, D. P., 54, 66, 67, 68, 69, 70
Keenan, J. M., 151
Keil, F. C., 191, 198
Kelley, H. H., 9, 55, 87, 88, 108, 109,
217–18, 225
Kelly, G., 4, 8, 11, 22–28, 31,
32, 37, 39, 43, 44, 45,
46, 80, 82, 89, 92, 94, 97, 104,
109, 119, 129, 138, 141, 218
Kendall, P. C., 6, 146, 218
Keton, J., 51, 52–53, 55, 66, 82, 92,
106, 240
Kihlstrom, J. F., 5, 6, 9, 12,
13, 25, 71, 74, 84, 99,
101, 108, 112, 115, 116, 117,
122, 124, 127, 129, 130–31,
132, 135, 137, 138, 139,
142, 144, 145–46, 147, 149,
150, 151, 152, 153–54,
156, 162, 185, 212, 217, 218,
219, 220, 222, 224, 225,
226, 228, 239, 240, 241
Kinder, D. R., 93, 105, 115, 117
King, G. A., 94, 98, 99, 104, 105, 118,
132, 136, 138, 153, 223
Kirson, D., 88, 89, 108
Klatsky, R. L., 94, 96, 98, 100,
102, 103, 105
Klee, S. H., 218
Klein, R. E., 16
Klein, R. P., 98, 129, 137, 140, 152,
186, 195, 217, 222, 223, 239
Klinger, E., 5, 116, 119, 138,
159, 160, 164–65, 169,
170, 172, 178, 179, 182, 187,
201, 219, 234
Klos, D., 177–78, 232, 241
Koeske, R., 115
Kogan, N., 12, 14, 16, 21
Kohlberg, L., 199
Kopp, C. B., 192, 195–97
Korn, H., 66, 172, 228
Kramer, R. M., 82
Kremer, M., 232
Kringlen, E., 193